April 30, 1968 — At Avery Hall, at about 3 a.m. students and faculty were seated on the steps. A group of uniformed police moved to Avery, stopped in front of the demonstrators and announced that they had to get through. They asked the demonstrators on the steps to get out of their way. No one moved.

Columbia Spectator, Volume CXII, Number 107, April 30, 1968

Photographs of students in front of Avery and Fayerweather Halls, taken by Richard Howard (CC 1970); May 6, 1968; University Protest and Activism Collection, Box 70, Folder 19; University Archives, Rare Book and Manuscript Library; Columbia University in the City of New York.

Reprinted courtesy *Columbia Spectator*.

Design, Create, Engage

Dean Amale Andraos

We live in a time of great uncertainty and change. Meeting its unprecedented challenges will be an urgent imperative for architecture in the coming years—but this moment might also inspire us to recognize and fulfill new potentials for a more equitable, sustainable, and creative world.

As global urbanization invites us to think relationally across cultures and contexts, climate change urges us to re-imagine how we live, move, and share. New types of housing, new forms of infrastructure, new possibilities for urban ecology, and new preservation technologies can all converge to foster more just societies. This work also moves freely between the virtual and the physical. Visualizing data is fundamental to re-presenting what we know—and how we know it—while rendering the future more tangible and participatory. A culture of making, meanwhile, is enabling new forms of collectivity and collaboration towards new experiences and material realities.

At the heart of many of today's challenges and opportunities are the disciplines and practices of the built environment—all of which are represented at Columbia GSAPP—and which together are moving the field in new directions. Fueled by the density and diversity of its encounters and perspectives, and combining creative experimentation and unbridled imagination with disciplinary practice and incisive critical thinking, the school has built its long legacy of excellence as an urban condenser of ideas.

In this time that demands new concepts around which to assemble and empower the next generation of architects, planners, urban designers, and real estate developers, Columbia GSAPP represents a unique environment that fosters the design of new modes of living and sharing, creates new forms of knowledge and practice, and renews our commitment to engagement with the world and the urgent issues of our time.

At GSAPP, we are inspired to nurture the bold creative thinkers, original designers and engaged idea makers of the next generation.

30 years seems like a long time, and yet, at the same time it's no time at all. This book, the 2017 edition of Abstract, marks the 30th year of its tradition as the annual publication of the work and activity of Columbia GSAPP, and as such it seems only appropriate to take stock of the role this book plays in the legacy and history of the school while acknowledging the ways in which it has changed, and will continue to change.

Yes, this book serves simultaneous documentary and promotional purposes for Columbia GSAPP, but more than that the past three editions of Abstract have attempted to build a broader audience for the process of educating the future leaders of the built environment in a generous, open-ended, and playful design. This in turn aims to foster greater diversity within our field in a reflexive manner. By doubling down on making architecture accessible without dumbing it down, we have aimed to provide greater context and agency to the student work included in a number of important ways.

With this goal in mind, the project of updating Abstract was critically oriented towards the creation of a parallel digital edition: not one that is identical to the print edition in a skeuomorphic fashion, but rather a networked, distributed version of the same visual work, which

Jesse Seegers

lives online and whose context evolves over time, which is reflected in a few ways: (1) The online student work archive, accessible at *arch.columbia.edu/student-work*, presents unedited repository of the pedagogical production as selected by faculty. (2) On our social media platforms and Instagram in particular, where our *@ColumbiaGSAPP* handle has grown from 2k followers in 2015 to over 60k followers by December 2017. As an example of the impact of this mission, the work of our students pinned up during final reviews is posted on the same day of the final critique and receives over 1.25 million 'impressions' in a single week. (3) Through our Digital Reader long-form publications on *arch.columbia.edu* which expand upon and provide more comprehensive descriptions of design studios than the limitations of the print edition allows, as well as facilitating the global dissemination of Columbia GSAPP design work to other parts of the globe, particularly cities in which the Urban Design program's Water Urbanism studios have taken place: Amman, Kolkata, Rio, and Madurai to date.

But what does all this have to do with the paper in front of you, you might ask? While this edition of Abstract includes a few new additions compared to previous years—notably a conversation about the architecture curriculum among the architecture faculty (p. 137) and design mantras for the political climate of 2016–17 dispersed throughout—its core contents demonstrate our commitment to representation as a political act. The amalgamation of papers, inks, and materials before you will last as a statement of purpose as much as documentation of a period in time, for a long time to come.

Advanced Arch. Studios
Juan Herreros,
Director

Advanced Arch. Design
Enrique Walker,
Director

Advanced Arch. Studio IV
David Benjamin,
Coordinator

Core Arch. Studios
Hilary Sample,
Director

Core Arch. Studio III
Hilary Sample,
Coordinator

Core Arch. Studio II
Mimi Hoang,
Coordinator

Core Arch. Studio I
Christoph Kumpusch,
Coordinator

Master of Architecture M.Arch

Advanced
Architecture
Studio VI

Advanced
Architecture
Studio V

Advanced
Architectural
Design

Advanced
Architecture
Studio IV

Core
Architecture
Studio III

Core
Architecture
Studio II

Core
Architecture
Studio I

The Master of Architecture (M.Arch) is a three-year professional degree program which brings together design thinking and making, cutting edge visualization and technology, and critical historical and disciplinary knowledge to actively shape the future of architecture, cities, and the environment. This is an exciting time for Columbia GSAPP: from the school's vibrant home in the heart of New York City, our inspiring faculty and students are committed to shaping a more equitable, sustainable, and creative world by engaging architecture and the built environment from a range of diverse and global perspectives.

The Master of Architecture program brings together imagination, experimentation and critical thinking towards new forms of practice. As an urban condenser of ideas, the school drives innovation and change through the leadership of our faculty, the excellence of our academic programs, the expansion of our interdisciplinary opportunities and the richness of our events and initiatives. To be part of the energy at GSAPP is to actively shape the future of architecture and the built environment, as students and faculty work together in a spirit of willful optimism, intellectual generosity, and creative entrepreneurship to design their own forms of engagement and modes of practice: never declaring what architecture is but always imagining together what it could be.

GSAPP's M.Arch program builds on the school's history of continuity and change. As one of the oldest and most prestigious of its kind, the program has also consistently led in advancing new possibilities for the discipline and the practice of architecture. One of our defining strengths is a commitment to global engagement, which transpires from the way we teach history to the extensive travel opportunities that students are presented with through design studios, interdisciplinary summer workshops, seminars, and collaborations across our global Studio-X network.

The program's commitment to environmental concerns has shaped the school's framing of the question of scale; buildings are not considered in isolation but rather embedded within scales of environment—from the material scale to the scale of a city. A focus on systems and relational thinking as well as an emphasis on process has enabled new interdisciplinary opportunities across programs, from joint studios (whether between architecture and historic preservation or architecture and planning) to all-school seminars which bring real estate development, urban design, and architecture together to think about climate change and its impact on cities.

Finally, our legacy of pioneering experimentation in digital technology and visualization, which always manifests in our students' signature graduating portfolios, is intersecting with a growing culture of making at the school. Our expanded maker space is enabling new opportunities for exchange and collaboration across the school and beyond—including our GSAPP Incubator in downtown Manhattan, which supports and fosters creative thinking and practice for our recent alumni.

To graduate with a Master of Architecture degree, a student is required to complete 108 graduate-level course points that are a combination of required courses from six different categories: Studio, History/Theory, Building Technologies, Visual Studies, Methods/Practice, and Electives.

At the heart of the M.Arch experience is an ongoing feedback loop between the space of the design studio and the space of the classroom. The studio sequence is divided into three semesters of Core Studios and three semesters of Advanced Studios. The Core Studio sequence begins with the question of architecture as boundary and gradually increases in scale and complex-

ity, up through GSAPP's seminal Housing Studio, which anchors architecture in its relation to the city as the fundamental question of inhabitation is examined across varying contexts, climates, and cultures. The Advanced Studio sequence begins with the innovative Scales of Environment Studio and ends with highly diverse and complex projects in which students claim a position vis-à-vis the field, and outline their interests for their future engagement.

In the classroom, students find the curricular sequences simultaneously autonomous yet complementary. The History/Theory sequence broadens students' perspectives through historical and theoretical examination and a commitment to an expanded, inclusive, and global view of architecture's past. The Visual Studies sequence focuses on drawing and making, opening up new modes of seeing and understanding that come to bear upon the design process. The Building Technology sequence prepares students to understand the environmental, structural, and material opportunities for design as well as their consequences for design decisions. The Methods and Practice sequence prepares students to engage as professionals within the field. Finally, the Elective sequence invites students to pursue individual interests in architectural, urban, and environmental topics, with the new Design Seminar category as a hybrid between a studio and seminar, in which the extended duration and expanded space of the former is augmented by a rigorous discussion series typical of the latter, pushing in directions the curriculum may evolve towards.

This year, Columbia GSAPP was ranked #2 among the country's top architecture schools by DesignIntelligence, a recognition of our standing today and a reflection on our future, as we transform new opportunities for architects and for architecture into reality for all our students and graduates.

The Advanced Studios are intended to build upon the ideas and skills developed in the Core Studios, working as laboratories of discussion and exploring different design processes and methods: setting the concepts and the narratives of the projects, describing the programs and their typological implications, making technical, energy and environmental decisions, activating the most appropriate graphic resources to the project's intentions. Nearly twenty studios each semester work on the explorations defined by their individual critics, trying to find new instruments, formats and approaches to everyday topics. Each syllabus carries out both an educational objective and an opportunity to develop a critical approach to a specific area shared by the instructor with their students. This means that an experimental attitude grounds our environment, while the coexistence of different ways of thinking stimulates dialogue and positive discussions in which the students learn to build, defend and rectify their arguments in a dialectical practice that is as important as drawing, making models or inventing a digital resource. In contradistinction to the Core Studios, the Advanced Studios combine M.Arch students with AAD professional degree students.

Today's architects' global practice—informed by social, cultural, economic, and environmental concerns that are re-shaping the world—is asking architecture for new agendas. In this sense, the Advanced Studios work as a laboratory of architectural design that in itself makes up an extraordinary accumulation of essays and research, in both conceptual and disciplinary fields, that can be considered a section of the present. We are all aware of this wealth and appreciate the special energy stored in this *white noise* that involves many instructors, teaching assistants and students working together. Throughout the semester, the Transfer Dialogues series offers two different types of events: the first is focused on making visible the diversity and intensity of work in other Advanced Studios, and the second brings in a selection of emerging offices to show the students how to develop a critical practice today. The intention is to open a new space for architecture and its parallel disciplines in the social, political, intellectual and economic arena with a critical position focused on the construction of the future.

Advanced Architecture Studio VI Spring 2017

1 2 3 4 5

COPULA HALL ¶ STEPHEN CASSELL, ANNIE BARRETT, CRITICS ¶ Two oppositional city-states partially occupy the same geographic territory. Citizens of both nations coexist side-by-side in an interwoven crosshatch of overlapping borders, yet are forbidden to acknowledge one another's existence due to deep cultural strife. These impossible architectural, cultural, and geographic circumstances are the setting for China Mieville's novel "The City and The City," which served as the site, program, and universe of this advanced studio. The improbable conditions of the text presented an equally conceivable parable of abiding cultural, economic, habitual, social, racial and/or ethnic discord. Moreover, the practice of architecture frames complex cultural and social relationships which are often impossible to solve; taking on any architectural project means becoming an expert in worlds previously unknown to the architect. So while the studio premise is imaginary, it equally stands for any, and every, critical architectural project. ¶ In an initial four-week project, each student produced a rigorous projective cartography of the text in their own visual language. Over ten days in Dkaha, Chandigarh and Ahmedabad, the studio explored the political, cultural, and formal themes of the studio through seminal 20th century projects constructed around the 1947 partition of India. ¶ Over the final six weeks of the semester, students developed their final projects: a design for a new Copula Hall—the key architectural protagonist of The City and The City that houses two interwoven seats of governance and their respective bureaucracies, and serves as both boundary and portal between the two worlds.

6 7 8

ABSTRACT TECHNOLOGIES ¶ KERSTEN GEERS, CRITIC, WITH ANDREA ZANDERIGO, CHARLES HAJJ ¶ For the 24th incarnation of Architecture Without Content, we arrive in Brooklyn via Japan and California. If our journey over the past years was often driven by an obsession with everything big, including its consequences and the places these big boxes inhabit, the latest episodes at our Laboratory for Architecture as Form inspired a radical scale shift in an attempt to find an architecture of the shared in the smallest of acupunctural interventions.

9 10

THE BOOK OF SINS: LUST. BARCELONA'S BARRIO XINO. THE ARCHITECTURES OF ILLICIT LOVE. ¶ CRISTINA GOBERNA PESUDO, CRITIC, WITH WADE COTTON ¶ The Book of Sins is a design research project that explores spaces related to what commonly are understood as immoral acts. Consequently, it is centered around architectural typologies that are often forbidden, forgotten, hidden, not publically revealed and insufficiently explored by the discipline. A past installment of this studio was Sloth, Barcelona's Party Scene After the Financial Crash. In this case, The Book of Sins explored Lust, the architecture related to sexuality in Barcelona's Barrio Xino o Raval, the city's historical red light district.

11 12

IMAGE CITIES CIRCUS: MODERNITY AND SPECTACLE ¶ MARIO GOODEN, CRITIC ¶ The circus is often a site of paradoxical juxtapositions of diversion, aesthetics, beauty, and seduction. In 1965, Henri Lefebvre's La Proclamation de la Commune analogized the relationships between the Paris Commune of 1781 and the carnival tradition. Lefebvre argued that the carnival, like the Commune, shatters the institutional framework within which they are traditionally contained. While the carnival and the circus are not necessarily synonymous, previous circus-type architectures such as Cedric Price's Fun Palace and Archigram's Ideas Circus were born of revolt against a certain kind of hegemony. ¶ On the other hand, European colonization in various parts of the world in the 18th through the 20th centuries was not only part of empire-building abroad but was also intended to reinforce hegemonic structures and promote nationalism and nation-building at home. Paradoxically, these colonial forays also revealed the desire, seduction, and spectacularization of the "other" among the horrors of imperialism. The studio explored the idea of the circus and relationships among paradoxical situations, contexts, and events in the former French colony of Senegal. The studio worked on various sites in Dakar, Senegal while exploring the post-colonial modernist visions for "l'Athènes de l'Afrique subsaharienne."

13 14 15

FLOATING NEW YORK ¶ LAURIE HAWKINSON, CRITIC, WITH GALEN PARDEE ¶ What if there could be "new ground" in New York City? If so, would this new ground be sited, anchored or moving? If anchored, then where? If not anchored—why not—and what or why would it move? What will this over-expanded city look like? How will it grow, accumulate and expand? How will it be made? What will it be made of? What if the 100-year flood line is the new water's edge? What will this change or affect? How will life be integrated into this new edge? ¶ The Mayor's Office plan for new ferry terminal sites, currently deemed "transportation deserts" on NYC's East River, serves as our starting point. The students proposed new terminals and new programs at the interface of water and land at these key locations. Prototype cultural programs for Museums, Recreation, Libraries, High Schools, Food Production and Community Centers together with the Ferry Terminal, demonstrate how this new life would be scripted on the water. The studio traveled to Venice and Rotterdam and met with experts in the field of coastal and river delta urbanization to see firsthand two cities that have lived next to and on water for centuries.

16
17

FROM THE INDUSTRIAL ESTATE TO THE ADVANCED NEIGHBORHOOD: TYPOLOGICAL CORRECTIONS & OCCUPATION PRACTICES ¶ JUAN HERREROS, CRITIC, WITH MAITE BORJABAD ¶ This studio focused on the types of sites that nobody would ever regard as the target of covetousness on the part of those who set the processes of change in motion. Nonetheless, their transformation has already begun. We refer to the apparently characterless outlying industrial districts, with their humdrum buildings in which thousands of anonymous people toil. ¶ Changes in systems of production and their strategic location on the edge of the city, near fast thoroughfares and on non-classified land, have converted these sites into the next target for real-estate speculation, which has set processes in motion of tertiary and residential occupation in what will most certainly become a new generation of urban districts. What seemed to be valueless fragments are now claiming their share of architecture in order to face their future. ¶ In this context, our studio developed three themes crucial to current circumstances: recycling the existing city (typological corrections), new ways of living (re-occupations), and the need to devise new design methods (emerging practices). ¶ The studio proposed a methodology to work simultaneously immersed in three dimensions: large-scale transformation of the city, typological reflection as correction of existing elements and the establishment of material, constructive and spatial systems associated with the deliberate choice of systems of representation.

18
19
20

ARCHITECTONICS OF MUSIC: TIME - SCALE ¶ STEVEN HOLL, CRITIC, WITH DIMITRA TSACHRELIA ¶ Iannis Xenakis (1922–2001) an engineer by training, who worked as an architect for Le Corbusier from 1947–1959, rejected conventional techniques of composition to invent new and elaborate scales for his music according to the laws of physical sciences. In a six-week exercise, until Midterm, students were challenged to make a 16×16×32" physical model according to their selected piece of music by composer Iannis Xenakis. As music has no "exterior," each study focused on capturing interior space, the quality of spatial overlap and the potential of genuine structure fused with the spatial energy of natural daylight. ¶ Each fragment of music served as the experimental conceptual departure for an architectural proposal along the waterfront of Patras, Greece, once an industrial port now being re-purposed with public programs. An imagined patron pledges €650 million to invigorate the city of Patras with a waterfront park and a pair of public pavilions for music and performance, including a 500-seat auditorium, as well as art education programs in collaboration with the University of Patras. ¶ The final review presentation included a sectional detail model of interior spaces in 1/50 scale and two-minute videos showing the interrelations between music, space and movement in time. ¶ www.architectonicsofmusic.com

21
22
23

REDESIGNING THE ACTOR NETWORK IN FUKUSHIMA ¶ MOMOYO KAIJIMA, YOSHIHARU TSUKAMOTO, CRITICS, WITH TAMOTSU ITO ¶ In 2011, the Tsunami Triple Disaster attacked numerous Japanese rural villages with beautiful natural landscapes and local lifestyles. After 6 years we see some recovery, except Fukushima, where many communities confront multi-layered problems caused by the Fukushima No.1 nuclear power plant accident. The studio focused on one of them, Odaka Ward in Minamisoma City. In 2016, after the inspection and decontamination process, evacuated local people finally came back to Odaka. However, people struggle to sustain local livelihoods because of harmful conditions, depopulation (currently only 10% of the pre-disaster population), unmanaged common capital resources, and a deteriorated landscape. We investigated and mapped the ecology of rural livelihood by applying the method of the Actor Network (Bruno Latour). Then, we proposed an architectural intervention into the network for a better future for Odaka, which many people like local leaders and NPOs have now started to aim for.

24
25
26

SETTLING THE NOMADS: SUPPORT STRUCTURES ¶ JOHN LIN, JOSHUA BOLCHOVER, CRITICS, WITH GEORGE LOURAS ¶ Ulaanbaatar, Mongolia is a city transitioning from a nomadic to sedentary lifestyle. The country evolved from a period of economic hardship immediately following Soviet withdrawal in 1989, to a democratic electoral system and free-market economy. The discovery of vast reserves of coal and copper made the capital city—Ulaanbaatar—the focus of rural migration. The ensuing optimism led nomadic herdsmen to sell their livestock and move to the city in search of a better life. When they arrive each claims a plot of land, builds a fence around it and erects a traditional felt tent or ger. ¶ The scale and speed of settlers has disrupted and pressurized the limited city resources as well as challenged basic infrastructure such as water, waste and social welfare. As this population has no prior experience of living amongst others—some state there is no word for "community" in Mongolian—it's a unique and urgent situation. ¶ The aim of the studio was to design transformative, incremental strategies for the ger districts. From hacking tectonic building systems, to growing micro-infrastructures, to large scale environmental systems, the studio rethought how the ger districts can act as a vital exchange point between nomadic and settled forms of living.

described this process and associated obsessions. The Monograph Studio is not a portfolio studio. A portfolio is objective. A monograph is subjective. A portfolio hastens. A monograph hesitates. A portfolio is defensive. A monograph is adaptive. The Monograph Studio reminds you, in the words of playwright Samuel Becket, to try again, to fail again, and to fail better.

43
44
45
46

OPEN WORK ¶ ENRIQUE WALK-ER, CRITIC ¶ Half a century ago, architecture became open-ended. Buildings would change and grow, architects argued, not unlike cities. They embraced impermanence, promoted flexibility, timed obsolescence, and welcomed uncertainty, just as Umberto Eco proclaimed the birth of the open work, and Roland Barthes pronounced the death of the author. Architects also questioned authorship. They would no longer strive to prescribe an outcome, let alone inscribe a meaning. Against the backdrop of modern masters and monuments, and as a result of cultural, social, and technological developments, buildings became systems. Paradoxically, architects would pioneer new building types, in unprecedented ways, by openly disregarding program. ¶ Design theories for open-ended buildings differed, but they all implied, almost invariably, free plans and modular units, as well as building components discriminated by their rate of renewal: frame versus clip-on, core versus capsule, structure versus envelope. By the mid-sixties, just a few years after speculation on openness had begun in earnest, several projects materialized. Over the following years, many changed: some according to plan, some according to other plans, or no plan. Many others did not. Some were demolished against the architect's will, some preserved against the building's principles. Today, they stand as monuments of architecture's attack on permanence. ¶ This studio addressed three open-ended buildings in Japan, namely: Kiyonori Kikutake's Tokoen Hotel, Arata Isozaki's Oita Prefectural Library, and Kenzo Tange's Yamanashi Press and Broadcasting Center. The brief was straightforward. Students joined a team, were assigned a building, and asked to double its surface. Do we

endorse openness, and observe, refine, or redefine the script? Do we argue against it, and monumentalize? What is at stake is to design in conversation with, and to take position on, a building and the arguments it advanced, and to tackle a longstanding question within the field, again, half a century later.

47
48
49

COLLECTING ARCHITECTURE TERRITORIES: CAMBODIA AND VIETNAM ¶ MARK WASIUTA, CRITIC, WITH EDUARDO TAZON ¶ This studio was a continuation of the evolving research project, Collecting Architecture Territories. The project contends that collecting is a practice that allows us to glimpse an emerging cultural logic of the early 21st century. It suggests that collecting processes draw together cultural artifacts, finances, resources, bodies, military controls, and new technologies within active spaces of accumulation, which we describe as territories of collection. ¶ In recent years the studio has focused on the Middle East. Following American foreign policy—which under the Obama presidency transferred resources, attention and diplomacy from the Middle East to those countries most influenced by China—this spring the studio sites shifted to Cambodia and Vietnam. Vietnam and Cambodia share a complex and related history. Both achieved independence from France and developed distinct forms of modernism in the 1950s and 1960s. Both were devastated by wars that have left indelible traces on their social, urban, and psychic structures. And both countries have emerged in recent years with contrasting political alignments and interests. With these histories and contemporary conditions in mind, each student analyzed a system of collection, from which they developed their own conceptual approach and design method. Bomb crater landscapes in Vietnam, water extraction in rural Cambodia, and cultural agencies in Phnom Penh were some of the collecting sites and operations that appeared in the student work.

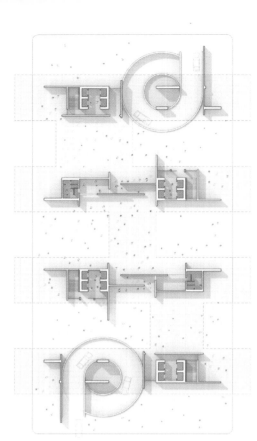

1

Grant McCracken

2

Brigitte Lucey

3

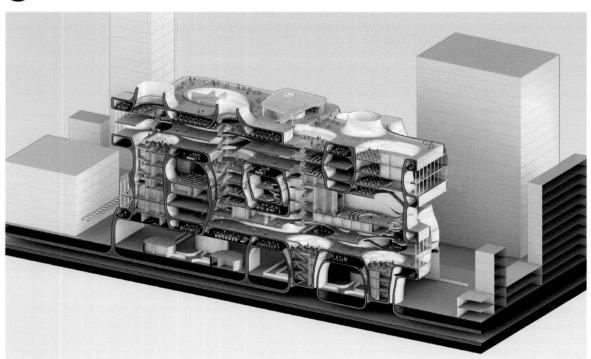

Ruosen Du

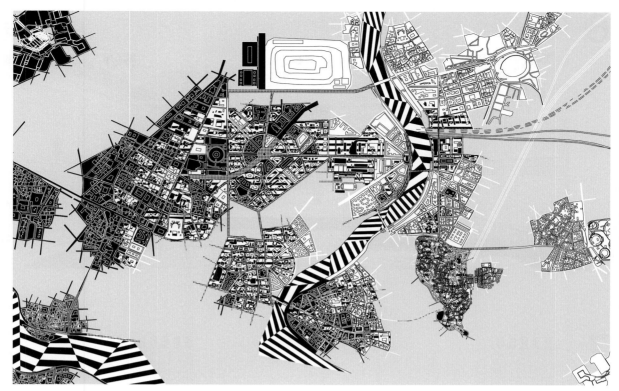

Alexandra Kurek

4

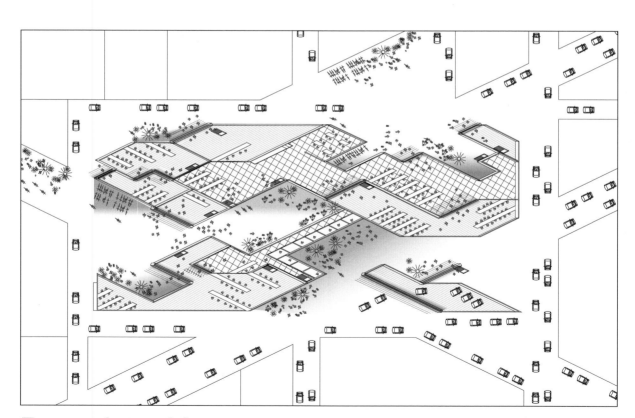

Bernadette Ma

5

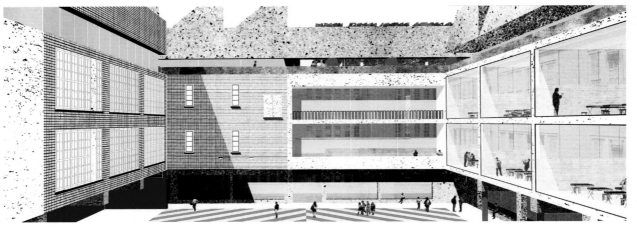

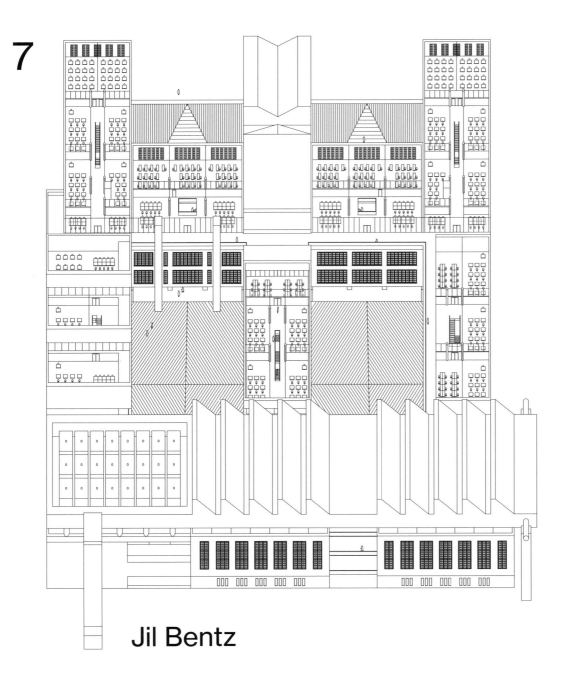

Jil Bentz

ADV ARCH STUDIO VI

Giovanni Cozzani

9

Naifei Liu

10

Troy Lacombe

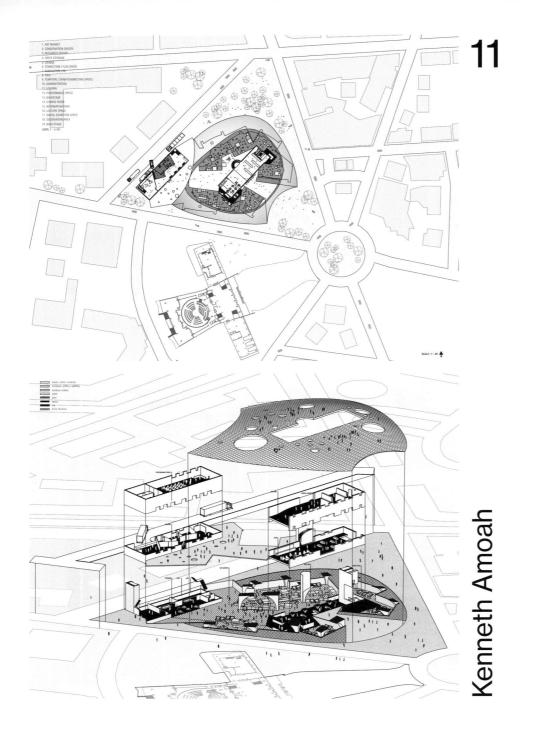

Kenneth Amoah

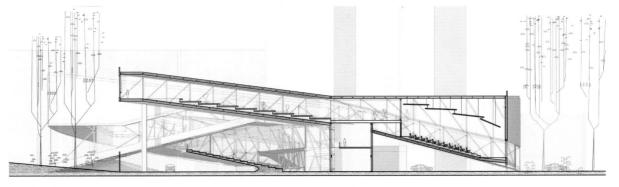

Wendy Huang

13

Chuhan Zhou

14

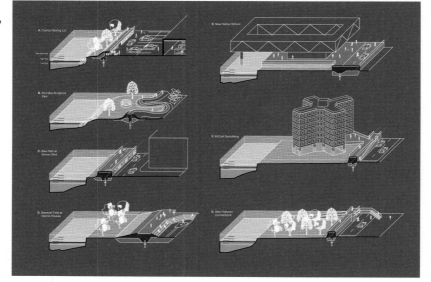

A. Costco Parking Lot

E. New Harbor School

B. Sololess Sculpture Park

F. NYCHA Retrofitting

C. Bike Path at Vernon Blvd

D. Baseball Field at Astoria Houses

G. New Walkway Connections

Mike Nickerson

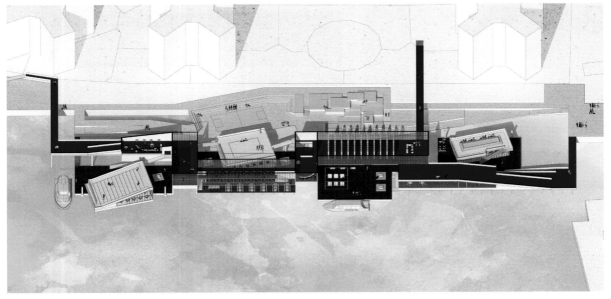

15

Ruoqi Fan

16

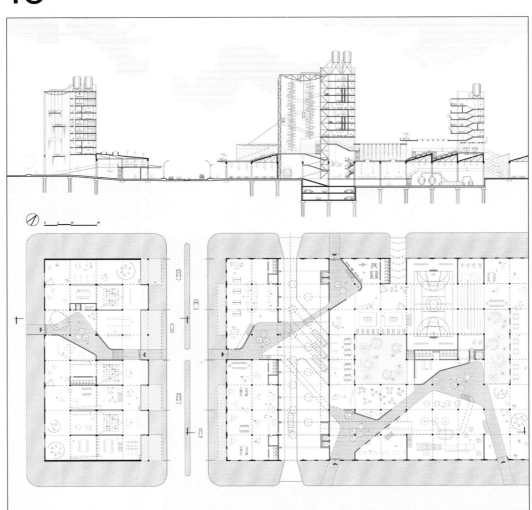

Rui Guan,
Wenzhao Zhang

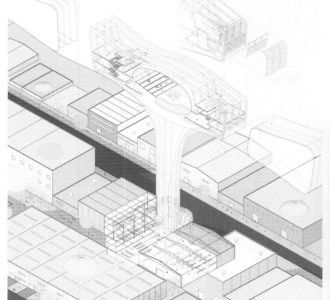

Jennifer Fang,
Kathy Xiao

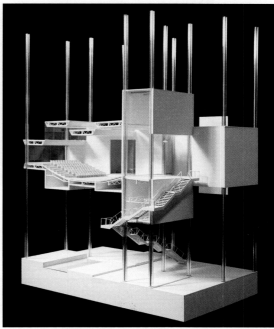

Jacobo Mingorance,
Colin Joyce

19

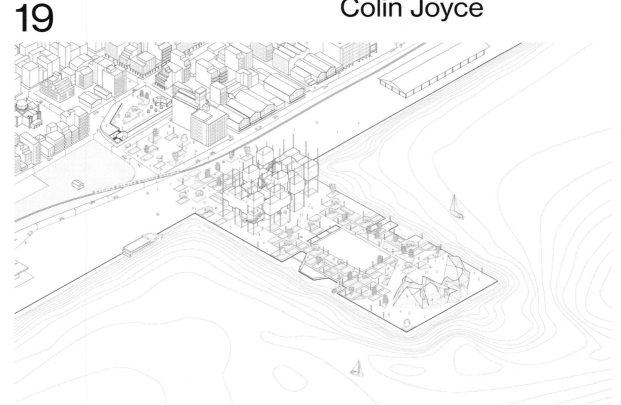

Jacobo Mingorance, Colin Joyce

20

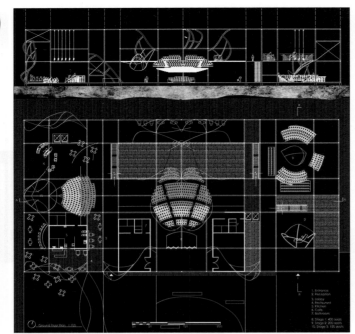

Tahsin Inanici, Qi Yue Hu

21

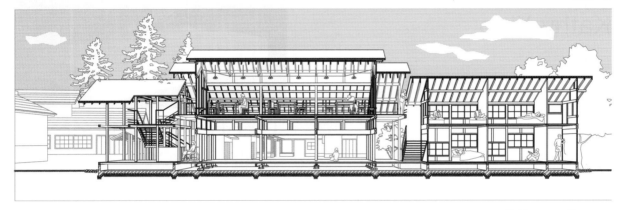

Zhe Cao

22

Yang Huang

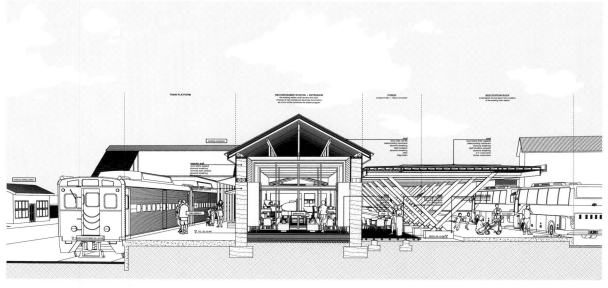

23

Roderick Cruz

24

Sun Yi

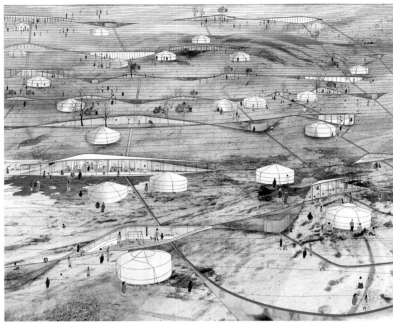

25

Shu Du

26

Julie Pedtke

28

Zoji Lin

29

Yujing Mandy Han

Qiu Jin

27

30

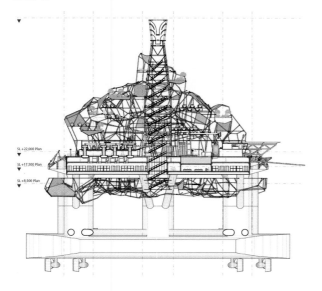

Chin-Yu Tsai,
Chia-Shan Hsu

Sunaina Shah

31

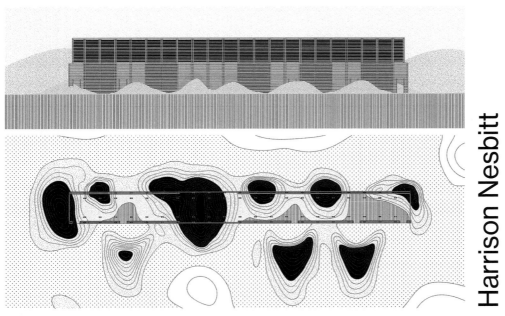

Harrison Nesbitt

32

33

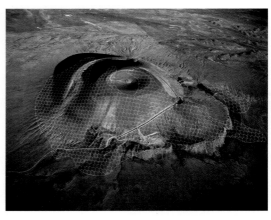

Su Jeong Lee

34

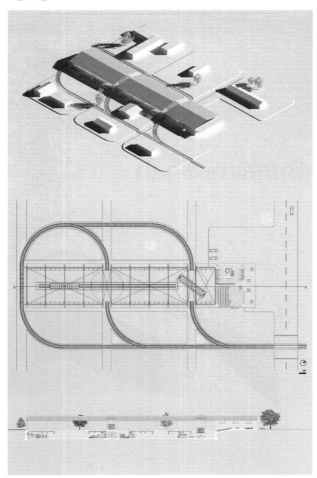

Stephanie Tager,
Nicholas Kazmierski

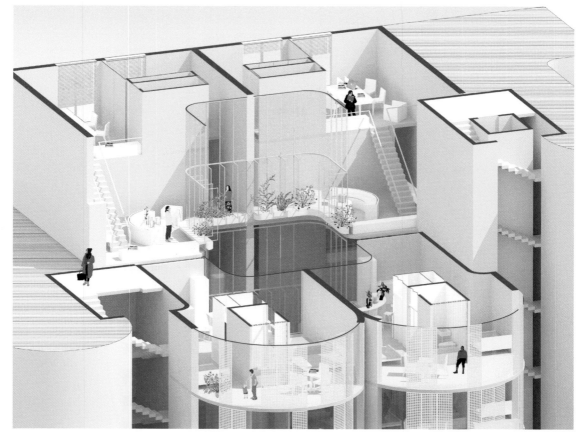

35   36

Kig Veerasunthorn, Wen Chou

Emily Mohr

Pei Zhou

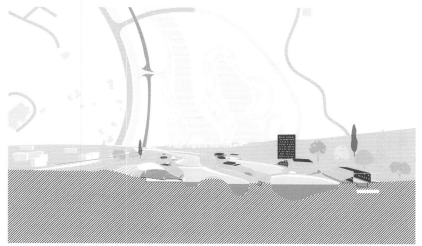

Amanda Hibbs

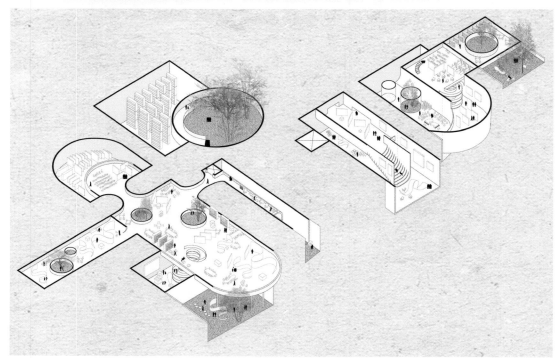

Wenmei Zhi

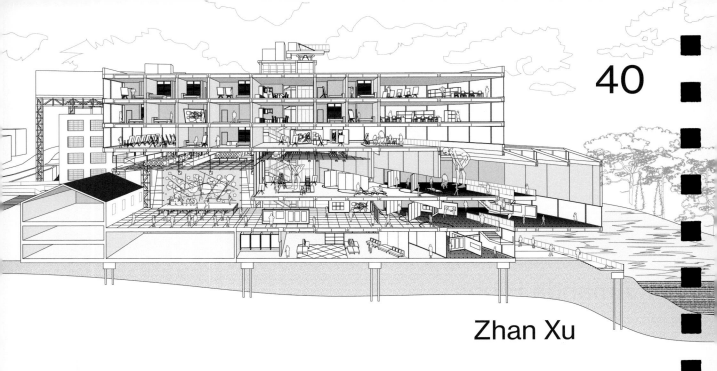

40

Zhan Xu

41

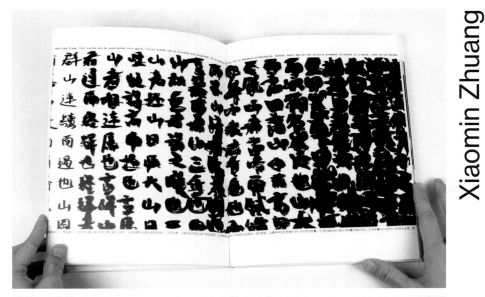

Xiaomin Zhuang

42

Amenah Alkendi

43

Jorge Cornet, Kavya Cherala, Boer Deng, Andrew Weber

Tigran Konstandyan, Karen Berberyan, Nila Muliawati Liem, Wantong Xu

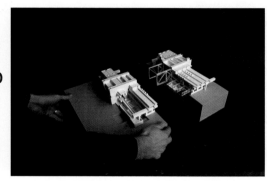

44

45

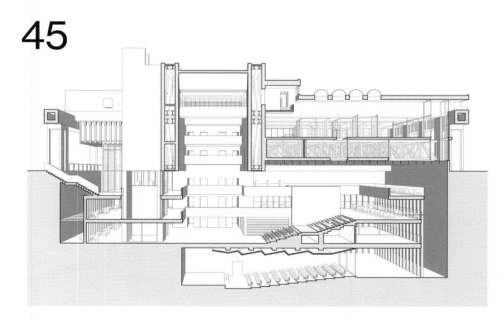

Tigran Kostandyan, Karen Berberyan, Nila Muliawati Liem, Wantong Xu

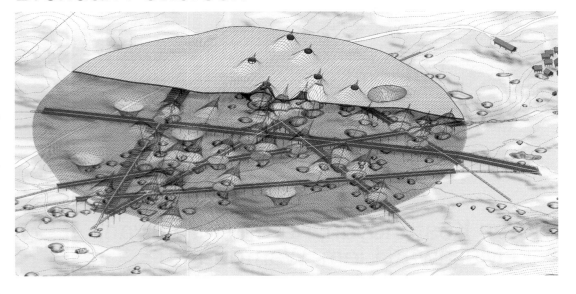

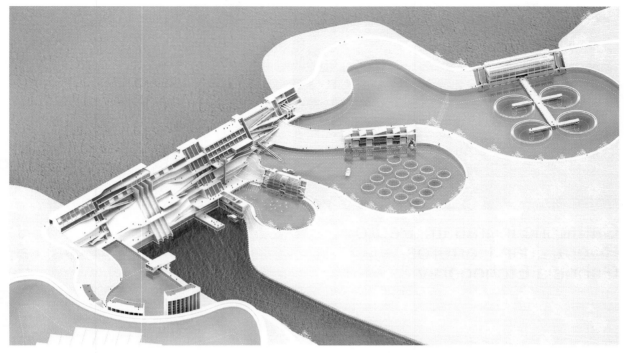

48

Lin Wu, Ye Yuan

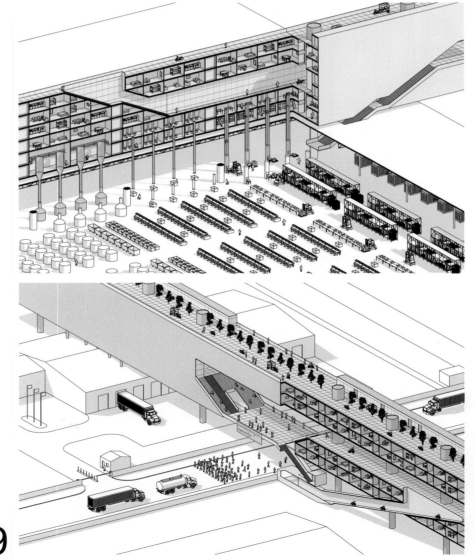

49

Kurt Streich

Catherine Ingraham, Pedro
Rivera, Juan Herreros,
Gabriela Etchegaray

Go Hasegawa,
Yoshiharu Tsukamoto

Tatiana Bilbao, Hilary
Sample, Juan Herreros

Kersten Geers,
Momoyo Kajima

Christian Wassman,
Garrick Ambrose,
Steven Holl,
Dimitra Tsachrelia

Barry Bergdoll, Stan Allen, Lucia Allais

Enrique Walker, Mimi Hoang, Kersten Geers,
Yoshiharu Tsukumoto, Momoyo Kaijima

Ilias Papageorgiou, Umberto
Napolitano, Eric Lapierre,
Amale Andraos

Nontsikelelo Mutiti, Gordon Kipping, Ignacio González Galán, Mabel O. Wilson

Liz Diller, Steven Holl, Antón Garćia-Abril

Jing Liu, Selva Gürdogan

Mark Wasiuta, Leah Meisterlin, Carlos Minguez-Carrasco, Farzin Lotfi-Jam, Maite Borjabad López-Pastor

Urtzi Grau, Joan Ockman, Eric Bunge, André Jacque

Galia Solomonoff,
Eduardo Arroyo,
Eric Bunge

Garrett Ricciardi, Julian Rose,
Ben Aranda, Ian David Volner

Mario Gooden, Eunjeong Seong,
Vishaan Chakrabarti,
Laurie Hawkinson

Advanced Architecture Studio V Fall 2016

1
2

THE VERTICAL CITY ¶ TATIANA BILBAO, CRITIC, WITH LAURA BUCK, GABRIELA ALVAREZ ¶ Since 2014, over half of the world's population lives in cities. Urban dwellers are a segment of the global population that will only continue to increase and, for this reason, cities of the future will need to adjust to gradual transformations, the unpredictable shifts in spatial and social structures intrinsic to organic growth. As an experimental response to urban expansion, this studio explored vertical densification from a decentralized perspective, translating urban typologies and civic life, hitherto developed primarily on the horizontal plane, into an upright dimension. ¶ To translate the city into a vertical expanse, students selected one typology and dissected it in order to design new possible connections. After individual typological research, the studio collectively focused on reconstructing a representative section of New York City in the form of a vertical, large-scale, exquisite corpse built model and section. The studio's aim was to mobilize student efforts as a collective that could achieve much more than individual work. ¶ With a seemingly incompatible series of projects, students learned that the key is to work from a position of uncertainty exploring possible connections and relationships between spaces. Only through improvisation can architects meet the challenges of the densely-populated areas of the future.

3
4

PRODUCTION+ ¶ LISE ANNE COUTURE, CRITIC, WITH LIAM LOWRY ¶ This studio envisioned architectural prototypes for a future "PRODUCTION + ZONE" along the Brooklyn Newtown Creek waterfront. The studio investigated architectural concepts with respect to a broad range of places of "production" that were appropriate for the waterfront site, including not only the production of objects and assemblies, but also the production of energy, food, materials, culture, events, content and ideas. The architectural proposals also anticipated and accommodated new concepts for desirable "byproducts" (the "+" in "Production+"). These other types of outputs, collateral programs or spaces, that offer an additional cultural, social, environmental or other collective benefit were seen as equally intrinsic to, or even the driver for, the development of design strategies and the ultimate architectural outcome.

5
6
7

THE MICRO MEGA CITY: MASS PROGRAMMING RANDALL'S ISLAND, A VISION FOR MANHATTAN INSPIRED BY ZAHA HADID ¶ MARKUS DOCHANTSCHI, CRITIC ¶ In 1983, Zaha Hadid expressed in her painting "The World (89 Degrees)" her excitement to integrate emerging technologies and a change in lifestyle to push and develop new possibilities in architecture. With new technology available today, architecture will have to continue to reinvestigate its foundations and possibilities. This studio explored new multifunctional cross-programmed housing typologies, and analyzed design methodologies. ¶ The site, Randall's Island, has many opportunities as it has challenges. The studio was challenged to investigate future housing typologies by cross-utilizing programs and utilizing new media tools. Booking systems like AirBnB have interrupted traditional industries and made the desire for ownership obsolete. Space sharing changed how housing can become systematically and economically "affordable." The housing market will drastically change, as will the way we live, work, and play. ¶ The Micro Mega City (MMC) on Randall's Island allowed for housing, recreation, and work to coexist with an unprecedented maximum efficiency and minimum cost.

8
9

THE WORK STUDIO: SPECULATING ON THE FUTURE OF WORK AT THE BROOKLYN NAVY YARD ¶ LAURIE HAWKINSON, CRITIC, WITH LEIGHA DENNIS ¶ What about WORK? The Brooklyn Navy Yard is no longer a vestige of what New York once was: instead, the Yard has become emblematic of how New York will adapt and transform toward the future. ¶ The agenda for this studio was to produce future designs for the Brooklyn Navy Yard site, envisioning new forms of working and collective urbanism for NYC dwellers. We speculated on the future of work, considering large-scale and small-scale drivers that might enable new forms of energy production, environmental resiliency, public policy, technology, and mobility. ¶ Students rethought the future of the workplace, and considered how work might inform their speculative models for collective urbanism. They positioned their projects within a spectrum of futures from probable, plausible, and possible to the impossible. ¶ What form does this work take as the concept of work evolves? The students proposed new programs for their collective space strategies.

10
11
12
13

INTERIM URBANISM ¶ NAHYUN HWANG, DAVID EUGIN MOON, CRITICS ¶ Under the logics of a post-'08 demographic economy and with persisting political and economic instabilities and inequalities at the global scale, increased mobility—both voluntary and forced— and related formats of living challenge the familiar notions of the ownership of the city and its inhabitants. As a part of the ongoing research and studio series "Interim Urbanism," this studio considered the architecture of "the stay," a working term that acknowledges the underexplored concept of a genre of architecture and urbanism that describes a spectrum of temporary habitation in all of its forms and intricacies. Aiming beyond the fascinations with the delights and limitations of the assumed ephemerality, the studio's goal was to reconsider the architecture of temporal habitation as a context and an instrument to reshape the city. The studio engaged the potentials in architecture of temporal habitation through a set of projects diverse in concept, location, and scale, and the forms of temporary occupation evolving to respond to new ideals of collectivity in the contemporary city.

14
15
16

FRACKED HOMES ¶ ANDRÉS JAQUE, CRITIC, WITH EDUARDO TAZÓN ¶ Starting in 2008, the hydraulic fracturing of Marcellus Shale (the largest volume of recoverable natural gas resource in the US) has rendered the homes and farms of Susquehanna County, in Northeastern Pennsylvania, the scene of a great controversy. The uneven confrontation of rural domesticity with massive extraction has mobilized activism and media attention, but together with that, it comprises a great deal of architectural design challenges. ¶ 1. What is the way architectural design can play a relevant role in the conflicts of the contemporary country-site? ¶ 2. What is the way architectural design engages with Nature, at a time in which Nature has become massively transformable by man, and an equally massive source of catastrophe, inequality, risk, and uncertainty? ¶ 3. What are the methodologies that can turn architectural design into a mediating force in ongoing uneven environmental conflicts? ¶ While cities might be becoming sanitized spaces for a safe and comfortable life, the countryside is progressively the place where a great number of architectural, technological, territorial and environmental transformations are taking place. The studio explored the potential of the RURAL's emerging leadership to redefine the focus of architectural engagement.

17

#CLOSERIKERS ¶ LAURA KURGAN, CRITIC, WITH GRGA BASIC ¶ Rikers Island is New York City's largest jail complex, located in the East River between the Bronx and Queens. Our studio considered what it would take—architecturally and otherwise—to close the jail at Rikers Island. We looked at existing proposals and the campaigns that have animated them, and proposed speculative, activist, and evidence-based design prototypes and infrastructures for its alternatives. Running for mayor of New York, Bill de Blasio often spoke of income inequality as "a tale of two cities," rich and poor. In this studio, we followed former Rikers inmate and now #CloseRikers activist Glenn Martin in approaching Rikers as a "third city." Martin calls it "a place where human beings, including children...are robbed of their sanity, their dignity, their families, their communities and sometimes, their lives." The notion of the "third city" tells us that this is a problem not simply of criminal justice, or inequality, or policy, but most importantly one of architecture. But architects have been slow to pick up on this, and most of the responses so far have been conventional, or worse. Our studio set out to change this.

18
19
20

TALES OF TWO BROTHERS: SPECULATIVE DOCUMENTATION, FUTURES, AND MORE ¶ JIMENEZ LAI, CRITIC, WITH TRUDY WATT ¶ Once upon a time there were two brothers: the North Brother Island and the South Brother Island. Located just on the backdoors of one of the densest and most important cities on earth, these two islands were strangely left alone as wilderness on the East River for the centuries as New York City developed into a metropolis. This studio took a closer look at these two small islands as architects, journalists and speculators, in hopes of learning something more about not just the past and present of Manhattan, but the United States at large. ¶ The studio used these two empty islands as platforms to imagine alternate realities. If architectural representation is a place to tell stories, the studio took a left-turn after the midterm. Our stories each had a political agenda—from Islamophobia

militarized architecture, architecture as city-states, or the import/export cycles between architecture on the two U.S. coasts, the students explored their ideas into architectural allegories.

21
22

NEW ERA GE STUDIO ¶ DOMINIC LEONG AND CHRISTOPHER LEONG, CRITICS, WITH JESSIE BAXA ¶ 21st century Western culture can be defined by two general socio-technological experiences: stress management and maximizing human potential. Both experiences could be described as the result of VUCA, a continual state of Variability, Uncertainty, Complexity and Ambiguity and exacerbated by the discontinuities between the biological speed of human evolution versus the technological acceleration of computing power (e.g. Darwin versus Moore's Law). ¶ Equally, as our collective experiences are increasingly hyper-mediated, we struggle to keep pace with the increasingly complex and continuous flows of information which govern our world. Many have theorized and forecasted this moment as either an existential crisis (Debord, Baudrillard, etc.) or as the next step on the path to technological transcendence (Elon Musk, Kurzweil, etc.), while architecture continues to search for its effectiveness as an antidote to the social anxieties of hyper-mediation or as an accelerator for unlocking human potential. ¶ This studio explored architecture's capacity to facilitate new forms of collectivity in response to the increasingly dominant culture of flow, agility, and relentless mediation. Beginning with research into forms of collective living movements and intentional communities, the students developed formal, material, organizational, scalar, and climatic techniques to speculate on new forms of collectivity in a non-urban setting.

23
24

THE WHY FACTORY @ GSAPP ¶ WINY MAAS, JAVIER ARPA, ADRIEN RAVON, CRITICS ¶ Offered by The Why Factory simultaneously at TUDelft, IIT Chicago and GSAPP, this studio was an invitation to look at the city through a multitude of scenarios simultaneously, and to test the capacity of adaption of a home, a block, a neighborhood, a city, a region... to the application of a new agenda. ¶ What if the average global temperature rises 6°C instead of 2°C by 2100? What if all national borders are eliminated? What about animal species that were basically neglected from urban life for decades? How does energy consumption define what a city can be? As new concerns arise, designers must devise a method for confronting the ever-increasing number of parameters that the city needs to address. ¶ Yet contemporary design rarely—if ever—takes those scenarios into account. Rather, design disciplines continue to engage the task of planning and designing for new settlement in fixed, singular and unresponsive ways that presume the preferred outcome is the only one worth elaborating. However, designers need to begin thinking in terms of scenarios, contingency and variability. On that score, students were confronted with a multitude of what ifs? that shaped their design. ¶ Students started the semester testing a series of hypothetical scenarios at the scale of the home and finally combined the resulting units into a 100×100×100 meter theoretical city block.

25
26

SPATIAL & PROGRAMMATIC ANOMALIES: BARRANQUILLA A DUAL CITY ¶ GIANCARLO MAZZANTI, CARLOS MEDEL-LÍN, CRITICS, WITH FELIPE ROBAYO ¶ Context: Barranquilla: historically known as the first multicultural metropolis that was developed in Colombia after Colonial times. By being established on the banks of the Magdalena River, it became the gateway to the Caribbean and the channel for most of the economic and cultural development of the country. ¶ The anomaly: heterotopias are forms relating to desires, which have grown and are expressed as shapers of the urban context where they take place. The problem is that the individual's desire is reduced to the potential of its realization. Therefore if this longing is not materialized, individuals lose the capacity to understand their self as part of the public realm, which is crucial to reach citizenship. ¶ A toy for the other(s): the first exercise looked to develop a TOY for learning about Barranquilla and its inhabitants using the stranger or foreigner as the active catalyst. The purpose was to allow the exchange of information, knowledge, products, services, objects, etc. ¶ The public building: we invited the students

to speculate on what a public building could mean in a city like Barranquilla. This raises the potential of architecture as a social catalyst, transforming city dynamics and allowing the degree of cultural sustainability necessary for the development of this city.

27
28

THE SPACE OF THE WALL: RE-CONCEIVING THE URBAN STADIUM ¶ GREGG PASQUARELLI, CRITIC, WITH ANGELICA TRE-VINO BACCON ¶ The architecture of cities can be defined as the strategic (or expressive, or opportunistic) manipulation of edges, surfaces, and apertures to define and enable certain human relationships—in other words, we build our walls and then our walls build us. In this context, however, the unbroken wall, the brutal wall, the pure wall, is widely accepted to be a city-killer: denying interaction, deadening sidewalks, inviting vandalism, ennui, and neglect. Of all the programs we design into our cities, the stadium/arena presents among the greatest challenges in this regard. An inversion of the preferred focus of urban attention tends to present the most impenetrable and problematic surfaces to the street. Throughout the studio, we interrogated the idea of the wall and tested strategies of control. We analyzed the thickness of the wall, the space of the wall itself, modulating to maximize performance in the challenging condition of the urban stadium edge.

29
30
31
32

THE URBAN ECOLOGY STUDIO: MANHATTAN PIER 52 URBAN BEACH ¶ RICHARD PLUNZ, PATRICIA CULLIGAN, CRIT-ICS, WITH AMY MOTZNY, ROB ELLIOTT, TYLER SILVESTRO ¶ The Fall 2016 Urban Ecology Studio—comprised of both graduate architecture and engineering students from Columbia University, working with place-based community stakeholders as clients—focused on Water

Urbanism and the next generation of development of cities on water in an era of increasing water-based hazards related to sea level rise, climatological change and extreme weather events. This studio worked in the context of one of the most important remaining public spaces on the West Side of Manhattan: the 5-acre waterfront peninsula situated between Gansevoort Street and Little West 12th Street at the nexus of the Whitney Museum and the High Line and the Hudson River Park. ¶ Work was coordinated with the goals of Hudson River Park Trust, which is the owner of the site and is currently considering plans for the peninsula development. Emphasis was on ecological restoration, public education, and a new urban/water relationship. Design and programmatic intentions were explored across scales, culminating in programmatic innovation and architectural design residing in an overall infrastructural and ecological framework concept and a detailed place-specific formal node.

33
34

ENLIGHTENMENT 2.0 ¶ PHILIPPE RAHM, CRITIC, WITH RAY WANG ¶ In his article "Why Has the Critical Run out of Steam," the French philosopher Bruno Latour states the impotence that postmodern argumentation (subjective and narrative) faces against contemporary crises, including global warming. Against a return of the obscurantism, Latour argues for a revival of the Spirit of the Enlightenment, which can be understood as a return to "reason", objective and universal. The Age of Enlightenment developed throughout the eighteenth century away from Royal courts and power; instead in new spaces for public speaking—coffee houses and salons. The public debate—free, critical and sitting on objective reasons and scientific methods—took shape around the shared heat of the coffee house or Salon and the intellectual excitement of coffee and tea. It invented new public space and forms of sociability, of political practice, intellectual and artistic life. ¶ Our design studio posed challenges at the programmatic and formal level. The program rethought the physical form of public speech, proposing to reinvent in different French regions the salons and coffee houses of the eighteenth century, inside of the digital and global era. The form was based on an updated architectural language, intensifying scientific principles of energy saving, terroir physical capacity, sustainable development, and climate, reaching a new form of beauty.

35

IN-FORMING ARCHITECTURE: ADAPTIVE TRANSFORMATION OF THE UNITED NATIONS HEADQUARTERS IN GENEVA, SWITZERLAND ¶ MARK RAKA-TANSKY, JORGE OTERO-PAILOS, CRITICS ¶ This studio, developed in collaboration with the United Nations, focused on adding a new programmatic intervention into their campus in Geneva, Switzerland. The campus began first as the Palais des Nations, infamous among designers for the rejection of Le Corbusier's competition scheme; the top five winning architects collaborated on the Art Deco complex the Palais des Nations from 1929–1938, with subsequent renovations and additions in the 1950s and 1970s. With the explosion of new forms of media, necessary for the ever more complex modes of global communication, a 50,000 square foot addition to engage the expansion of the United Nations Information Services and the Human Rights Council was proposed. From our contemporary moment looking both back and forward, from the past toward the future, the studio explored the informational and organizational logics and illogics of the Palais des Nations and the Geneva campus.

36
37
38

CONCEPT & SITE: REVISITING THE "GYM" ¶ BERNARD TSCHUMI, CRITIC; WITH ESTEBAN DE BACKER, JEROME HAFERD ¶ The studios run by Bernard Tschumi all start from the idea of "Concept." This semester, we looked at "Concept and Site," at how a concept affects a site, or a site affects a concept; how topography and social context can become an opportunity rather than a constraint. ¶ In 1968, Columbia University started to build a gym on Morningside Park, on the slope leading to Harlem (but accessible only from the summit above) for the exclusive use of Columbia College students. Considered insensitive and racially charged, the gym was eventually abandoned. More than 50 years later, our studio investigated how the gym (and other

programs) could have been designed on this challenging site.

39
40
41
42

PARADOXICAL EFFICIENCIES: EFFICIENCY AND EXORBITANCE IN ARCHITECTURE ¶ MARC TSURUMAKI, CRITIC, WITH MICHAEL SCHISSEL ¶ This studio was driven by a critical re-evaluation of notions of efficiency in architecture—recognizing that every efficiency implies a corresponding excess, exorbitance or waste. This coupling of efficiency to its opposite creates a fertile contradiction—an irrational residue—that can be used to hijack a narrow functionalist conception of efficiency. In an era of performance-driven optimization, this studio pursued extreme, perverse, or satirical efficiencies as a means of generating new programmatic and spatial opportunities. If the value of architecture exists to the precise degree that it transcends the strictly utilitarian, the work of the studio sought the point at which efficiency folds back on itself, to the point where it generates a productive exorbitance.

43
44

CATALYTIC DETROIT ¶ MABEL O. WILSON, CRITIC, WITH ZACHARY COLBERT ¶ Catalytic Detroit radically re-envisioned the future of an American rust-belt metropolis. Complex and sometime contradictory conditions of the present Detroit, such as border crossings, urban farms, stadiums, abandoned fairgrounds, and high-rises were re-imagined by the studio into future scenarios that offered analytical and critical perspectives on the city. We reconsidered "site" as a 21st century networked, relational and logistical condition existing within global flows of capital, material and labor. The studio sought catalytic opportunities, confluences and/or anomalies to leverage new architectural possibilities. Studies were further honed through a studio visit to Detroit to engage in further research on project sites and meet with activists,

developers, planners and architects re-visioning Detroit's future. With a rich body of research and parametric and analogue models as a catalyst, the studio developed architectural propositions in the form of videos on four sites that radically imagined Detroit in 2116. The studio conceived theses on the utopian or dystopian possibilities of the city's architectural and urban futures.

1

Harrison Nesbitt,
David Kagawa

2

Jonathan Izen

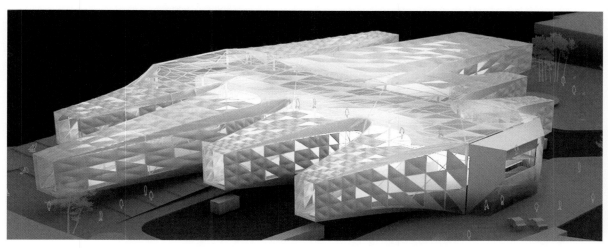

Eugene Chang

3

4

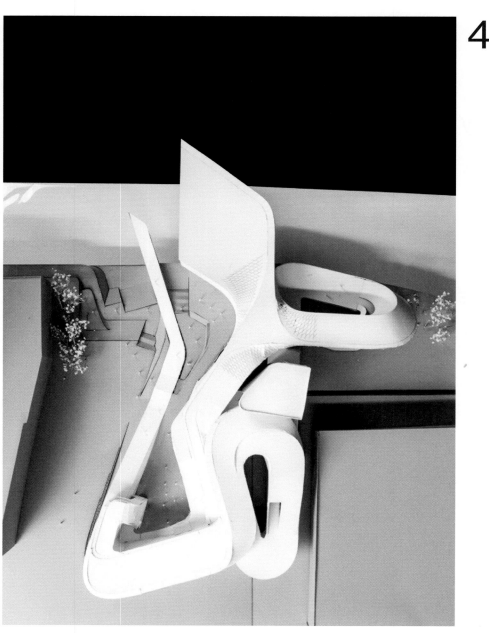

Ruizhi Wang, Sen Peter Zhang

5

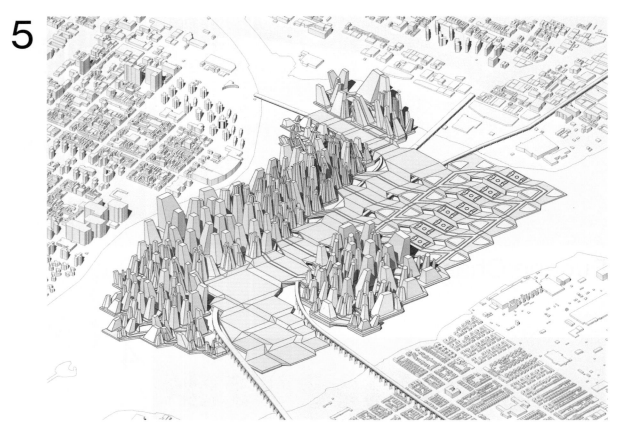

Anthony Zampolin

6

Naifei Liu

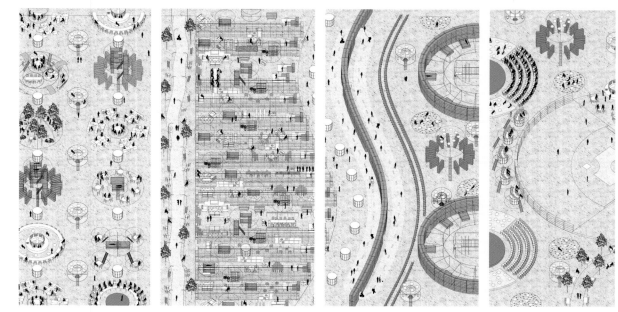

7

Chantal Jahn

8

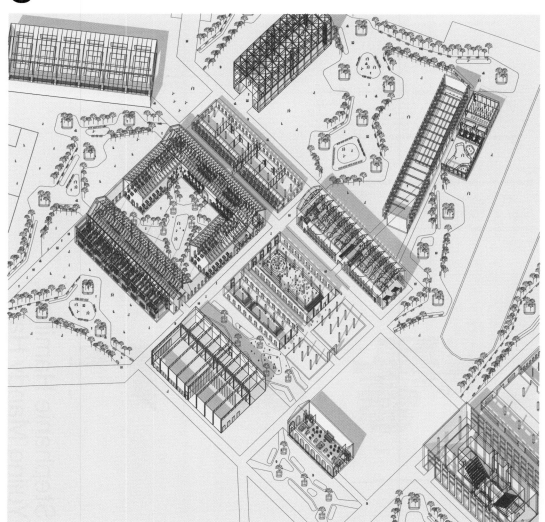

Nabila Morales Perez

9

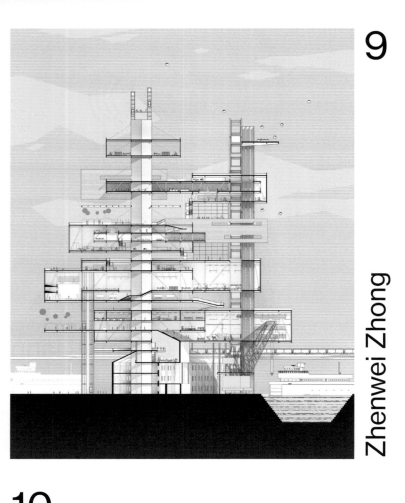

Zhenwei Zhong

10

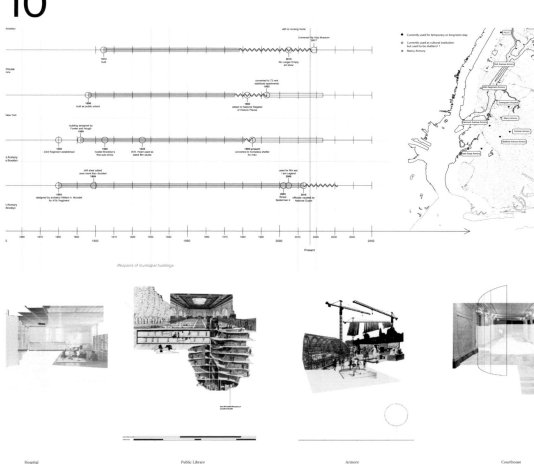

Hospital
as day care

Public Library
as job training center

Armory
as cultural and and recreational venue

Courthouse
as personal lounge

Stephanie Hamilton,
Yujing Mandy Han

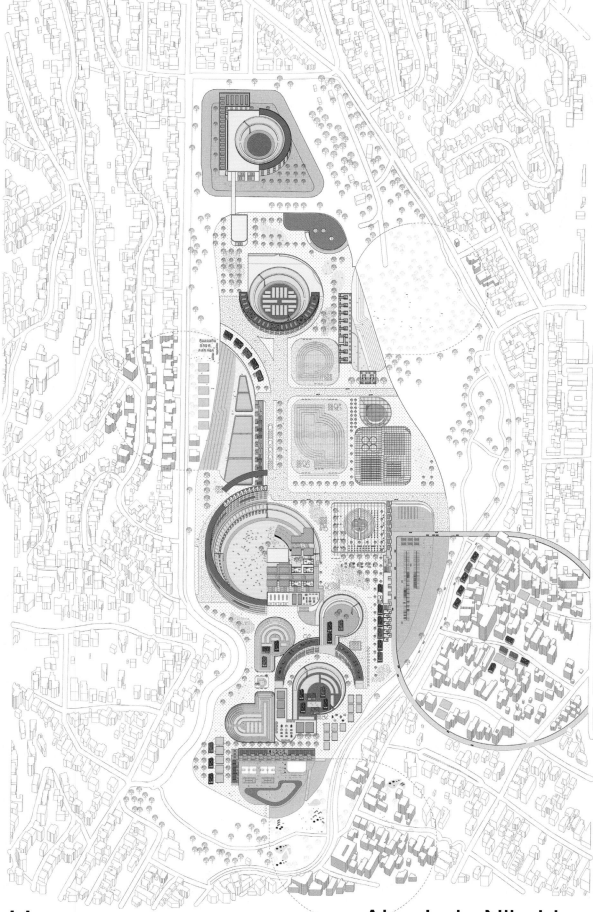

11

Alex Loh, Nila Liem

12

Stephanie Tager,
Kig Veerasunthorn

13

A.L. Hu, Sunaina Shah

14

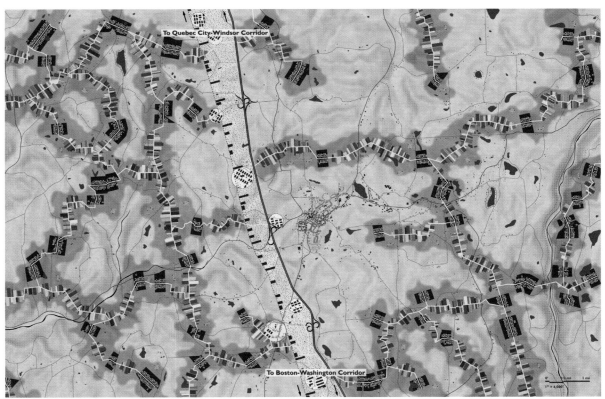

Kevin MacNichol

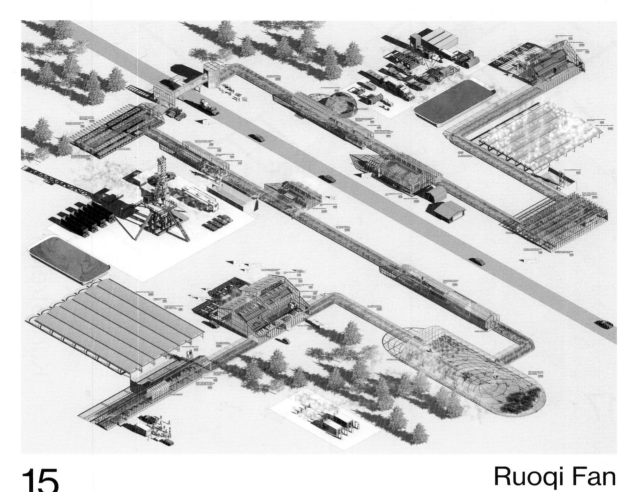

15

16

Ruoqi Fan

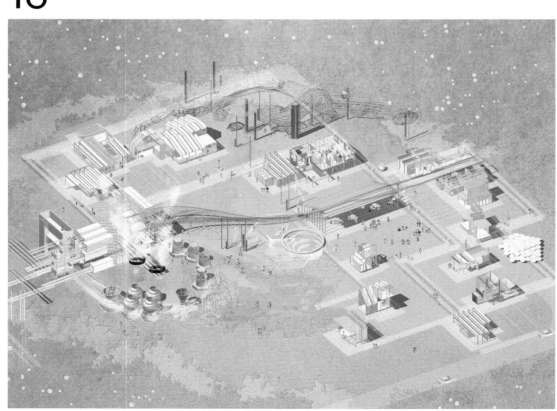

Pei Pei Yang

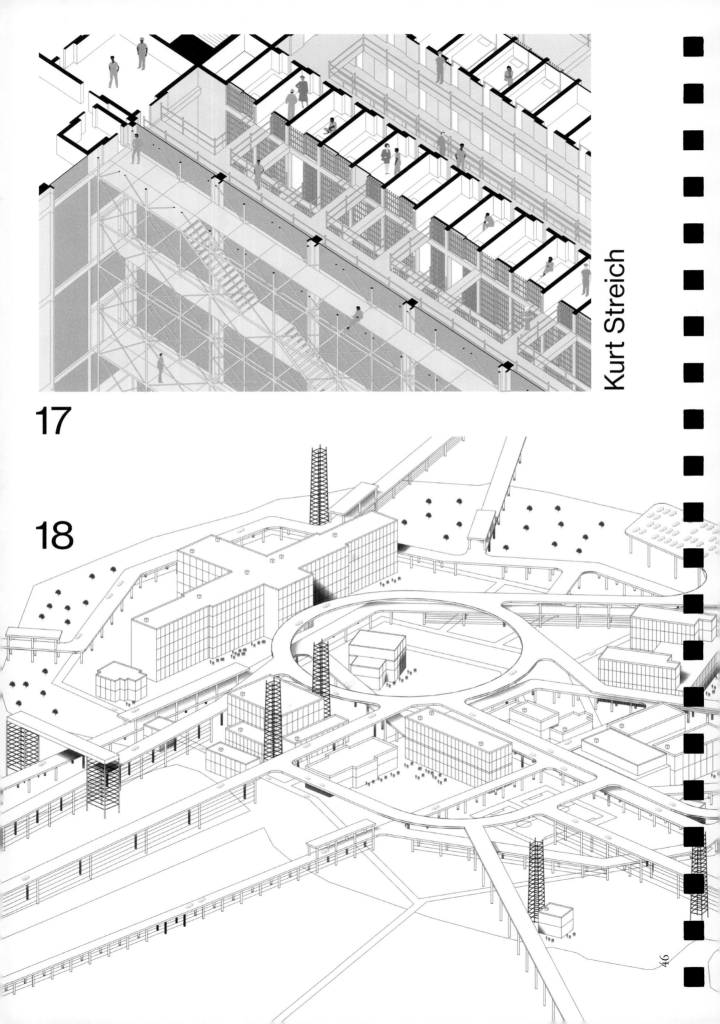

17

18

Kurt Streich

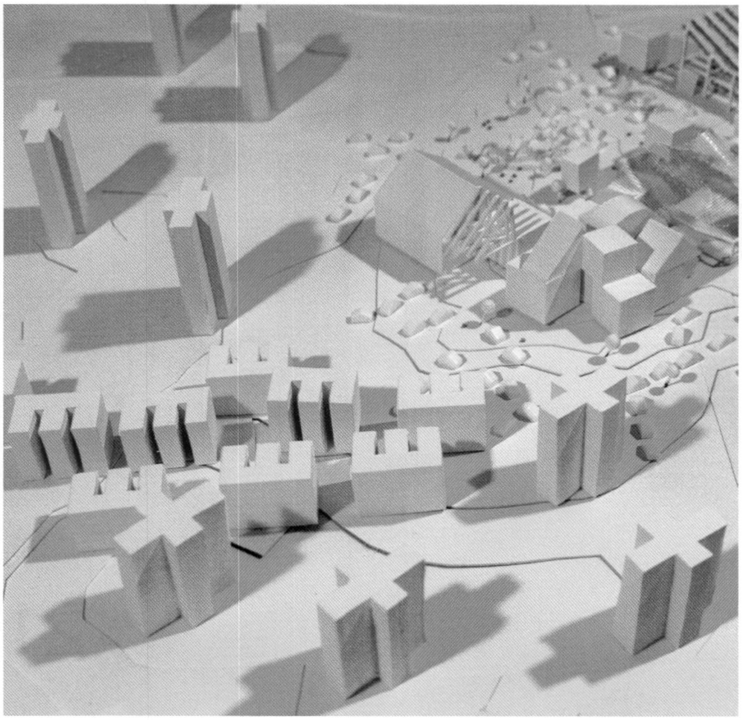

Emily Mohr

19

20

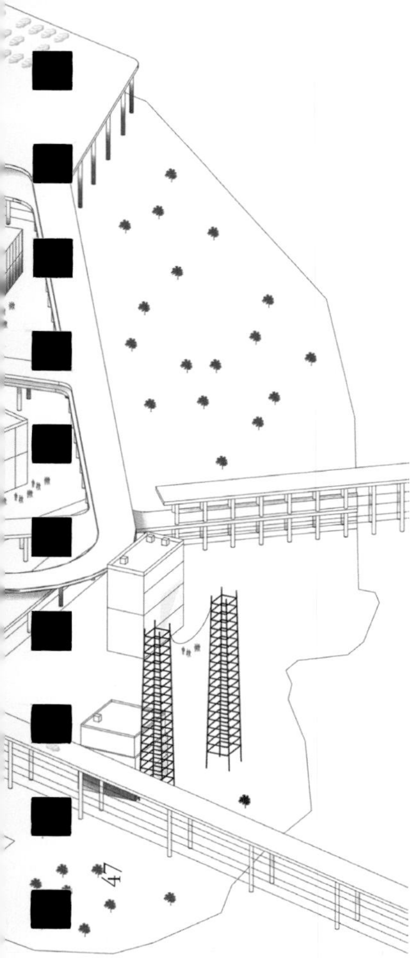

Sara Rad

47

Pei Zhou

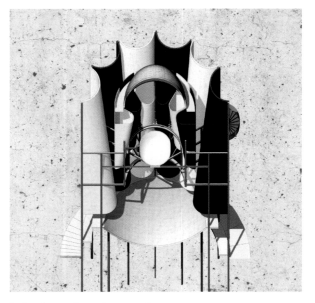

Valerie Lechene

21

22

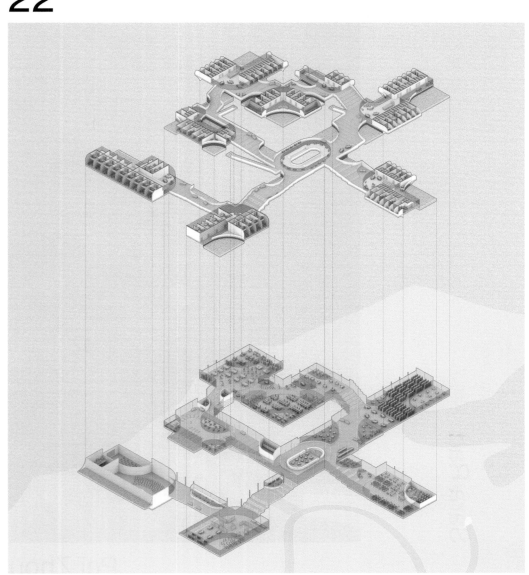

Thomas Smith, Lin Wu

Jean Gu

23

24

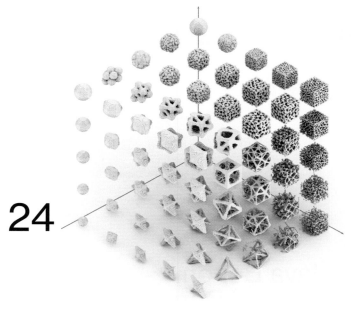

Michael Storm

Keren Bao, Zhe Cao

25

26

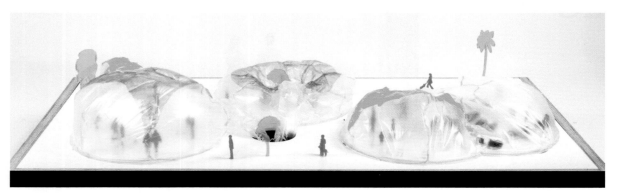

Dasylava Bolton,
Zhengmeng Dong

27 Jae Han Bae, Tigran Kostandyan

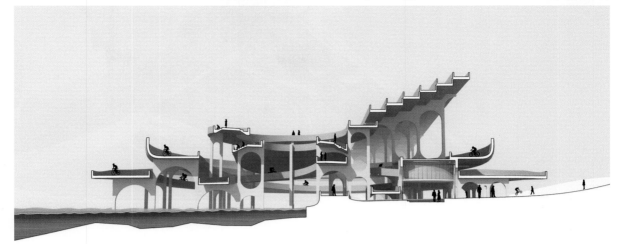

28

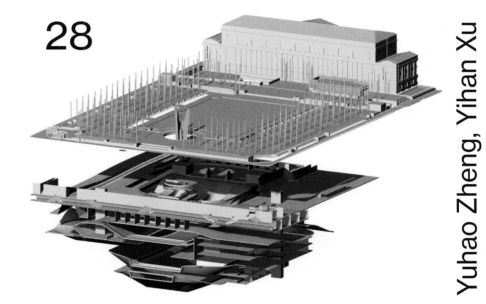

Yuhao Zheng, Yihan Xu

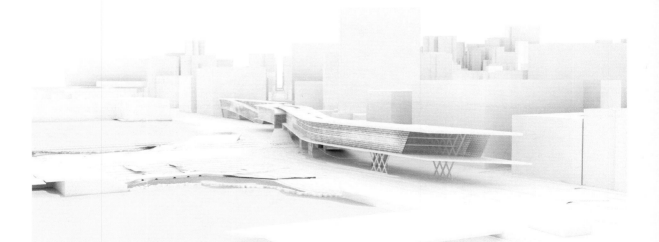

29 Elizabeth Cohn-Martin, Reza Dorrani

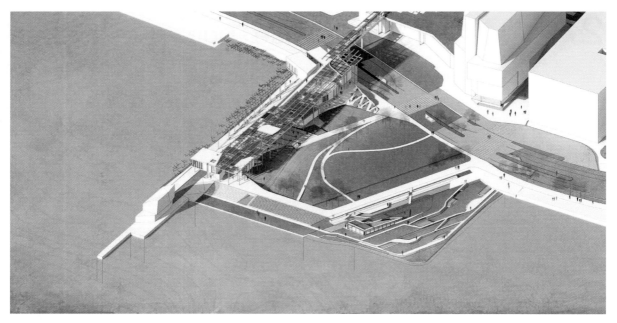

30 Karen Berberyan, Yang Jie

31

Yun Gong,
Shuo Zhang,
Yifang Hou

32

Ruosen Du,
Jingxuan Wu

33

Zhida Wu

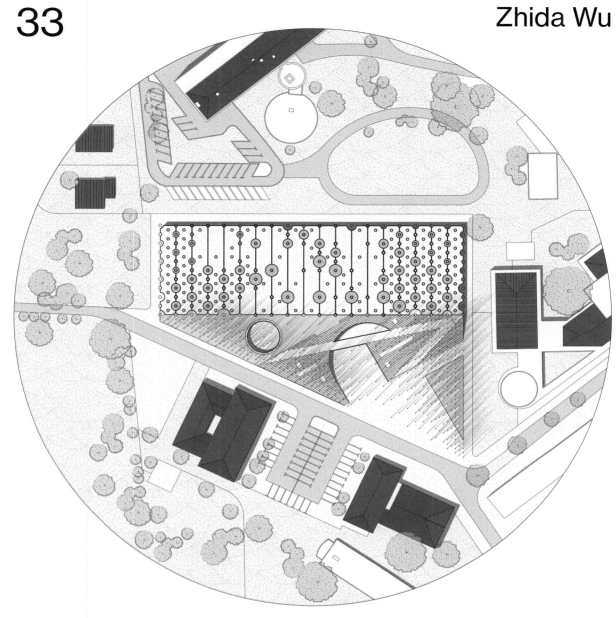

34

Sebastian Cilloniz

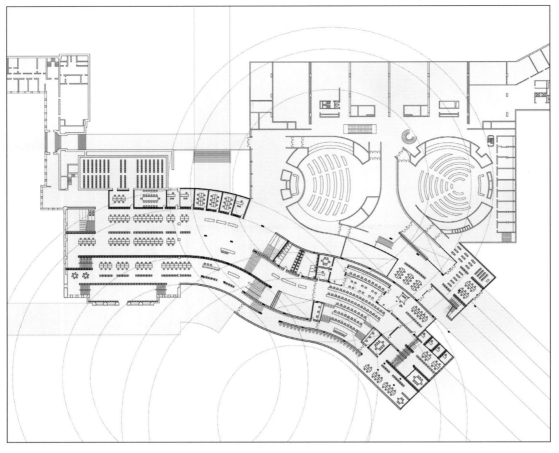

35

Andrew M. Luy

36

Yini Xu, Chung-Yi Lin

ADV ARCH STUDIO V

Chung-Yi Lin,
Yini Xu

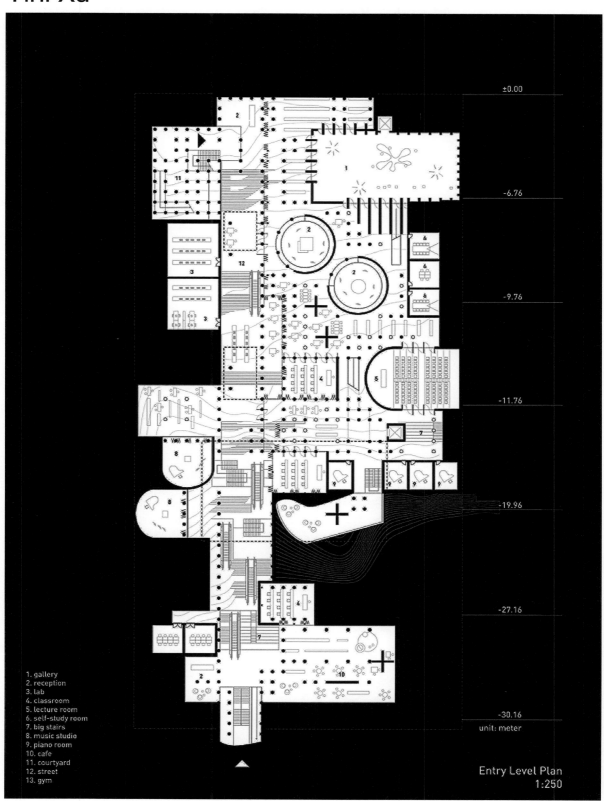

±0.00

-6.76

-9.76

-11.76

-19.96

-27.16

-30.16

unit: meter

1. gallery
2. reception
3. lab
4. classroom
5. lecture room
6. self-study room
7. big stairs
8. music studio
9. piano room
10. cafe
11. courtyard
12. street
13. gym

Entry Level Plan
1:250

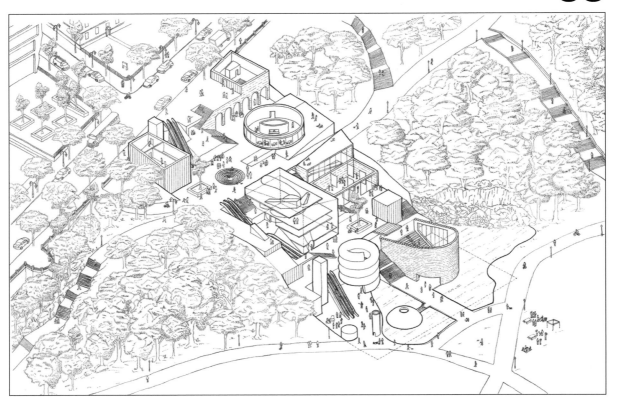

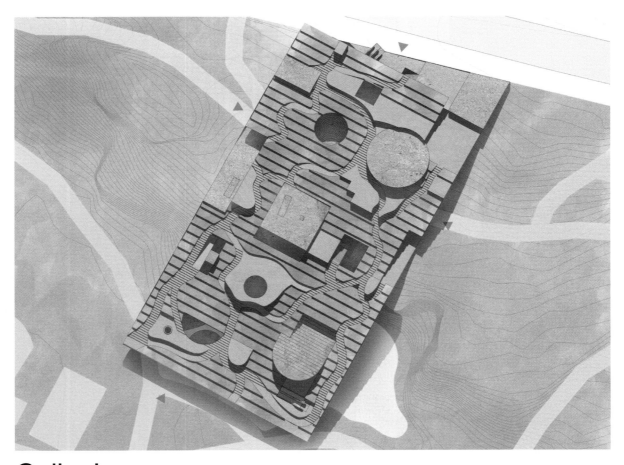

Colin Joyce,
Giovanni Cozzani

Siyu Zhao

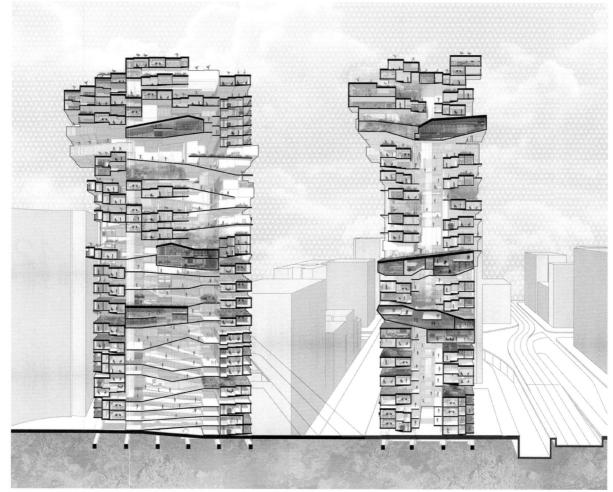

39

Ines Yupanqui

40

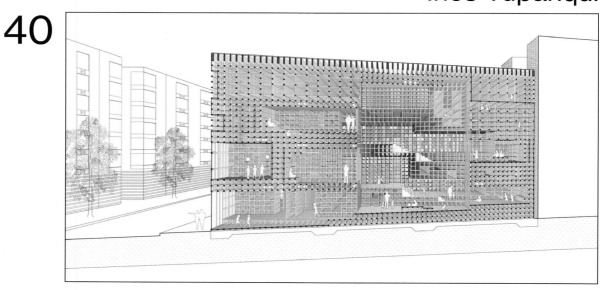

Mike Howard

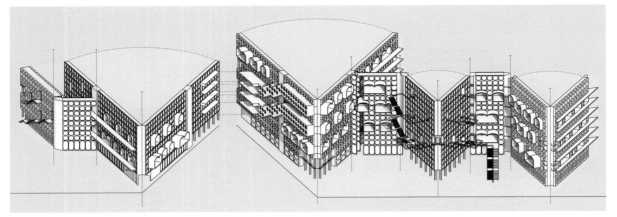

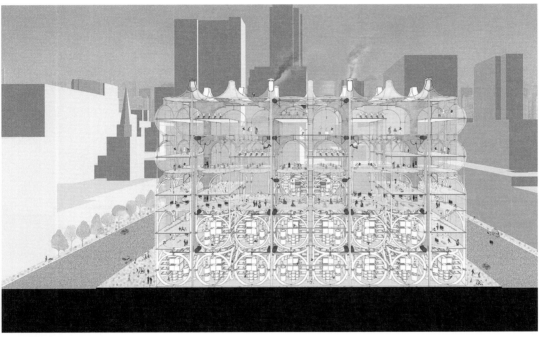

42

Qiu Jin

43

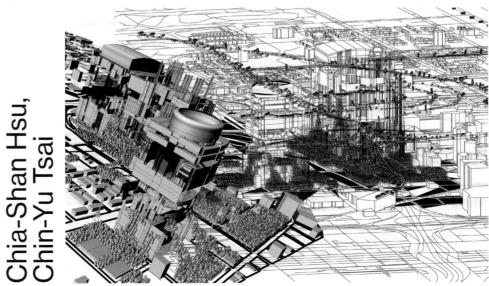

Chia-Shan Hsu,
Chin-Yu Tsai

Julie Pedtke

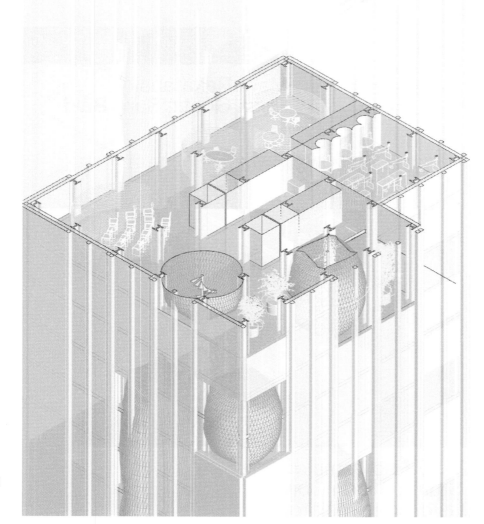

Patricia Culligan, Michael Waite, Nicole De Feo, Steven Chen, Celine Armstrong, Amy Shell, Victor Body-Lawson

Dominic Leong, Mimi Hoang, Jimenez Lai, Eva Franch i Gilabert, Alexandra Cunningham, Chris Leong

Mark Rakatansky, Erica Goetz, Sunil Bald

Danil Nagy, Ziad Jamaleddine, Susan Sturm, Alison Cornyn, Grga Basic, Leah Meisterlin

Marc Tsurumaki, Talene Montgomery,
Mark Rakatansky, Leslie Gill,
Erica Goetz, David Lewis

Bernard Tschumi, Jimenez Lai,
Reinhold Martin, Iben Falconer, Kate Orff,
Michael Sorkin, Anthony Vidler

The Master of Science degree in Advanced Architectural Design is a three-term program consisting of Summer, Fall and Spring terms. The objective of the program is to provide outstanding young professionals who hold a Bachelor of Architecture or Master of Architecture degree the opportunity to enter into an intensive, postgraduate study that encourages critical thought in the context of design speculation.

The program is viewed as a framework in which both academic and professional concerns are explored. Overall, the program emphasizes an experimental approach to research and architectural design rigorously grounded in multiple, complex realities. Specifically, the program seeks to: (1) Address the challenges and possibilities of global urbanization by exploring the city and its architecture in all its forms. (2) Engage in a complex definition of architecture, from the questioning of the program to the formulation of design strategies. (3) Produce architectural objects—both digital and physical—which reflect an open, critical engagement both with new and existing technologies. (4) Articulate architecture as a cultural practice that combines critical thought, design experimentation and ethical responsibilities in an interdisciplinary milieu. (5) Activate a wide debate on the contemporary conditions that critically affect the course of the discipline and the profession.

The program brings together a set of required studios with elective courses that are shared with other programs in the School and that promote intellectual cross-fertilization among disciplines. The advanced studios frequently utilize New York as a design laboratory— a global city that presents both unique challenges and unique opportunities. The program has long been a site for architects from around the globe to test concepts and confront changes that affect architecture and cities worldwide.

Advanced Architectural Design Summer 2016

1
2

HYBRID RESIDENTIAL INFRA-STRUCTURES IN THE BRONX: TYPOLOGICAL CORRECTIONS AND RE-OCCUPATIONS OF THE PROJECTS ¶ JUAN HERREROS AND IGNACIO G. GALÁN, CRITICS, WITH CHARLES HAJJ ¶ Architects' responsibilities go beyond the construction of new architectures, to concern the management of existing structures and of the built environment at large. This agenda demands devising alternatives to conventional architectural strategies (usually operating on one building at the time) with the aim of crafting comprehensive, integrated, and open large-scale strategies. In previous studios we have selected case studies located in central and consolidated areas of the city that are either in bad condition, infra-utilized or significantly vacant, in order to speculate upon alternative futures for them. This semester, we operated on a number of New York City social housing developments (popularly known as "Projects") in the South Bronx, as a physical fabric that is full of qualities but needs to be re-thought in order to address its current stigmatization and lack of urban integration. We proposed recycling solutions that considered both the potentials of re-occupying existing buildings as well as the possibilities derived from their transformation. Dealing with the characteristics of the current structures, their relationships, and their underlying potentials, each project designed a series of typological corrections activating processes of re-programming, re-densifying, re-scaling, re-signifying, etc.

3
4

IN SERVICE OF (2) ¶ PHU HOANG, CRITIC, WITH FELIPE ROBAYO ¶ The studio investigated today's "culture of service" to understand the contemporary definition of work, and in doing so, revisited the late-modernist categorization of servant and served program organization. Championed by the late modernist architects Louis Kahn, Cedric Price, Richard Rogers and Norman Foster, the utopian project of modular construction and flexible spaces was predicated on a social division between those who were served and their "servants" (workers). This social hierarchy has been replaced with a "culture of service" in which both the servant and served can provide service, most evident with the WeWork and AirBnB business models. It is increasingly difficult to determine who the "other" is in the so-called "sharing economy." The studio intersected two different architectural forms of service—the omnipresent incubator workplace with building infrastructure services—in order to ask what the role of service and "work" will be in architecture. Students proposed design alternatives to the incubator, in which an argument about the "culture of service" was tested in a contemporary workplace for a chosen program—a university, a hotel, or a data center.

5
6
7
8

POWERS OF N: ARCHITECTURES OF IMMERSION AND BEWILDERMENT ¶ MARIANA IBAÑEZ, CRITIC, WITH DOROTHY CONNOLLY-TAYLOR ¶ In 1977, Charles and Ray Eames made the movie "Powers of Ten and the Relative Size of Things in the Universe." From the smallest to the largest structures known to humans, from a carbon atom to the edge of the known universe, the movie depicts a world that can be understood linearly, is human-centric, and can be defined by its physicality. ¶ Forty years later, we know that there are things much smaller than atoms, that the universe is not empty and

quiet, and that our world is not only a vast collection of static elements, but a dynamic environment in a constant state of flux. ¶ Powers of Ten remains a fascinating artifact, and at the time it was made, presented an eye-opening view of the universe. As an art practice, the Eames were very effective in connecting the worlds of culture and technology. ¶ This studio—"Powers of n"—proposed an architecture embedded in a technological world that is non-linear, exists as a shared domain between human and non-human actors, and creates a complex entanglement of elements and relations. The work of the studio was positioned between reality and fantasy, in order to produce a systematic and rigorous description of space, context and environment, and simultaneously the tools and mechanisms for its transformation.

9
10
11

OCCUPY MIES, REVISITING MIDTOWN'S MODERNIST LEGACY ¶ ZIAD JAMALEDDINE, CRITIC, WITH SHARY TAWIL CHERBOWSKI ¶ What if, in a final act and perhaps a sign of rebirth, New York would kill its "sacred cows"—Seagram, CBS, the UN headquarters, etc.—by hacking, squatting, and occupying the "rationalist" modernist structures with a new architectural and urban agenda, taking a cue from the Occupy Wall Street movement, and a more socially-driven agenda. Instead of a city of (hollow) hyper-private vertical spears—a descendant of modernist corporate architecture—can we re-imagine a more democratic and inclusive city by reclaiming its ground as truly collective?

12
13
14

BEACHES OF NEW YORK ¶ AAD STUDIO, SUMMER 2016 ¶ ANDRÉS JAQUE, CRITIC, WITH EDUARDO TAZON AND ZHEHUI CHANG ¶ What is the way architecture defines the line between the ocean and the urban? What are the conflicts this line currently embodies?

What is the way design can take care of these conflicts, and the way it can reinvent the way we deal with them? ¶ Property markets, climate change, army veterans' benefits, associative summering, toxicity subrogation, the collective making of nature, and border regulation are all colliding in a very specific architectural entity: the "Beach Front." The architecture of the Beach Front both registers and participates in the production of all these realities, and provides an access point to reinvent them by means of redesign. ¶ Based on both analysis and field work developed in the most differentiated "Beaches of New York," the studio focused on the depiction of their materiality and on their performativity, and it discussed the conflicts each case is a part of. Each project proposed evolved scenarios in which the architecture of each beach front is reinvented to sense and intervene in the conflicts the line is part of.

15

LEARNING FROM FOOD ¶ JOAQUIM MORENO, CRITIC, WITH LIONEL ARY SLAMA ¶ Learning from Food was the encounter of the "learning from what surround us" attitude with a particular subject that breaches the division between inside and outside: Food; that portion of what surrounds us that we put in our mouths in order to construct ourselves. This outside that is consumed through the mouth is both nature and culture, which makes food a very problematic descriptor of both our objectivity and our subjectivity. Food is the substance through which we incorporate, through which we became bodies as well as subjects. Because it is a bridge, Food is an opportunity to problematize the relationship between science and nature, culture and nurture, individual and collective, choice and compliance, and intimacy and extimacy. These questions were incorporated through the reinvention of a precise locus: the domestic kitchen. The design problem of the studio was the kitchen, the material was food and the design strategy was digestion.

16
17
18

META-MORPHIC ¶ MARK RAKATANSKY, CRITIC ¶ This studio explored the experimental possibilities of metamorphosis, the transformative invention of spatial form as it is manifest in and through social and cultural formations. We utilized one of the world's largest and most legendary collections of cultural form and transformation, the Metropolitan Museum of Art, both its main Fifth Avenue location and the Met Breuer, as sites to explore new forms of curatorial and informational space-making. Already imminent in the artifacts of all of its collections are deep cultural informational networks that drew forth with new spatial and temporal relations in the proposed additions to the existing facilities. In the design process, the studio also engaged the conceptual issues raised in the Met Breuer exhibition *Unfinished: Thoughts Left Visible*, which explored how artworks might more evidently reveal aspects of the thoughts and techniques utilized to create their intended effects, such that we can perceive them in the midst of their transformative process, in the midst of a meta-level of self-consciousness in their shaping, in the formation of their form.

19
20
21

REVIVIFY: ENGAGING TABOOS OF THE 21ST CENTURY METROPOLIS ¶ KARLA ROTHSTEIN, CRITIC, WITH YVONNE KONSTANTINIDIS ¶ Through the filter of death and remembrance in the 21st century metropolis, the studio explored new typologies of secular-sacred space; imagining how our collective mortality may redefine how we build, share, and utilize urban public space. ¶ In response to a growing awareness of the environmental toll of traditional burial techniques, new technologies understand the corpse as fertile material. These processes confront the taboo of death and the body while creating a space within which we can fundamentally resituate our relationship to the environment. ¶ The studio's propositions were sited at two under-utilized but highly symbolic spaces in New York City; one a body of land surrounded by water (Hart Island), the other a body of water surrounded by land (Central Park's Reservoir). ¶ Spanning scales from corporeal to urban, work was produced through an iterative process of translation; a feedback loop across analytical drawing and critical material explorations enabling the transformation of concept into organizational, spatial and tectonic systems.

22
23
24

TYPOLOGY VERSUS THE CITY: REDRAWING THE BRONX ¶ HILARY SAMPLE, CRITIC, WITH EDUARDO TAZON AND ZHEHUI CHANG ¶ In this design studio, students examined three distinct building types: office, housing, and cultural, all of which have a relationship to urban design and infrastructure. The studio questioned typology and its relationship to the contemporary city. For instance, housing and office buildings are, by their very nature, examples of generic building types. Some may argue that working within a particular typology produces boring buildings. However, it is precisely the thorough understanding of an individual type and by extension the potential for multiple typologies (think housing) that allows one to understand what has motivated the peculiarities of a particular building. The specificities of urban context, such as the Bronx in New York City, the baseline of this studio, produce unexpected moments that alter type's original form and program potential.

25
26
27
28

ART AND ARCHITECTURE...AND A GAS STATION ¶ DAN WOOD, JAMES WINES AND MAURIZIO BIANCHI MATTIOLI, CRITICS, WITH SEO HEE LEE ¶ Working together with James Wines of Site, this studio looked at the problem of the urban gas station in Manhattan through the lens of contemporary art—both as a means to discover new concepts and forms and as a critique of architecture itself. Using the fact that gas stations in Manhattan are disappearing at the same time that the MTA is overwhelmed, and noting that taxi, livery and service drivers are by far the largest users of gas stations, the studio proposed that the gas station be reconceived as an important piece of public infrastructure and explored ways to make the new gas station an important element in the public life of the city.

1

Beomkyu Kim

2

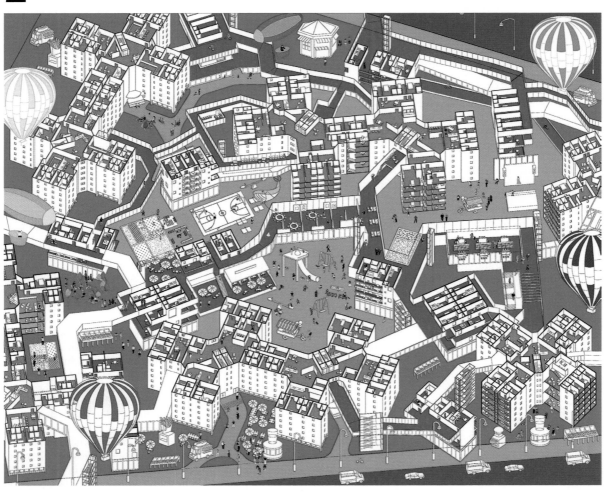

Siyu Zhao,
Shuying Mi

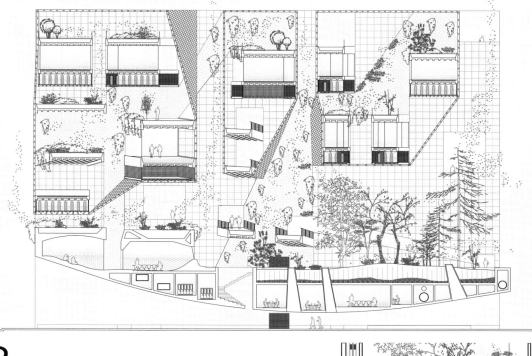

3

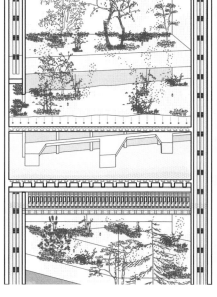

Sebastian Cilloniz, Tianji Liang

4

Wenmei Zhi, Zhiyun Wendy Huang

Sen Peter Zhang,
Anthony Zampolin

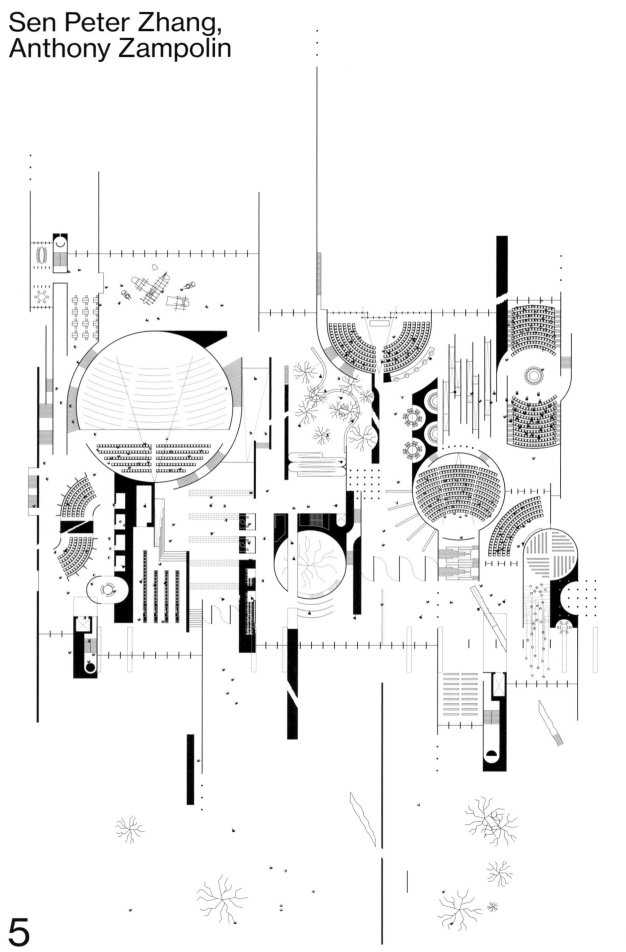

5

Sen Peter Zhang, Anthony Zampolin

Michelle Lozano, Yini Xu

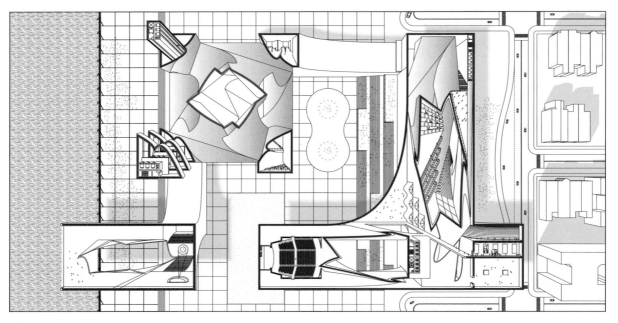

Sanghoon Jang, Kyle Wu

8

9

Sunaina Shah,
Wang Yuen, Leroy Tung

10

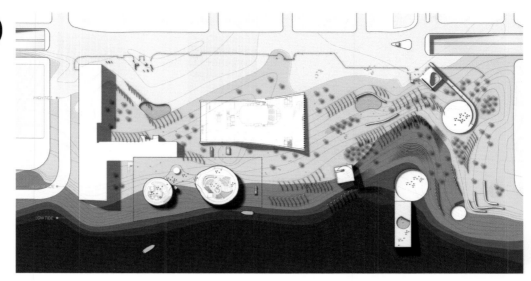

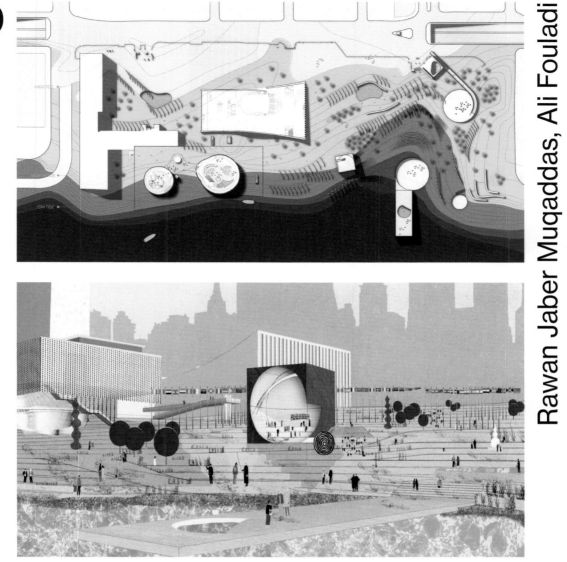

Rawan Jaber Muqaddas, Ali Fouladi

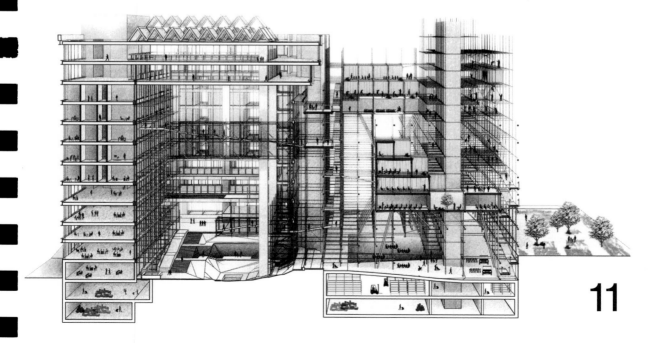

11

Nila Muliawati Liem,
Jiangjing Chen

Zhe Cao, Rui Guan

12

Ruosen Du, Yijun Wang

14

Shuo Zhang,
Zinan Wang

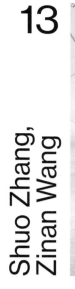

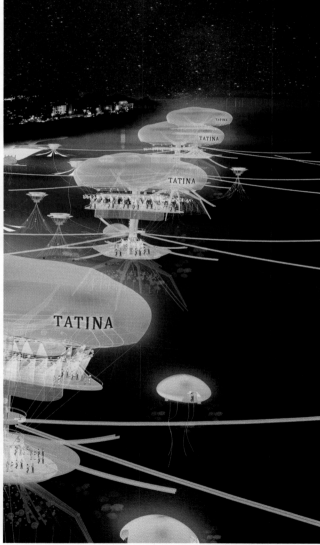

Ruosen Du, Yijun Wang

15

Keren Bao

16

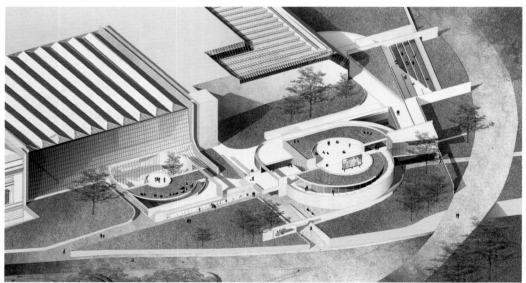

Jingxuan Wu

Jiayi Yi

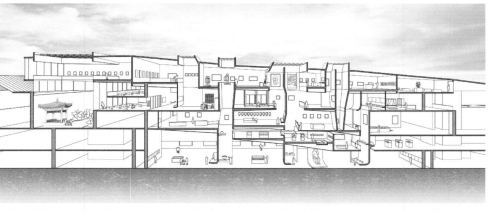

17

18

Chin-Yu Tsai

19

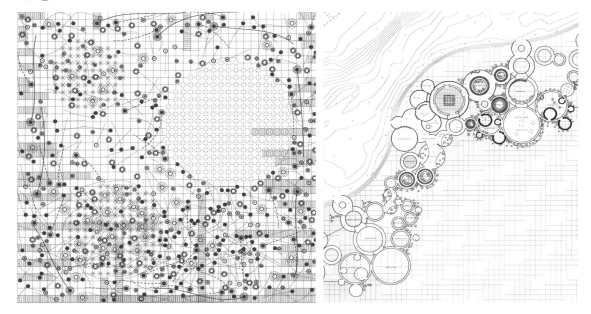

Kig Veerasunthorn,
Lin Wu

20

Zhan Xu, Jae Han Bae

21

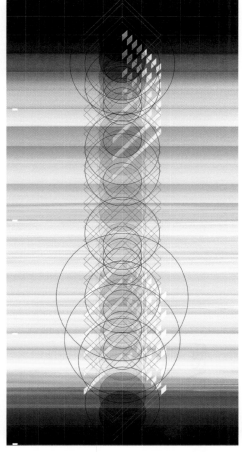

Kig Veerasunthorn,
Lin Wu

22

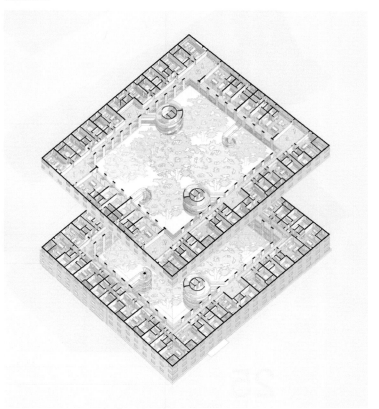

Sebastian Cruz

23

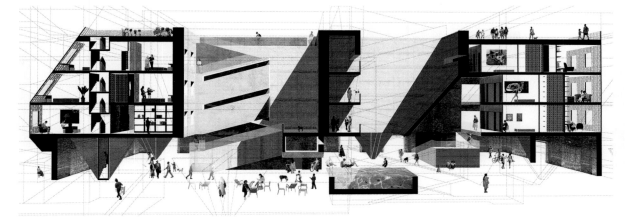

Jil Bentz

24

Karen Berberyan

25

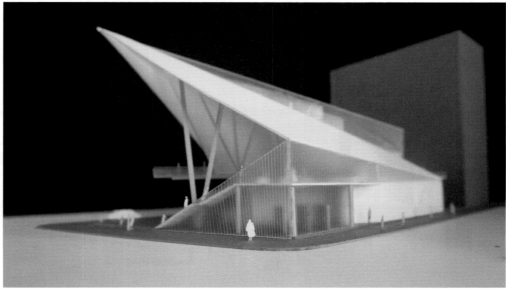

Ruizhi Wang

26

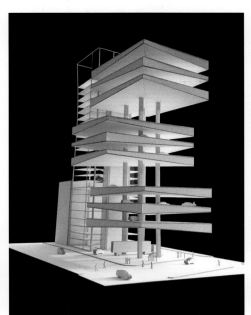

Stephen Smith

27

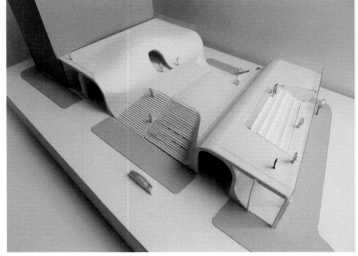

Cathy Yin

28

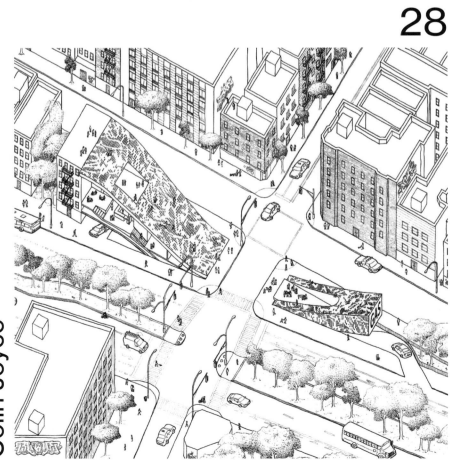

Colin Joyce

Scales of Environment

In the context of rapid urbanization and climate change, Advanced Studio IV develops a multi-scalar, ecological framework for designing the architecture, cities and landscapes of the future. The studio emphasized a common discussion across the class, while allowing each of the seven studios to explore unique ideas and approaches.

Environment & Technology

The studio explored past, present and future models of environment and technology. This exploration included a series of guest lectures and debates that focused on current innovative practices and on the study of environment and technology from a historical perspective.

Resilience

The studio built on the concept of design with resilience. Over the past few years, as climate change and the damage of natural disasters have accelerated, resilient systems have become appealing as a model for design with massive change, design with uncertainty and design with shifting and unknowable forces.

The Circular Economy

The Circular Economy is an emerging concept for a new era of design based on ecosystems with two types of nutrients: biological nutrients that are designed to circulate without unhealthy waste products, and technical nutrients that are designed to circulate without material impact. A recent report by the World Economic Forum explains, "In a world of close to 9 billion… the challenges of expanding supply to meet future demand are unprecedented…Ultimately the circular economy could decouple economic growth from resource consumption— truly a step-change."

Scale

The studio operated at multiple scales simultaneously. Over the course of the semester, we rethought materials, buildings, site plans and infrastructures. We investigated materials and buildings through an environmental lens, which included the consideration of embodied energy. Embodied energy—defined as the sum of all energy required to extract raw materials and then produce, transport, and assemble a product or building—accounts for an increasing percentage of overall energy consumption in architecture. By studying and designing with embodied energy, we engaged the tiny scale of the composition of materials and the enormous scale of global supply chains, as well as all of the scales in between.

Advanced Architecture Studio IV Spring 2017

1

2

AUTOMATIC—MACHINE LEARNING, ROBOTICS, LABOR, AND ENVIRONMENT ¶ DAVID BENJAMIN, CRITIC ¶ The ongoing story of humans and machines is a fascinating case study of technology in the 21st century, and it set the stage for Automatic: an architecture studio that engaged technology, environment, buildings, infrastructure, landscapes, ecosystems, numbers, images, stories, values, trade-offs, nature, and climate change. The studio combined technology with environment. It explored the latest generation of algorithms, robots, and artificial intelligence—and it interrogated several emerging frameworks related to themes of environment and technology, including the Circular Economy, Antifragility, and Hyper Nature. The studio also examined a range of design approaches, including multi-scalar design, new materials, and new software techniques. Within this context, the studio worked on architecture for education, energy, labor, and water bodies. Over the course of the semester, we generated proposals that were both quantitative and qualitative. We produced metrics, narratives, and images. We designed rules rather than fixed forms. We anticipated rapid change. And we welcomed shifting forces, unknowable crises, and uncertainty.

3

4

5

ARCHITECTURAL WILDS ¶ TEI CARPENTER, CRITIC ¶ The studio explored an expanded concept of environment to investigate how humans and nature can no longer be considered separate entities. Instead, we looked towards conditions of hybridity, entanglement, and dark ecology to motivate the design process. The semester began with material studies and an investigation into existing waste streams and then moved into a site analysis based on mining existing urban resources. The final studio project was for the design of a public high school located in Sunset Park, Brooklyn, which asked each student to propose a supplementary program to moderate each individual approach to education and environment. Projects from the semester included a floating school that makes and remakes itself over time, a school as tree and seed vault, and an infrastructural scale monument made of construction waste that encompasses a school.

6

7

AUTOSCALE ¶ VISHAAN CHAKRABARTI, CRITIC, WITH CHRISTOPHER JAMES BOTHAM ¶ Building on current trends moving away from vehicle-dominated lifestyles, the studio began with the assumption that 50% fewer vehicles are on the streets of Manhattan. Our focus of examination was not the technology that renders this change, but rather the question of what to do with an extraordinary amount of newfound space that can be re-appropriated from vehicular use. Throughout New York City today, streets take up 26.6% of our land area. Manhattan's land area is 22.829 square miles, meaning that streets comprise just over 169 million square feet of space. This, combined with the area given to parking on our streets, means that a 50% recoupment of the space presents a crucial opportunity for the next evolution of Manhattan's morphology. How do we re-think the city if the dominance of vehicular traffic subsides? What do we do with all this newfound space currently taken up by vehicles throughout the city?

8

9

10

COLLECTIVITY ¶ ADAM FRAMPTON, CRITIC ¶ Situated along the Brooklyn Queens Expressway and the Brooklyn Heights waterfront, this studio collectively designed a new campus for the applied life sciences. As a type, the campus is an ideal platform to examine collectivity: it consists of multiple, diverse and specialized yet interrelated buildings and disciplines of knowledge production. The campus is a dispersed ensemble of components that will operate together, connected to, rather than detached from, the post-industrial knowledge economy. Operating at several different scales, the studio investigated disciplinary theories of collectivity, from Fumihiko Maki's Investigations in Collective Form (compositional form, megastructure, group form), to O.M. Unger's Cities within the City and its model of the Green Archipelago of heterogeneous fragments. In doing so, the ambition was to engage questions such as: how does architecture resolve (or reveal) its own internal differences? What are the compound relationships between architecture and urbanism? How does architecture engage with, rather than retreat from, the broader environments of politics, the economy, and the city?

11

12

13

14

KNOWLEDGE CITY ¶ NAHYUN HWANG, CRITIC ¶ This studio, a part of the ongoing research and studio series "Knowledge City," explored the possibilities in architecture for knowledge production, exchange, and consumption, in the context of continuing socio-political and environmental crises and deepening inequalities. In doing so, the studio acknowledged the precarity and possibilities present in the contemporary knowledge economy. Challenging familiar spatial and institutional formats, the work considered the program of education a potent platform for experimentation for new configurations of collectivity in the city. It also explored new relationships between the goals of individuals, institutions, and the city, and the agency and opportunities of architecture in the milieu.

15

EXPERIENCE IS EVERYTHING ¶ OANA STANESCU, DONG PING WONG, CRITICS ¶ This studio's thesis was that experience is key to changing how we relate to the environment. Can we use visceral experiences to critically analyze a context, define a clear agenda, and design architecture that changes the public's relationship to the natural resources around them? ¶ To truly transform our relationship to water, we must first develop a deep appreciation of water through touching, feeling, smelling and tasting water. Only an inherent appreciation of our natural resources will shift the challenge of climate change from an abstract responsibility to a visceral belief, and create lasting and measurable political, social and technological progress. ¶ The studio explored design environments that not only change how we use water, but also how we fundamentally think about and care for water. The resulting project was a 600,000 square foot Water Center on Pier 40 along the Hudson River in Manhattan.

16
17
18

DESIGNING AGRICULTURE AND FOOD INFRASTRUCTURE IN THE HUDSON VALLEY ¶ CAITLIN TAYLOR, CRITIC ¶ In this studio we examined the shared themes of resilience, environment, and scale via a close study of the agricultural production and food infrastructure of the Hudson Valley. Specifically, we asked what role architects have in designing resilience into our food system at a variety of scales—from the regional, to the building scale, to the scale of an individual action.

1

Yanling Deng

2

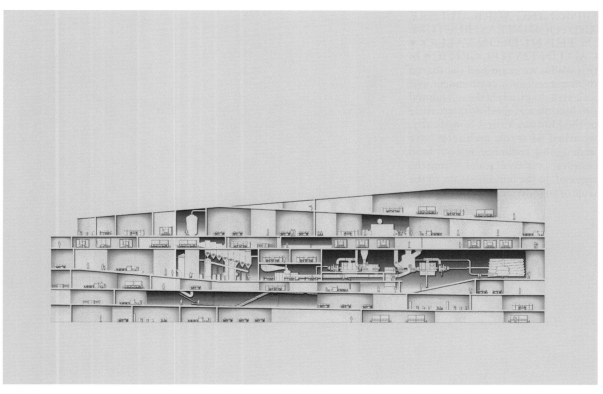

Abraham Murrell, Edward Palka

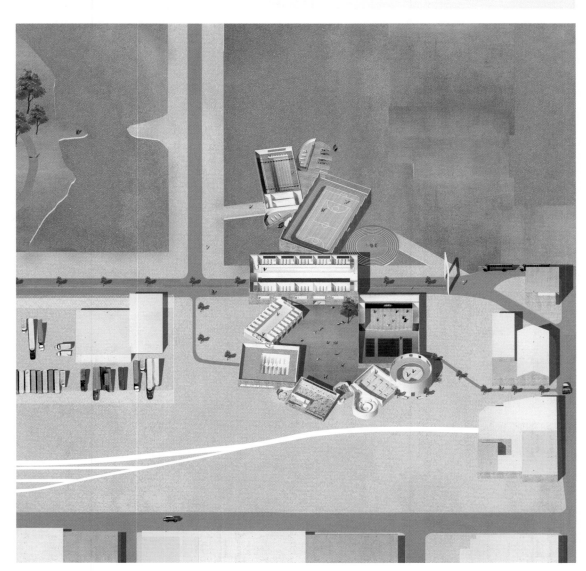

Ashely Kuo

4

Udit Goel

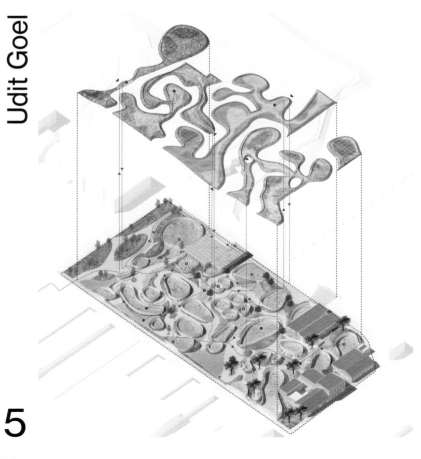

5

6

Alexis Irene Oppenheimer

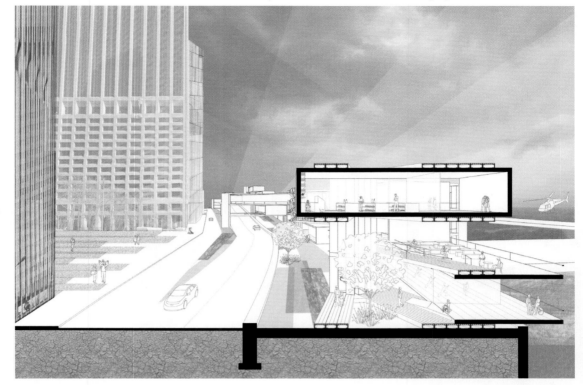

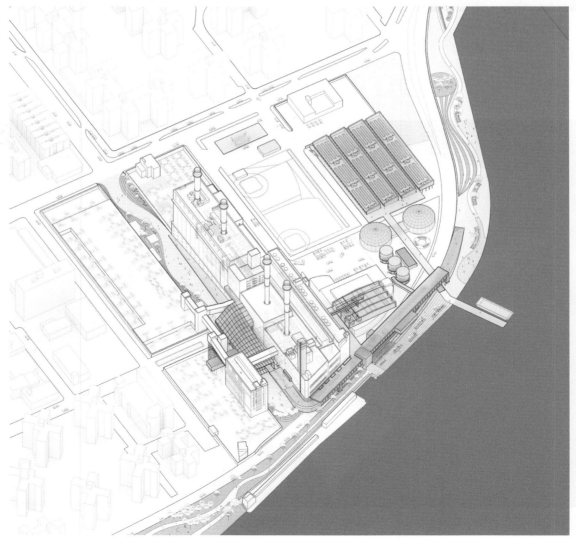

Kutay Can Biberoglu

8

Shuosong Zhang

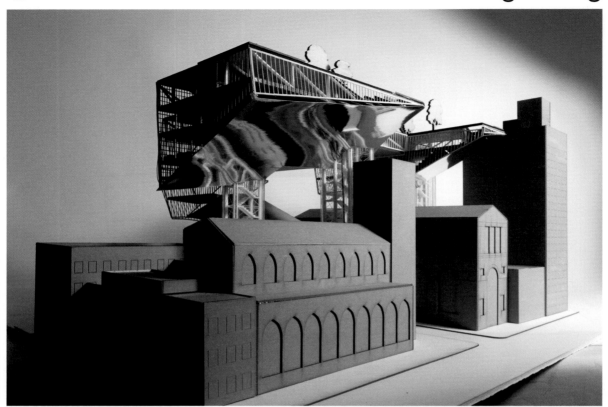

9

Andri Putri

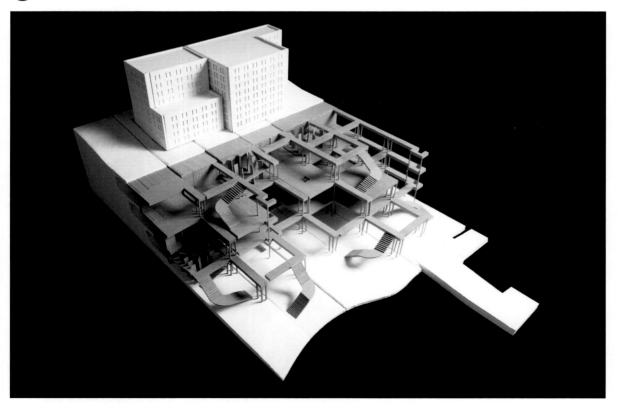

Shuosong Zhang

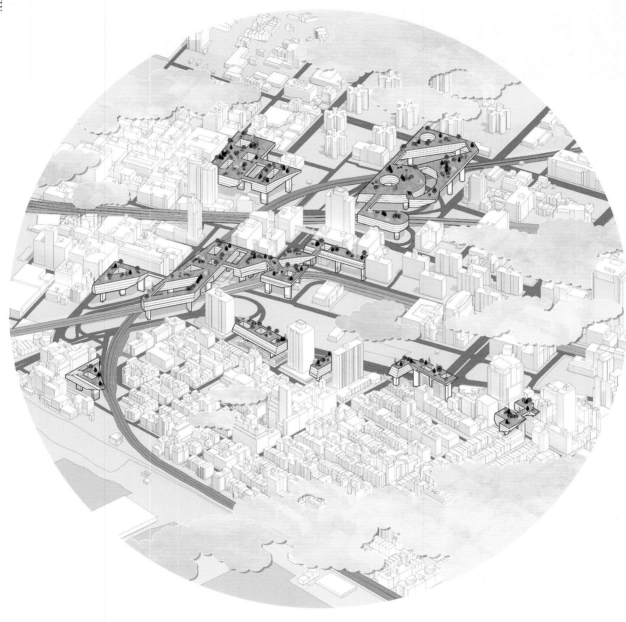

10

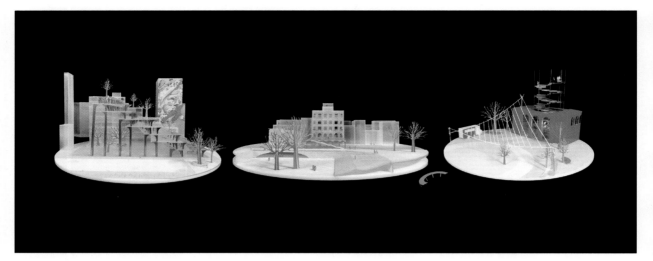

Quy Le,
Masha Konopleva

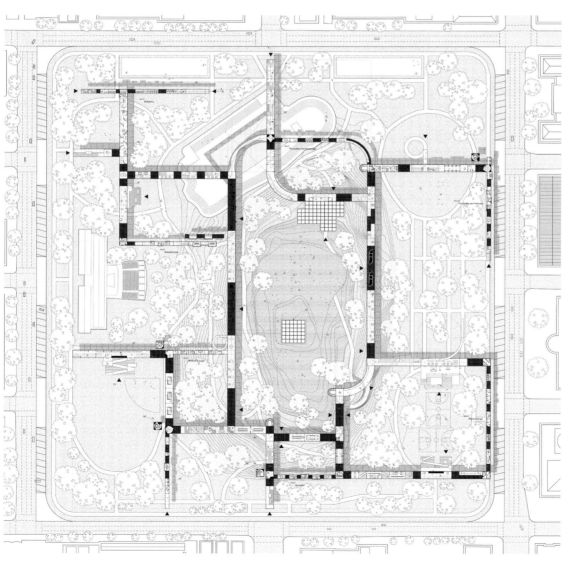

Adelaida Albir, Eugene Ong

Quy Le, Masha Konopleva

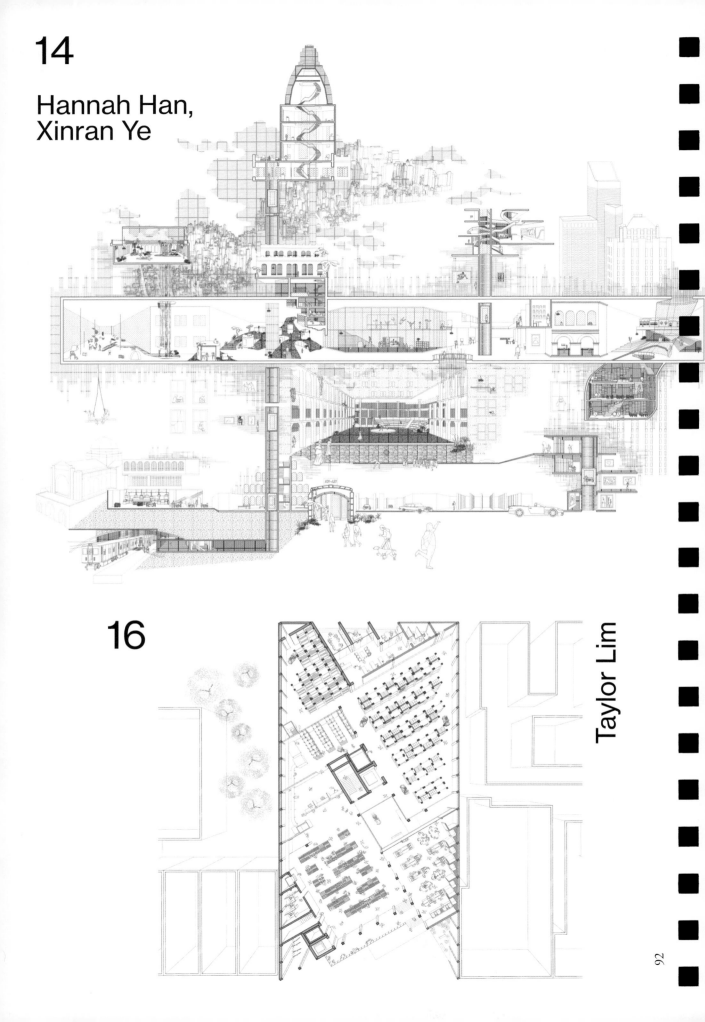

14

Hannah Han,
Xinran Ye

16

Taylor Lim

15

James Brililon

17

Veronica Watson

18

Aranzazu Gayosso

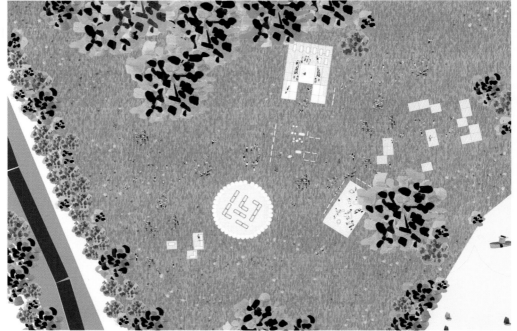

Troy Schaum, Anu Leinonen, Joshua Bolchover, José Aragüez, Oana Stanescu

Anthony Titus, Amale Andraos, Mimi Hoang, Anthony Acciavatti, Chris Woebken, Tei Carpenter, Caitlyn Taylor

Tei Carpenter

Advanced
Arch. Studio IV
Spring 2017
Juries

Ziad Jamaleddine, Amale Andraos, El Hadi
Jazairy, Rania Ghosn, David Eugin Moon

Nahyun Hwang, Marc Kushner, Adam Frampton

Hilary Sample, Director

At the GSAPP, the core design studios introduce students to architecture through an inclusive understanding of history, cities, typology and performance. Today, students engage the world through the increasingly global information on buildings, materials, structures, digital processes, media and communications. These digital processes and networks that were once theorized have become a commonplace part of our contemporary world. As a result, architecture is less and less of an exclusive and autonomous profession. These social aspects are perhaps the hardest things to teach within a school, but remain a critical part of the Columbia GSAPP pedagogy.

The core is structured through a sequence of carefully constructed design studios where students increasingly gain new knowledge through making, implementing ideas and experimenting with the problems of architecture: from form to materials, from small to large scale and from comfort to environment. Studios explore architecture within urban contexts from New York City and other cities around the world, situating experimental architectural thought within the world-at-large.

Rather than moving from the extra small to the large, the Core sequence builds in the small and the large in relation to one another throughout the first three semesters of the Master of Architecture sequence. After the first semester's focus on acquiring analytical and drawing skills, Core II takes as a project the design of an institutional building, and Core III culminates in the Housing Studio. This semester serves not only as a conclusion to the Core but also as a transition to the Advanced Studios, specifically transitioning to the Scales of Environment.

While the studios are structured to present knowledge about fundamentals of architecture as they apply to design, from the scale of a house to that of a building or housing project, the core sequence aims to inspire a shift in thinking about architecture in relation to the world.

States of Housing

Housing, as a design studio, is the last semester within the required series of core studios. It serves as a conclusion to the Core, as well as a transition to the advanced studios and specifically building up to Scales of Environment. While the studio is structured to present knowledge about fundamentals of architecture as it applies to designing housing projects, the studio aims to inspire a shift in thinking about architecture in relation to the world-at-large. There is perhaps nowhere better to study housing than at Columbia GSAPP with its nearly forty year history of offering housing studios focused on the deeply rich history of New York City. So, while this term, the studio focuses on a select site within the Bronx, the studio continually thinks beyond the familiar—reaching globally, never out of touch with advanced studios. While the core studios are structured sequentially, housing, because of its unique placement within the core, is also situated to absorb and be influenced by research in the advanced studios, while at the same serving to produce serious thinkers and designers about design through the problem of housing types.

This year's housing studio focused on the many different states of housing that we, as architects, typically encounter in practice. Throughout the term, each student examined the significance of public housing—both past and present—that are found within models in New York City and abroad, and, through team projects, speculated on the rich potential for contemporary urban housing types. The focus of the studio was twofold, research and analysis and a final architecture project. The first part of the studio was framed around methods of research and a preliminary understanding of urban housing within the Boroughs of New York City. Each studio was introduced to housing typologies through two specific assignments that focused on a large cross section of Manhattan's terrain to the Bronx to understand site and infrastructures followed by a precedent assignment that examined housing units, building programs and systems. The studio project was to design high-density mixed-use housing and public space with community amenities. Each assignment built upon the other throughout the term, first learning from the urban scale, and gradually zooming into the smaller human scale of the unit, aggregating all systems into a final design project that brought together the different states of housing in the development of the main studio site.

Core Architecture Studio III Fall 2016

1

2

3

4

HOUSING: DENSITY & LIGHT ¶ ERIC BUNGE, CRITIC ¶ The history of innovation in housing might be viewed as an ongoing contest between the apparent opposites of density and light. Encompassing many of the preoccupations of 20th century modernism, this contest was enacted across many frameworks, ranging from zoning, health and public policy, to organizational models and typologies, to experiential qualities of housing. Our section considered this unlikely pair of terms for inspiration in the design of contemporary housing. While the one conjures metrics and efficiency—the concerns of urbanism, but also mass, matter, intensity, and interiority, the other similarly conjures up metrics and health, but also absence, openness and the outdoors. As if in a chess game, increasing density seemingly requires a counter-move to increase light. Could the terms density and light be reconsidered and thought of together? Can we reframe relationships between density and light to create new models for housing? Can we challenge zoning codes as culturally biased frameworks, while embodying their objectives in terms of health? As designers of contemporary housing, students were challenged to develop their own approach to these questions throughout the semester, from concepts to organizational strategies, and from experience to representation.

5

6

7

HOUSING ¶ CHARLES ELDRED, CRITIC ¶ Type links the violence of real estate speculation to the possibility of creating (or destroying) a neighborhood. Type transmits the idea of a neighborhood as both a social community and a physical module of the city, and is its vessel for inhabitation—of people, their bodies, their lives lived (in towers, tenements, brownstones, lofts). Type underpins zoning, the regulation of a city's types, and of the strange hybrid mono-types that come into being—unquestioned by architecture—as the negotiation between the imperatives of regulation and of speculation. Furthermore, type embodies the latent possibility of inventing new techniques to negotiate these demands, to link all scales of domesticity, to engage the tensions between reproducible solutions and the hyper-specificity of unique sites. ¶ The studio engaged the persistence (and possible revitalization) of type, and speculated on how typological diversity, hybridization, and transformation might intersect with subjectivity and value in the design of housing.

8

9

FLOW II: A THOUSAND WAYS TO ENTER / THE GLOBAL AND THE DOMESTIC ¶ MARIO GOODEN, CRITIC ¶ This studio addressed Questions of Flow, Questions of Domesticity, and Questions of Space. "Considering the city as a dynamic complex system places emphasis on the interactions and connectivity of the flows through its infrastructures, and of the feedbacks and critical thresholds that drive the emergence of new spaces and urban morphologies that are animated by new modalities of culture." (Michael Weinstock from System City: Infrastructure and the Spaces of Flows). Within this condition, cities can be seen as emergent phenomena that exhibit characteristics of complex systems, are embedded within the systems of the climate and ecology, have cultural systems informed by history and geography, have infrastructures that provide services to cities, and have reciprocal interactions between them at a variety of spatial, temporal and organizational scales. Flows of capital, labor, goods, commodities, energy, waste, and data all impact the domestic body whose movement and migration patterns not only map and record these flows but also insinuate the question of what does it mean to dwell? Within this context can the architecture of housing remain static or fixed? What is its response when any of its streams are interrupted?

10

11

12

HOUSING ¶ ROBERT MARINO, CRITIC ¶ The influences that determine a housing typology fall into broad categories. The political and sociological category has to do with the organization of societies into progressively smaller groups, beginning with the city and ending with the individual. A primary need of each of these groups is a spatial one. Conventions and expected norms play roles in the distribution and organization of space. Rituals at every level dictate progression, security, visibility, and degrees of communality. It was a goal in the studio to identify a cross-section of American life, to determine its rituals, and to represent it in the most efficient possible way. The private lives of housing inhabitants were a major factor in the determination of architectural form. The designs therefore naturally evolved from the inside and revealed themselves on the outside. The result could not have been predicted at the outset of design. The will to create form by the architect was modified by life's necessities. This resulting architectural form can then be considered a Platonic one, engaged in providing the ideal living situation.

13

14

15

STATES OF HOUSING ¶ HILARY SAMPLE, CRITIC ¶ New York City has historically been at the forefront of new strategies for maintaining public health. Contemporary New York is no different, although the types of housing and health that exist today are radically different now. As part of the previous administration, Mayor Bloomberg's "New Housing Marketplace Plan" and the current city competition, adAPT NYC, New York City has sought proposals for housing composed of "micro-units." These new models for an affordable unit measure only 275 to 300 square feet. This introduces a paradox to the national obesity epidemic that has resulted in an increase in overall human proportion and dimensions. There is a debate over whether the city supports healthy individuals or whether the very nature of urban life attracts more active and healthy individuals. While this was one debate to consider, this studio sought to explore the relationships between health and housing, analyzed through the lens of stress. Stress is above all a physiological manifestation. For the purpose of the studio, the topic was explored through every possible meaning; no definition was off limits.

16
17
18

HOUSING ❡ GALIA SOLO-MONOFF, CRITIC ❡ This studio aimed to integrate the pragmatics of housing with art, culture, urbanity and environmentalism. Overcoming the tower-in-the-park scheme and suburban dispersion, the projects proposed new hybrids that connect urban density with landscapes and cultural contexts. ❡ For our studio, art was not a privilege for a few, but a constant, common, and popular search to transcend our finite selves. The integration of public housing residents into cultural networks was not seen as a luxury, but rather as a pragmatic alternative to advance the values of a democratic system. Our view was that proactive investments in housing, culture, sports and education offer better financial returns than reactionary investments in policing, health remediation or jails. ❡ Our goal, then, was to link every resident to the arts, culture, urbanity and nature; and provide every residence with sunlight and outdoor space. ❡ Aware, as we are, that achieving a pleasant, dense urban arrangement for all units is easier said than done, we delved into the large list of practical considerations with a view of architectural precedents in search for the right lessons from the past and a critical reassessment of future needs and desires.

1

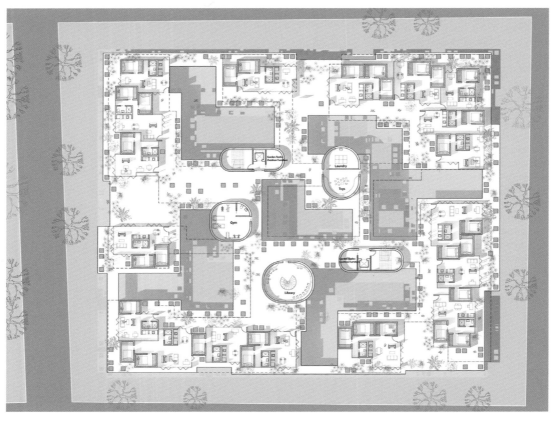

Lian Ren, Shuo Yang

2

Laura Lee, Laura Wu

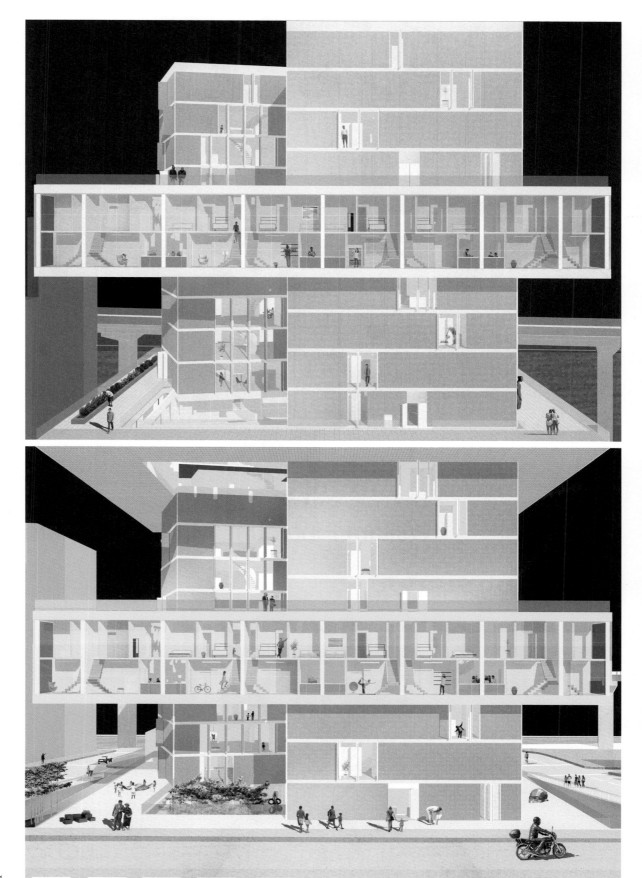

Ryan Leifeld, Joon Hyuk Ma

4

Tien Chen,
Mi Reuk Anh

5

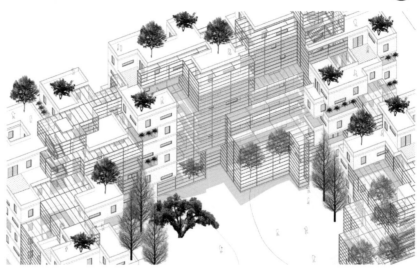

William Finnicum, Maddie Haslam

6

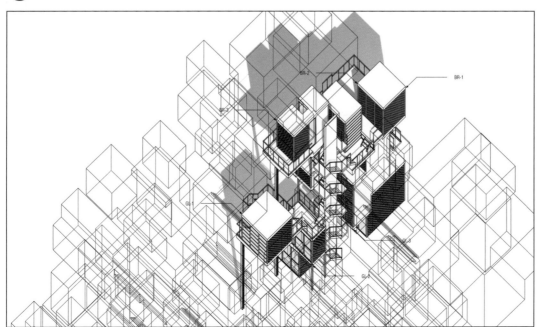

Udit Goel,
Randy Armas

102

CORE ARCH STUDIO III

Yu Hsuan Yang, Andri Putri

Jesse McCormick, Kutay Biberoglu

Minjae Kim,
Zachary White

9

10

Chen Mengze,
Eugene Ong

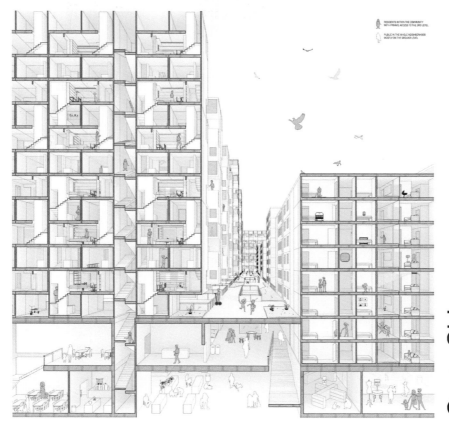

11

Coco Shi,
Shuosong Zhang

12

Qing Rui Teo,
Yanling Deng

Xiao Wei Lim, Yongwoo Park

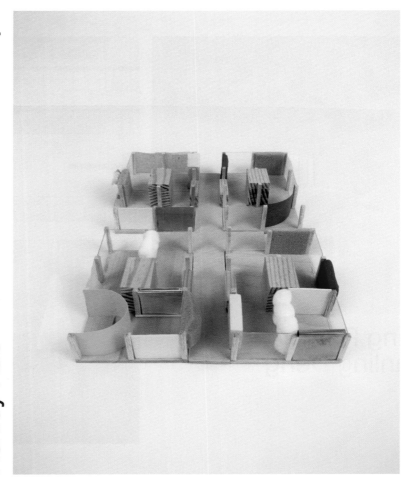

Andrea Chiney,
Ashley Kuo

Matthew Davis, Arianna Deane

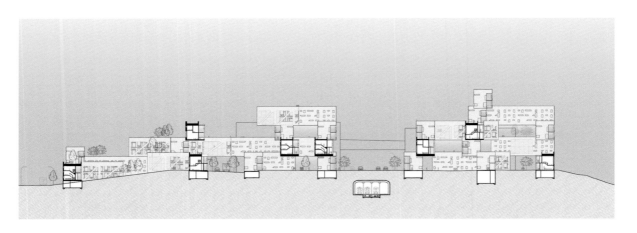

Edward Palka,
Abraham Murrell

17

Tonia Sing Chi, Colin Matthews

18

Anosha Zanjani,
Ranitri Weerasuriya

Zak Kostura, Ilze Wolff, Heinrich Wolff

James Moorhead,
Eunjeong Seong,
Jay Valgora,
Richard Plunz

Galia Solomonoff, Pedro Rivera,
Javier Arpa, Rosalie Genevro,
Matthijs Bouw, Mimi Hoang,
Abby Hamlin

Thomas de Monchaux, Reinhold Martin,
Leslie Gill, Dana Getman

Ryan Johns,
Tei Carpenter,
Esther Choi

Jinhee Park, Mpho Matsipa, Lindsey Wikstrom Lee,
Ignacio González Galán

The Library
(as Third Space)

The second studio of the core sequence challenges students to re-imagine a public institution whose architectural identity has been rapidly evolving. In this past election year, a crisis of facts and knowledge has marked our surreal reality. Now, more than ever, libraries and their civic, educational and cultural resources are essential to our pluralistic, open society. Each introduction of new media or technology, from the Internet to e-books to fake news, sparks a cycle of re-invention in how we access information and a re-examination of the library's role. Core II's inquiry examines the *container* and its *contents* by critically assessing relationships between: book/media space and public space; modes of private retreat and public engagement; intimate and collective work environments; structure, infrastructure, light and darkness.

Challenged to synthesize concepts with their corollary architectural language, students engaged at the scales of building, site and city, questions regarding:

What architectural form and identity should a 21st century library take? Acknowledging transformations in the book and information access, students posited how the library's physical manifestation relate to its increasingly virtual/placeless territories as well as its local urban contexts.

What should the future library offer and in what kind of environment? Students considered changes in modes of study and work and explored the spatial, structural, navigational and programmatic opportunities that have arisen.

Who is the future library for and how can architecture shape their interactions? Libraries open unto infinite digital worlds as well as the immediate world right outside its doors, unto past and future productions. What are the architectural opportunities for expressing new collaborative networks and urban communities?

Core Architecture Studio II Spring 2017

1
2
3

THE INFRASTRUCTURAL LIBRARY ¶ JOSÉ ARAGÜEZ, CRITIC ¶ This studio defined the Infrastructural Building as a three-dimensional organization that is capable of realistically housing a set of human activities but is not tied to any particular programmatic package. In other words, it is a material structure that transcends any specificity of form to program while retaining a fundamental "architecturalness." ¶ By rejecting any identity between spatial typology and program, the Infrastructural Building taps into the increasing necessity for buildings to accommodate change over time—while resisting any compromise on architectural qualities in the name of programmatic flexibility. Our premise was that, in further delineating The Infrastructural Building, the six propositions below underpin a design framework that facilitates historically significant contributions in the domain of architectural thinking: 1. Form-Program 2. Curated Equilibrium between Order and Differentiation: Toward Three-Dimensional Field Conditions 3. Beyond Separation between Floors 4. Structure as Spatial Medium 5. Distinctive Spatial Qualities 6. From Concealment to Integration of Services

4
5

FORM FOLLOWS PHOTON: LIBRARY OF LIGHT & SHADOW ¶ STELLA BETTS, CRITIC, WITH ANDREA CHINEY ¶ This studio explored the current changing nature and cultural significance of the space of the public library through the lens of light and shadow. ¶ If we assume that all public buildings have a right to light—a required minimum amount of light dictated by a presupposed building code, how does this change the city and its public buildings? What does it mean to design a building in the city that guarantees access to natural light? How might light and shadow, as an organizing principal, re-configure the contemporary library from the outside in and the inside out? ¶ Light, shadow, transparency, translucency and opacity are all controlled by mediating the inside from the outside. How much light is allowed in and how much light is emitting out of buildings all depends on the envelope (walls, floors and ceilings) of the structure. How does a desire for more or less light impact the structure and environmental performance of a building? What opportunities arise when trying to solve these problems? ¶ And as libraries expand their program and outreach, and books become less of the central focus, what is the public face of our Public Libraries?

6
7
8

INSIDE OUT—OUTSIDE IN ¶ BENJAMIN CADENA, CRITIC, WITH JOON MA ¶ Indoor public space has been relegated to the realm of transit and transaction (the mall, the station, the atrium, the store), yet in its diminished form, it remains stubbornly vibrant. As one of the few non-commercial public spaces left in cities where people can freely gather, libraries offer an opportunity to reconsider and restore the central role of public space indoors. ¶ In, out and around, the studio explored propositions for the library of the 21st century that can generate spaces that are an active part of the public realm and catalytic for civic engagement. Defining more connected and layered relationships from the room, to the street, and to the city, these architectural propositions reshape our experience of the city from the inside out.

9

10
11
12

LONG SPAN / SHORT SPAN ¶ ERICA GOETZ, CRITIC, WITH ABRAHAM MURRELL ¶ This studio posited that the integration of structure, space and natural light, through the nuanced composition of long-span and short-span spaces, can create both specificity and flexibility. Through the organization of the library's multi-faceted and evolving program, we created structural systems that provide for change while maintaining human-scale spaces that catalyze real interactions between people and the material world. ¶ As the very modes of learning are changing, how can a library provide both long-term flexibility and accommodate a diverse array of users and spaces for various types of learning? If not vertical partitions or standardized column grids to define internal space, then how can structure be used to organize program?

13
14

LIBRARY AS _____ ¶ MIMI HOANG, CRITIC, WITH XIAO WEI LIM ¶ Library as storehouse, as temple, as museum, as factory… Parallel to shifts in knowledge formats, information technologies, and modes of work and research, the library has aligned itself with various typologies that transform its role and identity. Largely operating symbolically, these metaphors have historically conveyed intentions relating to the library's architectural language and function as a civic and social institution. Our studio explored these alternate typologies as productive analogies—rather than symbols or metaphors. Through the lens of the following typologies, how can we radically reimagine the library's environment, structure, study carrels, reading rooms and stacks?; As garden?; As school?; As room?; As plaza? ¶ To a certain extent, these typologies are already rooted in the myriad environments of past and contemporary libraries. We drew from paradigms of the above typologies as well as instances found within library precedents, to critique and amplify their logics within our own projects. What opportunities for reinvention arise from rigorously interrogating the experiential, operational, environmental and other dimensions of these alternate typologies? At the macro and micro scales, we took cues from our chosen alternate typology and synthesized concepts with architectural and graphic presentation languages into a singular 21st century library.

15
16

THE BROOKLYN PUBLIC ¶ GORDON KIPPING, CRITIC, WITH PEI PEI YANG ¶ The public library has historically been an institution that makes information available to a public that may otherwise lack access. Yet today, the pervasive modes of information exchange question the primacy of this model. While we consume information from a massive diversity of sources, we also all produce and broadcast information like never before. Can the public library aid in this explosion of information exchange? While it continues to be a source of information, can it also be a receptor of information? Can we diversify the sources of information and directions of its flow? How do we define a public library for today and the foreseeable future which facilitates this information exchange? ¶ Diagramming was used extensively to develop and describe the program and the building. Flows of information, people and collections, vectors of structure, light and air, program spaces and their relationships to the context, and any other factors defining each project were diagrammed. Isolated diagrams were continually developed through an iterative process provoked by the contamination of each to one another. This culminated in idealized and multilayered project diagrams which guided the development of each public library as it was elaborated and made constructible.

17
18
19

THE LIBRARY FOR THE ILLITERATE ¶ CHRISTOPH A. KUMPUSCH, CRITIC, WITH EUGENE ONG ¶ The Library for the Illiterate is a space for books without words, where Architecture becomes the content. Each member of the studio investigated and researched one of the following types of illiteracy: Aspirational, Cultural, Digital, Emotional, Environmental, Financial, Health, Moral, Political, Sexual, Spatial, Spiritual and Technological. ¶ Libraries, being generally planned for the literate, are redefined—the studio aims to appropriate architecture into a device for information relating to both the Illiterate and the Literate. The Library for the Illiterate probes fusions between evolution and literacy, to suggest new roles for architecture that aim to reassess our collective, communicative, ecological and technological illiteracy, by placing a priority on learning from and transforming buildings and communities with architecture as a visual, experiential and virtual stimuli.

20
21
22
23

SYNERGISTIC CIVIC SANCTUARY ¶ KARLA ROTHSTEIN, CRITIC, WITH YONGWOO PARK ¶ A library in New York City is both an archive and a refuge. ¶ Cities need sanctuaries—havens for thought and exploration, vibrant places of unfettered civic life, spaces where beautiful ideas are synthesized with complex human realities, and where the most intimate space of contemplation can be curated within a truly public domain of social communion. ¶ Discrete interpretations and translations of sanctuary in the 21st century focused each student's independent explorations. Intensely iterative and diversely intertwined inquiry informed emergent logics, purposeful imagination, and potent spatial possibility. ¶ These public buildings are places of inspiration and introspection, sheltering spaces of immersive and catalytic experience. Sounds, smells, books, bodies, water, light and memories are sorted, aggregated, edited, enhanced, secluded and shared.

Joanne Chen

1

2

Maria Moersen

3

Sadie Dempsey

4

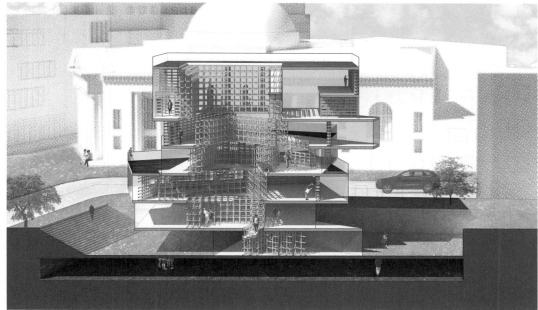

Charlotte Pang

5

Fiona Ho

6

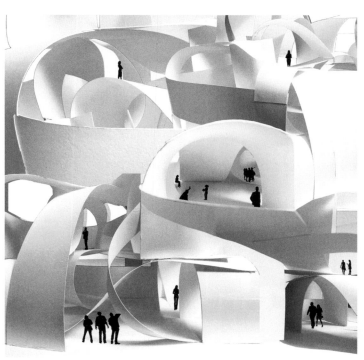

Russell Einbinder

7

Andrew Keung

8

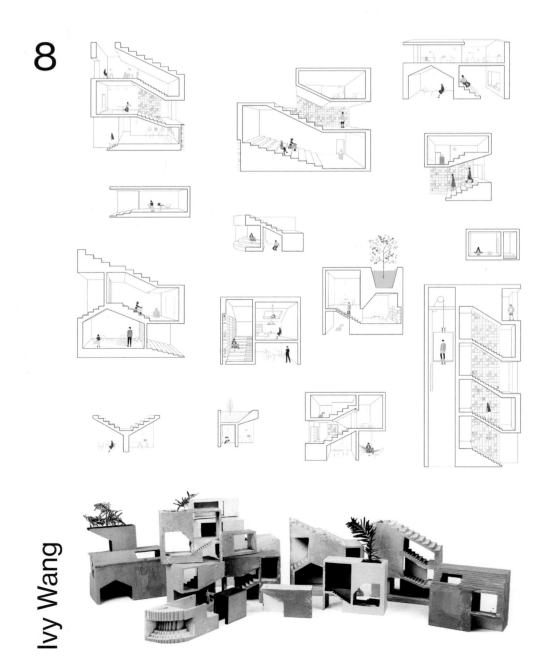

Ivy Wang

9

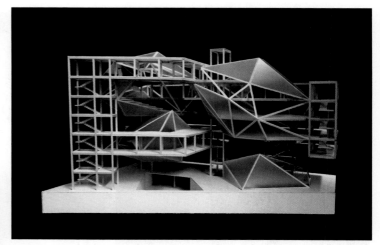

Gilmo Kang

10

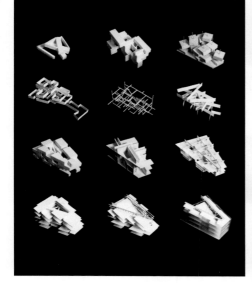

Wo Wu

11

Taylor Williams

12

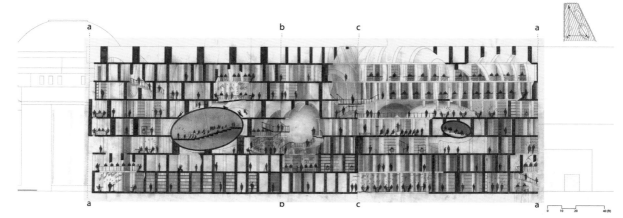

Charlie Hyoungjoo Yu

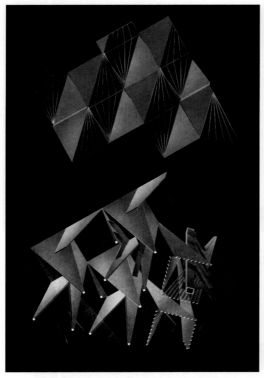

13

Po Emily Wincy

14

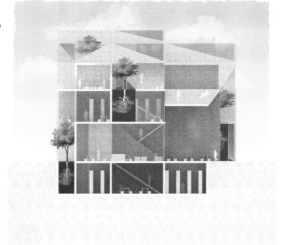

15

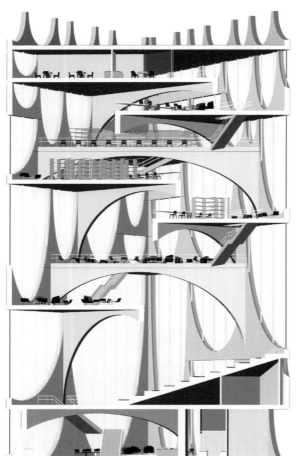

Xiaohan Sophie Su

Andrew Grant

16

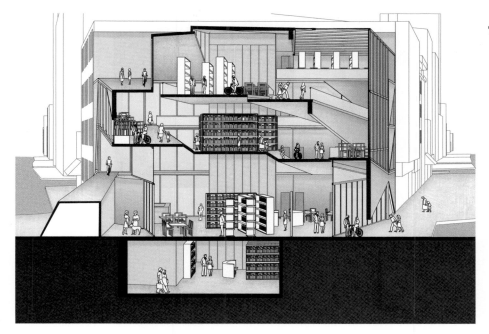

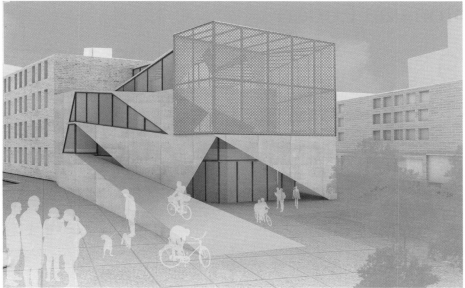

Luiza Canuto

17

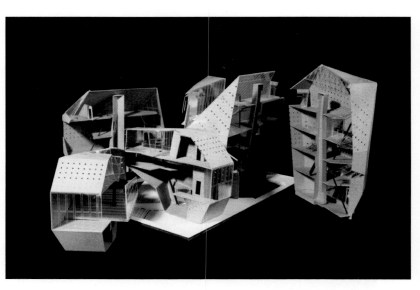

Min Jae Lee

18

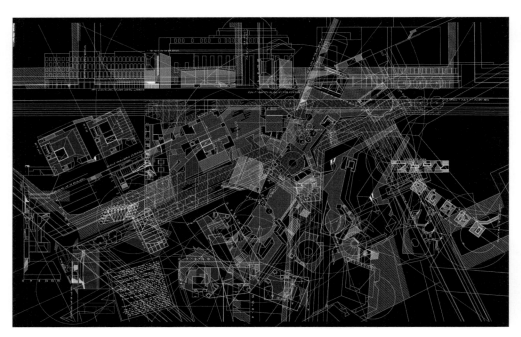

Stephan Anton van Eeden

19

Wenjing Zhang

20

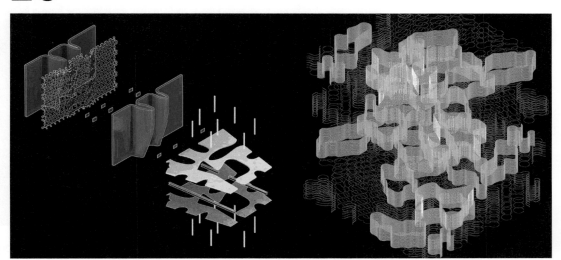

Alicia French

21

Zeynep Ugur

22

Dingpiao Chasce Tang

23

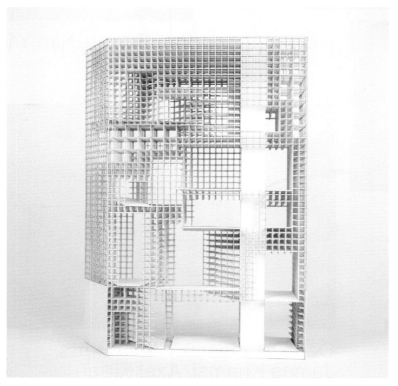

Yvette Liu

Hrag Vartanian, Youmna Chlala, Nora Yoo, Anthony Titus

José Aragüez, Diana Cristóbal, Michael Young, Gordon Kipping, Phoebe Springstubb

Eric Bunge, Kim Yao, David Allin

Ilias Papageorgiou, David Leven, José Aragüez, Hilary Sample, Chris McVoy, Amale Andraos

Oana Stanescu, Stella Betts, James Khamsi, Axel Killian

Core Arch. Studio II Spring 2017 Juries

Chris Leong, Christy Cheng, Koray Duman, Erica Goetz

Mimi Hoang, Marion Weiss, Lynn Rice, Eric Bunge, José Aragüez

Christoph Kumpusch, Rosalyne Shieh, Mabel O. Wilson, Galia Solomonoff

Dan Wood, Ignacio González Galán, James Slade, Mimi Hoang, Amina Blacksher, Gordon Kipping, Matthew Bremer

In Core I, students are introduced to fundamental concepts about architectural thinking and ways of making that draw connections between form, environment, performance, and site. The studio investigated and worked with[in] multiple interpretations of ground. Ground was no longer accepted as the default abstract horizontal plane, but as a conditional, relational, aesthetic, and contextual space.

Assignments built in strategic sequence, each reinterpreting conditions of ground. Drawing and modeling investigations offered diverse ways of seeing and reading form, building up layers and processes of making.

The studio considered architecture in relation to or with something else, such as Architecture [and] program, Architecture [and] site, Architecture [and] environment, Architecture [and] politics; always Architecture [and] ... This supposition guided the creative process and opened opportunities to integrate architecture within multiple contexts. Students learned the fundamentals of architecture, and simultaneously questioned them, to establish connections between Architecture [and] ...

Architecture [and] the city. While it is important to first understand and learn fundamentals, we are at a moment where architecture and the city are never separate. The studio progressively became more integrated into New York City throughout the semester.

Our foundational ground shifts with modifiers or syntax: infrastructural field conditions, vantage points, lines of inquiry, energy vectors and planes of dissection. We developed an architectural language through a series of Archi-Types that moved between scales: from the human to the urban, the architectural detail to the master plan, the micro conditions of materiality to macro tectonics.

This language translated into four projects investigating four central conditions, each of which reconsidered the conception of ground and challenged the fundamental statics of architecture: kinetics versus virtual motion and force.

The studio was our space for conceptualization, critical exchange, and graphic and material production. High energy, open-mindedness, and passionate engagement were the prerequisites for Core I. In studio we worked intensely and collaboratively; ideas were valued and clearly represented; constructive criticism and bold design responses constituted our primary means of communication.

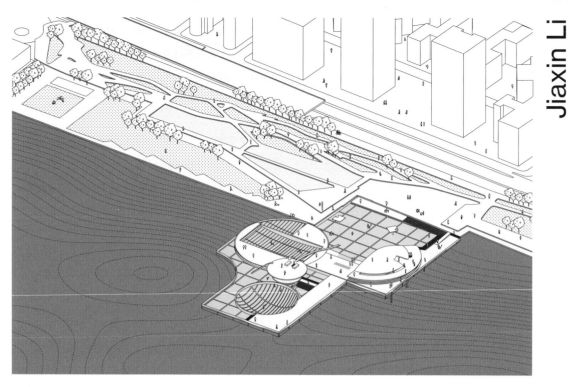

1

Jiaxin Li

2

Emily Wincy Po

Gin Jin

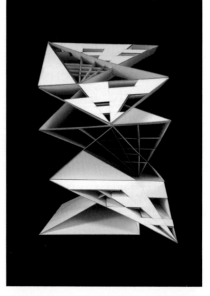

3

4

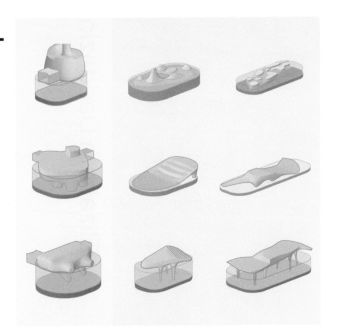

Andrew Keung

Yvette Liu

5

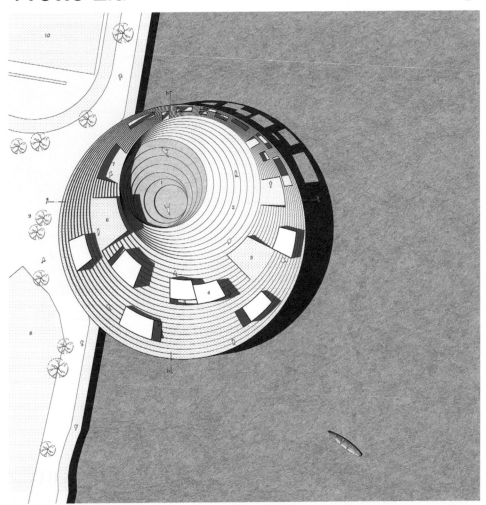

6

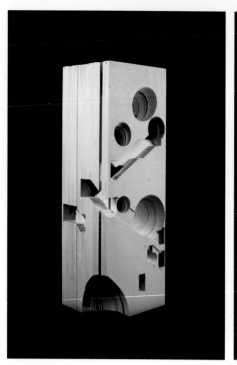
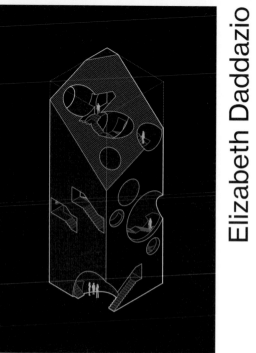

Elizabeth Daddazio

7

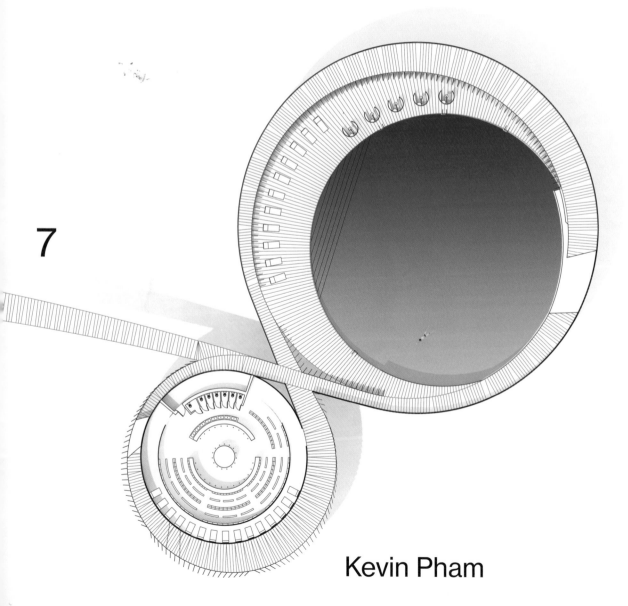

Kevin Pham

8

Wo Wu

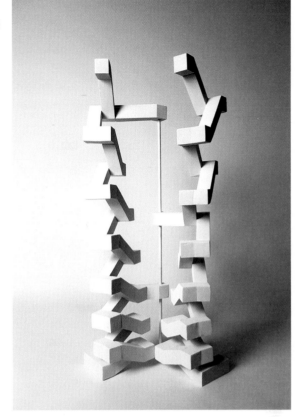

9

Fiona Ho

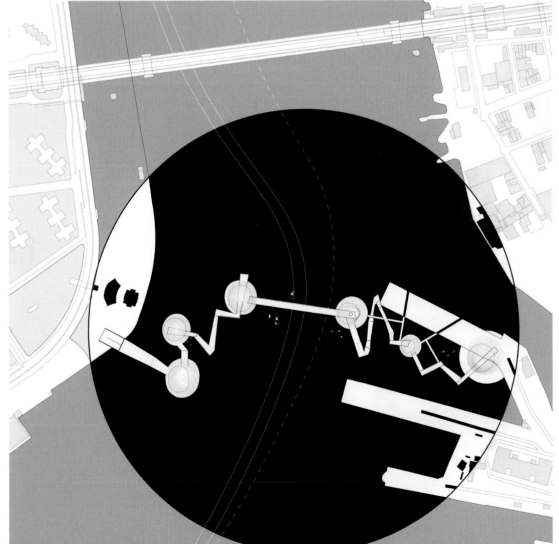

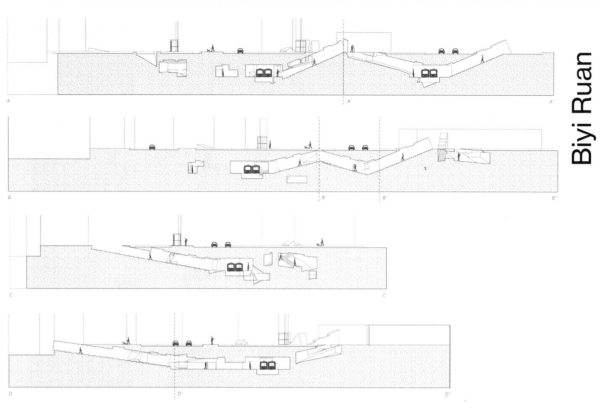

10

James Waxter

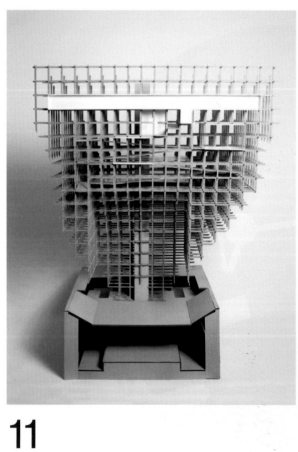

11

12

John Sanchez

13

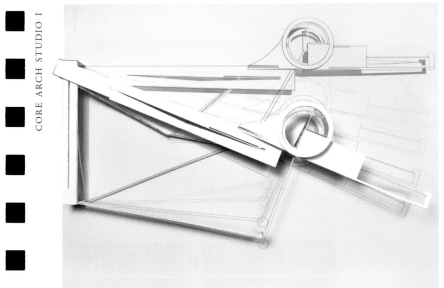

Sarah Rutland

14

Travis Tabak

15

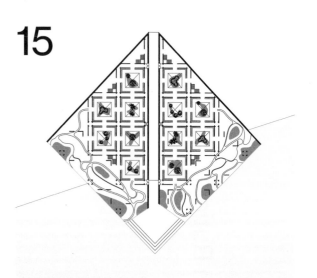

Quentin Yiu

16

Kate Wang

17

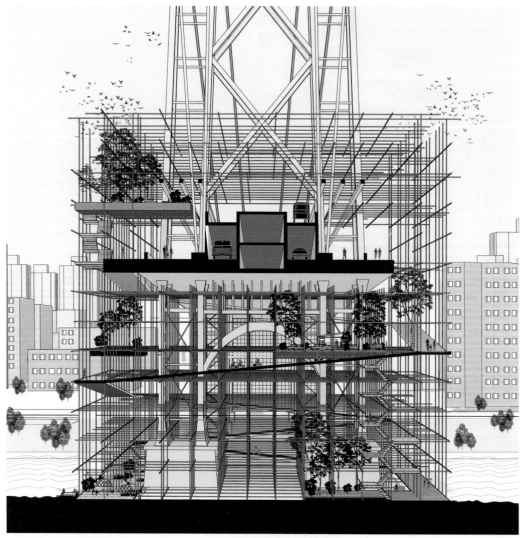

Katinka Bosch

18

Marcos Arriaza

19

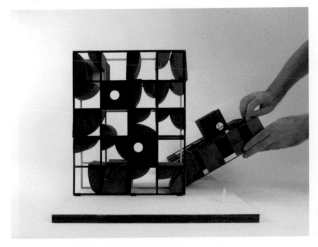

Stephan Anton
van Eeden

20

Stephan Anton
van Eeden

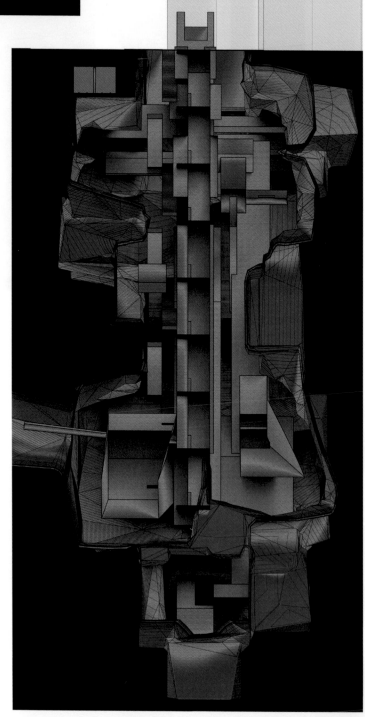

21

Marcos Arriaza

AA

Three years ago we launched a series of discussions around the curriculum—M.Arch Core in particular—to explore whether it embodied some of the ideas and questions we think the school should actively pursue: questions related to scale and environment, history and how we teach, global engagement and comparative modernities, representation and visualization, and of course technology and the way it functions in architecture and pedagogy today. So, I thought we could discuss some of the changes we made to the curriculum and reflect more holistically on whether these changes constitute a kind of body or form that can be shaped further as we move forward.

The question of representation has always been central to the school—students are taught to be critical of modes of representation, but also encouraged to push the envelope, especially if we consider the legacy of the paperless studio, et cetera. Laura, you always had very strong opinions about where to start with the students. They shouldn't start with the two-dimensional and then move to the three-dimensional, but rather immediately be immersed in three dimensions. The first changes were to the Visual Studies Sequence. [PP. 179-196] And now that these changes have been implemented, I'd like to reflect on some of the connections and decisions we made, and think about their evolution over history.

LK

The official visual studies curriculum really started to change around 2004 and was built on what Bernard Tschumi (former Dean, Columbia GSAPP, 1987–2003) started with the paperless studios. We made a very strong decision to take the word "computer" out of the visual studies curriculum and to place it more centrally within the school. But at the time, that center didn't exist as there was only one required visual studies course. So the decision to expand the Visual Studies Sequence meant that the computer could spread across the programs, which in this case meant primarily to the Master of Architecture and the Master of Advanced Architectural Design (AAD).

There were two required courses in this newly conceived Visual Studies Sequence, one of which was the computation course run by Josh Uhl. [P. 184] We flipped these courses so that computation would be taught in the first semester, which was incredibly unusual in architecture schools across the country. Despite the pervasiveness of computation in architecture curriculums, the belief that you have to start with the hand persisted—and that belief is something we really challenged.

Since then, the range of courses in the Visual Studies Sequence has really evolved; all of the workshops underscore how technology is not only useful to design but also how it impacts the way we think through design problems and conceive of the tool itself. Over the last 10 to 12 years, technology has changed from being a single software to a range of different things: it's Rhino and scripting and GIS or it's a robot and a video program.[PP. 186-188] It's really a set of tools executing multiple tasks simultaneously rather than one tool at a time.

We ask recent graduates to submit proposals for workshops in the Visual Studies Sequence, which keeps the curriculum up-to-date. That's how Appitecture, [P. 185] robotics, model-fabrication technologies, and new methods of collage entered into the curriculum, which is just fantastic. I'm constantly evaluating new workshops with Josh Uhl and with teaching assistants, having conversations with them about where they think things are going. In this way, the Visual Studies Sequence is directed by both students and faculty.

Now we're getting to an exciting point where I think that these things are starting to move across the curricular programs at GSAPP. The Urban Planning Program is much more amenable to the new data-centric Urban Analytics Concentration [P. 269] and the Historic Preservation Program is working with new tools and forms of representation [PP. 293–295] as well as the latest modes of object replication and preservation.

DB

Yeah, the Historic Preservation Program leapfrogged into the future; the students use some of the most cutting-edge technologies.

LK

My new statement describing the Visual Studies Sequence explains how today there are quantitative methods, qualitative methods, and "translational" methods, as I'm calling them, which refer to the workflow. [P. 183] Even though the focus tends to be on the quantitative, I think that qualitative research methods are something that we should really pursue. The field of humanities has new research methods as well; I'm trying to see how these emerging methods can complement one another.

There are now three strains of courses in the Visual Studies Sequence that cut across the whole curriculum, so it's gradually taking hold across the entire school. That said, the issue of requirements is hard as very few visual studies classes are required as part of the curriculum.

AA

Participants

AA   Amale Andraos
      Dean

JH   Juan Herreros
      Director, Advanced Studios

EW   Enrique Walker
      Director, Advanced
      Architectural Design
      Program

HS   Hilary Sample
      Director, Core Studios

RM   Reinhold Martin
      Director, History &
      Theory Sequence

LK   Laura Kurgan
      Director, Visual Studies
      Sequence

CS   Craig Schwitter
      Director, Building Science
      & Technology Sequence

DB   David Benjamin
      Coordinator, Scales of
      Environment Studios

But that's also liberating. The Visual Studies Sequence has taken on its own life in a strong way.

LK

Yes, it's definitely become a track through the school, and, as we know, there are positives and negatives to this freedom. If a certain set of students only take courses in visual studies without taking courses in the History & Theory Sequence, the balance is upset. It's tricky because we don't want to go back to incorporating theory into the Visual Studies Sequence. So, figuring out why students register for each track and what that implies is an effort that could be facilitated by the school.

AA

It's interesting because, with regards to the students, there is a culture bubbling up. I think the feedback that you invited and that the students have contributed to with the Skills Tree—a publicly-available online pedagogical tool which has become a part of the school's identity—reflects the fact that today it's not about choosing between Maya versus Rhino software, but instead, about combining all of these different ingredients to define new methods of representation. That attitude has infiltrated the design studio, through questions of narrative, storytelling, and video. It's no longer just about drawing.

Your questions about the role of history and its position within and alongside forms of visualization have also informed the Arguments Series [P. 230] within the AAD program, which brings a very strong historical, theoretical, and discursive context to that program. Reinhold has brought some of these questions to the History & Theory Sequence itself—and it has become more integrated within the studio sequence.

LK

Right, the architecture program is characterized by two different approaches—a parametric or post-parametric approach and a more analog and narrative approach. In the Urban Design Program, it's a narrative approach and GIS-based approach; in the Urban Planning program, it's quantitative methods and qualitative methods; and in the Historic Preservation Program, all kinds of new methods are being used to replicate the world.

AA

There were two big moves that affected the Design Studios. First, we carved out space for other activities and different formats in the curriculum: Discussions on Wednesday and Transfer Dialogues on Fridays. These act like a kind of glue. Second, there was a sort of relational thinking established in the second-year curriculum: Hilary Sample posited housing as a lens to look at different contexts globally [P. 97] and a col-laboration between David Benjamin and Kate Orff used questions relating to scales of the environment to think beyond the scale of a building. P. 81]

HS

In terms of rethinking the three semesters of Core Studio [PP. 96-136], students work from a small to large scale—ending with a project on housing. Exploring cities, New York City specifically, is a great opportunity for the students, but the goal is to also look beyond our immediate context and engage with other cities and programs like Studio-X. [PP. 247-258] So, it's through those terms that we want the students to rethink the visualization of housing, for instance, and to engage with the broader history of housing.

The Core Studio shifted to two days per week with a third day dedicated for lectures by invited guests. This was an argument about how we engage with housing through architecture: that it is not just a way to solve, or attempt to solve, certain problems, but that it can address those issues in a broader way through the basics of representation, for example. Often even despite the increasing access to drawing technologies and programs, there are still fundamental questions about how to draw a plan.

Students are presenting plans, but which plans? How do we locate the heart of an idea in a plan? Where do we look for solutions? We're exposing them to these questions first in studio, but also in person—because to see these plans materialized in different contexts is something else. For instance, we studied the plans for Mario Pani's first social-housing project in Mexico City and then were able to actually tour four different apartment types, which I think was eye-opening for the students. It also put the onus back on them to consider how they start to draw plans and who they cite. That's one very direct question that came out of this push to rethink drawing and rethink the references for housing.

AA

This expansion of references has been really interesting—and you're making a booklet of references from cities all over the world.

HS

We call them "cut sheets"; we're working on them with all of the Studio-X directors and the faculty. Students are certainly bringing their own examples too, some from places they're from and others from places they've been to. And in fact, some of these references were new to us. So I think, regarding the way that Laura was talking about students and teaching assistants influencing the curriculum, there's definitely an audience. While maybe in the past students were more willing to accept what was given, now perhaps because of the subject of housing, they're definitely more invested in developing their own clear position. It's interesting to figure out how to negotiate that. To what degree can you take that interest and make it both representative of the Core Studio and a collection of broader visual materials?

AA

Related to the question of scale, David, there was a desire to converge the programs to more creatively tackle systems of infrastructure at different scales—material, building, and territorial—and to tie all of these together through questions of representation and technology. Kate Orff was brought in from the Urban Design Program to contribute towards shaping the Advanced 4 Studio. [p. 81] Do you want to talk about the Scales of Environment studio as a way to think about climate change? Specifically, how the issue is not just a problem to solve, but rather a problem to think through?

DB

Yes, part of the initial move was to recognize where the Scales of Environment Studio sits in the program as a whole. It's the first advanced studio of the M.Arch Program, so it's coming after the three Core Studios, after the Housing Studio. We were interested in bringing together the very diverse Option Studios that we have in Advanced Studios 5 and 6 for example, and facilitate cross-studio discussions. The shift to two days for studio instruction and one half-day for open-ended discussion was an interesting shift—it allows us to bring in a type of conversation that is parallel to the individual student projects. It also creates the space for students to broaden their approach.

The studio addresses questions of environment through scale. And with environment, we're trying to go beyond default reactions to sustainability, beyond green washing and a surface-level treatment of the environment. Scale is one of the most helpful angles for us in this exploration—from the scale of a brick to the scale of a site plan and everything in between. And there are some studios that literally start with material; my studio has done that [P. 84] and Tei Carpenter is doing that this semester. [PP. 85-86] On the other end of the spectrum you have Vishaan Chakrabarti's studio that starts with the scale of urban infrastructure. [P. 87] Each student is responsible for developing his or her own take on the environment and on scale in this mix of possible approaches. This has really encouraged critical thinking around the environmental issues we face today.

AA

And this criticality was also the idea behind the Transfer Dialogues—to create a kind of studio culture that, in Juan's case, reflects on the question of practice and on the concepts and questions that emerge from all of the studios, to detect intersections, overlaps, and shared intensities.

J H
Yes, the Advanced Studios [PP. 5-95] are a crucial moment of concentration in the curriculum—a space to define how a community is changing in terms of how it's reading, thinking, making decisions, and transmitting and communicating its ideas.

When I say reading, I'm referring to the conditions of a project—not only how to understand a site, place or community, but also references, history, everything. The challenge is how to introduce all of these aspects in a project; how to construct an argument and study the narrative of a work, with the understanding that these are all design decisions. Communication is related to graphic systems and every other tool for explaining content. It also pushes one to reflect and rethink the content. This is exactly what the Advanced Studios aim to do.

The Transfer Dialogues is a re-inscription of all this. It tries to answer the question: "what am I doing?" It attempts to discover the moment of this inscription and what empty areas we should fill. In the last few semesters, the question of how the Advanced Studios could be linked to the idea of immediate practice has arisen very clearly. How is practice a design exercise itself as opposed to a break between academia and reality? Practice can be the most theoretical work for a young architect. The Transfer Dialogues aims to discuss and describe how young and not so young practices are working.

This is interesting because the first year is truly pedagogical; it tries to understand history and the studio as very specific ingredients and manifestations of the school's personality. The next step is to talk about how these histories and ingredients affect practice, or how they are worked out through practice.

A A
What's also interesting for me is that the Transfer Dialogues merge rather than separate the classroom and the studio; it carves out a space for discourse in the studio. These dialogues are characterized by a sense of openness and diversity; they pose history as a series of questions rather than a single canonical narrative. Reinhold, do you want to talk about that?

R M
This is and has indeed been an ongoing conversation for the past three years now and there are a couple of dimensions to it.

One, is that we also began with format, and similarly to the studios, made

adjustments here and there. In the past, the Core Studio teaching method was a classic lecture course, which implied a certain kind of knowledge: delivered in a broadcast form and assimilated by the students. We decided to change that by replacing the lecture course and the first two required classes for the History & Theory curriculum. What was once Architectural History 1 and 2 is now Questions in Architectural History 1 and 2 [P. 223] and these courses take place in a seminar-style classroom rather than a lecture hall. So even the place, the site in which this occurs is different; there's an architectural component to it.

The idea was to open up historical knowledge as a question rather than as a fixed body of information to be delivered. It's very interesting: professional architecture education remains the single form of professional education in this country that requires some kind of historical knowledge formally in its accreditation and for professionalization protocols. Hence, the history curriculum, and we have a particularly robust version of this.

The question is: Why does this matter? Who cares? Why do you need this? Given the way things have changed historically, the way our world has changed and how we have participated in those changes, it seems to me and to others that one of the key differences has to do with historical knowledge. Rather than being seen as a kind of repository of categories—like precedents or forms of knowledge, ancient or modern, to be more or less faithfully reproduced or acknowledged—historical knowledge ought to be considered something that one understands oneself as belonging to, as participating in.

We've described this frequently as an effort to elicit, enhance, and nurture historical consciousness among students. That doesn't mean the information is less important. It means that the relationship to that knowledge is different.

The second part of this is, by extension of this logic, to understand oneself as a participant in historical processes rather than just a recipient—a critical participant that asks questions such as: To whom does this speak? And on whose behalf does this kind of knowledge speak? Hence our ongoing effort to displace the inertia of Eurocentrism that has defined not only this curriculum, but virtually every architecture curriculum in the country in different ways, and to model a way of dealing with it. Many of our colleagues are doing this in other schools of architecture, but we are modeling a different way of addressing the question of what could be called provincial—displacing the sort of Eurocentrism with a more

cosmopolitan or comparative perspective on modernity by performing this as a series of questions rather than as a new set of answers to replace the old answers.

The effort to globalize the history curriculum, and to think about whose histories we teach, goes hand in hand with the changes in the format and content of the class.

A A
The AAD Program has been doing this already for a long time. It was constructed as "design and discourse" program where students, already with professional backgrounds, could come in for three semesters and be given this critical distance. Enrique's method of crafting of the AAD Program around the Arguments Lecture Series and his work with Juan on the Transfer Dialogues, combined with the legacy of the program developed by Reinhold, gave the program a very strong identity. I want to build on that; I see the AAD program as a perfect intersection of design and discourse.

E W
It's exactly true. The Arguments series, which was added to the AAD Program curriculum a few years ago, has become a key component, and intersects some of the questions raised in the History & Theory Sequence and the Transfer Dialogues. It has also had an incredible impact on the AAD studio culture at large. The Arguments series examines the various practices and platforms an architect engages within the field—journals, books, exhibitions, installations, and so on—through debates on specific projects with a number of guest lecturers. This series has allowed us to put emphasis on the notion of "argument," and stage a different conversation on the ways in which architecture advances positions through projects. In other words, we have changed the lexicon in order to change the nature of the conversation. The series has also allowed us to indirectly train a number of Architecture Ph.D. students, who act as instructors, to engage in design-related discussions that they might not otherwise.

A A
We've made a lot of changes to our approach towards technology, and yet for me it's the part that that we can conceptualize even further. What's happening with STEM (Science, Technology, Engineering and Math) now is really interesting; schools with post-professional equivalents to the AAD Program have gotten STEM accreditation because the technology component is central in the curriculum. Enrique is adamant that the AAD Program does not become that.

Yet I think Craig, who organized the *Architecture + Technology: Pedagogy in an Age of Disruption* conference [PP. 160–161], has managed to recast and reshape the Building Science and Technology Sequence—so that it not only progresses differently, starting with the environment and then moving to structure, but also incorporates some kind of critical, or at least a historical dimension. I wanted to talk more about that—and also discuss what we can do in the future and how we can continue to rethink the way we make things and our connection to materials.

C S

One of the important things that the Building Science and Technology Sequence can do is get closer to the studios—or have a more symbiotic relationship with them. This is something that was previously missing at Columbia GSAPP. So for the three Core Studios we've made sure that fundamental technology courses required for accreditation are embedded into the systemic learning phases of the curriculum, from the scale of the object in Core Studio 1 to broader systems in Core Studio 3. [P. 208] By the time students reach Advanced Studio 4, they are equipped to think at different scales with various technology tools at their disposal.

The conference revealed the possibility of curating a whole series of additional technology courses. We've been asking ourselves: what are the areas we really want to champion? And how do we want to go about that? We have around 20 elective courses and phenomenal professors across different areas of building technology and architecture technology-related fields; it's a real resource. Frankly, going forward, I think it would be really productive to push our technology sequence closer to visual studies, to better understand some of the interfaces there, and to really push those interfaces.

L K

There have been a lot of overlaps between the Visual Studies Sequence and the Building Science and Technology Sequence in terms of incubating courses and projects. When students start out they don't necessarily know the implications of a certain technology, but as those courses and projects mature, students have shifted over into the Technology Sequence, which means a better understanding of those tools.

J H

Also, in the Advanced Studios students have the chance to discuss their work with engineers, who not only review technical aspects of their projects, but also establish connections between their design decisions and the technologies they are based on. Since those design decisions imply arguments, students often feel compelled to trace their histories.

R M

That's an interesting question. And it just happened, not necessarily by design, to be addressed in the revised Questions in Architectural History class last fall. Mabel Wilson, Zeynep Celik Alexander, and I wound up emphasizing technological questions, in a way that's a little different than some of the more recognizable narratives around architectural building technologies in the field.

For example, we spent a fair amount of time discussing steam engines— what you do with them and what they do—and waterworks. Technologies from other moments in history are nonetheless still with us in various forms and aren't necessarily building or construction-related technologies.

You could say something similar for visualization technologies. In other words, there are various ways in which the profession was changed when blueprints and/or other forms of reproduction entered the scene. So while obviously retaining an emphasis on construction-related technologies, broadening the scope of the conversations we have at GSAPP, would be another interesting way of dealing with questions concerning modernity and its aftermath.

A A

Yes, and a way of locating oneself and one's architecture, both past, present, and future, within these trajectories.

WE WON'T BUILD YOUR WALL

Student-made signage on
Avery Hall, January 2017

Columbia GSAPP Design Mantras, 2017

Taken together, these statements can be read as a sort of
time-sensitive mantra for the disciplines of the built
environment, a set of pedagogical imperatives that have
emerged from the school, and a statement of engagement
as an institution. We understand these six statements,
dispersed throughout this book, as an urgent call to action
for Columbia GSAPP, and we recognize their relevance
and implications for the larger global community of
which the school is inextricably embedded within. They
address issues of political engagement, social equity,
representation, pursuing action on climate change,
global perspectives, cultural diversity, and developing
professional practice in all disciplines of the built
environment in which we study and practice.

Columbia Books
on Architecture
and the City

Exhibitions

Events

Events

At Columbia GSAPP, public programs play an integral role in fulfilling the school's responsibility of hosting a diverse and lively community where unwavering intellectual generosity and the desire to communicate and exchange are at the foundation of how we learn and grow together. This year, GSAPP events continued to address the state of architecture and design practice through the critical examination of climate and environment, technology, representation, and social justice. The volatile political atmosphere of the past year has brought to the forefront an even greater sense of urgency for action across all sectors of the built environment, calling into question the responsibility of architects and designers in this moment.

To grapple with the ever-changing "new normal", GSAPP events have considered the role of architecture as a tool for grassroots mobilization and critical resistance. How are architects and designers engaging and empowering local communities to have a voice in urban design and planning? How can design thinking and skills be employed to visualize, represent, and play a critical role in shifting or creating pressure on public policy? At the same time, we have considered the power of architectural narrative and speculative design as a method for revealing and interpreting current social,

FALL 2016 LECTURES
Vincent de Rijk
Adam Caruso and Peter St John,
    Caruso St John
Malo Hutson
Catherine Johnson and Rebecca Rudolph,
    Design, Bitches
Fuensanta Nieto and Enrique Sobejano,
    Nieto Sobejano Arquitectos
Gregg Pasquarelli, SHoP '94 M.Arch
Walter Hood
Laurel Broughton and Andrew Kovacs
Emilio Ambasz
Fulong Wu
Anupama Kundoo

SPRING 2017 LECTURES
Christian Kerez
Tatiana von Preussen '07 M.Arch, Catherine
    Pease, and Jessica Reynolds, vPPR
Virgil Abloh
Martin Beck
Zeynep Çelik Alexander
    (The Detlef Mertins Lecture on the
    Histories of Modernity)
Peter Cook
Konstantinos Pantazis and Marianna Rentzou,
    Point Supreme
Li Hu, OPEN Architecture
Momoyo Kaijima, Atelier Bow Wow
Fabrizio Barozzi, Barozzi Veiga
Francine Houben, Mecanoo
    (The Paul S. Byard Memorial Lecture)

FALL 2016 DISCUSSIONS
Processing Design: Making & Modeling
    Billie Faircloth, Mariana Ibañez,
    Joshua Jordan, Quayola
Search and Research
    Giovanna Borasi, Matthew Buckingham,
    Michael Meredith, Nader Tehrani
Conflict Urbanism
    Eyal Weizman, Enrico Bertini '88 M.Arch,
    Laura Kurgan, Grga Basic, Dare Brawley,
    Juan Saldarriaga '09 MSUP & '12 M.Arch,
    Violet Whitney, Michael Storm
Interpretations: Destabilizing Ground(s)
    Daniel Barber '10 PhD Arch, Kian Tajbakhsh,
    Lindsey Wikstrom '16 M.Arch, Caitlin Blanchfield,
    Nina V. Kolowratnik, Susan Schuppli, Sampson
    Wong, ESTAR(SER)
Outlaw Territories
    Felicity Scott, Brian Larkin, Reinhold Martin
Preservation as Battle Zone
    Erik Fenstad Langdalen, Jorge Otero-Pailos,
    Bryony Roberts
Making a Place for Work
    Carlo Bailey '15 M.Arch, Patrice Derrington,
    Amanda Ramos, James Sanders '82 M.Arch
Interface: Negotiating Convergence in
    Architectural Technology
    John Cerone, Ben Gilmartin, Thorsten Helbig,
    Craig Schwitter
GSAPP Books: Columbia in Manhattanville
    Amale Andraos, Caitlin Blanchfield,
    Deborah Cullen-Morales, Reinhold Martin,
    Eric Washington

cultural, and technological conditions and projecting future possibilities, to consider "what if." Using a strategy common to the work of writers and artists, speculative and imaginative designs for the near future take a current scenario to an extreme endpoint, in order to enact a highly tangible and often prescient expression of the now.

Rapid technological changes in architecture over the past decade have also had a transformational impact on design, fabrication, and construction, with digitization altering both the means of thinking about design and the means of production. What is the meaning of "making" in design processes? What does the age of digital tools and fabrication mean for design education? Technology is not a solution alone, but it is enabling greater integration, accessibility, and innovation within the design and construction process, as well as interdisciplinary thinking and collaborative practice. But what is perhaps lost in the narrative of "disruption" is that it is not necessarily the technology itself that is currently sparking radical change within the field, but rather the ways in which we perceive value, with human efficiency and well-being taking precedence over resource performance. How might architects more effectively measure and act upon both quantitative and qualitative data with greater consideration for the effects on human experience?

SENIOR DIRECTOR OF COMMUNICATIONS AND EVENTS Steffen Boddeker, CO-DIRECTORS OF EVENTS AND PUBLIC PROGRAMS Paul Amitai, Lyla Catellier, STUDENT EVENTS CREW Joanne Chen, Aalekh Hirani, Sara McGillivray, Graham Nichols, Andri Putri, Justin Romeo, Shruti Shubham

Air Drifts
Kadambari Baxi, Janette Kim, Meg McLagan, David Schiminovich, Mark Wasiuta

Incubating New Work
David Benjamin '05 M.Arch, Christopher Barley '09 M.Arch, Wade Cotton '15 M.Arch, Isabelle Kirkham-Lewitt '15 M.Arch, Marcelo López-Dinardi '13 MS CCCP, George Valdes '12 M.Arch

Architecture Practice and the City: Johannesburg and Rio de Janeiro
Mpho Matsipa, Marta Moreira, Pedro Rivera, Mabel O. Wilson '91 M.Arch, Heinrich Wolff, Ilze Wolff

SPRING 2017 DISCUSSIONS
The First 100 Days: Day 1
Architectural Narratives
Rama Allen, Kai-Uwe Bergmann, James Ewing, Ziv Schneider, Cassim Shepard

Who Builds Your Architecture?
Kadambari Baxi, Laura Diamond Dixit, Tiffany Rattray '14 M.Arch, Lindsey Wikstrom '16 M.Arch, Mabel O. Wilson, Jordan Carver '11 M.Arch '12 MSCCCP, Amale Andraos, Phillip Bernstein, Andrew Ross

The First 100 Days: Day 27, Design + Social Justice
Ifeoma Ebo, Ingrid Haftel, Quardean Lewis-Allen, Betsy MacLean '06 MSUP, Quilian Riano, David Smiley '86 M.Arch

Performing History
Kate Gilmore, Andrés Jaque, Bryony Roberts, Xaviera Simmons

When Ivory Towers Were Black
Sharon Egretta Sutton '73 M.Arch, Reinhold Martin, Senator Bill Perkins, Mabel O. Wilson

The First 100 Days: Day 64, Dismantling
Vishaan Chakrabarti, Laurie Hawkinson, Reinhold Martin, Valerie Stahl

The Building
Stan Allen, Amale Andraos, José Aragüez '10 MSAAD, Bernard Tschumi

New York 2140
Kim Stanley Robinson, Reinhold Martin

Magnetic City
Justin Davidson '90 GSAS '94 DMA, Amale Andraos, Fred Bernstein

Cooking Sections
Daniel Fernández Pascual, Alon Schwabe, Jesse Connuck, James Graham

Shenzhen/Hong Kong: Enclaves, Edges, and Experiments
Jonathan Bach, Joshua Bolchover, Adam Frampton, Ou Ning

Designing with Communities
Sharon Davis, Louise Braverman, Amale Andraos

Architecture Practice and the City: Amman and Istanbul
Nora Akawi '11 MSCCCP, Selva Gürdoğan, Ammar Khammash, Mehmet Kütükçüoğlu, Gregers Thomsen, Ertuğuçar, Mabel O. Wilson

Conflict Urbanism

To mark its inaugural year, The Center for Spatial Research presented its work on "conflict urbanism" in Aleppo and Colombia. The event engaged participants in a discussion about the role of conflict in structuring urban space and the politics of representation in zones of discordance, disruption, and violence as they contribute to the making and remaking of cities.

The roundtable featured Eyal Weizman, Professor of Spatial and Visual Cultures at Goldsmiths, University of London and Director of the Centre for Research Architecture and Enrico Bertini, Assistant Professor of Computer Science and Engineering at NYU Tandon School of Engineering as respondents to the work presented by CSR researchers and students: Laura Kurgan, Juan Francisco Saldarriaga, Grga Basic, Dare Brawley, Violet Whitney, and Michael Storm.

The center point of *Conflict Urbanism: Aleppo* was an interactive web-based map representing the intensifying violence in urban Aleppo after five years of civil war in Syria. The map combined layers of high-resolution satellite images together with data gathered from multiple perspectives and sources to show the historic city from 2012 to the present. Using the logic of a typical geographic information system (GIS) map, the Conflict Urbanism: Aleppo project overlapped these layers, as it explored two kinds of evidence: evidence about the physical destruction of the city and evidence about how urban warfare is tracked and monitored from a distance.

Conflict Urbanism: Colombia traced the trajectories of Colombians who were forcibly displaced between 1985 and 2016 as a result of the decades long conflict between state and non-state actors. The project visualized conflict at the scale of the country through a single government-created dataset that will shape transitional justice efforts. The visualizations that resulted reveal the paths of more than eight million people displaced by war while critically examining how this conflict has been recorded.

Conflict Urbanism: Colombia is a collaboration with the Masters on Peacebuilding at Universidad de los Andes in Bogotá, Colombia.

Speakers
Grga Basic, Enrico Bertini, Dare Brawley, Laura Kurgan, Juan Francisco Saldarriaga, Michael Storm, Eyal Weizman, Violet Whitney

From top: Laura Kurgan, Eyal Weizman, Urban Design student Zarith Pineda, Third year M.Arch students Michael Storm and Violet Whitney.

Who Builds Your Architecture?

FEBRUARY 3, 2017

Who Builds Your Architecture? (WBYA?) is a coalition of architects, activists, scholars, and educators that tackles the pressing question: who builds your architecture? to examine the links between labor, architecture and the global networks that form around building buildings. As major architectural projects unfold in the Middle East, Asia, Africa and around the globe, and as architects from the US increasingly work abroad, we explore the ethical, social and political questions that emerge under these relatively new circumstances. From workers' rights to construction practices to design processes to new technologies *WBYA?* investigates the role of architecture and architects: what it is and what it could be.

We name our group in the form of a question in order to jumpstart a discussion amongst our colleagues in architecture as well as collaborators in related disciplines. For us, this one question sparks many other inquiries where

we need to rethink ethics, new technologies, professional practice, activism and education. Ultimately, our aim is to investigate contemporary forms of globalization where architecture takes central stage, and to address critical questions, such as:

—What are the architects' ethical responsibilities toward those who erect their buildings around the world?
—Where do these construction workers come from and what does architecture demand from them?
—How do new technologies transform construction methods as well as communication? Addressing labor-intensive manual labor? Or workers' rights? Or site oversight?
—If low-cost labor enables architects' uninhibited creative expression, what is the human cost?

Speakers

Kadambari Baxi, architect and professor,
   Barnard College
Jordan Carver, writer and PhD student,
   New York University, American Studies
   (M.Arch '11 / MSCCCP '12)
Laura Diamond Dixit, architect and PhD candidate,
   Columbia GSAPP
Tiffany Rattray, architect, Studio Tack (M.Arch '14)
Mabel O. Wilson, architect and professor,
   Columbia GSAPP (M.Arch '91)
Response by Amale Andraos, Phillip Bernstein,
   and Andrew Ross

Top: Kadambari Baxi.
Lower (l—r): Kadambari Baxi, Tiffany Rattray,
Laura Diamond Dixit, Mabel O. Wilson, and
Dean Amale Andraos.

The Center for Urban Pedagogy (CUP)
Quardean Lewis-Allen, Founder and CEO,
  Made in Brownsville
Betsy MacLean, Executive Director,
  Hester Street Collaborative (MSUP '06)
Quilian Riano, Founder and Principal, DSGN AGNC
Moderated by David Smiley, Assistant Director,
  Urban Design, Columbia GSAPP

100 Days

THE FIRST 100 DAYS: DAY 1
JANUARY 20, 2017

GSAPP faculty and students gathered to discuss, organize, and plan for changes to come during the Trump administration. The series continued with special guests throughout the semester.

THE FIRST 100 DAYS: DAY 27
DESIGN & SOCIAL JUSTICE
FEBRUARY 15, 2017

The GSAPP community and invited guests discussed the role of architecture as a tool for grassroots mobilization and critical resistance. How are architects and designers engaging and empowering local communities to have a voice in urban design and policy? How might GSAPP students use their skills for grassroots initiatives? Invited guests presented case studies on how design thinking and skills can visualize, represent, and play a critical role in shifting or creating pressure on public policy.

Speakers
Ifeoma Ebo, Senior Design Advisor, NYC Mayors Office
  of Criminal Justice
Ingrid Haftel, Community Education Program Director,

THE FIRST 100 DAYS: DAY 64
DISMANTLING
MARCH 24, 2017

The policies of the Trump administration will influence how architects, planners, and designers can plan for and build sustainable and functional housing and infrastructure. A number of existing regulations and programs, from funding for the National Endowment for the Arts (NEA) to the Obama administration's Affirmatively Further Fair Housing (AFFH) rule, are currently at risk.

Faculty and students reflected on the range of ways that the Trump administration could dismantle the administrative state and impose or rescind policies that limit progressive contributions to infrastructure and the built environment. By contextualizing what is at risk of being undone, the panelists also considered potential avenues for resistance through emphasizing what is worth protecting in the new administration.

Speakers

Vishaan Chakrabarti, Associate Professor, Columbia GSAPP and Founder, Practice for Architecture and Urbanism (PAU)

Laurie Hawkinson, Professor, Columbia GSAPP and Partner, Smith-Miller + Hawkinson Architects (SMH+)

Reinhold Martin, Professor, Columbia GSAPP and Director, Temple Hoyne Buell Center for the Study of American Architecture

Valerie Stahl, PhD candidate, Columbia GSAPP Urban Planning

Top page, from left: Ingrid Haftel, Betsy Maclean, Ifeoma Ebo, Quardean Lewis-Allen, Quilian Riano, Isabelle Kirkham-Lewitt, Quardean Lewis-Allen, Betsy Maclean '10 MSUP, Ifeoma Ebo. Lower page, top, from left: Laurie Hawkinson, Vishaan Chakrabarti, Valerie Stahl.

When Ivory
Towers Were Black

FEBRUARY 23, 2017

When *Ivory Towers Were Black* (Fordham University Press, 2016) tells the untold story of how an unparalleled cohort of ethnic minority students earned degrees from Columbia GSAPP during the Civil Rights Movement. The panel discussed the role of the university in communities and disruptions as potential catalysts for transformational change in academia and society.

The book follows two university units that steered the school toward an emancipatory approach to education, in particular, the school's Urban Planning program, revealing fierce struggles to open the ivory tower to ethnic minority students and to involve them, and their revolutionary white peers, in improving Harlem's slum conditions. It tracks the unraveling of this groundbreaking experiment as white lash against reforms wrought by civil rights legislation grew. Through its first-person

Performing
History

FEBRUARY 17, 2017

Performing History addressed performance as a medium for critically engaging cultural history. While permanent monuments can idealize and cement historical narratives, performances can render visceral the complexities of social histories. All of these speakers experiment with inserting history into everyday life, creating public experiences that slip between past and present.

Speakers
Kate Gilmore, Artist and Associate Professor,
SUNY Purchase College
Bryony Roberts, Architect and Visiting Professor,
Columbia GSAPP
Xaviera Simmons, Artist and Research Scholar,
Harvard University
Moderated by Andrés Jaque, Architect and
Adjunct Associate Professor, Columbia GSAPP

Top to bottom: Xaviera Simmons,
Bryony Roberts.
Lower page, top to bottom:
Mabel O. Wilson, Sharon E Sutton.

New York 2140: Kim Stanley Robinson

APRIL 6, 2017

Presentation by Kim Stanley Robinson on the release of his latest novel, New York 2140 (Orbit, 2017) and discussion with Reinhold Martin

The waters rose, submerging New York City.

But the residents adapted and it remained the bustling, vibrant metropolis it had always been. Though changed forever.

Every street became a canal. Every skyscraper an island.

Through the eyes of the varied inhabitants of one building Kim Stanley Robinson shows us how one of our great cities will change with the rising tides.

And how we too will change.

portrayal of how a transformative process got reversed, *When Ivory Towers Were Black* can catalyze contemporary struggles for equality as crushing race- and place-based injustices multiply and historically marginalized students remain excluded from the elite city-making professions.

Speakers
Sharon Egretta Sutton (M.Arch '73), Author, *When Ivory Towers Were Black*
Reinhold Martin, Director, The Temple Hoyne Buell Center for the Study of American Architecture
Senator Bill Perkins, (D, WF) 30th Senate District
Mabel O. Wilson (M.Arch '91), Architect and Professor, Columbia GSAPP

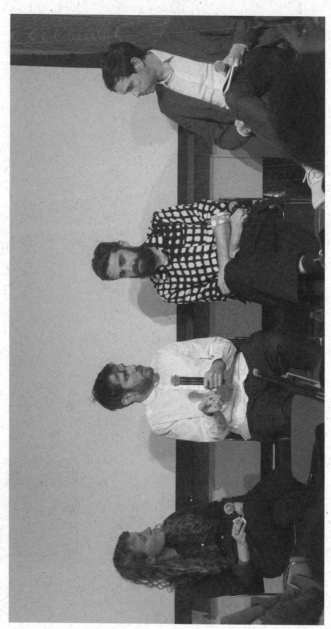

possibility and implications of selling back the remains of the British Empire in London today. *The Empire Remains Shop* worked as a platform to investigate and explore postcolonial spatial implications behind the 'exotic' and the 'tropical', conflict geologies, the financialization of ecosystems, 'unnatural' behaviours, the ecological perception of 'invasive' and 'native' species, the architecture of retiring to former colonies, or the construction of the offshore and Special Economic Zones.

Top: Maite Borjabad López-Pastor '15 MSCCCP. Lower (l–r): Jesse Connuck, Alon Schwabe, Daniel Fernández Pascual, and James Graham.

APRIL 14, 2017

Cooking Sections (Daniel Fernández Pascual & Alon Schwabe) in conversation with James Graham and Jesse Connuck

Empire Shops were first developed in London in the 1920s to teach the British how to consume foodstuffs from the colonies and overseas territories. Although none of the stores ever opened, they intended to make foods such as sultanas from Australia, oranges from Palestine, cloves from Zanzibar, and rum from Jamaica available and familiar in the British Isles. *The Empire Remains Shop*, a public installation that opened in 2016, speculated on the

Cooking Sections:
The Empire Remains Shop

Top: Selva Gürdoğan.
Lower, from left:
Ammar Khammash, Ertuğ
Uçar, Ammar Khammash,
Mehmet Kütükçüoğlu,
Selva Gürdoğan, Gregers
Thomsen, Nora Akawi,
and Mabel O. Wilson.

Architecture Practice and the City: Amman & Istanbul

APRIL 28, 2017

Architecture Practice and the City was a Studio-X initiative engaging design practices whose work addresses key debates taking place in their respective cities. Discourse on the city was explored through the examination of specific projects.

Speakers
Ammar Khammash, Khammash Architects
Nora Akawi, Director, Studio-X Amman, and
 Adjunct Assistant Professor, Columbia GSAPP
Mehmet Kütükçüoğlu and Ertuğ Uçar, Partners, TEGET
Selva Gürdoğan and Gregers Thomsen,
 Directors, Studio-X Istanbul, and Partners, Superpool

Imaginary Futures

Imaginary Futures brought together architects, designers, artists, and scientists to discuss the relationship of speculation, imagination, and cognition, illuminated through a series of case study presentations by practitioners working at the intersection of design, "near futures" fiction, and technology. The event posited that the current state of architecture and culture at large call for a reimagining of architectural practice as well as a re-envisioning of the world in which it operates. Beyond the physical built environment, architecture is a platform for speculation and critique, a domain for interrogating the implications of technological and cultural change as it impacts the evolution of our cities and societies. Architecture is inherently a form of speculative fiction, with the architectural imaginary providing alternative visions of the future. *Imaginary Futures* sought to reflect the limitations of our current realities while attempting to transcend them through investigations at varying scales: the city, the object, the body, and the mind.

Speakers
Fiona Raby, Katie Torn, Chris Woebken, Liam Young, Laura Kurgan, Tei Carpenter, Christoph Kumpusch, Daphna Shohamy

9.23.2016

Top page: Laura Kurgan, Daphna Shohamy, Liam Young, Katie Torn, Chris Woebken, Tei Carpentner, Fiona Raby, Christoph Kumpusch Bottom page, clockwise from top right: Liam Young, Katie Torn, Fiona Raby, Chris Woebken, Christoph Kumpusch, Tei Carpenter.

153

Fitch Colloquium: Preservation and War

The *2016 Fitch Colloquium* brought together some of the world's leading experts in historic preservation to discuss urgent questions around preservation and war. The regulation of modern warfare in many ways preceded and shaped that of modern preservation. Military codes of conduct, such as the pioneering 186⸱ ⸱ber Code, became the basis and inspiration for na⸱ ⸱ ꞈnal and international preservation laws. The experienc⸱ ⸱f World War II, and the now famous work of the Monuments Men, was a powerful catalyst for the creation of preservation institutions during peacetime, from the National Trust of Historic Preservation to UNESCO. To what degree, we may ask, is preservation thinkable outside of militarization, and its prewar—war—postwar continuum? What is the range of acceptable preservation actions and nonactions in the face of today's wars, when spectacles are made of the dynamiting of monuments and the killing of preservationists?

Speakers

Azra Akšamija, Lucia Allais, Leila A. Amineddoleh, Zaki Aslan, Erica Avrami, Zainab Bahrani, Julián Esteban-Chapapría, David Gissen, Rodney Harrison, Nikolaus Hirsch, Mark Jarzombek, Laura Kurgan, Rosalind C. Morris, William Raynolds, Laurie Rush, Clive van den Berg, Tim Winter.

Organized by Jorge Otero-Pailos.

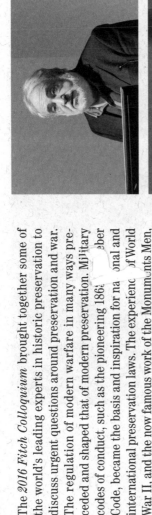

Top page, left to right:
Rosalind C. Morris, Azra Akšamija.
Bottom page, clockwise from top right: Julián Esteban-Chapapría, Laura Kurgan, Zaki Aslan, Zainab Bahrani, Jorge Otero-Pailos.

The Museum Boom in China: Innovations and Global Aspirations

Top page From left: Aric Chen,
Alexandra Munroe. Lower page,
top row from left: Zhu Pei,
Ou Ning, Wu Hung, John Rajchman.
Group photo (l–r): Jeffrey Johnson,
Zhu Pei, Steven Holl, Aric Chen,
Weiping Wu

10.14.2016

The Museum Boom in China featured architects and curators discussing the intensive development of cultural projects over the past decade. Concurrent with China's rapid urbanization, a museum building boom has taken place, producing almost 100 new museums a year and harkening the importance of culture in the identity of a new China. With ambitions to hastily increase museum per capita numbers to international standards, challenges persist in filling the abundant spaces with content. How many museums does China need? Can the museum in China redefine its role in society, whether socially, politically or culturally? And, what new architectural forms and spatial organizations are being invented to accommodate these new possibilities? The forum at GSAPP also addressed these issues while reflecting the broader international context. How have global influences and pressures impacted the proliferation of new museums in China? How has what has been happening in China influenced museums globally?

Speakers
Aric Chen, Jean DeBevoise, Steven Holl, Wu Hung, Jeffrey Johnson, Alexandra Munroe, Ou Ning, Zhu Pei, John Rajchman, Mark Wasiuta, Weiping Wu

Co-Organized by Jeffrey Johnson and John Rajchman. Supported in part by Weatherhead East Asian Institute.

Exhibition Models: Curating Architecture

Sarah Herda   Sylvia Lavin   Irene Sunwoo

Exhibition Models examined new curatorial practices, scholarship, and institutional experiments that are redefining the agency of architecture exhibitions. Presentations and panels offered case studies and considered the format, role, and impact of exhibitions in different settings ranging from academic venues, alternative spaces, and well-established institutions to project-based architecture biennials and triennials.

Speakers

Lluís A. Casanovas '13 MSAAD, Beatriz Colomina, Cynthia Davidson, Ignacio G. Galán, Beatrice Galilee, Joseph Grima, Sarah Herda, Rory Hyde, Wonne Ickx, Sylvia Lavin, Andres Lepik, Reinhold Martin, Isabel Martínez Abascal, Carlos Mínguez '12 MSCCCP, Alejandra Navarrete '11 MSCCCP, Vanessa Norwood, Marina Otero Verzier '13 MSCCCP, Mónica Ponce de León, Fernando Portal, Felicity Scott, Galia Solomonoff, Nina Stritzler-Levine, Irene Sunwoo, André Tavares, Mark Wasiuta

Top page, from left: Sarah Herda, Sylvia Lavin, and Irene Sunwoo. Lower page, counterclockwise from top left: Galia Solomonoff, Mónica Ponce de León, Fernando Portal, Ignacio G. Galán.

Architecture + Technology: Pedagogy in an Age of Disruption

2.10.2017

The *Architecture + Technology* symposium set out to evaluate the current role and potential of technology, while interrogating the strategies by which it is being taught, in order to arrive at relevant modes of practice that are in tune with the disruptions that are now emerging. Through presentations and discussion, the participants examined technology's impact on the field of architecture beyond building-centric technology and evidence-based design—specifically, how advancements are changing ways in which we perceive value, with human efficiency and well-being taking precedence over resource performance. How might architects more effectively measure and act upon both quantitative and qualitative data with greater consideration for the effects on human performance? How might we respond to the increasing urgency within architectural education to adapt to meet industry demands?

Speakers
David Benjamin, Lise Anne Couture, Anna Dyson, Jens Dyvik, Billie Faircloth, Nick Gelpi, Ben Gilmartin, Michael Ulrich Hensel, Mimi Hoang, Kasper Guldager Jensen, Vincent Loubière, Scott Marble, Forrest Meggers, Kiel Moe, Silvia Prandelli, Ingeborg Rocker, Hilary Sample, Craig Schwitter, Kevin Slavin, Meejin Yoon

Organized by Craig Schwitter.

Cities and Climate Action: New Orleans, Rio, NYC

Cities and Climate Action brought together government officials and policymakers from New Orleans, Rio de Janeiro, and New York City to discuss the critical role that cities play in driving the agenda on climate change where federal governments are failing to adequately assist cities in their efforts to respond to vast environmental, economic, and cultural impacts. The event addressed the work currently being undertaken in three coastal cities, connected in their roles as key regional economic and cultural centers, each acutely vulnerable to the effects of rising sea levels. The conversation proved to be prescient in light of the US federal government's subsequent withdrawal from the Paris Agreement and the counter response from US cities and states committing to adhere to the international climate accord.

Speakers
Adam Freed, Jeffrey Hebert, Michael Kimmelman, Kate Orff, Rodrigo Rosa, Weiping Wu

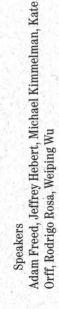

163

Top page, from left:
Jeffrey Hebert, Adam Freed.
Bottom page (l-r): Michael
Kimmelman, Jeffrey Hebert,
Rodrigo Rosa, Kate Orff,
Weiping Wu, and Adam Freed.

DIRECTOR OF EXHIBITIONS Irene Sunwoo, ASSISTANT DIRECTOR OF EXHIBITIONS Adam Bandler, M.ARCH EXHIBITIONS CREW Nabi Agzamov, Valentina Angelucci, Vanessa Arriagada, Tim Battelino, Axelle Dechelett, Ying Huang, Deniz Onder, Emily Po, Shruti Shubham, Elif Unsal, CCCP EXHIBITIONS CREW Jake Cavallo Andrew Davis, Aastha Deshpande, Marwah Garib, Jean Im, Paul Provenza, Betzabe Valdés

GSAPP Exhibitions 2016–2017

The GSAPP Exhibitions program is a platform for testing and developing curatorial strategies and exhibition related research. The program conceives, designs and launches several exhibitions each year. Core GSAPP exhibitions analyze and expose important and under-examined architectural projects and practices from the postwar period. Other exhibitions emerging from collaboration with contemporary artists and architects seek to provide models for new forms of architectural speculation and spatial practice.

The Arthur Ross Architecture Gallery, the primary venue for the exhibitions program, serves as a space for experimenting with the spatial and visual organization of architectural documents, drawings, photographs and archives. As a university research gallery, its mission is to provide a context for architectural research and to explore exhibition formats complementary to this research. After appearing at the Ross Gallery many GSAPP exhibitions travel to museums and to other institutions nationally and internationally. Apart from those shown in the gallery several exhibitions are produced and developed for Avery Hall, where they take place regularly throughout the year.

GSAPP Exhibitions relies on the work and dedication of students from the CCCP, M.Arch and AAD programs in their roles as researchers, installers, fabricators and gallery assistants. Through this student involvement, through research that resonates with other projects at the school, and through exhibition related conferences, conversations and panel discussions, GSAPP Exhibitions aims to be an active and critical participant in the architectural debates formed at the school, in the city and within a broad international forum.

CURATOR Giovanna Borasi & CCA, EXHIBITION DESIGN MOS Architects (Hilary Sample and Michael Meredith), GRAPHIC DESIGN Christian Lange, INSTALLATION PHOTOGRAPHY James Ewing

The Other Architect

Organized by the Canadian Centre for Architecture (CCA), Montréal, *The Other Architect* examined how architects have expanded their role in society to shape the contemporary cultural agenda without the intervention of built form. On display were twenty-three case studies dating from the 1960s to today that illustrate how international and often multidisciplinary groups applied experimental attitudes and collaborative strategies to invent new tools and alternative methods outside of traditional design practice. *The Other Architect* identified a range of experiences that pushed beyond the established domains of academia and the usual dynamics of editorial and institutional activities to develop architecture as a field of energetic, critical, and radical intellectual research.

The architects included in the exhibition challenged the concept of individual authorship in favor of establishing networks and partnerships with permeable roles: AD/AA/Polyark, AMO, Anyone Corporation, Architects Revolutionary Council (ARC), Architectural Detective Agency (ADA), Architecture Machine Group (AMG), Art Net, Atelier de recherche et d'action urbaines (ARAU), Center for Urban Pedagogy (CUP), CIRCO, Corridart, Delos Symposion, Design-A-Thon, Forensic Architecture, Global Tools, Institute for Architecture and Urban Studies (IAUS), International Laboratory of Architecture and Urban Design (ILAUD), Lightweight Enclosures Unit (LEU),

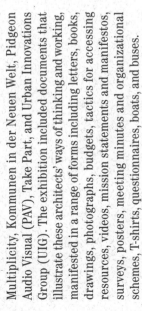

9.16–12.2.2016

Multiplicity, Kommunen in der Neuen Welt, Pidgeon Audio Visual (PAV), Take Part, and Urban Innovations Group (UIG). The exhibition included documents that illustrate these architects' ways of thinking and working, manifested in a range of forms including letters, books, drawings, photographs, budgets, tactics for accessing resources, videos, mission statements and manifestos, surveys, posters, meeting minutes and organizational schemes, T-shirts, questionnaires, boats, and buses.

The Other Architect, like the case studies it examined, is a research project in its own way, contributing to a new reflection on the role of the architect and inspiring and proposing unexpected ways of practicing architecture today. It responds to the question of how we can position architecture beyond building, as an original site for the production of ideas.

CURATOR Irene Sunwoo, ASSISTANT CURATOR Adam Bandler, GRAPHIC DESIGN Glen Cummings, MTWTF, INSTALLATION PHOTOGRAPHY James Ewing

Stagecraft: Photos & Models

Confluent advances in photography and the rise of mass media throughout the twentieth century steadily fueled the production of architectural models as photogenic objects. As a hybrid form of architectural representation, model photography flourished for its ability to realistically envision a building in a future site, give form to complex theoretical concepts, and demonstrate radical proposals of monumental scale. Pivotal in the promotion of commissioned projects, model photography also cemented the iconic status of unbuilt visionary architecture—such as Mies van der Rohe's Berlin skyscrapers, Frederick Kiesler's Endless House, Louis Kahn's City Towers in Philadelphia, and Kenzo Tange's Plan for Tokyo. Yet the techniques and possibilities of this enduring intersection of architectural media have been increasingly overlooked within professional practice and education, as digital tools and platforms dominate the contemporary production of architectural representation—from video animations to 3D-printed objects to hyperrealist, outsourced renderings.

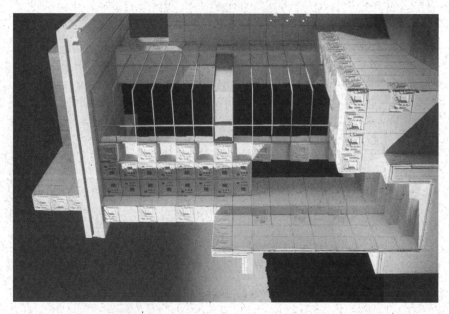

Stagecraft: Models and Photos explored the synergy between architectural models and photography as a wellspring of architectural invention. For this exhibition, the Arthur Ross Architecture Gallery commissioned architectural photographer James Ewing to photograph six models of notable twentieth century buildings, culled from the archives of Columbia University's Graduate School of Architecture, Planning and Preservation.

Ewing's photographs invite a reexamination of the ways architectural creativity and thinking unfold through the picturing of objects and the crafting of images. Using the gallery as a photography studio for several weeks, Ewing experimented with a range of lighting, framing, and staging techniques that drew upon his research on the history of model photography. He studied the archive of model photographer Louis Checkman, located at the Avery Drawings & Archives Collection at Columbia University, took inspiration from the work of Balthazar Korab and Ezra Stoller, and exchanged ideas with Jock Pottle, a prolific model photographer active during the 1990s and early 2000s.

As photographic subjects, the models—displayed alongside Ewing's photographs—were a unique pro vocation. Rather than simulate whole buildings or strive for realism, the models illuminate moments of structural ingenuity and architectural craftsmanship. Representing projects by Le Corbusier, Frank Lloyd Wright, Gerrit Rietveld, Jørn Utzon, Norman Foster, and Peter Zumthor, the models were produced by students during the 1990s and early 2000s as part of historian and Columbia professor Kenneth Frampton's pedagogical exploration of the history of architectural tectonics. The models are testimony to the students' tactile intelligence and historical engagement with the "poetics of construction"—a term coined by Frampton. In dialogue with these objects, Ewing's photographic illustrations offer a meditation on how the cross-fertilization of material and visual modes of representation can prompt new ways of seeing, making, and understanding architecture.

CURATOR Irene Sunwoo, ASSISTANT CURATOR Adam Bandler, GRAPHIC DESIGN Rob Carmichael, SEEN, INSTALLATION PHOTOGRAPHY James Ewing

Liam Young: New Romance

Liam Young: New Romance was the first US solo exhibition of Australian-born architect Liam Young—one of the most distinctive and adventurous voices in contemporary architecture today. At the core of his multidisciplinary practice is a continuous interrogation of the present realities of cities. Through research expeditions, storytelling, documentary film, and performance, Young extrapolates and exaggerates existing networks, systems, and technologies to imagine possible future urbanisms. The exhibition presented three short films—*In the Robot Skies* (2016), *Where the City Can't See* (2016), and the debut of *Renderlands* (2017)—and charted his recent work in fiction film and his experimentation with new cinematic tools. Each framed as a love story, the trio of films reveals Young's emerging interest in world building: the design of a cinematic universe in which narratives evolve.

In the Robot Skies tells the story of two teenagers who communicate through a hacked drone from within the digital confines of a high-rise council estate in London. Filmed by drones programmed with specific cinematic rules and behaviors, the film embraces the drone as an

Young harnesses the popular medium of fiction film and cutting-edge visualization technologies to open up critical conversations on the role of current digital infrastructures in shaping future cities. Based on intensive research and innovative production methods, his cinematic worlds and speculative scenarios present exciting advances in architectural representation and design. As documentation of Young's process, the exhibition featured a selection of specialized props, materials, and research that helped build each world.

instrument of visual storytelling, and as the catalyst for a network of surveillance activists and hackers. *Where the City Can't See* follows a group of young factory workers as they drift through a smart city in a driverless taxi. Shot entirely with laser scanning technology, the film explores emergent subcultures in a city ruled by urban management systems and CCTV surveillance. *Renderlands* is a mixed reality romantic fantasy that chronicles a digital renderer's virtual construction of a dream city. Set in an outsourced video game company in India, the film uses scavenged VFX movie models and 3D game assets—remnants of cancelled production jobs on studio hard drives—to present a contemporary utopia in the thickness of the screen: a virtual city of demolished landmarks, drowned streetscapes, alien invasions, and synthetic actors.

Columbia Books on Architecture and the City

The books and magazines published through the Office of Publications at Columbia University's Graduate School of Architecture, Planning, and Preservation (GSAPP) are enduring records of the school's intellectual life. They reflect the scope of intellectual work at GSAPP and the stakes within architectural discourse today, ranging from long-term research projects to conferences and exhibitions. In thinking about architecture and the city, they draw on the knowledge of architects, scholars, planners, engineers, artists, theorists, and curators, among others. Yet even in their diversity, the school's publications capture only a small fraction of what is happening in the world of architecture. Our commitment to print includes broadening the notion of publication, exploring a range of formats to help make ideas accessible across a wider range of media.

During the 2016–2017 academic year, Columbia Books on Architecture and the City published many new books. *Social Transparency: Projects on Housing* by Michael Maltzan looks at the architect's projects with the Skid Row Housing Trust in Los Angeles, and is the newest in our GSAPP Transcripts series, as well as the first in the series

Transcripts on Housing. Published in advance of the opening of Columbia's Manhattanville campus, *Columbia in Manhattanville* brings architects, planners, historians, and educators together to document the making of the campus and to engage in the contested history of public planning and the private university. Edited by Esther Choi and Marrikka Trotter, *Architecture is All Over* collects contributions from scholars and practitioners on the dual meaning of the title: that architecture is simultaneously everywhere and finished. Working with Avery Archives on the anniversary of Frank Lloyd Wright's 150th birthday, *Wright's Writings: Reflections on Culture and Politics 1894–1959* traces the discursive work of the architect through a set of essays by Kenneth Frampton alongside images of Wright's literary output. Produced on the occasion of the exhibition *Stagecraft: Models and Photos* at the Arthur Ross Gallery, *Modeling History* is both a book on the material legacy of Kenneth Frampton's course Studies in Tectonic Culture and an envelope for the photographic prints by James Ewing exhibited in the show. Other exciting projects this year include *Trace Elements*, a riff on the architectural monograph by Aranda\Lasch;

Water Infrastructure, a toolkit for questions of water use and distribution; and *Blue Dunes: Climate Change by Design*, a chronicle of the proposal to build artificial barrier islands along the Mid-Atlantic coast of the US.

DIRECTOR OF PUBLICATIONS James Graham, ASSOCIATE EDITOR Isabelle Kirkham-Lewitt, MANAGING EDITOR Jesse Connuck

Social Transparency: Projects on Housing — Authors: Michael Maltzan, Hilary Sample, and others
Designer: Neil Donnelly; Specifications: 144pp, Paperback; Dimensions: 5 × 7.5 in. ; ISBN: 978-1-941332-19-1

s needed,
cess to an ATM.

s needed,
eriors that are not
om the exterior.

s needed,
ich color palette.

s needed,
curity and sense

s needed,
uld be designed
to other
of isolated
projects within
ct's office.

173

Columbia in Manhattanville — Editor: Caitlin Blanchfield; Designer: Common Name; Specifications: 144pp, Paperback; Dimensions: 6 × 9 in.; ISBN: 978-1-941332-23-8

HELICAL BUILDING
An Interview with Elizabeth Diller and Charles Renfro

Diller Scofidio + Renfro were
new facilities for the Columb
be housed in two buildings b
and Broadway and Twelfth A
just broken on these structu
of the second phase of cons
a new design voice within th
interview with editor Caitlin I
Charles Renfro discuss desi
pedagogy, helical circulatior

I'd like to begin with your design
process. How did you conceive of
the concept for the new Columbia
Business School building?

Charle

on very close student, faculty
We didn't want this to be a pl
at the top and the students w
of the building. Our first strat
populations together in orde
and unpredictable interactio
and the students.
    We were also inter
programmatic hierarchies of
of a traditional graduate sch
lounges and dining facilities
We envisioned these progra
might say—that would sprea
defined program elements s

Columbia in
Manhattanville

Amale Andraos
Carol Becker
Caitlin Blanchfield
Lee C. Bollinger
Elizabeth Diller
Steven Gregory
Maxine Griffith
Tom Harris

Architecture is All Over — Editors: Esther Choi and Marrikka Trotter; Designer: Neil Donnelly
Specifications: 288pp, Paperback; Dimensions: 6.5 × 9.25 in.; ISBN: 978-1-941332-30-6

Modeling History — Author: Kenneth Frampton and Amale Andraos; Photographer: James Ewing
Designer: MTWTF; Specifications: 63pp, Paperback; Dimensions: 8.5 × 11 in.

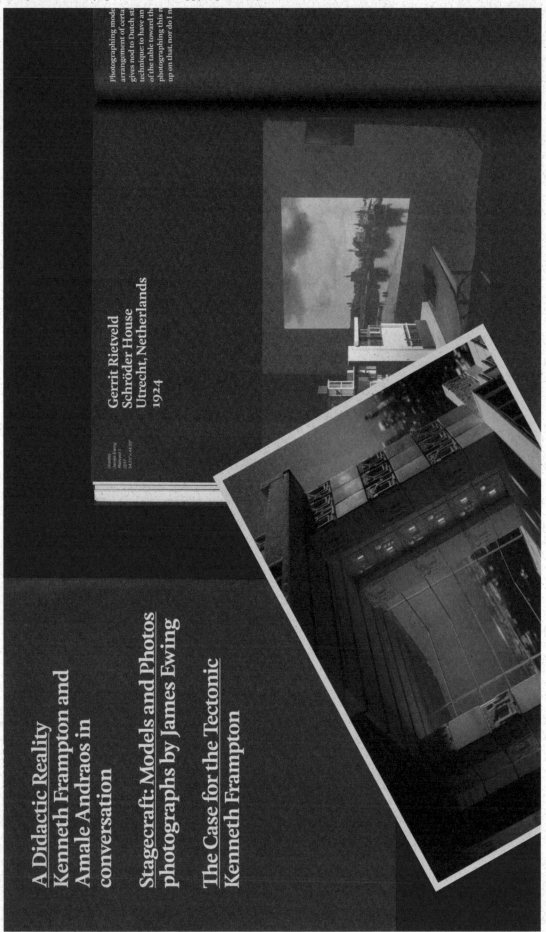

Gerrit Rietveld
Schröder House
Utrecht, Netherlands
1924

A Didactic Reality
Kenneth Frampton and
Amale Andraos in
conversation

Stagecraft: Models and Photos
photographs by James Ewing

The Case for the Tectonic
Kenneth Frampton

Trace Elements — Author: Benjamin Aranda and Chris Lasch; Designer: Kristian Henson; Specifications: 160pp, Paperback; Dimensions: 4.75 × 7.5 in. ; ISBN: 9781941332337

Water Infrastructure — Author: Bry Sarté and Morana Stipisic; Designer: Manuel Miranda Practice; Specifications: 172pp, Paperback; Dimensions: 7 × 10 in.; ISBN: 978-1-941332-26-9

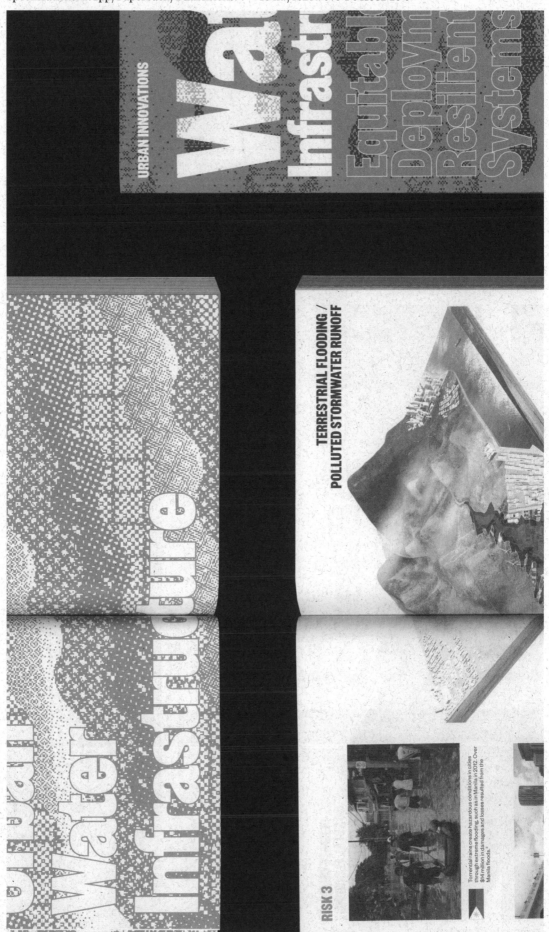

Blue Dunes: Climate Change by Design— Editors: Jesse M. Keenan and Claire Weisz; Designer: Yeju Choi; Specifications: 288pp, Paperback; Dimensions: 6.75 × 9 in.; ISBN: 978-1-941332-15-3

Avery Review

EDITOR James Graham, MANAGING EDITOR Isabelle Kirkham-Lewitt, CONTRIBUTING EDITORS Alissa Anderson, Caitlin Blanchfield, Jacob Moore

On the presidential inauguration of Donald J. Trump, the *Avery Review* released a special online and limited edition risograph-print issue, entitled *And Now: Architecture Against a Developer Presidency (Essays on the Occasion of Trump's Inauguration)*. The project continues to develop, and will be published as a book by Columbia Books on Architecture and the City in the fall.

The *Avery Review* is premised on the idea that the review and the critical essay are vital but still under-utilized ways of exploring the ideas and problems that animate architecture, and we hope to push these genres beyond their most familiar forms, whether journalistic or academic. Our aim is to explore the broader implications of a given object of discourse (whether text, film, exhibition, building, project, or urban environment). Published monthly during the academic year at www.averyreview.com, the journal aims to enrich the digital culture of architecture writing, opening new space for intellectual creativity and spirited criticism. Be it through the juxtaposition of books and buildings, meditations on constructed landscapes, or incisive critiques of architectural showmanship, our reviewers and essayists test their own intellectual commitments and convictions—theoretical, architectural, and political—through engagement with the work of others.

2016–2017 marked the *Review*'s third year. In addition to continuing the same dogged commitment to the critical essay, the *Avery Review* focused explicitly on architecture's obligations and long-standing complicities in response to the current political climate.

KNOW YOUR AXO

Columbia GSAPP Design Mantras, 2017

Taken together, these statements can be read as a sort of
time-sensitive mantra for the disciplines of the built
environment, a set of pedagogical imperatives that have
emerged from the school, and a statement of engagement
as an institution. We understand these six statements,
dispersed throughout this book, as an urgent call to action
for Columbia GSAPP, and we recognize their relevance
and implications for the larger global community of
which the school is inextricably embedded within. They
address issues of political engagement, social equity,
representation, pursuing action on climate change,
global perspectives, cultural diversity, and developing
professional practice in all disciplines of the built
environment in which we study and practice.

Visual Studies
Laura Kurgan, Director
Joshua Uhl, Coordinator

Design Seminars
Amale Andraos

Building Science
& Technology
Craig Schwitter, Director

History & Theory
Reinhold Martin, Director

Visual Studies

Laura Kurgan, Director & Joshua Uhl, Coordinator

Visualization is never just presentation—it is a way of thinking, designing, and drawing spaces at all scales. In a series of courses across all programs, the Visual Studies sequence exposes students to a wide range of tools and techniques and foregrounds both their uses and their limits. The sequence seeks to initiate interdisciplinary dialogues across the school and address the dynamic nature of our visual culture.

The courses and workshops are divided into three broad sets of methods in visualization: quantitative, qualitative, and translational (hybrid). The variety of trajectories possible within the sequence of classes, required and elective, promote an individual exploration of visualization, fostering innovation and creative methods. Courses are either full semester (3 credits) or half semester (7 week, 1.5 credits). Teaching generally follows a "flipped classroom," with students acquiring skills in tutorials outside of class and devoting class work to methodological and creative discussions exploring the limits and underlying concepts which guide those techniques.

1
2
3
4

ARCHITECTURAL DRAWING AND REPRESENTATION 1 ¶ FALL 2016 ¶ JOSHUA UHL, DANIL NAGY, BIKA REBEK AND FARZIN LOTFI-JAM, INSTRUCTORS ¶ Recent shifts to a "paperless" architecture continue to have a profound impact on the field of architecture and its modes of representation and analysis. Beyond severing the longstanding relationship of the line to paper, the extraction of the vector to a virtual realm is accompanied by a simultaneous influx of data. With this new data saturation, the position of the architectural drawing is in flux. The field of architecture is slowly moving away from its longstanding roots of projection-based representation and drawing, in favor of a virtual model. The embedded data within the virtual model anticipates a certain adaptability or temporal quality which stands at odds with the fixity of traditional techniques. In this course, we engaged drawing's new temporal nature and tried to harness its potential. What does it mean to make a drawing in the "Post-Projection" era? What is lost when an understanding of the constructed nature of a drawing is gone and the tools of projection are relegated to a secondary role? What can be gained through understanding these tools more completely and then re-appropriating them in contemporary investigations?

5
6
7
8
9
10
11
12

ARCHITECTURAL DRAWING AND REPRESENTATION 2 ¶ SPRING 2017 ¶ DAN TAEYOUNG, FARZIN LOTFI-JAM, LEIGHA DENNIS, LYDIA XYNOGALA, INSTRUCTORS ¶ Architecture can be described as the practice of crafting imaginary worlds, and manifesting these imaginaries into various forms of existence. Operating in a role between artist and activist, novelist and politician, illustrator and manager, architects balance on a spectrum between constructing the imaginary and discovering the real. On one hand, the drawing performs an imaginary to an audience. Drawings patiently explain highly intricate systems, argue for spaces that don't exist yet, whisper the complex ecologies of a site, and evoke the indescribable. Like written language, drawings are expressive communications through form, medium, and grammar. On the other hand, drawing is a process of thinking through doing, as a way to discover our real designs. Much like spoken language, drawings can perform in the murky space between intention and improvisation. ¶ The goal of Architectural Drawing and Representation 2 is to generate critical and playful debate, to experiment with representational tools and strategies, and to take active risks. To do so, the course is structured as a series of experiments with three "hypotheses" to be tested, challenged, debated, agreed with, or rejected: 1) Drawing is a form of thought; 2) Our tools and workflows affect what we represent; 3) The audience influences the drawing; How, through representation, can we move beyond mimesis and verisimilitude in order to represent these shared matters of concern? How, through representation, can we gain new modes of thinking that can enable us to be more thoughtful and exploratory designers?

13
14
15

ARCHITECTURAL PHOTOGRAPHY ¶ FALL 2016 & SPRING 2017 ¶ ERIETA ATTALI, INSTRUCTOR ¶ Architectural photography primarily deals with the relation between artifacts and their environments, or the dipole of building and landscape; cities are but a special case of this model of thought. Urban landscapes have their own seasons, circadian rhythms, and sociopolitical ecosystems. From historical centers and high-density commercial developments, to suburban sprawls and post-industrial brownfields, urban landscapes enmesh past, present, and future. ¶ New York City has an almost singular presence in the history of photography; a city reflected in a mosaic of images created by true masters like Alfred Stieglitz, Berenice Abbott, Garry Winogrand, Bruce Davidson, William Klein, among others, but also by less known foreign photographers who were enthralled by the magnetic presence of the city's urbanity. These series of images that span almost two centuries create an undeniable visual memory, etched in our cultural consciousness.

16
17

PARAMETRIC REALIZATIONS ¶ FALL 2016 ¶ MARK BEARAK, INSTRUCTOR ¶ Parametric modelers are commonly used in the development of digital architectural models, but they are rarely taken to the point of becoming physical realities. This course looked at the process of generating parametric algorithms and then turning those models into physical realities. Students worked in groups to design a product that was the physical realization of their scripted protocol.

ENCODED MATTER ¶ FALL 2016 & SPRING 2017 ¶ EZIO BLASETTI, INSTRUCTOR ¶ This workshop investigated non-linear systems and self-organization in the design and prototyping of architectural immersive environments via computational generative methods. At present, computational techniques are predominantly employed in the optimization, rationalization, or surface decoration of more traditionally created forms and spaces. This research instead focused on the inherent potential of computation to generate space and of algorithmic procedures to engage self-organization in the design process. Encoded matter operated as an open source design laboratory. Participants engaged closely with computational processes in order to develop an aesthetic and intuition of complexity that resides in a balance between design intent and emergent character. ¶ Encoded matter proposed a parallel study between material behavior and computational systems. The participants were encouraged to conduct and document a series of material experiments in dialogue with their computational research. A critical parameter in this workshop was to develop the potential beyond finite forms of explicit and parametric modeling towards more non-linear algorithmic processes. The goal was the development of an exquisite and novel architectural language that is inextricably tied to the process of its own production.

18

APPROACHING CONVERGENCE ¶ SPRING 2017 ¶ BIAYNA BOGOSIAN, MAIDER LLAGUNO MUNITXA, INSTRUCTORS ¶ Approaching Convergence introduced the theoretical and technical framework for the generation of design question oriented spatio-temporal visualizations. The working methodology advocated in this course focused on converging varied inter-operational platforms to develop custom toolsets for each proposed design question and its corresponding visualization and analysis methods. This approach enabled our students to gain an advanced knowledge of data driven parametric and algorithmic design tools. We used the city of Seoul as the case study of the investigations. Through lectures and hands-on exercises, our students employed various custom toolsets based on Grasshopper and its extensions, along with Geographical Information Systems (GIS) and remote sensing analysis.

19
20
21
22
23

ULTRAREAL ¶ FALL 2016 & SPRING 2017 ¶ JOSEPH BRENNAN AND PHILLIP CRUPI, INSTRUCTORS, WITH JENNY FANG ¶ The use of perspective and rendering is often an afterthought. With the abundance of 3D modeling software and the ability to see every angle of a project instantaneously, renderings are often thought of as a last minute tool for representation. Ultrareal challenged its participants to not only think of rendering as a method of presentation, but also a tool for design. We encouraged the use of perspective and rendering early and often in the design process. In addition to learning techniques for creating ultrarealistic images, students learned a workflow that encourages

early exploration. We focused on color, light, material, context, reflection, and opacity throughout the course of the entire semester. We also looked for inspiration in many places, including art, photography, and cinematography.

24
25

GRAPHIC ARCHITECTURE PROJECT II: DESIGNING IMAGES ¶ FALL 2016 ¶ TERRI CHIAO, INSTRUCTOR ¶ In this class, we considered the architectural image as a critical and personal tool of visual persuasion. With an emphasis on individual stylistic and conceptual development, we aimed to foster each student's visual voice through a series of diverse image-making exercises over the course of the full semester. ¶ In the first part of the semester, students completed weekly exercises exploring form and counterform, constructed landscapes, photographic series, typophoto, oppositions, and invention. Throughout the semester, we considered the relationships between multiple images as a crucial aspect of designing images, producing image sets and photo books that investigate series and sequence. Assignments were structured to encourage exploration through play, experimentation, rigor, and critical thinking. Discussions and readings centered around abstraction, narrative, and image construction. ¶ In the second part of the semester, students worked on one multi-part, five-week project culminating in the creation of a visual book that builds a story through images. Combining graphic narrative and physical book prototyping, we created distinct visual experiences based on each student's subject of choice.

26
27
28

GRAPHIC ARCHITECTURE PROJECT 1: DESIGN AND TYPOGRAPHY ¶ FALL 2016 & SPRING 2017 ¶ YOONJAI CHOI, INSTRUCTOR ¶ In this course we examined, in rather minute detail, aspects of presentation: that is the visual rhetoric employed to convey design concepts. We were especially interested in how diverse forms of representation—plan,

section, elevation, perspective, diagram, and rendering—combine with typographic language in complex graphic and discursive narratives. ¶ We investigated these conceptual issues through extremely practical assignments. In so doing, this class introduced basic 2D design as a component of complex message making. In the first half of the semester, we focused on 2D composition and typography. We examined the details of letterforms and investigated type design and typesetting from a historical and visual perspective. We also considered typographic hierarchy and systems and looked at the composition of graphic space using both typography and images. ¶ In the second part of the semester, we began with a lesson in simple but refined typesetting, followed by assignments that dealt with layered content, working with more sophisticated design systems. We continued to explore the use of grids for managing complex information and for the graphic articulation of two-dimensional space. Using the visual and conceptual tools developed in the first section, we combined graphic devices with narrative content.

APPITECTURE ¶ SPRING 2017 ¶ MARK COLLINS AND TORU HASEGAWA, INSTRUCTORS ¶ Mobile phones are an expansive platform for spatial computation. Taking on the role of software developer, architects are well poised to deliver compelling experiences that build strong connections between information and space. Space can be mapped, tagged, generated and experienced through these now ubiquitous devices. The goal of this seminar was for each student to develop a spatial app, an open-ended prompt that means to stimulate thinking on the notion of situated technologies. Students were led through the iPhone SDK, a powerful set of tools and APIs that let them harness the array of sensing, processing and actuating technologies available through mobile computing.

29

INTERACTION & ENVIRONMENT ¶ FALL 2016 ¶ TIM GAMBELL, FLORIAN MEWES, INSTRUCTORS ¶ This class was about the overlap of interaction and environment—that is, how people interact with machines in a spatial context. With reference to the design of exhibitions, mobile apps, and physical computing, we reconsidered conventional screen-oriented interactive design from a perspective that includes sequence, scale, and site-specificity. By designing interactive experiences, we investigated how interactions change spaces and how spaces affect interactions.

FUNDAMENTALS OF DIGITAL DESIGN ¶ FALL 2016 ¶ MARK GREEN AND JOHN CERONE, INSTRUCTOR ¶ Fundamentals of Digital Design investigated modes of authorship and graphic communication in architecture and design. A wide range of imagery was used to conceive, coordinate and materialize the built environment and to map various types of information and data associated with it. The techniques of representation are not only a critical player in the communication of one's idea, but they become part of the study, problem solving, and aesthetic of that idea. Therefore, understanding the range of techniques and representational methods of architectural drawing is essential to both the development and realization of one's ideas. ¶ This course investigated the concepts, techniques, and representational methods of computer aided "drawing" in architecture. Students studied the operative relationship between 2-D and 3-D data, exploring the reaches of their analytic and representational potential. While the class was a foundational course in architectural computing, it built on the student's advanced ability to question, shape and interrogate space and time.

LINES NOT SPLINES: DRAWING IS INVENTION ¶ FALL 2016 & SPRING 2017 ¶ CHRISTOPH A. KUMPUSCH, INSTRUCTOR ¶ This intensive workshop format course was rooted in three propositions: that drawing is as much a way of seeing as it is a means of representation, that drawing is not bound to digital versus analog categorizations and that drawing remains the primary vehicle to record, communicate and create architecture. ¶ We reviewed the "Top Twenty Great Architectural Drawings," as a series of case studies linked to a film project on the drawing process. We attempted drawings of one line and drawings of 1,000 lines in the same spans of time. We drew what we see, what we cannot see, what we want and what we wish we could achieve. The word "rendering" had no place in this seminar. ¶ Students surrendered their typical drawing habits in favor of a rigorous drawing routine, which challenged notions of style, assumptions about "start" and "finish" and ideas about surface, shadow and scale. Diverse media were deployed; subjects included studio work, urban fragments, body parts and inward visions. Students left the course with sore hands, bright minds and a thick portfolio of new work.

RE-THINKING BIM ¶ FALL 2016 & SPRING 2017 ¶ JOHN LEE AND BRIAN LEE, INSTRUCTORS ¶ What is the place of BIM in architecture? Is it only meant for production, or can architectural design benefit from the real time feedback of Building Information Models. BIM can and will change the profession—this generation is responsible for how that will happen. Not having to deal with professional demands, students in this course were able to explore BIM strategies, which are not possible in the workplace. These virtual buildings are requiring that architects be extensively aware of all aspects of design. The intention of this workshop was to develop a thorough understanding of BIM, most importantly how we can intervene in the BIM process to ensure it is not strictly about efficiency, but instead utilize its capabilities as opportunities for design. How is the time gained from these tools reappropriated? How can the concepts of parametric modeling infiltrate, magnify and redefine the design process? Using software that forces rigor, can we learn from it and re-apply those logics to other aspects of what we do? Often out of familiarity, architects favor one design medium over another. This workshop insisted on interoperability between various platforms, magnifying the strengths of each tool. We investigated the process of integrating multiple parametric platforms simultaneously into a single architectural project.

INTEGRATED PARAMETRIC DELIVERY ¶ FALL 2016 & SPRING 2017 ¶ JOHN LEE AND BRIAN LEE, INSTRUCTORS ¶ Emerging technologies in architectural design find their own time and place to be implemented. Too often the tool controls the design. When utilized effectively, advanced parametric design methodologies will facilitate numerous iterations, enabling a more resolved final product in a time-restricted setting. Designers often favor one tool over another, mainly out of familiarity. This workshop insisted on interoperability between various platforms, magnifying the strengths of each tool. We investigated the process of integrating multiple parametric tools simultaneously into a single architectural project.

HACKING THE URBAN EXPERIENCE ¶ FALL 2016 & SPRING 2017 ¶ JOHN LOCKE, INSTRUCTORS ¶ This course sought to assert the relevance of the fabrication skills at our disposal as potentialities for social and environmental relevance. Through the re-appropriation and re-imagining of existing urban conditions, the student designed and fabricated a working prototype that embraced the messy reality of our city and promoted community involvement. The students pushed the notion that learning occurs through making, doing, and interactivity while giving primary focus to the designing of experiences in lieu of objects. At the conclusion of the course the student produced a full-scale urban intervention and observed and documented their relevant successes or failures. ¶ Material workshops were held to encourage students to explore constructions from inflatables to parametric agglomerations using quotidian materials. Ultimately, the student came out of the course with a healthy respect for two core concepts: firstly, an increased skill in the use and applicability of the building skills we have developed for solving design issues using unorthodox materials in unconventional settings; and secondly, that there is an opportunity for architects to regain lost relevance by inserting themselves through unsolicited proposals into the public consciousness as stewards of urban well being.

30

DATA MINING THE CITY ¶ FALL 2016 ¶ DANIL NAGY, INSTRUCTOR, WITH VIOLET WHITNEY ¶ Data Mining the City is a seminar studying the application of Big Data and Machine Learning methods to urban research and design practice. In this semester, the class focused primarily on Artificial Neural Networks, a promising branch of Machine Learning which has achieved substantial advances in recent years, solving problems which were once thought to be beyond the scope of machine intelligence. ¶ The first half of the class consisted of an accelerated crash course in the tools and technologies of Artificial Neural Networks. The second half was devoted to targeted discussions and workshops focusing on how these technologies can be applied to urban planning, architecture, and design. During the second half, students worked in groups to develop a research project that applies Machine Learning to a given problem in their field.

31
32
33

GENERATIVE DESIGN ¶ SPRING 2017 ¶ DANIL NAGY, INSTRUCTOR, WITH VIOLET WHITNEY ¶ Generative design taught students how to leverage the power of natural evolution and advanced computation to derive novel, high-performing solutions to complex design problems. The basis of the generative design method is the design space model, which combined a set of input parameters for generating a wide variety of design solutions with one or more measures used for evaluating the performance of each design. Once the design space was specified it was connected to a Genetic Algorithm which autonomously searches through the large space of possible designs to find the most optimal solutions.

34
35
36

GRAPHIC ARCHITECTURE PROJECT 3: GRAPHIC NARRATIVES ¶ SPRING 2017 ¶ MICHAEL ROCK, JI EUN RIM, INSTRUCTORS ¶ Why does James Bond drink martinis? ¶ The question begins to tease out some of the complex operations at work behind narrative: how parts stand for wholes, the evocative power of mood, and the narrative potential latent in precisely encoded details. This course interrogated narrative strategies through the practice of analytical reading, viewing, and most importantly, making. As a hybrid workshop and seminar, the first half of the semester was comprised of short, focused assignments, in conjunction with readings and films that examined a particular aspect of narrative technique. Each week, students critiqued and discussed each other's work, and were each required to deliver a presentation on the supplementary material during the course of the semester. Through these exercises students rehearsed the grammar of storytelling, considering narrative aspects of time, sequence, pacing, repetition, hierarchy, tone, audience, representation, and voice. ¶ The second half of the semester concentrated on a multi-week book project that used each student's own studio work as its subject. Through an engagement with the book, a discrete narrative tool, students came to better discern and frame the most vital and significant aspects of their individual projects. This process prompted students to cultivate their unique voice.

MAPPING FOR ARCHITECTURE, URBANISM AND THE HUMANITIES ¶ FALL 2016 ¶ JUAN FRANCISCO SALDARRIAGA, INSTRUCTOR, WITH EMILY FUHRMAN ¶ This course provided an introduction to mapping theory and geographic information systems tools. Through the use of open-source GIS software and open data students learned how to critically use mapping tools and geographic data for spatial analysis and representation. In this course, students worked through a series of web tutorials and hands-on in-class exercises to gain a better understanding of how these tools and data can be leveraged to analyze, represent and study past or present urban phenomena. In addition to using existing data, students were also able to create or bring their own sets of data and questions from other courses in order to work with these in the class.

37
38

DATA VISUALIZATION FOR ARCHITECTURE, URBANISM AND THE HUMANITIES ¶ SPRING 2017 ¶ JUAN FRANCISCO SALDARRIAGA, INSTRUCTOR, WITH BUCK WANNER AND MARK MADERA ¶ This course provided an introduction to data visualization theory and methods for students entirely new to the fields of computation and information design. Through a series of in-class exercises and take-home assignments, students learned how to critically engage and produce interactive data visualization pieces that can serve as exploratory and analytical tools. The course was part of a larger initiative hosted by the Center for Spatial Research to teach courses in the critical use of digital tools across fields in architecture, urbanism, and the humanities. ¶ The course was centered around a semester-long data visualization group project, through which the students learned the basics of data visualization, data analysis, data collection, programming and version control. However, even though the course taught specific visualization tools, the main conceptual thread centered on how to work with data, both in the humanities and in architecture and urbanism. Students defined their final projects around their own interests, and brought their own datasets into their final projects.

MONTAGE CITY: FILMMAKING AS URBAN OBSERVATION ¶ FALL 2016 & SPRING 2017 ¶ CAS-

SIM SHEPARD, INSTRUCTOR ¶ This workshop immersed students in the theory and practice of cinematic montage—that is, the sequence and juxtaposition of moving images—as a pro-active strategy of interpreting the built environment of cities. Students produced short videos that analyze and represent a particular New York City site's sense of place in terms of the social practices of its users. ¶ The focus was preparing students to look closely at what is around them—on how people use, navigate and interact with the built environment—by working through a series of formal and intellectual methods in montage filmmaking. Key selections from the history of poetic non-fiction cinema—from the first experiments in moving images in the 1880s to the European city-symphonies of the interwar years to the birth of the verité tradition in the 1960s—informed the production of original video montages that investigate urban conditions in particular sites in and around New York City. Each week, workshop participants met for discussion about works-in-progress. Students in the fall semester made videos exploring Newtown Creek, the Subway Station at 125th and Broadway, Columbus Circle, Houston Street and many more. During the spring semester, students investigated border conditions, thresholds, the liminal spaces of commuting and the maintenance of public space from Times Square to Paley Park to the Staten Island Ferry.

METATOOL ¶ FALL 2016 ¶ DAN TAEYOUNG, INSTRUCTOR ¶ The architect's tools are their most prized possessions, akin to bodily prostheses: tools are augmentations that not only alter what can be done, but what can be represented and thus what can be conceptualized. It could even be said that the architect is indelibly influenced by the logic and agency of those tools. ¶ This critical architect might ask: Where does the tool come from? What does the tool want to do? What new tools can be created? ¶ METATOOL takes the thesis that architects not only should be able to use tools, but also should have the ability to design new critical/experimental design tools themselves. The course was grounded in a solid technical understanding of computational tools and workflows, anchored around a set of conceptual/critical texts and group discussions. Rhino/Grasshopper was used as a meta-tool: a tool that enables the creation of other tools. However, the course was not about software itself, but about experimenting with design processes, as well as collaborative structures. Playful tools create new forms; experimental voting systems create new dynamics between collaborators; data-driven models attempt to democratize access to design decisions. The task at hand was to understand and design tools and their agencies.

VIABLE UTOPIAS ¶ FALL 2016 ¶ DAN TAEYOUNG, INSTRUCTOR ¶ Viable Utopias begins from a materialist premise of practice: the output of a firm's practice is heavily influenced by the firm's own reproductive labor, or the methods with which the firm supports itself. Articulated in one manner: the means of production influences the end goals of the work. Said in another: the business model of the firm influences the conceptual bent of the practice. What does it look like to practice differently? What would it look like to realize alternative modes of architectural practice? ¶ Viable Utopias was a course at Columbia GSAPP in Fall 2016 in co-designing organizational and pedagogical architectural culture. The course was about how collective work takes place, to research, design, and playtest ways of working collectively, and the course itself was an experimental 'space of play' to test methods of working together. The course was first proposed to Dan Taeyoung by A-Frame, a GSAPP student collective in early 2016; the syllabus was co-designed together over summer 2016. ¶ Our course was cooperatively facilitated, and structured as series of working groups anchored around a weekly class structure. Each week, a pair of participants facilitated a two-hour meeting, and helped re-orient the direction of the curriculum. Much of the output of our course was process-based, such as contact improvisation or exercises along Augusto Boal's Theater of the Oppressed. Working groups emerged, created and facilitated by participants including: ¶ Experimental Video: exquisite corpse video making, passion projects around "objects of desire" ¶ Documentation: Methods of recording, collective authorship ¶ Authority: Holacracy, the Tyranny of Structurelessness, management science, subjective nature of authority and power, authority bias, communicating experiences of authority. ¶ After our class, there are no clear answers, but renewed questions and proposals: Should we assemble and practice together? Should we design our relationships and organizational structures with each other? Should we deliberately design modes of collaboration so we can create newer, healthier, alternative modes of practice in the near future?

39

X-INFORMATION MODELING ¶ FALL 2016 ¶ LUC WILSON, INSTRUCTOR ¶ In this course, students created 3D data-driven analysis systems to facilitate the design of buildings and cities focused on five primary points: integration of competing objectives, pairing external data sources with custom spatial analysis, visualization of data, iteration of multiple options, and ultimately, design decision making through the use of metrics and data. ¶ In the first half of the semester, teams of students worked together to develop a custom evaluation system, using it to design and iterate development scenarios for New York City. Through this process students were asked to create new drawing types that could effectively communicate the intent of their parametric design systems for evaluation and critique. In the second half students took the concepts and techniques developed at the building scale and focused them on the urban scale. Teams paired various data sets such as PLUTO, energy use data, twitter, and weather data with spatial evaluation techniques to analyze, and ultimately propose urban-scale interventions in the city. ¶ Throughout this course students developed flexible and reusable digital tools that allowed them to quickly test and iterate thousands of scenarios, pair external spatial analysis with urban data sets, and develop a data-driven approach for decision making.

ALGORITHMS AND URBANISMS ¶ SPRING 2017 ¶ LUCIEN WILSON, MONDRIAN HSIEH, INSTRUCTORS ¶ The proliferation of urban data has resulted in an equal growth in accessibility of data exploration tools. Data-driven techniques have become indispensable not only in the exposure of issues, but as essential methods in urban storytelling. ¶ This course mixed students from Architecture, Urban Design, and Urban Planning to explore data visualization and algorithmic methods as a medium for urbanistic communication. Students brought their current educational material into the folds of other departments, and in working together interrogated their own industry's canon. Through data exploration, visualization and spatial analysis, students developed projects to investigate new methods of design and development in New York City. ¶ Projects were proposals to intervene in the process of city building, with students creating planning and design models informed by data and vetted through testing and their own expertise. Subjects included the effects of gentrification on the city, how to leverage growth over displacement, and the future of a flexible legal structure for short term sublets. ¶ Teams worked with course

instructors to grow projects, develop workflows to exchange data, and test proposals. In developing the workflows, data analysis and visualization we worked with and tested a number of techniques and softwares.

1

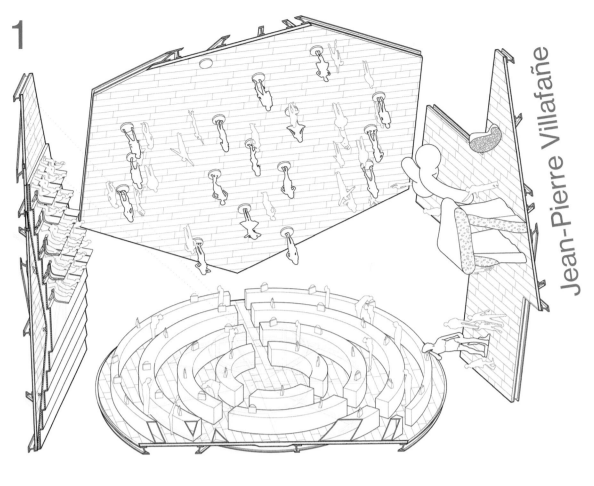

Jean-Pierre Villafañe

2

Kuan He

3

Kilmo Kang

4

Quentin Yiu

5

Mayrah Udvardi

6

Taylor Z. Williams

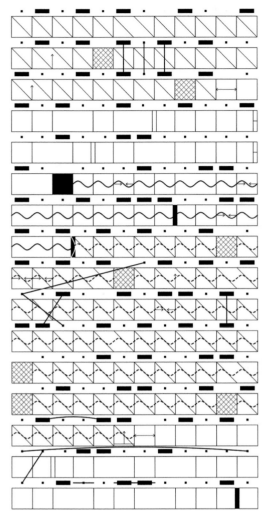

7

Kate Wang

8

Travis Tabak

9

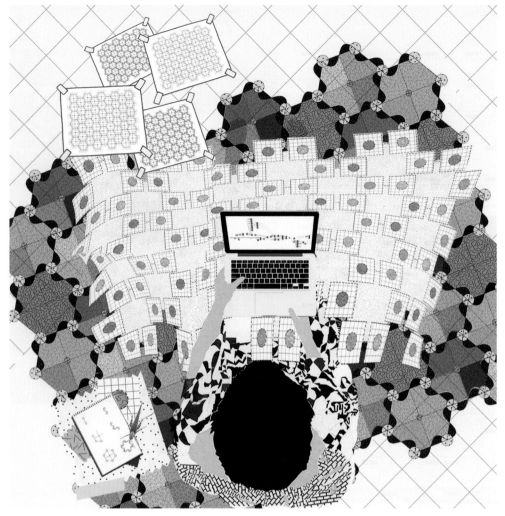

Sadie Dempsey

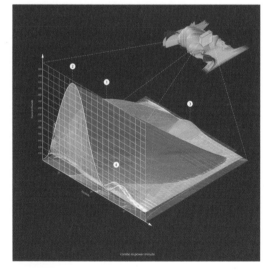

10

11

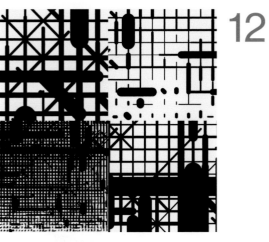

12

13

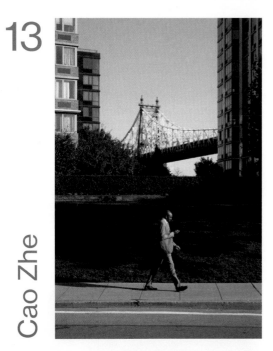

Caitlin Sills

Cao Zhe

Chu Li

14　15

Boekum Kim

16 Kig Veerassunthorn

Alejandro Ciudad-Casafranca, Ella Yini Xu

Zhenwei Zhong, Chuhan Zhou

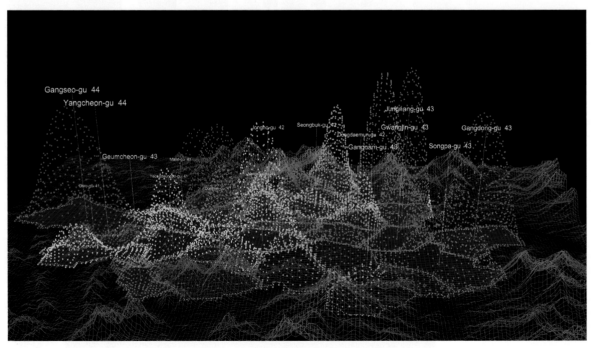

18

19

Abraham Murrell

Ali Fouladi, Zahid Nawaz Ajam

20

21

Hannah Han, Dylan Belfield, Zara Gilbert

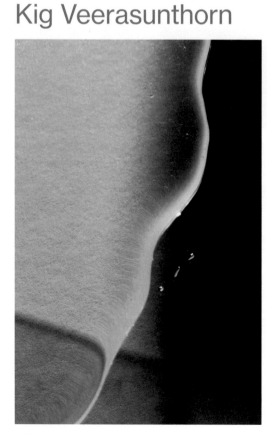

26

Andri Putri

27

Harrison Nesbitt

28

David Kagawa

29

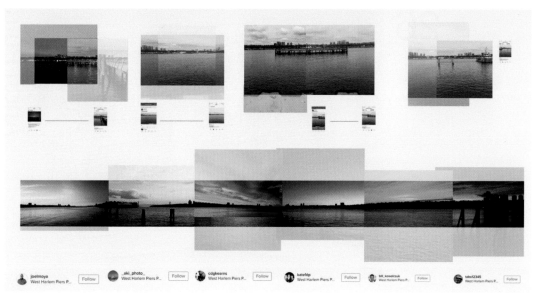

Soojung Yoo

30

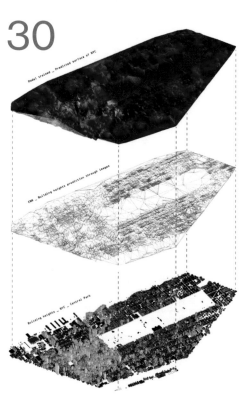

31

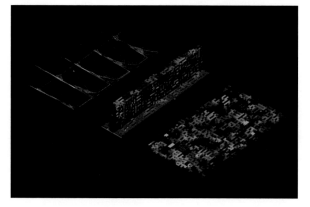

Zachary White

Nicklaus James Sundholm,
Shuman Wu, Carmelo Ignaccolo

32

Cory Archie

Laura Lee

33

34

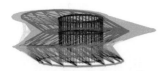

Corina Wright

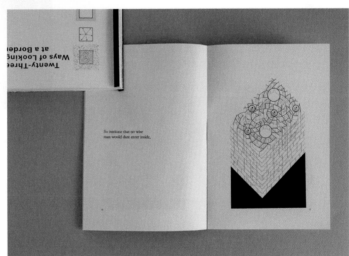

Nabila Morales Pérez

35

Ayesha Gosh

36

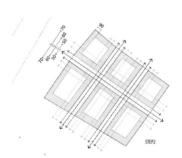

37

Andrei Zaiatz, Valerie
Lechene, Jeffrey Wayno

38

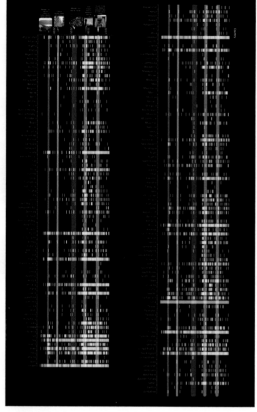

Ge Zhao, Maria Khan,
Jianghanhan Li,
Majed Abdulsamad

39

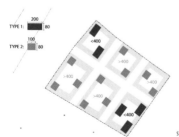
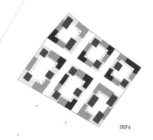
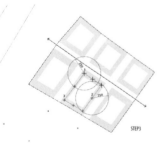

STEP1

STEP2

STEP3

STEP 4

STEP 5

STEP 6

Hong Li, Ruoqi Fan, Haochen Yang

Today, we understand technology as constantly and rapidly changing. Recognizing the limitations of a traditional track-based program to keep pace with these changes and foster further exploration, our architecture curriculum is instead predicated on this evolution. It moves towards hybridization, blurring the boundaries of each sequence—History & Theory, Visual Studies, Technology, and the Design Studio—to create new possibilities for intersections but also entirely new types and formats for teaching and learning.

Technology-related questions around the analysis and visualization of data, for example, cut across the entire Visual Studies Sequence. As a result, a number of seminars now straddle these two fields, initiating a "Visual Technology Sequence" that brings technology and visual studies together in fresh ways.

Following the Housing (Core III) and Scales of Environment (Advanced IV) Lecture and Workshop series as well as the Advanced Studios' Transfer Dialogues, which intensify arguments on and around the studio curriculum through conversations with invited guests and faculty, a new set of Design Seminars and Workshops have been launched to explore specific material and fabrication technologies, with equal emphasis on the design process. While the Design Seminar sits at the intersection between practice and discourse, the Workshop proposes a hybrid between studio and seminar—the extended duration and expanded space of the studio augmented by the rigorous discussion of the seminar.

To hybridize the various sequences of the architecture curriculum is to argue for the necessary and productive mingling of history & theory, technology, practice, and design-related investigations. Informed by interdisciplinary perspectives, these new hybrid courses not only expand the space between the material, architectural, and urban scales but also invite an ongoing critical perspective—always pushing the boundaries of the curriculum and the nature of the curriculum itself to become something else. We might not know what the "else" is yet, but we can already begin to recognize it in the faculty syllabi and in the work of the students. These classes encourage this evolution as seeds for engaging the future.

Amale Andraos

AGONISM AND ARCHITECTUR-AL COMMUNICATION ¶ SPRING 2017 ¶ CRISTINA GOBERNA PESU-DO, INSTRUCTOR ¶ Agonism and Architectural Communication was a research seminar that explored how various types of non-traditional media construct up-to-date architectural discourse and how Agonism, or critical thinking, is introduced in their conceptualization, design, and content. Due to the availability, multiplication, and speed of current communication channels, architects today not only need to be skillful in a wide range of broadcasting technologies but also be aware of the latest international conversations on architectural representation. Taking into consideration that architecture is currently produced and consumed not only by drawings, models, and descriptive or academic writing, this course focused on the historical and current use of non-traditional media such as theatre, film, sound, creative writing, alternative publishing, exhibitions, education, documentaries, etc. and their use as tools for constructing critical positions on current disciplinary affairs. The final result of the course was an exhibition and a book of interviews with OFFICE, Atelier Bow Wow, Bernard Tschumi, Common Accounts, Cooking Sections, Liam Young, and Takk, among others.

NEW FORMS OF CONTEMPO-RARY ARCHITECTURAL PRAC-TICE ¶ FALL 2016 ¶ NIKOLAUS HIRSCH, INSTRUCTOR ¶ The workshop/seminar aimed to reflect on new forms of contemporary architectural practice. The focus was the increasingly multifaceted and yet threatened role of the architect. Today we face a paradox: the field of architecture is both expanding and contracting, both characterized by a multidisciplinary practice, and—contrary to the classic self-image of the generalist architect-genius—a marginalized expert for one building element, the formal packaging into facades. ¶ In this disciplinary context the workshop/seminar critically investigated the conflicting question of trans-disciplinary collaboration. We discussed the potentials and contradictions of the "architect in the expanded field" (to rephrase a quote from Rosalind Krauss, ostensibly a notion that has been debated at GSAPP in recent years). Squeezed between art and engineering, between an increasing number of consultants, controllers, developers, philanthropists, etc., the contemporary architect has to creatively search for a new position.

TRANSURBAN STATES OF AMERICA ¶ FALL 2016 ¶ AN-DRÉS JAQUE, INSTRUCTOR ¶ City, suburbia and countryside, as spatial categories, are no longer able to explain or project the demarcation of daily life. Having breakfast, engaging politically, or developing relationships are all processes happening in different spatial modes—namely the interscalar transience between constellations of heterogeneous entities distributed around the world, occupying simultaneously urban and non-urban space. The seminar explored what happens to architectural design when facing this spatial mode that we will call TRANSURBIA. To explore its architectural specificity and ways for architectural practices to become relevant in its design were the goals of the TRANSURBAN STATES OF AMERICA seminar. ¶ The work was based on the discussion of selected readings, organized as pairs, where architectural thinking finds parallels with in the social sciences. Together with this, the participants in the seminar collectively produced a collection of architectural designs directly addressing nine perspectives to approach TRANSURBANISM in the US.

BOOKS, FIGURES, OBJECTS ¶ SPRING 2017 ¶ HILARY SAMPLE, INSTRUCTOR ¶ In this advanced design-research seminar, students were exposed to both the design work related to books, figures, and objects as well as the thinking and making behind their production. Mirroring its title, the seminar was organized into three independent sections: books, figures, and finally objects. Each section consisted of a series of lectures given by the instructor that presented examples; offered a workshop component which explored how to make something or explain the instruments of representation; and included extracurricular experiences such as a visit to Avery library, a museum, or a gallery. In addition, a series of guests, all key figures in the framing of design thinking and curating of design objects today, were invited to the seminar. The seminar explored specific architects who work outside of their respective disciplines to design object-things that might not so easily be classified as Architecture-as well as industrial designers, artists, and graphic designers. These figures included: Anni and Josef Albers; Aino Aalto and Alvar Aalto; Donald Judd; Ronan & Erwan Bouroullec; Jean Prouve; Isamu Noguchi; Petra Blaisse; Rita McBride; and Katharina Grosse, among others. The seminar used this idea as a starting point, and looked to those who are making books, objects, and figures as a way forward to a better understanding of the relationship between design and architecture.

ART AS PUBLIC INFRASTRUC-TURE ¶ SPRING 2017 ¶ GALIA SOLOMONOFF, INSTRUCTOR, WITH BRIAN KENET ¶ Art as Public Infrastructure was a seminar dedicated to investigating the emergence of Art Institutions and the effects in urban regions around them. The premise was that as cities around the world seek to nurture 21st century industries, lively urban centers, and harmonious communities—while simultaneously adapting to a whirlwind of social, technological, and environmental changes, all under severe budgetary constraints—it is crucial to understand the ways in which a given city expresses its values, enhances its identity, and quantifies its growth. ¶ The seminar investigated the interrelationship between art, architecture and economic development, evaluating different localities were art institutions were deployed. In some struggling communities, these institutions had a positive transformative effect and triggered healthy organic economic growth, while in others, similar institutions triggered uncontrollable gentrification and displacement. ¶ Drawing from an array of contemporary and historical examples, the seminar examined the efforts and successes of private cultural institutions such as the Guggenheim Museum, Basel Art Fair, Dia Center for the Arts, as well as governments operating at city, regional, and national scales. Selected precedent cities from Bilbao to Beacon, New York to Miami demonstrated how art institutions acted as urban catalyst, imparting physical as well as demographic transformations.

PEAK FLOW ¶ FALL 2016 ¶ TROY CONRAD THERRIEN, INSTRUC-TOR ¶ As a discipline modeled on artistic genius as an animating principle—call it 'design'—architecture is a fragile anachronism in a world whose foundation is increasingly built on bedrock of computation. Computation introduces a new physics into the idea economy. Silicon Valley has mastered these dynamics through an emerging apparatus of rituals and beliefs. Their success has spawned a new Prometheanism for reliably driving the critical path of history by 'inventing the future' with a steady flow of original ideas that have tamed the unpredictability of genius. Flow has replaced fixity as the steady state of contemporary innovation. Architectural thinking and practice—planning, vision, design—is not only anathema to this age of agility, it is a liability. This seminar explored the Silicon Valley idea space, the nature of digital technology, and its consequences for the social mind and body through architecture practice. The writing of Venkatesh Rao served as our compass to the weird terrain of contemporary Californian ideologies, from the Dark Enlightenment of Peter Thiel to the Bayesian rationality of the Singularitarians; the theories of Boyd and Bannon in strategic disciplines like politics, business, war, forecasting, and sport; and new spiritual forms, from technopaganism to SoulCycle.

MAKE. ¶ SPRING 2017 ¶ LOT-EK, ADA TOLLA & GIUSEPPE LIGNANO, CRITICS ¶ "Stop it and just DO. Try and tickle something inside you, your 'weird humor.' You belong in the most secret part of you. Don't worry about cool, make your own uncool. You are not responsible for the world—you are only responsible for your work, so do it. And don't think that your work has to conform to any idea or flavor. It can be anything you want it to be."–Sol LeWitt ¶ The premise of this workshop was to produce work that is experimental, personal, difficult, ugly, dirty, weird and investigative—rather than definitive in presenting conclusions. The seminar was about MAKING, and the work was physical, a 12"x12"x12" volume repeated through the basic materials of architecture: Concrete, Plastic, Metal, Glass, Masonry, Wood. ¶ Through MAKING the students explored and questioned their obsessions. They discovered and invented, followed and drove, commanded, and listened. The material was an opportunity and a constraint. The material was malleable and rigid. The material was vague—they chose it. In twelve weeks, the students produced six models—six volumes each responding to one of six materials.

Steven Smith

Jamie Waxter

Mike Nickerson

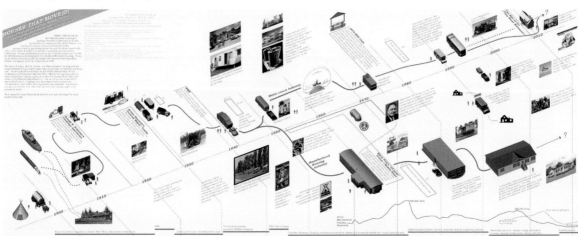

Arianna Deane

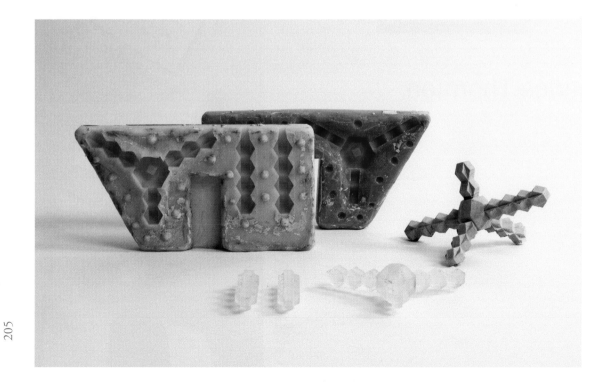

Brigitte Lucey

Qiu Jin

Charles Thornton

Goberna Seminar

For the next generation of architects, technology has become a greater and more differentiating force than ever before. As computational power increases at exponential rates and data becomes ubiquitous, formal methodologies in architectural design are giving way to an evidence basis. New modes of making in architecture are being disrupted through changes in manufacturing, materials and information technologies in a globalized world. While bricks and mortar may have been central to earlier methods of architecture, today the focus is squarely on performance of design in the built environment. Does design drive greater productivity? A better sense of community and wellbeing? Lower energy use? Less material waste? Broader and shared economic development? The subjective narratives of decades past on these subjects are today turning into data and hard facts. Performance and its measurement and verification have become a function of an architecture searching for the right solutions.

Urban conditions continue to drive discourse on the global stage. As cities grow globally and see the impact of unprecedented migration, the effects of design are ever present. Scarcity of resources, driven by rapid population growth and demographic change, need to be addressed head on by the architectural community. Energy, and its efficient performance in buildings has become the critical issue across architecture to address the questions of global climate change. Even while working harder inside the building construct, architects must think outside the building boundary, to wider notions of integration in systems including water, transportation, waste and energy. These are the pieces of a global puzzle that will be waiting for students as they graduate.

The technology sequence is fundamental in changing the course of architecture. It is an integral part of the school and training for the next generation of architects that will shape our built environment. Students must explore and experiment as always, but realize that abilities to rationalize and prove are more interconnected with design as it touches every aspect of development across the world.

ARCHITECTURAL TECHNOLOGY 1: ENVIRONMENTS IN ARCHITECTURE ¶ FALL 2016 ¶ SHANTA TUCKER, INSTRUCTOR ¶ This course addressed the fundamentals and application of environmental control systems in buildings. Heating, cooling, ventilation, lighting, and acoustics were discussed based on the physical laws that govern the exchange of energy between building and environment and how they relate to human comfort. Electrical, plumbing, fire protection and circulation were introduced in this context as required systems to make buildings fit for occupation.

ARCHITECTURAL TECHNOLOGY 2: STRUCTURES ¶ SPRING 2017 ¶ ZACHARY KOSTURA, INSTRUCTOR ¶ Some of the most prolific architectural works of the post-renaissance era have resulted from great architects and engineers working closely at every stage of the design process. These fruitful relationships demonstrate that the division of responsibilities once held solely by the majester operis into a wide array of technical disciplines —often led by the modern architect —has not hindered the viability of delivering a holistic end product. In fact, it has offered an opportunity to preserve harmony between innumerable aspects of design, planning and construction, while emboldening us with the capacity to embrace rapidly emerging technologies that promise to enhance our design process and built environment. ¶ This class provided students with an understanding of what "structural design" means and how it is carried out. Students gained familiarity with basic elemental forms, structural assemblies and systems and new and emerging materials. Through project-based and hands-on work, the class worked together to gain an intuitive understanding of structure, empowering everyone to integrate into architectural concepts a level of structural coherence and technical inspiration that allows load resisting systems to both perform and intensify the spatial experience.

ARCHITECTURE TECHNOLOGY 3: ENVELOPES ¶ FALL 2016 ¶ SILVIA PRANDELLI, INSTRUCTOR, WITH EUGENE CHANG ¶ This course explored the design of building skins to comply with a set of performance standards while turning an architectural concept into a finished system. Potential materials and systems were explored for different areas of the building that satisfy the architectural and functional constraints along with the performance goals. ¶ The class was taught as lectures that included case studies of real projects as well as an introduction to tools that improve a system's performance and optimize the envelope geometry. ¶ The final aim of the course was to teach students the process of defining an envelope strategy while conceiving complex geometry systems and to give an overview of the different parties involved in the decision making process in the American and overseas markets.

ARCHITECTURAL TECHNOLOGY 4: INTEGRATED DESIGN— BUILDING SCALE ¶ FALL 2016 ¶ SARRAH KHAN, INSTRUCTOR ¶ The key to functional balance and synergy is interweaving the complex and, at times, conflicting building systems. This integrated approach has repeatedly been shown to inspire compelling buildings, new spatial paradigms and the creative courage to solve complex, hard-to-define problems. In this course, student teams designed and integrated the building systems for a theatre in Red Hook, Brooklyn. The designs demonstrated systems expertise in fire protection, structures, mechanical, electrical and plumbing. In addition, the systems were synthesized in an integrated and innovative way.

INTEGRATED DESIGN: URBAN SCALE ¶ SPRING 2017 ¶ CRAIG SCHWITTER, INSTRUCTOR, WITH WEN ZHOU ¶ Integration is about problem solving collaboratively across disciplines. True collaboration requires a base level of knowledge of disciplines other than one's own in order to ask the right questions, to be open-minded to the answers, and to have the design dexterity to translate answers into built form. Architects, engineers, planners, developers, communities, and government agencies attempt to collaborate every day. Some find ingenious ways to shape cities through architectural insertions. Others just seem to fight against each other despite seemingly having the same underlying goals on what makes better cities. ¶ This class was the second half of students' experience developing proficiency with integrated design at Columbia. This time students dealt with systems you do not control. Urban-scale systems extend through the regional watershed, the local sewer shed, the city's electrical grid, highway networks, food systems, micro and macro-economic systems, and waste management networks. Buildings may plug into these systems, or these systems may plug into a building. Either way a building doesn't work without effectively connecting to and supporting these and many other urban scale systems. Integration at building scale is formalized and structured. Integration at urban scale is less defined.

1
2

PLACE: PROJECTIVE LANDSCAPES AND COLLECTIVE ECOLOGIES ¶ FALL 2016 ¶ MARK BEARAK, DAVID BROWN, INSTRUCTORS ¶ Designing the Future of Canopies for Governors Island ¶ New Yorkers have a long history of embracing outdoor spaces, from Central Park to the Hudson River to Brooklyn Bridge Park. The park is a gathering space for the entire city, a melting pot of cultures and activities. The city's newest park is on Governor's Island, a short ferry ride from both the Financial District and Brooklyn. This seminar provided an opportunity to work with the Friends of Governor's Island (FoGI) to contribute to the future of this new public space through the construction of a semi-permanent structure for shade and shelter. The participants were asked to balance the unique history and urban design of Governors Island, the concept of a master-planned community, the ecology associated with the park, the landmark status of the buildings and the nature of canopy design and independent fabrication.

3

FAST PACE / SLOW SPACE ¶ SPRING 2017 ¶ BRIGETTE BORDERS, MARK BEARAK, INSTRUCTORS ¶ Fast Pace/Slow Space explored the capabilities of digital technology by challenging students to create a system with an innovative use of materials and joinery, and then to test that system by programming it as an architectural folly or space of repose. ¶ Parametric and computational software offer designers a high degree of specificity which can be used to create complex forms, intricate details, and material efficiency, yet high-level results become insignificant if construction methods are too complicated to be timely. This course focused on the marriage of complex form and logical assembly, with detailing, hardware, and construction methods informing design decisions from the onset. ¶ Students designed an installation or environment with slow pace sensibilities, while utilizing details that allow for high-speed assembly and disassembly. The class explored the nature of digital processes, material techniques, and fabrication processes in the human environment. Students generated unique solutions that satisfy architectural requirements, building standards, cost ceilings and aesthetic aspirations, and efficiency of time.

EVOLVING EPIGENESIS ¶ SPRING 2017 ¶ JOHN LOCKE, MARK BEARAK, INSTRUCTORS ¶ This class focused on nature's emergent processes of creating unforeseen uniqueness. The results of this exploration led to the construction of a permanent pavilion on Governors Island this past spring. ¶ The measure of success for the project was for the structure to reflect the natural environment in which it was built: a building in nature that is both of nature and for nature. Exploring the theory of epigenesis we were able to look at the way that environment factors into evolution: nature vs. nurture. Building on this concept, the project was meant to evolve over time. This year represented the seed of the design, and then future iterations will evolve, morph and grow the pavilion annually. Nothing was prescribed or pre-defined; the project was the physical realization of the organic growth of form.

4

ART OF OBJECT ¶ FALL 2016 ¶ AARON BERMAN & JONATHAS VALLE, INSTRUCTOR ¶ In this course, students explored the intersection between Art, Architecture, and Object. Through the use of various digital design and fabrication techniques, students conceived a concept and fabricated an "object" directly related to human perception. Students developed a strong conceptual argument for their object, and then tested, expanded, and refined their argument throughout the semester. This testing ground took place in the form of physical prototypes, designed to analyze techniques, materials, and methods.

VDC AND THE DIGITAL DOMAIN ¶ SPRING 2017 ¶ JOHN CERONE AND SCOTT OVERALL, INSTRUCTORS ¶ The traditional drawing set has had a good, long run. But the future points elsewhere. Tomorrow's architects will work in a virtual, cloud-based environment, encouraging owners, architects and contractors alike to form strategic relationships and deliver built work. The reason to do this is simple. By demystifying the process of construction and presenting complex processes in a manner that even non-specialists can immediately comprehend, architects can access the knowledge of every stakeholder in real-time. The result is broader, more fruitful, more fluid, and with far more equitable collaborations—and that means better-performing buildings. ¶ At the heart of the process is a set of evolving tools and techniques that

have come to be known as Virtual Design and Construction—VDC. In a multi-dimensional, 4D+ environment, VDC is the process of digitally simulating the complexities of a design project. This can include geometric rationalization, systems development/ fabrication, logistics analysis and cost estimation, from concept through construction—or fabrication through assembly. This seminar demonstrated the principles of VDC and other key technical processes, focusing on how architects utilize emerging technologies to promote collaboration throughout all phases of design, production and operation. Technology-focused lectures were paired with, and informed by, presentations of real-world precedents from current project work. The course shared the current state of construction communication in the AEC industries—and why it must be radically changed.

ADVANCED MODELS IN ARCHITECTURAL SIMULATION ¶ SPRING 2017 ¶ MARK COLLINS AND TORU HASEGAWA, INSTRUCTORS ¶ The focus of this seminar was construction automation and the technologies that enable computing systems to sense and act in the physical environment. Modern design software lets us harness computation to direct the making of a staggering amount of design information. In this seminar, we looked at the complementary techniques and technologies that enable the physicalization of that design intent. The seminar explored the collapsing line between the physical world of bricks and the digital world of bits through a dissection of innovative projects and their associated algorithms and hardware. Students worked with a powerful simulation platform to develop and quantify their own novel construction systems. A special emphasis on digital simulation of physicality, kinematics and path planning helped students to develop innovative construction methodologies augmented by a new generation of machines.

INNOVATION, TECHNOLOGY AND ARCHITECTURE ¶ SPRING 2017 ¶ LISE ANNE COUTURE, INSTRUCTOR ¶ This seminar was an exploration of a varied cross-section of innovation and potential drivers of change with respect to the physical and spatial aspects architecture. This seminar included research of a wide range of state-of-the-art technologies, such as self-assembling structures, programmable materials, 3D and 4D printing, robotics, biodesign, AI and IoT, sensor technologies, as well as other developments in material

sciences and strategies or intelligence transferred from other disciplines and industries. The class was interested in speculating from a design perspective on the aesthetic, cultural, spatial and formal implications that might result from the application of these diverse cutting edge NextGen developments in technology. The seminar was interested in exploring disruption, paradigm shifts and game changers that have the potential to drive innovation in architecture today and in the not so distant future.

WIRED SKINS ¶ FALL 2016 ¶ TODD DALLAND, ROBERT LERNER, COLIN TOUHEY, INSTRUCTORS ¶ "Wired Skins" looked at the building skin as an active membrane, collecting energy, moving to respond to dynamic loads or solar orientations. The course explored how new materials such as shape memory polymers, flexible photovoltaics, and industrial textiles can be employed to make building skins that are dynamic—functionally and visually. We took a hands-on approach to research and development, learning about materials and methods through fabrication and testing, devising test procedures and implementing testing. While architects enjoy pushing the limits of technology, architectural fabricators are often key members of the design team, determining what is realistic technically, within project budgets and time frames. The course focused on developing the discipline of design from the fabricator's point of view, by testing ideas in a fabrication work-shop environment. Students researched and presented their own case studies of projects in which the expertise of the fabricator played a significant role in realizing the project.

TRANSFORMABLE DESIGN METHODS ¶ FALL 2016 ¶ MATTHEW DAVIS, INSTRUCTOR ¶ Architects have long imagined a built environment that is fundamentally dynamic. Portable buildings, retractable coverings, kinetic facades, and spaces that morph: these transformable structures have become part of the lexicon of architectural possibilities. Despite persistent interest, examples of truly dynamic buildings are few and architectural design remains focused on the development of objects that are essentially static. This course explored transformation itself as a design parameter that can be shaped, crafted, and optimized.

MAN MACHINE & THE INDUSTRIAL LANDSCAPE ¶ FALL 2016 ¶ SEAN A. GALLAGHER, INSTRUCTOR ¶ Industrialized communities are prevalent in every corner of the world today, and as a result the global population is now more urban than rural. Over the next century, existing and developing metropolises will have to reconsider traditional relationships between industrial and public territories in order to accommodate and sustain an increased level of demand for space and services. ¶ This course examined past and present strategies for meeting the growing industrial and infrastructural demands of our society. It identified areas where industrial technologies and/or landscapes might be recalibrated to serve future infrastructural networks that establish new relationships between the public, local ecology and industry. The course framed an understanding of the means and methods of industrial activities ranging from mining to waste management with a focus on current and future techniques of material extraction, refinement, and redistribution. ¶ Students produced writings and drawings analyzing and reimagining the current state and potential futures of industrial processes and sites. Students were encouraged to use their research assignment as a way of investigating interesting and unfamiliar industrial processes, but more importantly as a means to initiate a thesis for why and how architects can influence the necessary change in our urban environments.

5
6
7
8
9

ADVANCED CURTAIN WALLS ¶ SPRING 2017 ¶ ROBERT HEINTGES AND DAN VOSS, INSTRUCTORS, WITH EDWARD PALKA ¶ This course offered an intense exposure to the custom curtain wall in a lecture/seminar and technical studio format. It was the intent of the course to provide graduating students with a comprehensive understanding of the technical concepts and specific skills necessary to undertake the actual practice of designing, detailing, specifying and administrating the custom curtain wall. Although the course emphasized current and emerging technologies of the curtain wall, discussion of specific technical issues and methodologies

focused on those aspects that directly inform contemporary architectural design. Case studies of contemporary examples were used throughout to illustrate the technical content of the course.

10

THE ANATOMY OF ARCHITECTURE ¶ FALL 2016 ¶ A. JAY HIBBS, INSTRUCTOR ¶ In this seminar, we analyzed the primary technical systems—structural, mechanical and enclosure—of specific prominent post-WWII built architecture. Construction documents from a select group of buildings served as the core source of information, with supplementation from other published resources. This detailed investigation focused on the interrelationship between the structural, mechanical and enclosure systems, construction methods and materials, and the architectural form. The examination of the building systems emphasized the way in which each informed and impacted the others as well as their ultimate effect on the creation of the architecture. ¶ While this course emphasized the "how" of architectural technology, it also stressed the "why" of technology choices and determinations. It was a fundamental premise of this course that the creation of architecture must be guided by an overarching architectural intention and that this vision of the architecture forms the approach to all design decisions—from planning to detailing. As such, an objective of this course was to understand the architect's attitude regarding building systems and how the architectural intention of the specific building was realized, reflected and/or amplified by the choice, manipulation, interaction and execution of the building systems. Students investigated the principles behind the methods of construction as well as the reason certain construction methods and systems were created and employed.

11
12

ASSEMBLING ALL SORTS ¶ FALL 2016 ¶ RYAN LUKE JOHNS, INSTRUCTOR ¶ Parametric digital design tools and computer-aided manufacturing have enabled a non-uniform, curvilinear and mass-customized architecture. While this conceptual plasticity of the first digital turn has relieved architects of the monotony

of the mass-produced detail, the apparent freedom of digitally fabricated architecture still remains bound to industrially produced, standardized components (blanks, bars, bricks and sheet stock). Designs are generated in a digital world of infinite possibility, and are materialized (often wastefully) into a world constrained by the 4×8 sheet. ¶ This seminar explored alternative methods of designing details and assembly techniques which derive their non-uniformity, in part, from irregular or found building materials. By defining the material morphospace of a chosen component type (stones, branches, wood scraps, broken glass, etc.) students developed algorithmic methods for constructing experimental models which are not only adaptable enough to tolerate such material deviation, but benefit from it. These assembly techniques were prototyped at the small-scale using the school's UR3 Robot, computer vision, custom end-effectors (grippers, suction cups, depth sensors, etc.), and Processing/Grasshopper interfaces. ¶ More student documentation, including project videos, can be found on the course site: assemblingallsorts-sp17.tumblr.com

13
14
15
16

MATERIAL THINGS ¶ SPRING 2017 ¶ JOSHUA JORDAN, INSTRUCTOR ¶ This course introduced students to fundamental properties of materials and analog and digital construction techniques, in the combined format of a seminar and physical workshop. It provided hands-on experience with individual and cooperative building skills, focusing on the connectivity of analog and digital methods, as well as encouraging a type of engagement with making that is analytical and creative. ¶ The title of the course was literal in that it is a hands-on workshop concerned with the nature and performance of materials, examined and tested through direct experience. The title was also a reference to our necessary attachment to materials and material things as designers, and a nod to the positive cultural institutions that emerge around the act of making. As such, the course examined the relationship between materials and methods by engaging (through discussion and workshops) the conceptual and historical themes that establish making as an act of design thought. This included discussion of the history of making as part of design education, making countercultures, and the reexamination of craft vis-à-vis digital fabrication.

SUSTAINABILITY AND EXISTING STRUCTURES ¶ FALL 2016 ¶ NICO KIENZL, INSTRUCTOR ¶ The built environment plays a critical role in society's environmental footprint. Buildings account for 39% of primary energy consumption and 72% of all electricity consumed domestically. Given the urgency to address climate change, owners, designers and policy makers are therefore focusing on improvements to the built environment as a key mechanism to reduce greenhouse gas emissions. While much of this work in recent years has focused on efforts for new buildings, it is becoming increasingly clear that only improving new buildings will not result in the significant changes needed to avert catastrophic climate change. ¶ This course built on the core environmental systems course and challenged students to apply the lessons from that class to the realm of existing building improvements. Students learned how to survey building system concepts and create base documents of the project's architecture as well as the HVAC and energy systems. Students learned qualitative and quantitative approaches to analyze technical and architectural problems and how to develop innovative integrated solutions. Sustainability was a driving focus for the projects and students learned how to critically evaluate current industry developments and benchmarks alongside their design process.

SUSTAINABLE DESIGN ¶ FALL 2016 ¶ DAVIDSON NORRIS, INSTRUCTOR ¶ Sustainable strategies and techniques covered: principles of bioclimatic design, bioclimatic site design, sustainable water and waste treatment, regional bio-climates and related building types, building as thermal skin, passive heating, passive cooling, natural ventilation, daylighting, sustainable building systems, advanced sustainable technologies, sustainable materials and products, indoor air quality and environment. As a matter of sustainable design, the designer must meld these nominally separate sustainable building topics into an integrated sustainable design that successfully juggles potentially conflicting functional demands along with the building's broader, deeper and more poetic architectural objectives. ¶ To engage in this complex functional/poetic exercise, students designed a

High School of Environmental Design (HSED), to be located on the same site (Central Park) but transposed to one of four typical climates (cold, temperate, hot dry and hot wet). Each week, we assessed the lesson's architectural and sustainable implications and integrated them incrementally into students' designs. ¶ While the course introduced students to "advanced sustainable technologies," it prioritized sustainable principles and practices to be deeply embedded in the building's siting, orientation, core, envelope, circulation, primary materials and finishes. This not only assures that the building's sustainable performance endures independent of changes in technology but that its message of a more balanced integration of the natural and man-made persists into deep time.

ARCHITECTURAL DAYLIGHTING ¶ SPRING 2017 ¶ DAVIDSON NORRIS, INSTRUCTOR ¶ Architectural Daylighting introduced students to "light space," which is defined not by the conventions and restrictions of Renaissance perspective but rather by hemispherical space and perspective mapped onto the curved surface of the skydome in accordance with the diurnal and seasonal path of the sun. Within this hemispherical space, students were introduced to how light dynamically transforms static architecture with light and shadow that paints abstract forms onto walls, with color fields generated by the setting sun that fill a space with light thick as water, with sunlight on a field of tiny prisms that refract a thousand pointillist suns. Creating these daylight effects in architecture requires not only a general knowledge of light/space/material interactions but also an ability to model them. To accomplish this, students learn quantitative (computer model) and qualitative (architectural scale model) analytical techniques. The final project was to explore and develop a daylighting intervention in their studio project that united the qualitative and quantitative pathways. To do so they tested and recorded their intervention using an architectural scale model in natural sunlight. Under these conditions the photon does not lie.

ARCHITECTURAL ACOUSTICS ¶ SPRING 2017 ¶ RAJ PATEL, INSTRUCTOR, WITH LEAH GUSZKOWSKI ¶ The course began with a historic overview of human interaction with sound in the built environment. Fundamentals of acoustics were explained over a series of three classes, using images, video, listening, sound creation, sound visualization and measurement. An assignment entitled

"Boom Box" required students to apply the gained knowledge to construct a lightweight sound isolating enclosure for a loudspeaker. ¶ A field trip was taken to two significant but very different sites in New York City, where sound plays a pivotal role in the experience. This provided context to examine the historic development of buildings for music, opera, and theatre, and the relationship between technology, architecture and art. These classes also investigated sound and space, thinking about how different types of buildings sound as well as understanding the impact that noise and vibration have on design in the built environment. ¶ A visit to the Arup SoundLab allowed students to experience a wide range of acoustic design issues discussed in previous classes, and to learn how sound is used proactively in the design process. ¶ In the final assignment students delivered a project called "Sound Space," which was built around sound as the core driving concept.

TECHNOLOGY IN TRANSITION ¶ FALL 2016 ¶ CRAIG SCHWITTER, INSTRUCTOR ¶ As architectural practice evolves through the most recent information and digital cycle, it is only now catching up to the disruptive innovations that a broader spectrum of technology is advancing. How does ubiquitous availability of data change architectural planning? How does quantitative evidence start to shape the stories of development—economic and strategic—and what methods are we using to harness this in practice? How do post-digital tools that enable computation rather than simply representation impact the very foundation of creativity in the design profession? ¶ But is innovation in architecture different than other industries? How does innovation move the profession and the form of our built environment forward—a process that seems rapid and yet painfully slow all at the same time? Is innovation simply the ability to render and even fabricate a more complex shaped building? Or does it have a broader and deeper meaning to the ability for architecture to build society? ¶ This seminar explored some of the most disruptive innovations in architecture today—disruption at the building scale, where we are moving from a digital toolset that documents to a digital environment that computes. Disruptions in global scale issues, such as energy and productivity and the opportunity to tame climate change. Disruptions in urban density that drive city planning with predictive behavior mapping and use of social media.

17
18
19
20

were to become normative. Finally, we evaluated modular architecture critically, and considered questions such as: Would the widespread adoption of modular architecture inevitably lead to homogenization and dull uniformity? Can it be a tool for urban revitalization? Is it adaptable to a range of climates? Does it offer sustainable solutions? Can modular architecture be expressive of cultural distinctions?

SURFACE, SCREEN & STRUCTURE ¶ FALL 2016 ¶ JOE VIDICH, RETO HUG, INSTRUCTORS, WITH MARK MADERA ¶ This course focused on the design and digital fabrication of panelized cladding systems developed from sheet metal and folded to gain rigidity and form. These systems were designed for the NEW INC building, a museum-led incubator and co-working space located adjacent to the New Museum on the Bowery. Utilizing the simple masonry façade of the NEW INC building as our canvas, this course challenged students to develop a comprehensive cladding strategy in response to the diverse architectural fabric developing along the Bowery and the complex program within the incubator itself. ¶ The cladding systems were designed to perform as functional shading, ornamental expression and graphic branding, while engaging with the city at multiple scales. Students were challenged to design thoughtful solutions that spatially and functionally resolved their concepts within a strict set of intrinsic and extrinsic constraints: light transmittance, structural loading, thermal expansion, CNC machine limitations, assembly logistics, material properties and building cost analysis, among others.

MODULAR ARCHITECTURE ¶ FALL 2016 ¶ DAVID WALLANCE, INSTRUCTOR ¶ We are on the cusp of an unprecedented and transformative change in the way we design and build our cities. Architects will increasingly be called upon to design multi-story urban buildings using modular techniques. To design in a modular language requires a fundamental shift in thinking at the conceptual level as well as a working knowledge of modular technology. This course focused mainly on a design problem, in which we developed a modular solution to a multi-story urban infill building on a site in located in NYC. ¶ Our method was interdisciplinary, and we learned to think in terms of business strategy, financing, marketing and sales, as well as the more familiar terrain of design and building technology. We speculated on how the role of the architect might evolve if an industrialized approach to building

21
22
23
24
25
26
27

TRANSITIONAL GEOMETRIES ¶ FALL 2016 & SPRING 2017 ¶ TREVOR WATSON, INSTRUCTOR ¶ This course encouraged exploration and development in two different ways. The first was an abstract study of tiling principles, which looked at different tileable "frame" conditions. Strategically-placed nodes overlaid on these frames allowed the tile to be flipped and rotated so that adjacent nodes formed new relationships; these adjacent relationships allowed a single tile to create a seemingly random pattern over a large surface. The second means of development was from iterative feedback in fabrication. Students developed their own designs based on in-class tutorials in concrete casting and mold-making. There were no "perfect" molds, but through the feedback-driven design process, students built on these new understandings and pushed beyond with each successive iteration. Subsequently, each mold became a test of something new, attempting to push the boundaries into an unknown result so that the class as a whole could learn and develop.

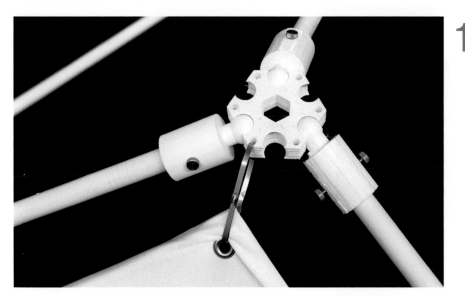

1

Kathy Xiao, Christopher Brockhoft, Kimberlee Boonbanjerdsri

2

Stephanie Tager, Vanessa Arriagada

3

Jiayi Yi, Siyu Zhang, Naifei Liu, Wenjing Zhang, Stephen Charles Smith, Ruizhi Wang, Anastasia Sytenko, Rawan Jaber Muqaddas, Keren Bao

4

Harrison Nesbitt,
Mustafa Khan,
Gabriel Luiz-Larrea

5

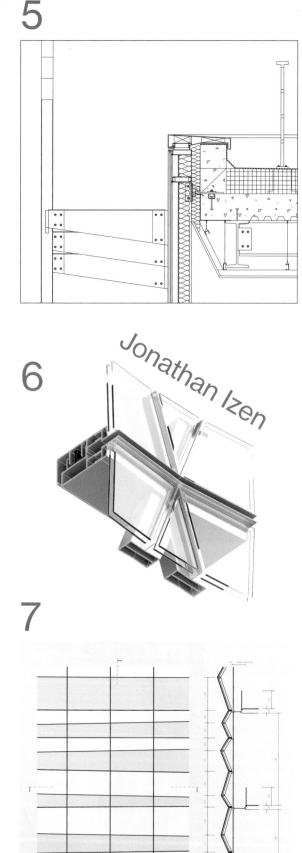

Andrew Luy

6

Jonathan Izen

7

Stine Pedersen

8

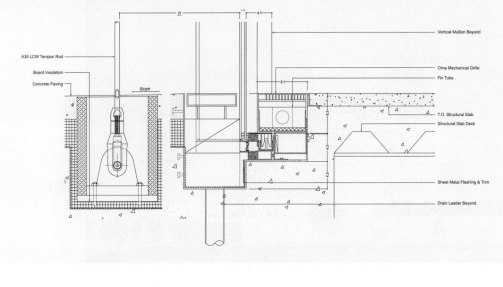

A35 LCW Tension Rod
Board Insulation
Concrete Paving
Slope

Vertical Mullion Beyond
Orna Mechanical Grille
Fin Tube
T.O. Structural Slab
Structural Slab Deck
Sheet Metal Flashing & Trim
Drain Leader Beyond

David Kagawa

9

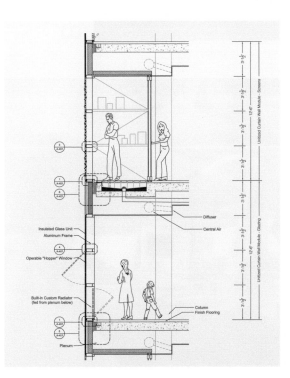

Insulated Glass Unit
Aluminum Frame
Operable "Hopper" Window
Built-in Custom Radiator
(fed from plenum below)
Plenum
Diffuser
Central Air
Column
Finish Flooring

Unitized Curtain Wall Module - Screens
Unitized Curtain Wall Module - Glazing

Michael Nickerson

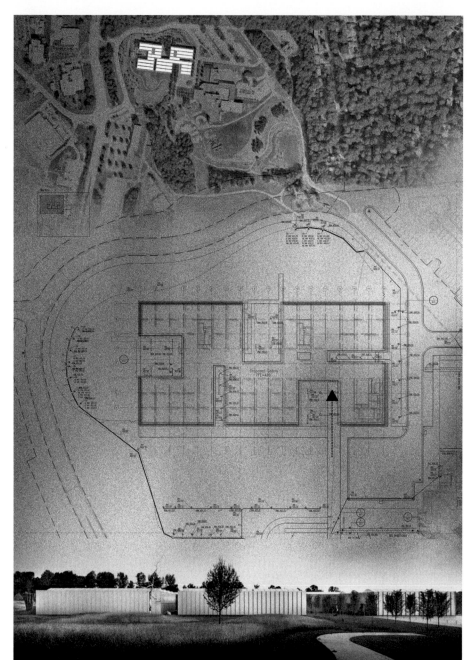

10

Boer Deng

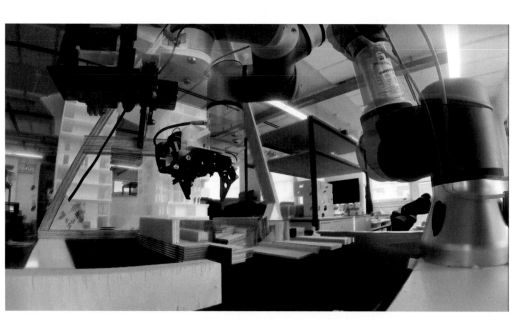

11

Zhida Wu

12

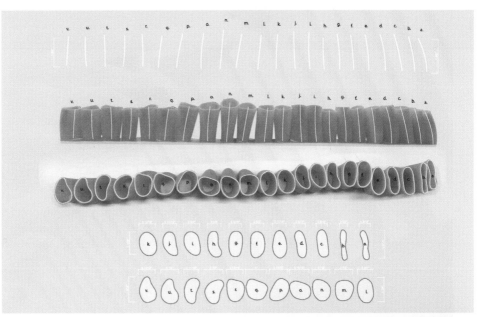

Eugene Chang

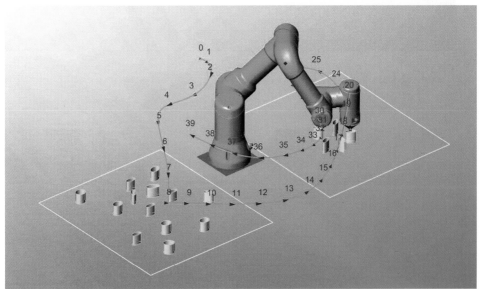

13

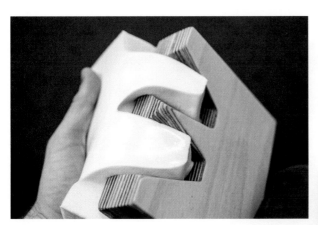

Sadie Dempsey

Violet Ding

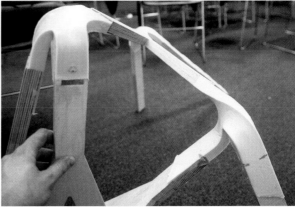

14

15

Corina Wright

16

Kevin MacNochol,
Naifei Liu, Chuhan Zhou

17

Group Fuzz

18

Group Rany

19

Group Damet

20

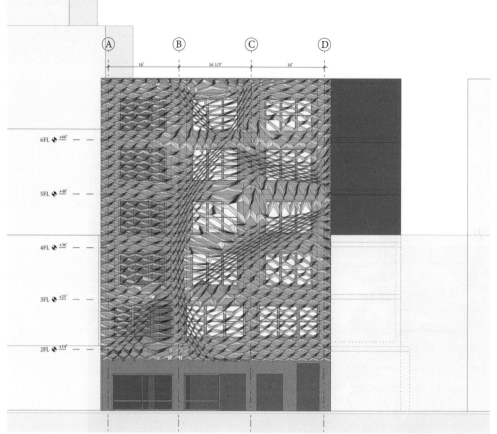

21

Jonathan Izen

Da Ying

22

Sanghoon Jang

Qing Teo

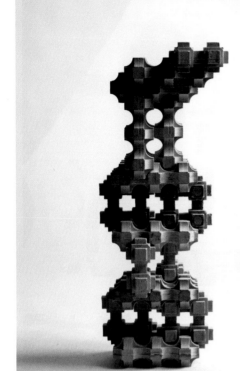

23

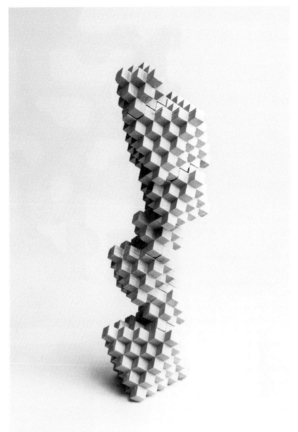

24

25

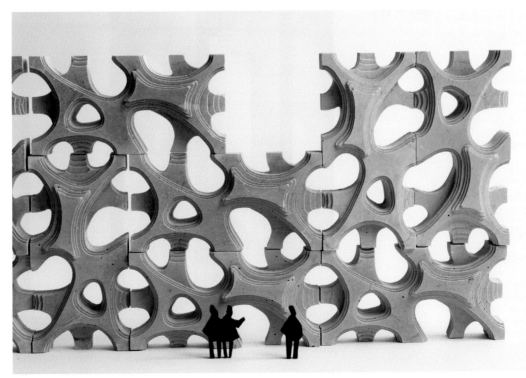

Paul Provenza

26   27

Wo Wu

Quentin Yiu

The History and Theory of Architecture curriculum at Columbia GSAPP aims to develop a critical, historical consciousness among students preparing for diverse forms of architectural practice. Central to this is a worldly understanding, in depth and in breadth, of a complex artistic, societal, cultural and technological past. The bearing of that past on contemporary debates and practices is an important focus, as is the relation of architectural history to other disciplines. From the outset, the curriculum equips students with questions suited to ongoing historical inquiry into a "global" or planetary past, including an ecological past, with an emphasis on both continuity and change.

The process of critical inquiry begins in the first year, with the two-semester core sequence, "Questions in Architectural History," focused on the interaction of architecture and modernity across two centuries and taught by a group of senior history and theory faculty. In addition to introducing students to key examples, themes and relationships, the course asks whose history is being studied, how, and why. The sequence continues into the second and third years with a series of distribution requirements that allow students to pursue selected topics in greater depth, while ensuring exposure to a range of geographically, culturally, and historically diverse contexts and subject matter. Students may also take related courses in humanities departments across the University to meet or supplement these requirements.

QUESTIONS IN ARCHITECTURAL HISTORY 1 & 2 ¶ FALL 2016 ¶ REINHOLD MARTIN, ZEYNEP CELIK ALEXANDER, MARY MCLEOD AND MABEL O.WILSON, INSTRUCTORS ¶ SPRING 2017 ¶ KENNETH FRAMPTON, FELICITY SCOTT, MARK WIGLEY, INSTRUCTORS ¶ This two-semester introductory course explores selected questions and problems that have, over the course of the past two centuries, helped to define architecture's modernity. ¶ The course treats the history of architectural modernity as a contested, geographically and culturally uncertain category, for which periodization is both necessary and contingent, beginning with the apotheosis of the European Enlightenment and the early phases of the industrial revolution in the late eighteenth century. The fall semester covers the "long" nineteenth century and the spring semester covers the "long" twentieth century, up to the present. Both situate developments in Europe and North America in relation to worldwide processes including trade, imperialism, nationalism, and industrialization. Continuity and change are emphasized. ¶ The course also treats categories like modernity, modernization, and modernism in a relational manner. Rather than equate modernity with rationality, for example, we ask: How did such an equation arise? Where? Under what conditions? In response to what? Why? To what end? Similar questions pertain to the idea of a "national" architecture, or even a "modern" or a "postmodern" one. To explore these and other questions, the course stresses contact with primary sources. In addition to weekly readings, the syllabi list key buildings, projects, and documents, along with at least one primary text, through which such questions may be posed. Many of these buildings, projects, and texts have long been incorporated into well-developed historical narratives, mostly centered on Europe. Others have not. The aim, however, is not to replace those narratives with a more inclusive, "global" one. It is to explore questions that arise, at certain times and in certain places, when architecture is said to possess a history. ¶ The course format prioritizes discussion and critical reflection. Students enroll in one of three seminar-style classes, each led by a different faculty member in collaboration with a PhD Teaching Fellow. In addition, Teaching Fellows conduct smaller weekly sessions to support and elaborate upon the main class. All three course sections discussed primary texts and background reading, but with different secondary readings assigned at the discretion of individual faculty. ¶ Overall, the aim is a semester-long dialogue, with active student participation, that unfolds, explores, and contextualizes questions and problems that inform and challenge the historical imagination and ultimately, enhance historical consciousness.

1
4

ECHOING BORDERS ❡ FALL 2016 ❡ NORA AKAWI, NINA V. KOLOWRATNIK, INSTRUCTORS ❡ This seminar took as its starting point our understanding of territoriality, which is still heavily rooted in our imagination of the world as divided into compartmentalized, distinct, and mutually exclusive political formations. The class situated itself at the tension between the rising density and rate of forced displacement on the one hand, and the static definitions of contemporary citizenship and human rights on the other. ❡ Considering that frontiers are physically manifested through fences and trenches, but also through international networks of border patrol, technologies of body identification, access to natural resources, shelter, jobs, and healthcare, and fluctuating policies and regulations, the projects developed in the class attempted to redraw contemporary borders with a focus on elements of movement and detention—challenging the static representations of what are in fact unstable and volatile conditions. Through theoretical readings and discussions, research on migration policies and regulations, mapping and drawing exercises, and field research travel to the Jordan Valley, Dead Sea, Negev Desert, and the occupied Golan Heights, student projects in Fall 2016 focused on questions of forced displacement in relation to memory and erasure, representations of Bedouin territories and connection to the land, and access to infrastructure and particularly to water resources.

(RADICAL) FUNCTIONALISM IN LATIN AMERICA ❡ FALL 2016 ❡ LUIS E. CARRANZA, INSTRUCTOR ❡ This seminar focused on the conceptualization, theorization, and materialization of functionalist architecture throughout Latin America between the 1920s and 1940s. This architecture responded to the tremendous lack of public infrastructures (such as schools or housing facilities) as well as to what was then considered "bourgeois" aesthetic practices; practices that were in seeming opposition to social projects and ideals for the advancement of the population and culture in general. The research of this seminar was centered on understanding and carefully investigating functionalism—an abstract utilitarian architecture primarily intended, in this context, for the masses—which manifested itself most powerfully in the urban centers of Argentina, Brazil, Mexico, and Uruguay and in the artistic, social, political, and ideological messages from the architects and patrons who enabled and defined it. Specifically, the seminar focused on four themes: the design, material, and structural bases for functionalist architecture; the new aesthetics that these propose; the translation of these to other non-public structures; and the tensions that developed through the introduction of local materials, formal references, furnishings, and art. This seminar analyzed and evaluated work in Latin America with the goal of critically evaluating it while developing an "archive" about the diverse practices and productions.

MODERN ARCHITECTURE IN MEXICO: FROM THE EUPHORIA OF TRANSPARENCY TO THE CANONIZATION OF COLOR, 1945–1976 ❡ SPRING 2017 ❡ LUIS E. CARRANZA, INSTRUCTOR ❡ Centered primarily on the role of the state, on material, artistic, and typological experimentations, and on the transformation and "Mexicanization" of modern architecture, the class looked at how Post-War Mexican architects and intellectuals developed an architecture that both reinforced and challenged their strong cultural legacy while addressing the globalizing and homogenizing forces of modernity. Mexico's positive economic outlook at the time, dubbed as the "Mexican miracle," encouraged and promoted the government to undertake large modern public works programs that continued the social, cultural, and architectural projects engendered by the Mexican revolution of 1910–1920. At the same time, Mexican architects experimented with new materials and industrial products in their design for office buildings, private residences, and public spaces that reflected contemporary international practices and aesthetics. Post-war architectural debates were centered on how to present Mexico as simultaneously modern while having deep historical roots and traditions. The use and manufacture of public space also changed in the 1960s as seen by the student uprisings, their violent suppression, and the architectural-minded planning for and branding of the 1968 Olympic games. In the mid-1970s, we see the international mythification of Luis Barragán's architecture: hailed as the clearest expression of "Mexican" modern architecture.

2
3
5
6

THEORY OF CITY FORM ❡ FALL 2016 ❡ VISHAAN CHAKRABARTI, INSTRUCTOR, WITH SKYLAR BISOM-RAPP ❡ Theory of City Form is a survey course that examined the myriad forces and factors that directly govern or indirectly influence the size, shape and nature of cities. The class covered explicit theories regarding the form of cities as well as explore many interdisciplinary, critical approaches to understanding urban outcomes that can loosely be categorized under the broad umbrella of "Urban Studies." Questions addressed included: What do we mean when we talk about city form?; Why do cities look the way they do?; What explains differences in the way different cities look?; Is a general theory of city form even possible?; How could a critical understanding of the factors which drive urban form influence practitioners in the allied urban professions?

ARCHITECTURE OF COLONIAL MODERNITY: HISTORIES OF URBANISM AND SPACE WITHIN SOUTH ASIA, AFRICA, AND THE MIDDLE EAST ❡ SPRING 2017 ❡ CHRISTOPHER COWELL, INSTRUCTOR ❡ The imprint of European colonialism is still acutely felt upon much of our modern world—its cultures, cities and wider urban environments—despite its apparent consignment to the history books. This seminar course, using the tools of postcolonial theory and contemporary historical research, will focus upon the colonial histories of early 19th to mid-20th century South Asia, Africa, and the Middle East. The course examined the latent and overt ideologies and concepts that shaped European expansion within these territories, through architecture, urbanism and material space. A particular focus, due in part to a pioneering body of critical literature, was upon British imperial expansion and consolidation within South Asia. Each week, a theme was introduced and discussed that situates architecture and urbanism at the junction of space, the material environment, and colonial knowledge formation, and examined how these interlink. These themes followed a general chronology, building up methods to expose various modes of modernity at work within and against colonialism—in particular, to find out how both concepts interact. The themes followed a general sequence: from wider theoretical inquiries to historically specific case studies; from knowledge and information systems to space and material construction; and from histories of representation to histories of performance.

DISPLACING GOD: ARCHITEC-TURE, MODERNISM, AND THE SECULAR ¶ SPRING 2017 ¶ MA-RIA GONZALEZ PENDAS, IN-STRUCTOR ¶ This seminar explored the shifting role played by religion in various historical conceptions of architectural modernism, and cross-referenced contemporary theories on secularism with physical and discursive evidences drawn from the field of architecture and design. While still absent in most canonical histories of modernism, the production of religion has been crucial to the shaping of core ideals of art and architectural modernism, and buildings continue to act as significant instruments for the intersection of politics and religion—tensions that continue to define conflicts over nationalism, tradition and modernity in ever so urgent manners. Not a course on churches or mosques alone, and avoiding the study of these typologies in relation to theology, this research-based seminar analyzed alternative spaces where religion has operated historically: from theoretical narratives and exhibition practices to notions of technology, space, and pedagogy; from processes of urbanization to forms of technocratic governments; from museums to universities. In the course of our inquiry, we considered these as the "shadows" of secularism, which study helped us debate and better understand the often-deceiving displacements of the religious sphere under regimes of modernization. ¶ A crucial concept of inquiry was that of "secularism," with which we engaged through the pivotal theories of Talal Asad and Charles Taylor. As per their work, the secular has by now proven to be a notion all too intertwined with the Western Christian narrative on progress and religion to be anything but absent from the public sphere. A core objective of the course was to theorize the built environment for the evolving production of the secular. In addition to its commitment to theory, the seminar was global in its approach to historical contexts, looking at case studies in Northern Europe, the Iberian Peninsula, North and Latin America, and the Middle East.

ART POWER & SPACE IN THE MIDDLE EAST ¶ SPRING 2017 ¶ MARIO GOODEN, INSTRUCTOR ¶ At the heart of the issues challenging contemporary art practice in the twenty-first century Arab world is the lack of a written historical context—an art historical context or discourse to place, view, articulate and evaluate this new artistic production. To start with, many of the region's modern historical developments are contested on various levels and, secondly, contemporary productions reject their segregation as an "other." Adding to the complexities is the nature of the contemporary production itself, which is highly interdisciplinary and crosses the boundaries between traditional forms of representation, curatorial strategies, performance, and image making. ¶ While the region remains as it was in the early decades of the 20th century—beset with wars and colonization in its various guises, from imposed rules by foreign powers to military occupation and now globalization—these conditions do not prevent artists from producing art, but they do, however, influence the parameters of representation and reception of art. ¶ The seminar examined the production, consumption, and dissemination of Middle Eastern art and the subversive strategies of artists to engage in new spaces for social and political critique. The seminar sought to uncover pedagogies and methodologies for artistic practices to locate new sites of meaning in contested territories and among contradictory landscapes.

CLIMATIC IMAGINARIES ¶ FALL 2016 ¶ JAMES GRAHAM, INSTRUCTOR ¶ Climate is often seen as an externality, changing or otherwise, to be accommodated or ameliorated by design. Though this scientific and solutions-focused approach is indeed fundamental to the contemporary practice of architecture and urbanism (not to mention politics, government, and daily life), this seminar explored a different proposition—namely, that our environment is not just a resource to be managed or a ongoing circumstance to which we must adapt, but is instead one of the chief figurations of shared cultural values. "Nature" is, in a very real sense, what we see in it. It is both historical and epistemic. Our conception of things like air, ocean, rock, ice, and weather conditions our engagement with them, and climate registers on many levels within our lived realities. Furthermore, climate has long been present within the disciplinary history of architecture, and this longer history has much to say about our suppositions about what buildings are and do. We explored climate as it refracts through ideas like political ecology, corporeality, and architectural enclosure.

ESSAYS ON ARCHITECTURE ¶ SPRING 2017 ¶ JAMES GRAHAM, INSTRUCTOR ¶ This seminar examined the role of critics, criticism, and the essay form in shaping how we understand architecture both in public life and within architectural discourse. We considered reviews as testing grounds for the author's own intellectual commitments (theoretical, architectural, political) as those ideas are refracted through the work of others. Readings included foundational texts in critical theory, histories of reviewing and essay writing, and predominantly the essays themselves. We explored the complex responses to buildings across generational shifts through selected case studies, and contemplated the possibility that the history of architecture is in fact a history of essays on architecture. We considered current trajectories within architectural writing and publishing, particularly a recent resurgence in the essay format (spawned in part by the rise of digital publication formats). Finally, we examined the essay as a means through which to connect the discourse of architecture with a broader political life.

ADVANCED PROFESSIONAL PRACTICE ¶ SPRING 2017 ¶ ROBERT HERRMAN, INSTRUCTOR ¶ This class investigated legal and financial structures imbedded in architectural practice following a debate format. Students, coached by Herrmann and invited guests, discussed topics such as agreements, fees, management, marketing, intellectual property, practice in foreign countries, corporate structure and strategies for architecture firms' growth. ¶ Topics included executing projects in foreign countries, contractual issues related to consulting teams, teams' fee allocation and structure, capturing fees for additional services, developing realistic project fees, budgets and schedules, arbitration and litigation.

CIRCULATION ¶ SUMMER 2016 ¶ PHU HOANG, INSTRUCTOR ¶ The Circulation seminar, formatted as walking tours of case studies, explored the generative role of circulation in architecture. Current building practices have increased the disciplinary specializations—architect, façade architect, interior architect, landscape architect, retail design architect—that are required to deliver a complete building. A result of this "hyper-specialization" is that architects are increasingly asked to only design the "core and shell." Much of this work can be understood as the spaces that exist in-between the gross and net surface areas, such as the circulation, envelopes, structure, voids and mechanical/electrical rooms. This seminar concentrated on the importance of circulation in both the concepts and practice of architecture. The seminar also reevaluated the disciplinary segregation and understood circulation as inextricably linked to all layers of architecture—where program, collective events, environment, structure and infrastructure co-exist. The lobbies, corridors, ramps, stairs, elevators and terraces that constitute circulation were renewed by understanding them as a primary design element of architecture.

BUILDING ISLAM, AN INCOMPLETE HISTORY OF THE MOSQUE ARCHITECTURE ¶ FALL 2016 ¶ ZIAD JAMALEDDINE, INSTRUCTOR ¶ Building Islam was not about Islamic buildings; nor was it an attempt at forming a comprehensive history of the built environment of the Islamic world. Instead the class aimed to critically re-formulate (re-build) the field of inquiry of the history of the architecture of the mosque— the most "Islamic" archetype. ¶ Architecturally, at every historical turn, the mosque proved itself to be one of the most hybridized, ever-evolving religious buildings that still stands as a living witness to the historical multiplicity of Islam (a threat to 21st century religious extremists' flawed, nihilistic regime of intolerance). Here, reading and writing an alternative architectural history of the mosque became an integral part of a cultural war against an autonomous and reactionary discourse that wants us to believe (not unlike the Orientalist counterpart) in the pre-determinism of the Islamic cultural landscape.

CONFLICT URBANISM: LANGUAGE JUSTICE ¶ SPRING 2017 ¶ LAURA KURGAN, LYDIA LIU, INSTRUCTORS ¶ This was the second in a series of multidisciplinary Mellon seminars on the topic of Conflict Urbanism, offered as part of a multi-university initiative in Architecture, Urbanism and the Humanities. This year, we focused on the role of language as a major force in shaping cities, using New York City as our laboratory. Over the course of the semester, students fused fieldwork with theory to create web-based projects exploring how language both unifies and divides the city. Through a series of hands-on tutorials, students developed skills in critical cartography, data management, and web mapping to equip them in communicating their findings in novel and creative ways. Students used ethnographic methods to explore their own communities and discover ones they had never had access to before. The projects they created highlight the myriad of ways language shapes our city from the dynamics of employment (Food Carts) to the assumed literacy of riding the subway

(Navigating Illiteracy) and the way languages disappear and reappear throughout the city (Boundaries and Border Crossings). To view all of the projects in the seminar, visit http://c4sr.columbia.edu/courses/conflict-urbanism-language-justice.

BUILDING CHINA MODERN, 1919–1958: EXPERIMENTS FOR A NEW PARADIGM ¶ FALL 2016 ¶ AMY LELYVELD, INSTRUCTOR ¶ The quest for an architecture both modern and Chinese has been going on for significantly more than a hundred years. Early in the last century a desire for this kind of language of building, one that could be both international and specific, was a common puzzle the world over. But in China, the quest started early and continues to this day, running parallel with changing ideas of "China"—the place and nation—a concept radically reconstrued at least four times in the course of the same period of time. ¶ The seminar investigated experiments in new Chinese building in three of these moments—around the May 4th Movement (1919), by Nationalist China (1927–48) and the inaugural years of the People's Republic (1949–58)—periods representing distinct mindsets but in which the reimagining of Chinese architecture and China itself was equally all-important. ¶ Students built individual semester long projects around caches of primary resource material each identified in Columbia's deep research collections. The archival material was used to explore case study "experiments" in modern Chinese building—buildings which purposely broke with certain aspects of tradition while safeguarding others—in terms of the qualities of "new" and the character of the building (and other discourses) they represent.

URBAN ECOLOGY ¶ SUMMER 2016 ¶ JING LIU, INSTRUCTOR ¶ In this seminar, we conducted empirical studies on a series of urban typologies in the boroughs of New York. The four locations we ventured to were: Queens, Sunnyside Gardens, Brooklyn Navy Yard, Governors Island and Manhattan Chinatown, each of which fall loosely under the categories of living, working, leisure, and mixed-use. The typologies were selected based on their unique physical characters, historical importance and demographic specificity. Additionally, we suggested that the transformation they are currently undergoing could reveal something curious about our contemporary urban life.

ARCHITECTURAL VISUALIZATION SINCE 1900 ¶ FALL 2016 ¶ REINHOLD MARTIN, INSTRUCTOR ¶ As a rule, architects do not build. They

draw, write, annotate, diagram, model, map, sketch, photograph, animate, and otherwise visualize objects, spaces, and territories; they make visual and verbal presentations; they compile visual and written analyses and reports; and they issue visual and written instructions. ¶ This lecture course introduced key episodes in the history of architectural visualization, in a variety of geographic and cultural contexts across the "long" twentieth century. The approach was thematic; it followed a loose chronology built around concepts, problems, and practices associated with international modernism and its aftermath. In and through these, we observed architectural knowledge being constructed, drawings and buildings interacting, and ideas, techniques, and imagery circulating. ¶ Each lecture considered a specific set of techniques within the history and theory of modern and contemporary architecture, the history of technology, and theories and practices of visualization. Drawings, models, photographs, and other visual artifacts were analyzed in depth. Some readings situated these examples historically, while others offer conceptual orientation. Together, the lectures offered a historical perspective that reframed concerns shared among different aspects of the GSAPP architecture curriculum, including the design studios, visual studies, and the technology sequence. ¶ The history of architectural visualization is also a history of globalization. Architectural discourse and techniques move constantly across a variety of national, cultural, and geographic boundaries, both historically and in the present. The lectures therefore also emphasized problems and effects of visual translation, standardization, reproduction, interface, transformation, site, and circulation that accompany this movement. ¶ Material covered included diagrams, travel sketches, orthographic projection, axonometric projection, perspective, the representation of movement, construction drawings, urban cartography, architectural and aerial photography, rendering, and stages of digitalization, from the period around 1900 to the present. Through these visual materials we witnessed the ongoing invention and dissemination of "architecture" as a category in a manner that explains much about contemporary assumptions.

PHILOSOPHIES OF THE CITY ¶ SPRING 2017 ¶ REINHOLD MARTIN, INSTRUCTOR ¶ This seminar read key theoretical texts from the late nineteenth century to the present that address the city and urbanization as objects of critical, philosophical reflection. An important contribution to such thought was made by a variety of German thinkers concerned with the modern metropolis. The seminar began there and followed the problem forward, to the present, with a particular focus on the interactions of capital and culture, and to the social relations of urbanization, technological development, decolonization and financialization, including the role of architecture and urbanism therein. The aim was not a philosophical metalanguage but rather, the elaboration of a critical, theoretical discourse. Special attention was paid to the constitutive role of buildings, space and infrastructures within this discourse.

"BUILT IN UNCERTAINTY": SHADRACH WOODS, A SEARCH FOR A SYSTEM RESEARCH COLLOQUIUM ⁋ FALL 2016 ⁋ MARY MCLEOD, INSTRUCTOR ⁋ This colloquium investigated the architecture and thinking of Shadrach Woods and the firm Candilis-Josic-Woods, using the archives of Shadrach Woods, located in Avery Library. It was the intention of the class that students gain a detailed knowledge of these drawings and papers, conduct interviews (taped and transcribed oral histories), select documents for a publication, and write introductions to texts and descriptions of projects for this publication. The course was envisioned as a research workshop for a book to be published by GSAPP of Shadrach Woods' writings with some illustrations of projects. While the focus was on primary research, it was hoped that students would also gain a solid background in architectural developments relevant to the practice of Candilis-Josic-Woods (notably, the architecture and planning theories of Le Corbusier, CIAM, Team 10) and a knowledge of contemporary social, economic, and cultural currents in postwar France and in the United States (such as colonial housing, postwar reconstruction in France, the Grands Ensembles and housing policy, emergence of the Welfare State, the development of mass leisure and consumer society, the Lindsay administration and New York City urban development, American architecture education, etc.). In conjunction with the seminar, there were also a series of presentations by individuals who worked with or studied with Woods (such as Waltraude Woods and Peter Papademetriou) and by scholars who are familiar with aspects of the firm's work or the cultural context of the period.

MODERNISM AND THE VERNACULAR 1900–PRESENT ⁋ SPRING 2017 ⁋ MARY MCLEOD, INSTRUCTOR ⁋ This class explored the intersections between modern architecture and what is sometimes called "vernacular" building from the early 20th century to the present. Other adjectives that have been used to describe buildings erected by non-architects (though often with considerable qualification) are "indigenous," "spontaneous," "anonymous," "informal," "folk," "popular," "rural," and "primitive." This interest in vernacular forms also relates directly to concerns for "tradition" and "regionalism," which modern architects have either embraced or dismissed with seemingly equal fervor. The working hypothesis of the seminar was that modern architecture, despite its commitment to technology and modernization, was deeply involved with ideas about vernacular buildings, and that the nature and meaning of this fascination with indigenous structures changed over the course of the century.

THE THEORETICAL TURN IN ARCHITECTURE: 1960–2000 STRUCTURALISM/POSTSTRUCTURALISM ⁋ FALL 2016 ⁋ MARY MCLEOD, INSTRUCTOR ⁋ This seminar examined some of the theoretical and critical approaches current in architecture debate from 1960 to the beginning of the 21st century. The course focused in particular on the question of meaning in architecture, beginning with approaches influenced by semiology and structuralism to establish an architecture of greater signification, and concluding with recent trends influenced by poststructuralist theories that challenge the possibility of architectural meaning. The last class addressed the current reaction against theory, and the emergence of anti-theoretical "theories" (technological determinism, Neo-Pragmatism, sensationalism, etc.). Certain classes considered general theoretical approaches, usually originating in philosophy or literary criticism; others examined specific currents in architecture in relation to these theoretical approaches.

STRUCTURAL DARING & THE SUBLIME IN PRE-MODERN ARCHITECTURE ⁋ FALL 2016 ⁋ RORY O'NEILL, INSTRUCTOR ⁋ Many works of pre-modern architecture are daring, poised at the very edge of structural stability. Others are well-supported, but strive to give an illusion of precariousness or even of levitation. This seminar invited students to explore the sublime effects of precarious architecture through visual and literary representations, as well as simulation models that examine the dynamic behavior of ancient and medieval monuments. Discussion topics included: the a priori and culturally specific aspects of daring architecture; the ancient and medieval sense of the sublime and aesthetics; environmental psychology; and strategies for reading architectural forms. Students presented

two or three readings during the semester, participated in class discussions, and wrote a short midterm essay and a final research paper.

CITY AND COUNTRYSIDE IN CHINA ⁋ FALL 2016 ⁋ NING OU, INSTRUCTOR ⁋ When looking into the mutation of urban and rural China, this course asked the following questions: Why were the Chinese peasants always the victims? How can one empower or animate the grassroots people? As a professional, how can architects or urban designers promote social change? Is a practical utopia possible in reality? This course explained how China took the land and labor from the countryside in order to expand the city, raised spatial production in urban areas, and brought the economy to a new scale while producing a host of social problems. It also examined how "ruralism" worked as the opposition to urbanism and gave birth to a new politic. Special attention was paid to the critical thinking and practices of the New Rural Reconstruction Movement led by some Chinese intellectuals.

CURATORIAL PRACTICES AND PLACE MAKING ⁋ SPRING 2017 ⁋ NING OU, INSTRUCTOR ⁋ In an era of globalization driven by neoliberalism after the end of Cold War, "non-places" (Marc Augé) grow increasingly similar worldwide, while unique "places" maintain their differences. The biennales or mega-exhibitions that became popular from the late 1990s on helped to shape the global spectacle of cultural production, created a great deal of opportunities for transnational travel, and brought the role of "curator" to a central stage at the same time. But today, with hundreds of biennales around the world, it has become both a game of power within certain professional circles and a repetitive machine of production and marketing. Curators are only "Ausstellungsmacher," they're likely making the exhibitions into "non-places." This course paid attention to the practices of artivism, social engagement, community art, site-specific art, public architecture, public landscape projects and those anti-globalization curatorial projects that try to transform "non-places" into "places," in order to see and understand how artists, architects, designers and curators work together to connect people, to activate social life, to shape identity, and to create new locality.

ARCHITECTURE, THE FREE MARKET AND THE DEGRADATION OF CIVIC SPACE ⁋ SPRING 2017 ⁋ NICOLAI OUROUSSOFF, INSTRUCTOR ⁋ The seminar looked at how a variety of social and economic forces—from the shrinking of state power to the rise of the unregulated free market and globalization—have shaped contemporary architecture since the end of the Cold War. ¶ We began with a brief overview of how Modernism's failure to deliver on its promise of a better society helped to forge the values of the generation of architects who rose to prominence in the 1980s and 1990s, drawing them away from seemingly intractable social issues and closer to the world of art and high culture. ¶ From there, we zeroed in on a number of trends that have shaken architecture over the past few decades: the changing nature of cities and the urban audience in the wake of globalization, the impact of branding, and the increasingly cozy relationship between architecture, art, fashion and money. We looked, too, at how some contemporary architecture operates as a form of "camouflage"—obscuring rather than clarifying meaning, cloaking urban space in an aura of cultural enlightenment, and creating the illusion of social diversity where there is none. ¶ Finally, we discussed different ways of talking and writing about architecture, with the aim of helping students develop a critical voice of their own.

BELFAST, IRELAND: CITY CENTER IN DEVELOPMENT CONTEXT ¶ SPRING 2017 ¶ RICHARD PLUNZ, INSTRUCTOR ¶ This studio comprised both architecture and urban planning students in a joint project tasked with exploring scenarios for redevelopment of the City Centre of Belfast, Northern Ireland, including its reintegration with the surrounding city. The client and sponsor was the Belfast City Council and its Office of City Centre Development. Beginning in 1969 as a consequence of the sectarian conflicts in Belfast, strategies were implemented for partitioning the city, including a "ring of steel" around the City Centre that drastically reduced accessibility during daytime and effectively closed it to the public at night. The Centre was deliberately maintained as a "neutral" (i.e. uninhabited) zone. While the "ring of steel" no longer functions, the cumulative negative effects of this long period of isolation is evident. This studio was tasked with investigating the reintegration and renewal of the City Centre in concert with the de-partitioning process for the entire city. Proposals for the City Centre included heightened pedestrian linkages; investment in renewed transportation networks; rebuilding of "shatter zones;" and options for next generation cultural production. Both spatial and economic redevelopment of the City Centre was considered, in the

context of future economic potentials for Northern Ireland and with particular reference to options for new global investments in a post-Brexit era.

READING BUILDINGS, WRITING BUILDINGS ¶ SPRING 2017 ¶ MARK RAKATANSKY, INSTRUCTOR ¶ This seminar explored a variety of techniques in the close reading of buildings that have been engaged to investigate the significance of the built environment. In every reading—whether by an architect, critic, historian, or theorist—the building is re-constructed in the act of writing. While it is not possible to discern some absolute intentions, what can be discerned and explored are various forms of attention in and of the building. These forms of attention can lead to various hypotheses regarding the relations of its architectural and cultural intentions. As writing is itself an act of design, one can track how these writings are constructed so that an intended argument is proposed, developed, and articulated through the narrative and rhetorical attentions in its design as it tracks the attentions of the building under investigation. We explored not only written forms of close reading that have proved influential in the past, but also investigated new forms developing in the digital humanities: how innovative modeling and visualization procedures can move beyond merely documenting a building to provide new forms of critical and historical analysis. Formal techniques were utilized to draw forth questions of cultural meaning, and questions of meaning were utilized to draw forth questions of form, developing corroborating evidence to cross-reference the building's architectural and cultural positions.

MILITARY URBANISM ¶ FALL 2016 ¶ VICTORIA SANGER, INSTRUCTOR ¶ Warfare shaped the cities of Early Modern Europe (ca. 1450–1800). It configured shifting border networks and impacted the fate of towns. Specifically, the technology of gunpowder artillery and its accompanying bastioned defense systems restructured towns for parading, circulation and surveillance and equipped them with standardized architectural typologies. ¶ Sébastien Le Prestre de Vauban (1633–1707) stands at the center of these changes. As military engineer to France's King Louis XIV, he crystallized and catalyzed political and planning trends in all European cities that had been developing since the mid-fifteenth century. Vauban was seen by his contemporaries as a master of the art of attacking and defending bastioned fortifications with geometrical rigor. He was, in fact, also an accomplished

and prolific "urbanist." He approached his projects as multi-faceted, posited on demographic and economic surveys. His towns were not only safe and solid but also decorous and detailed. From splendidly ornamented gatehouses with standardized plans to town markets to the individual barrack bed, he aspired to total spatial mastery. He built nine new towns and one hundred sixty cities in total. ¶ This course looked at 17th century France as a tale of origins. France was arguably the most important military and political force of the latter part of this period. How has this period shaped our modern cities and borders and could things have evolved differently? We probed the Early Modern period for how city walls and national borders did or did not contain the roots of nationalism and xenophobia. We analyzed walls as places of exclusion: from border to interior, across enemy lines, to princely capitals and overseas colonies. The "open city" began with Paris in 1670 and rose in the 18th century as cities such as Washington D.C. were marked by the ideals of the Enlightenment. Walls began to be dismantled or not included in plans for new cities. Yet cities continued to be places of surveillance, and fortification, while on a larger scale, walls were still a part of their design. The next generation of Romantics emphasized the destructive and irrational nature of combat, theorized as "total war" by Carl von Clausewitz. In the second half of the nineteenth century, Violet-le-Duc exposed the ever-growing scale and costs of warfare between nation states in the Industrial era, looking ahead to World War I. In the last session we made spatial and philosophical comparisons with forms of current warfare such as the use of drones, the global threat of terrorism, cyber warfare, and systems of urban surveillance methods as cities once again become military targets. ¶ The structure of each seminar session was part lecture and part reading discussion. Students brought their own viewpoints as historians and contemporary designers to the table. Readings were selected for their informational content, their historical importance and their methodological diversity. In the last few sessions, students shared and discussed their individual projects.

EUROPEAN URBAN CARTOGRAPHY 16TH–19TH CENTURIES ¶ SPRING 2017 ¶ VICTORIA SANGER, INSTRUCTOR ¶ This course presented a critical period in the history of Western urban cartography. The 16th through the 19th century witnessed expansion and mechanization of cities and their maps evolving from the Age of Discovery and the invention of the printing press to the

Industrial Revolution. ¶ Today, maps are no longer seen as objective vehicles of data. We will look at city maps from a variety of angles: as tools combining planning, documenting, and governing while also being artistic and symbolic form in their own right. They are also works using different techniques made by graphic artists and craftsmen on paper and other media. How might all these aspects interact? The class focused on a few major European cities and colonial cities and it worked with facsimiles and original maps in New York collections. Throughout the course, students were encouraged to criticize digital presentations of historic maps and make parallels with contemporary methods of cartography such as Google Earth and GIS. Students presented original map analyses in the final sessions which they wrote about for their papers.

ARCHITECTURE, HUMAN RIGHTS, SPATIAL POLITICS ¶ FALL 2016 ¶ FELICITY D. SCOTT, INSTRUCTOR ¶ This seminar investigated contemporary trajectories of architectural research and practice that intersect with questions of human rights, notions of democratic public space, and spatial politics. We asked what role the discipline plays (or might play) in current debates over questions of political representation, defense, the organization of territory, surveillance, warfare, political conflict, and cultural heritage as well as in questions of citizenship, diaspora, humanitarian intervention, and justice. These questions mark a profoundly fascinating and highly complicated field of study, and there is a growing body of important literature pertaining to them. The seminar provided a forum for considering aspects of this literature and practices associated with it, as well as for identifying new lines of research and further critical prospects for the discipline of architecture. ¶ Architecture and the city have long been understood to provide an infrastructure for citizenship and democracy—for instance in the sense of organizing and of giving a formal and aesthetic identity to public space and to cultural and political institutions. In the first half of the 20th century, modern architecture was largely identified with ideals of social progress and radical spatial transformation, and the discipline soon came to be embraced after the Second World War by the United Nations as having a role to play not only in addressing rights issues, such as housing, but in the world of international relations. Such enlightenment ideals are not without their own difficult legacy, and specific critiques of human rights and humanitarian intervention and aid were addressed during the class.

Architecture and urban sites have also, of course, frequently been the location of (or even provided techniques for) inequity, colonization, terrorism, and exclusion, raising the question of the discipline's possible responsibility to address its imbrication within such forms of violence. Finally, as was addressed in the seminar, architecture's current role in the organization of public space is further complicated by the increasingly interconnected and mediated if dispersed condition we know as globalization, and by the post-national politics to which it has given rise. Indeed, the very notion of space and of a public within it has been profoundly transformed since World War II, raising questions and significant critical prospects for architecture. ¶ To investigate this complex set of issues, students addressed relevant work and research by architects and architectural theorists as well as working through important literature and critiques of human rights, public space, the public sphere, surveillance, and citizenship. We looked at topics including camps, borders, apartheid planning, as well as architectures of warfare, displacement, and occupation. In addition we identified and discussed contemporary practices that have forged critical and strategic interventions within these fields.

PROFESSIONAL PRACTICE ¶ FALL 2016 ¶ PAUL SEGAL, INSTRUCTOR ¶ The purpose of this course was to give students an understanding of the framework and processes by which designs become buildings. Topics included the relationship between Owners and Architects and Owners and Contractors, covering the duties, obligations, rights and remedies of each. Additionally, the course covered the public constraints or the public/private relationships by which individuals—owners and architects—have their rights limited for the sake of the public good. Through these topics students learned how to protect their designs from concept to realization, as well as some of the ethical and moral issues of practicing architecture. There was considerable discussion about the current state of the profession, where it is headed, and how to shape its future. Active student participation and debate was required.

ITALIAN RENAISSANCE ARCHITECTURE 1400–1600 ¶ FALL 2016 ¶ DANIEL SHERER, INSTRUCTOR ¶ The course provided a historical overview of the major figures of Italian Renaissance architecture from 1400 to 1600—Brunelleschi, Alberti, Leonardo, Bramante, Raphael, Antonio da Sangallo the Younger, Michelangelo, Giulio Romano, Sanmicheli, Sansovino, Palladio, and Serlio. Stressing the dialectic of rule and license implicit in the revival of the classical code, we studied the diverse cultural and artistic factors that entered into the project of forging a new language based on antiquity yet moving beyond its example. Topics covered included the social and cultural implications of the link between architecture and humanism; the role of architecture in elaborating new urban strategies, chiefly in Florence, Urbino, Mantua, Rome, Venice, and Milan; the search for a new type of canon that simultaneously presupposed and challenged the authority of Vitruvius and the study of ancient buildings; the emergence of new conventions of graphic representation based on orthographic and perspective projection; the rise of the treatise and its articulation of universally applicable theoretical norms, which, rather than hindering, served to spur on a new awareness of the potentials of invention; the transformation of architecture by print culture, whose mechanical reproduction of image and text revolutionized the dissemination of theory; the theorization of an architecture which draws both on the example of the other arts and on the precepts of nature; access to theory and the antique, and a new consciousness of the possibilities of the discipline, based on the historicity of architecture and the city; and the relation of architecture to new uses of visual representation that helped inaugurate the modern era.

URBAN HISTORY I: CONFIGURATIONS OF THE CITY FROM ANTIQUITY TO 1800 ¶ SPRING 2017 ¶ DANIEL SHERER, INSTRUCTOR ¶ Focusing on the configuration of architecture in urban space, this course followed the evolution of the city through a series of exchanges between typological, morphological and topographical factors. The first part addressed the typological transformation of the agora and acropolis and the emergence of paradigmatic urban forms from 5th century Athens to the rise of Rome. We then studied the formal and functional dimensions of domestic and civil architecture in the Roman Empire from Augustus to Constantine. Turning to the medieval period, we isolated continuities and discontinuities between classical and Christian conceptions of the forma urbis, analyzing the typological refunctionalization of ancient monuments and the interplay of urbanization and its territorial contexts. This provided a prelude for our discussion of new urban strategies and architectural languages associated with utopian schemes, aristocratic and communal use of public space, and the rise of new towns in the Italian Renaissance. The second part of the course charted the emergence of new urban models and architectural interventions from the inception of the Baroque era to the end of the ancien régime.

THE CONTEMPORARY: ARCHITECTURE AS CONCEPT FROM 1968 TO THE PRESENT ¶ SPRING 2017 ¶ BERNARD TSCHUMI, INSTRUCTOR, WITH JONAH ROWEN, CECIL BARNES, JEROME HAFERD, AND ESTEBAN DE BACKER ¶ The "Architecture as Concept" seminar took as its starting hypothesis that there is no architecture without a concept; that concepts are what differentiate architecture from mere building. The course attempted to demonstrate that the most important works of architecture in any given period are the ones with the strongest concept or idea rather than simply those with the most striking form or shape. ¶ The seminar discussed projects or buildings from 1968 to the present in terms of their ability to mark the history of ideas and concepts in architecture. Differences between concepts, "partis," diagrams and compositions as well as between concepts, percepts and affects were central themes. ¶ This year a new discussion format was introduced in the form of a "debate" or trial. Students, in pairs or threes, were asked to engage in a debate either "for" or "against" the shared case study building. Using the analogy of a court case, the building was the suspect, one student the prosecutor, another, the defense lawyer. Expert witnesses from within and outside the class were called. The main goal of the exercise was to discover whether the original framing theme and theory surrounding a given project is still relevant today.

ARGUMENTS ¶ SUMMER 2016 ¶ ENRIQUE WALKER, INSTRUCTOR, WITH CRISTÓBAL AMUNÁTEGUI, JOSEPH BEDFORD, ERIK CARVER, ADDISON GODEL, DIANA MARTINEZ, POLLYANNA RHEE, NORIHIKO TSUNEISHI, AND FEDERICA VANNUCCHI ¶ This course examined the state of contemporary architecture culture through the lens of current intellectual projects in a wide range of practices within the field. Organized around a series of case studies—from exhibitions to installations, from journals to books, from research projects to educational projects—this course's main goal was to interrogate ongoing projects for these spaces of architectural production, and in turn to examine different positions within the field. In brief, the course scrutinized the formulation of agendas and projects—that is, arguments—and the way in which

they take part in the advancement of architecture. ¶ Specifically, this installment of the course took on four spaces of architectural production (books, collective exhibitions, individual exhibitions, and journals), and devoted two sessions to each of them. Each session was divided into two parts. The first, conducted as a seminar and supported by selected readings—with the course instructors operating individually—examined a specific space of architectural production. The second, conducted as a guest lecture and an open debate with the course instructors operating as a team, interrogated a project for that space. The ultimate aim was to engage current debates within the field.

METROPOLIS ¶ SUMMER 2016 ¶ ENRIQUE WALKER, INSTRUCTOR ¶ The modern metropolis—cauldron of social transformation, technological innovation, and aesthetic experimentation—is inseparable from the equally modern notion of an international "avant-garde." However, in the course of their myriad encounters throughout the twentieth century, both categories—the metropolis and the avant-gardes—have become virtually unrecognizable. In their place have emerged new configurations, new challenges, and new possibilities. This course examined arguments and design theories formulated for—and through—the city after "metropolis." This is the global city, the financial capital of advanced capitalism. But it is also the city after the city—the result of massive urbanizations stemming from regional and global migrations, as well as massive dispersals that trace back to the decades immediately following the Second World War. The course scrutinized in detail architectural objects and the debates surrounding them, positioning these objects within the cities they imagine. In each case, we traced multiple, genealogical affiliations—the alliances they forge, the subjects they conjure, the pasts they construct, the futures they project, the others they exclude—and find a decisive realignment of the ways in which architecture and urbanism operate, as well as multiple opportunities to re-imagine the city—architecture's recurring dream—yet again today.

DESIGN THEORIES ¶ SPRING 2017 ¶ ENRIQUE WALKER, INSTRUCTOR ¶ In Aldo Rossi's article "Architettura per i musei," which was originally delivered as a lecture at IUAV in April 1966, Rossi examined the question of "design theory." The proposition he advanced, in retrospect particularly polemical, if not altogether questionable, reveals the aspiration as well as the shortcoming of

his then-imminent book, L'architettura della città. A theory of design, Rossi argued, is an integral part of a theory of architecture, and the first goal of an architecture school. However, Rossi warned that design theories are rare and usually tackled by the most naive or the greatest of men. ¶ Rossi's main reference was not an architect, but a writer, Raymond Roussel: in particular his posthumous publication, *Comment j'ai écrit certains de mes livres*, which explained the method he had used to write some of his books. Rossi himself expected to eventually write a book that would explain the way in which he designed some of his buildings, but never actually did. In the preface to the second edition of *L'architettura della città*, he briefly mentioned a design procedure based, not unlike Roussel's method, on combining predetermined objects. His design theory, however, remained unformulated. ¶ If design theories were rare then, as Rossi claimed, they have become rarer since. Design and theory have actually forked. This seminar speculated on their intersection. Specifically, it examined the ways in which architects have since the mid-sixties theorized their design practices. The seminar focused on eleven programmatic books by practitioners; each session interrogated one book and scrutinized the arguments it articulated, the objectives it pursued, the critiques it entailed, and, in turn, the design theories it implied. Ultimately, this seminar traced the trajectories of architectural design as a theoretical question over the past five decades.

COLLECTING ARCHITECTURE TERRITORIES ¶ SPRING 2017 ¶ MARK WASIUTA, INSTRUCTOR ¶ This seminar was a continuation of the evolving research project, Collecting Architecture Territories. The project contends that collecting is a term, practice, or condition that allows us a glimpse of the emerging cultural logic of the early 21st century. It argues that one of the most significant developments reshaping the intersection of art and architectural practice over the last three decades is the veritable explosion of institutions and foundations that have emerged out of private art collections. ¶ The emphasis upon territories in the seminar recognized that the contemporary proliferation of various collecting activities—no longer concentrated solely in traditional urban centers—are dispersed globally. Territory is understood not only as spatial proximity and physical terrain, but also as something actively produced, an operational space defined by different types of cultural production, consumption, governance, investment, communication, and development.

The seminar asked students to develop descriptive strategies for elucidating the spatiality and territoriality of new regimes of collection. Student work took into account diverse factors such as new art-architectural practices, the globalization of the art market, initiatives for urban development, practices of preservation, branding strategies, cultural policies, financial investments, and tax laws.

EXTREME DESIGN ¶ SPRING 2017 ¶ MARK WIGLEY, INSTRUCTOR ¶ Where is architecture in a time of extreme design in which the weather, body, brain, genes, debt, networks and personal/collective identities are being self-consciously designed and "design thinking" has become a ubiquitous mantra? Design has dramatically transformed human capacity yet architects and architecture schools act as if the inhabitants of rooms, buildings, neighborhoods, cities, landscapes and ecosystems are relatively stable defined figures and that the role of architecture is to physically and psychologically shelter that figure. Architecture is treated as a form of protective care, even as the preservation of a particular idea of the human, insulating people from the radical transformation of their multiple environments and even insulating them from the radical transformation to their bodies and brains. The human figures that are represented by designers occupy a very narrow range of physical type, age, health, abilities, ethnicity, groupings, interactions and behaviors. Architects aspire to enhancing human life yet those that engage directly with the dramatically reconstructed body and brain are treated as if engaging in a form of science fiction even as such transformations have become everyday. The idea of this class was to produce a kind of catalog of all the dimensions of the human body and brain that are being redesigned (artificial body parts, plastic surgery, neuroprosthetics, drugs, bioprinting, gene editing, biomimicry, gender reassignment, body on a chip, biofeedback, etc.) and to consider the implications for the design of objects, buildings and environments.

AFFORDABLE HOUSING ¶ SPRING 2017 ¶ GWENDOLYN WRIGHT, INSTRUCTOR ¶ The term "affordable housing" first emerged around fifty years ago. It reveals dire inequalities in housing opportunities around the world, especially as neo-liberal political economies have replaced earlier welfare-state programs and the very idea of a "right to housing." As a result, municipal governments, local philanthropies and religious organizations have had to take a role in providing alternatives to market-rate housing that is increasingly unattainable for ordinary people. These affordable alternatives are inherently tied to local conditions and specifically local economies, as well as sponsors and residents, both their specific needs and opportunities. This seminar explored the legacy of affordable housing prototypes as they have evolved in a wide range of settings over the past fifty years including New York, northern and southern California, Vienna, Paris, Singapore, and Shanghai.

HISTORY OF THE AMERICAN CITY ¶ FALL 2016 ¶ GWENDO-LYN WRIGHT, INSTRUCTOR ¶ This course explored the volatile, seemingly chaotic yet cohesive forms of American cities, which have long been the quintessence of the modern metropolis: a synthesis of raw unregulated development, precise professional master plans, broad-based cultural and transnational exchanges and unexpected local anomalies. Lectures began with colonial-era origin myths, then nineteenth-century developments and focusing on the twentieth-century metropolis. Each class took up a specific historical epoch and formal typology—housing, commerce, finance, industry, etc.—juxtaposing general trends across the country with a focus on one particular city. We covered both unique creations and generic spatial forms, problems and creative inventions. ¶ While the last lecture concentrated on contemporary cities, every class examined repercussions of earlier decisions on the present day. Who decides where "downtown" is located? How have Americans envisioned homes—and housing? What are Americans' attitudes about the natural environment, especially in cities? How does infrastructure affect the efficiency and equity of a city? We emphasized a fundamental aspect of historical inquiry: the past affects what is possible in the present and what people can imagine about the future.

COLONIAL/POSTCOLONIAL ARCHITECTURE ¶ SPRING 2017 ¶ GWENDOLYN WRIGHT, IN-STRUCTOR ¶ Colonialism has had a powerful effect on the architecture of housing, schools, civic buildings, infrastructure and tourist facilities around the world, as well as the larger scale of urban plans and environmental developments. The seminar examined the impact of European powers, as well as colonial architecture under the U.S., Japan, the USSR, and China. Colonial cities touted some of the earliest examples of modern architecture and urbanism, purportedly signs of the benefits for local and foreign residents, yet modernism's progressive demands for equality and autonomy also gained a foothold. ¶ After analyzing historical precedents, the seminar looked at more recent "postcolonial" repercussions of these phenomena—not only in Lahore, Seoul and Nairobi but also in New York, London, Paris and Shanghai. The key issues extend from historic preservation and affordable housing reform to new towns and the very concept of "global cities." Contemporary designers are still caught in these tensions, both western architects who seek work abroad or innovative non-western architects—some now peripatetic themselves.

MODERN HOUSING ¶ HIS-TORY AND THEORY, FALL 2016 ¶ GWENDOLYN WRIGHT, INSTRUCTOR ¶ This seminar explored key themes and examples of twentieth- and twenty-first-century modern housing. We focused on fundamental questions about continuities and innovations. How have architects addressed cultural norms about "home" and "housing" over time? We ranged across multiple scales from the individual body, the room and the wall to larger composites of housing complexes, production systems, social services, environmental factors and economic challenges. ¶ The first half of the class surveyed and compared a broad range of examples from iconic social-democratic housing estates of Europe in the 1920s and progressive American enclaves of that era, to more recent prefab prototypes in Sweden, informal barrios in Caracas, the mix of market-rate and social housing in Amsterdam and affordable housing in the United States. Students in the Housing Studio worked with students from other programs and other departments across the university. ¶ Students presented research projects during the last third of the class. They also commented on one another's presentations with great insight, which quickly lifted the level and self-awareness of everyone's work. Topics included UN-Habitat proposals for the Middle East, John F.C. Turner's work in Latin America, contemporary projects in Sao Paulo's favelas, UDC projects in Brooklyn, Joseph Eichler's suburbs in northern California, Chinese gated communities, post-WWII and more recent housing projects in Mexico City, barracks for illegal immigrants and the use of recycled materials in recent housing.

1

Britta Ritter-Amour

2

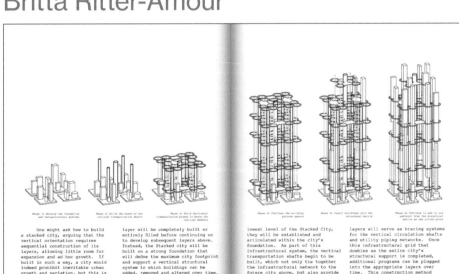

One might ask how to build a stacked city, arguing that the vertical orientation requires sequential construction of its layers, allowing little room for expansion and ad hoc growth. If built in such a way, a city would indeed prohibit inevitable urban growth and variation, but this is not the construction model for the Stacked City.

Change is inevitable, thus it is unrealistic to suppose that an entire layer will be completely built or entirely filled before continuing on to develop subsequent layers above. Instead, the Stacked city will be built on a strong foundation that will define the maximum city footprint and support a vertical structural system to which buildings can be added, removed and altered over time. Infrastructural systems must be one of the first things built in a city and because they are located on the lowest level of the Stacked City, they will be established and articulated within the city's foundation. As part of this infrastructural system, the vertical transportation shafts begin to be built, which not only tie together the infrastructural network to the future city above, but also provide the structural support for the future buildings.

Similarly, the transversal access platforms distributed between layers will serve as bracing systems for the vertical circulation shafts and utility piping networks. Once this infrastructural grid that doubles as the entire city's structural support is completed, additional programs can be plugged into the appropriate layers over time. This construction method simply transfers inevitable city development from the horizontal surface, where it traditionally happens, to the vertical plane.

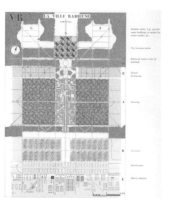

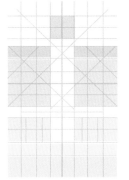

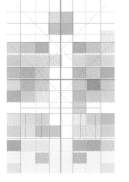

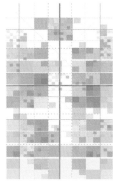

Stella Ioannidou

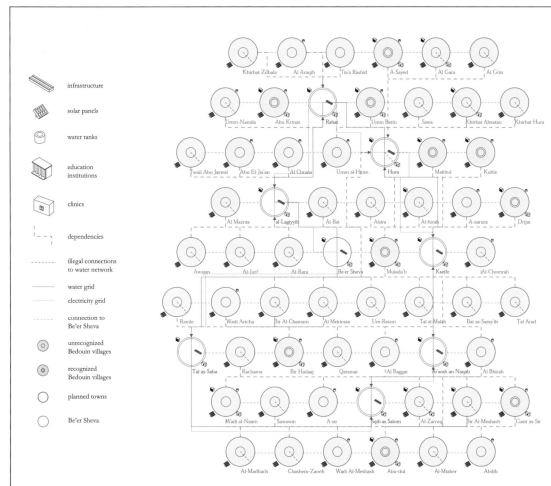

Udit Goel, Masha Maria Konopleva

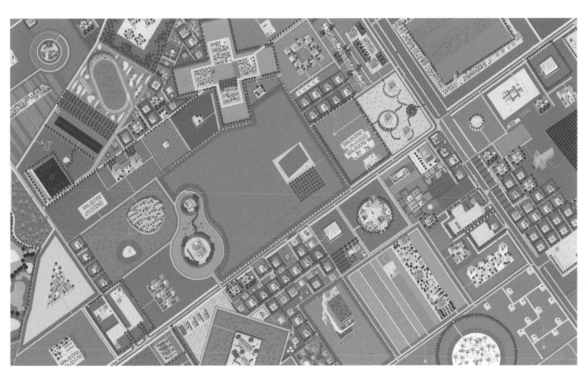

6

Violet Yi Ding

TOWARDS
THE
PLANETARY

Columbia GSAPP Design Mantras, 2017

Taken together, these statements can be read as a sort of
time-sensitive mantra for the disciplines of the built
environment, a set of pedagogical imperatives that have
emerged from the school, and a statement of engagement
as an institution. We understand these six statements,
dispersed throughout this book, as an urgent call to action
for Columbia GSAPP, and we recognize their relevance
and implications for the larger global community of
which the school is inextricably embedded within. They
address issues of political engagement, social equity,
representation, pursuing action on climate change,
global perspectives, cultural diversity, and developing
professional practice in all disciplines of the built
environment in which we study and practice.

Research

Global

1

2

Temple Hoyne Buell Center for the Study of American Architecture

The Temple Hoyne Buell Center for the Study of American Architecture was founded in 1982. Its mission is to advance the interdisciplinary study of American architecture, urbanism, and landscape. A separately endowed entity within the Graduate School of Architecture, Planning, and Preservation, the Center sponsors research projects, workshops, public programs, publications, and awards.

During the 2016–2017 academic year, the Buell Center organized a number of public events to conclude its multi-year research project, House Housing. This project elaborated a critical, historically informed analysis of architecture's engagement with real estate development. In the summer, the Center exhibited House Housing: An Untimely History of Architecture and Real Estate (July 12–September 10, 2016) at New York's Center for Architecture. In the fall and spring, House Housing: An Untimely History of Architecture and Real Estate, traveled in pieces to the Oslo School of Architecture and Design as a part of the Oslo Architecture Triennale (November 7–27, 2016) and to GSAPP's Studio-X in Rio de Janeiro (March 9–May 20, 2017). All exhibitions were accompanied by public programming. For more information on all of the above, please see house-housing.com.

Also during the academic year, the Buell Center hosted events related to its new long-term research project, "Power: Infrastructure in America," which examines local and regional infrastructural systems in the United States as sites of governmentality operating at many scales. On November 29, 2016, the Center screened Air Drifts, a film about trans-boundary air pollution and new territories of global responsibility, which was followed by a conversation with its creators, Kadambari Baxi, Janette Kim, Meg McLagan, David Schiminovich, and Mark Wasiuta. On April 6, 2017, the Center hosted the New York Times bestselling science fiction author Kim Stanley Robinson to read from his most recent book, New York 2140, which envisions New York City after a catastrophic sea level rise. The Center also participated in GSAPP's "100 Days" series, which gathered faculty and students to discuss, organize, and plan for potential changes in the built environment during the Trump administration. And on May 12, 2017, continuing under the "Power: Infrastructure in America" research theme, the Buell Center convened a workshop of scholars to discuss the practice of "Emergency Management" in Flint, MI and Detroit, MI and other municipalities around the country.

Further, on March 31–April 1, 2017, the Buell Center hosted its biennial Dissertation Colloquium, which brought together an international group of select doctoral students working on dissertation topics related to the history, theory, and criticism of American architecture, urbanism, and landscape. This year's colloquium featured a keynote address by Joseph Heathcott, Associate Professor of Urban Studies at the New School and the 2016 Mellon Distinguished Fellow at Princeton University School of Architecture, entitled "Angels of Memory Guard the City in Freefall."

These selected projects represent an ongoing research agenda that reflects the Buell Center's commitment to the articulation and discussion of challenging issues confronted by its various, overlapping constituencies. For more information, please see buellcenter.org.

Reinhold Martin
Director

Jacob Moore
Assistant Director

Jordan Steingard
Program Manager

1   Kadambari Baxi presents at Air Drifts, in collaboration with: NASA-GMAO (Global Modeling and Assimilation Office), Nov 29, 2016
Buell Dissertation Colloquium
2   House Housing Exhibition, Center for Architecture, New York
4/5   House, Housing Exhibition, Oslo School of Architecture (AHO), Oslo Architecture Triennial

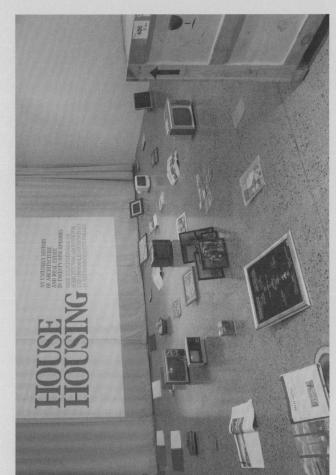

3

5

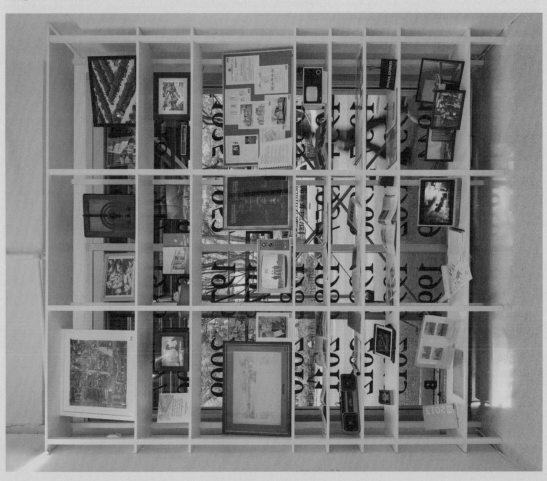

4

Center for Spatial Research

The Center for Spatial Research (CSR) was established in 2015 as a hub for urban research that links design, architecture, urbanism, the humanities and data science. CSR supersedes, and builds on the work of, the Spatial Information Design Lab. It sponsors research and curricular activities built around the critical use of new technologies of mapping, data collection, analysis, and visualization. Through these initiatives, CSR fosters data literacy and critically interrogates the world of "big data" in order to open up new areas of urban research and inquiry.

The 2016-2017 year has brought further work on our multiyear research theme, Conflict Urbanism; an exhibition in the Oslo Architecture Triennale; two exhibitions in the Istanbul Design Biennial; several public events and lectures; new interdisciplinary courses: the Summer Faculty Institute Mapping for the Urban Humanities, and three semester-long courses, Conflict Urbanism: Language Justice, Data Visualization for Architecture Urbanism and the Humanities; and the launch of the critically acclaimed Brain Index.

During Fall 2016 CSR together with GSAPP Events hosted a symposium on the role of conflict in structuring urban space and the politics of representation in zones of discordance, disruption, and violence as they contribute to the making and remaking of cities. CSR Researchers presented ongoing research efforts and were joined by Eyal Weizman of Goldsmiths and Enrico Bertini of NYU. Also during the fall CSR organized a conversation around new uses of mapping in humanities classrooms among Columbia University Faculty and Deans. During the spring semester CSR sponsored a series of lectures titled Conflict Urbanism: Language Justice. These lectures focused on the role of language in structuring cities, bringing together speakers to address the ways that urban spaces and their digital traces are physically shaped by linguistic diversity, and to examine the results of languages coming into contact and conflict. This lecture series was organized in conjunction with the seminar of the same title.

Laura Kurgan
 Director
Dare Brawley
 Program Administrator
Juan Francisco Saldarriaga
 Associate Research Scholar

Michelle McSweeney
 Associate Research Scholar
Jochen Hartmann
 Design Associate
Grga Basic
 Associate Research Scholar

1 Conflict Urbanism: Colombia map of reported internally displaced people

CONFLICT URBANISM: COLOMBIA

Over the course of the last thirty years, almost seven million Colombians have been forced to leave their homes and towns and move to safer locations. Thousands more have been victims of sexual violence, threats, land-mine explosions, homicides and massacres. Conflict Urbanism: Colombia maps and visualizes these crimes in hopes of better understanding the patterns and urban ramifications of the Colombian conflict.

The project was exhibited at the Oslo Architecture Triennale, in September—November, 2016 and has been released online as an interactive website with several different visualizations of this complex dataset. To view the full project visit: http://c4sr.columbia.edu/conflict-urbanism-colombia.

Laura Kurgan, Principal Investigator; Juan Francisco Saldarriaga, Principal Investigator; Angelika Rettberg, Principal Investigator; Dare Brawley, Research Associate; Anjali Singhvi, Graduate Assistant; Stella Ioannidou, Graduate Assistant; Patrick Li, Graduate Assistant; Mike Howard, Graduate Assistant; Jeevan Farias, Graduate Assistant

CONFLICT URBANISM: ALEPPO

Since 2012, the people of Aleppo—one of the oldest continuously-inhabited cities in the world—have been exposed to catastrophic violence. Many

Center for Urban Research (CURE)

an on-going dialogue between the center and real estate practitioners.

Community Engagement in the Real Estate Development Process

Seeking to understand this socio-economic mechanism of building delivery, with the formulation of an analytic, evaluative, and predictive framework, and with the objective of proscribing improvements rather than just being descriptive, two case studies were underway during this period:

- The West Harlem neighborhood has been explored for its history of community engagement, the manner in which the urban development process has been encoded in the built fabric, the changing context of public policy and the uncovering of successful instances of community collaboration and consideration.

- The rebuilding of Lower Manhattan after the devastation of September 11, 2001 has been examined through the lens of the different entities that directed the formal, social and economic outcomes of the district. The level of authority of the various entities has changed and conflicted over the past 15 years, and the outcomes can be read in the light of the intentions of those who dominated at the respective phases of redevelopment.

Additionally, for continually checking and encouraging these research initiatives, CURE maintained iterative industry engagement such that topic selection and dissemination of investigations was

industry challenges, and held two industry symposia:

- Tech Unbundled (Sep 30, 2016), panel moderated by Marc Holliday
- FormForward 2017 (Mar 31, 2017), hosted by CURE research scholar Josh Panknin

CURE's research in real estate technology also gained significant credibility with the recent creation of an informal partnership between CURE, Columbia Entrepreneurship, and MetaProp NYC. This partnership provides a strong and credible forum for discussion and idea formulation. Additionally, the partnership is jointly providing Pre-accelerator sessions for selected ideas for real estate technology, with the first such session commencing in May 2017.

The CURE research in real estate technology also supports the creation of a curriculum aimed at making the M.S.RED program and CURE the true global thought leader for real estate technology and real estate education. By creating an extensive ecosystem of research, education initiatives, and industry engagement and partnership, CURE sets the stage for producing transformative technology for the built world and also an unparalleled advancement in the abilities of graduating students.

Patrice Derrington
Director

During the 2016–2017 academic year, CURE focused on research in two key areas:

1. The fundamental process of real estate development: the critical dissection and evaluation of that process with specific emphasis on the socio-economic dimension of that process especially that which occurs in the community engagement phase.
2. Formulating a strategy to effectively embrace the evolution of technology to help address challenges of the real estate industry.

The project was exhibited at the Istanbul Design Biennial in October—November, 2016. To view the full project visit: http://c4sr.columbia.edu/conflict-urbanism-aleppo.

Laura Kurgan, Principal Investigator; Madeeha Merchant, Research Associate; Grga Basic, Research Associate; Dare Brawley, Research Associate; Jamon Van Den Hoek, Research Associate; Mike Howard, Graduate Assistant; Carmelo Ignaccolo, Graduate Assistant; Nadine Fattaleh, Graduate Assistant; Michael James Storm, Graduate Assistant; Violet Whitney, Graduate Assistant

2

3

thousands have been injured, died, or fled. Our project focuses on their city and what has been done to it compiling new forms of evidence documenting urban damage.

The project is an archive and a resource centered on an open-source, interactive, data-rich map of the city of Aleppo at the neighborhood scale. Drawing together three scales of evidence—the high resolution satellite view, the low resolution satellite view, and citizen journalist captured YouTube videos—the project presents multiple case studies that explore different aspects of the conflict and how it has been documented. Triangulating between these different scales the project has revealed astonishing and devastating city-wide and hyper-local patterns in the war.

2 Conflict Urbanism: Aleppo, Informal Control Damage
3 Conflict Urbanism: Aleppo, Low-Res High-Res Sequence

Avery Library

The world's leading architectural library supports the work of students and faculty at the School by providing a wealth of research materials as well as outstanding research support and access services. Orientation tours of the library—offered to students at the beginning of the fall and summer semesters—are strongly recommended. The Avery Architectural Library was founded in 1890, following a gift to Columbia by Samuel Putnam Avery. The University's Fine Arts Library was added in 1978, and the re-named Avery Architectural and Fine Arts Library now holds more than 650,000 non-circulating books and periodicals related to architecture, urban planning, art history, archaeology, historic preservation and the decorative arts.

The Avery Classics collection comprises more than 40,000 rare books beginning with Alberti's De Re Aedificatoria (1485) to modern masterworks such as Olafur Eliasson's Your House (2006). The Classics collection also has important holdings of graphic suites, periodicals, manuscripts, broadsides, photographs, and printed ephemera. The American collection is one of the most extensive in existence. Avery Library also includes

the Ware collection of more than 9,000 circulating books on architecture, urban planning and real estate development. Avery's collections are searchable through CLIO—the Columbia University Libraries online catalog.

More than 2 million documents make up Avery's Drawings and Archives collection, including original drawings by masters such as Frank Lloyd Wright and Le Corbusier; original photographs by Lewis Hine, Joseph Molitor, Samuel Gottscho and others; and the archives of many major American practices, such as Richard Upjohn, Alexander Jackson Davis, Greene & Greene, Warren & Wetmore, Harold van Buren Magonigle, Stanford White, Wallace K. Harrison, Gordon Bunshaft, Philip Johnson and the Guastavino Fireproof Construction Company among many others. The collection is a major source for exhibitions and for primary research in architecture. Available by appointment, the collection welcomes students, scholars and professionals.

Avery Library also produces the Avery Index to Architectural Periodicals. Begun in 1934, it is the most extensive periodical index in the field of architecture and provides citations to more than 860,000 articles in architectural and related periodicals. The Avery Index is accessible to students and alumni as one of the databases offered through the Columbia Libraries website.

Avery Library began a long-awaited process of renovation and expansion in 2003. Phase one consisted of the creation of a new Miriam and Ira D. Wallach Study Center for Art and

1

1   Avery Library, photograph by Ofer Wolberger
2   Feminist Architecture Collaborative, F-Architecture
3   QSPACE Coded Plumbing exhibitions with the Van Alen Institute and GSAPP End of Year Show
4   QSPACE at the GSAPP Incubator, photograph by Tim Schutsky

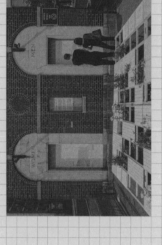

VAN ALEN INSTITUTE

GSAPP EOYS

3

4

2

GSAPP Incubator

The GSAPP Incubator is an initiative that provides recent graduates with a collaborative environment to explore new ideas and projects at the intersection of culture, technology and the city. It blends a professional setting and a culture of entrepreneurship with the communal creative energy and rigorous discourse experienced by students during their time at GSAPP. The program expands the territory between academia and the profession, and it allows members to share experiences and skills while building their professional networks and connecting to critical issues in New York and beyond.

Located in the heart of the downtown creative scene at 231 Bowery, the GSAPP Incubator is a unique university-led initiative that spans multiple disciplines and draws on the strengths of the school and its faculty, the resources of NEW INC and the New Museum and the proximity to Lower Manhattan's technology industry. Directed by Assistant Professor David Benjamin, the co-working space encourages discovery and open exchange among a diverse group of participants who are engaging in topics and interdisciplinary methods that expand the possibilities of architecture. It supports experimental and alternative modes of practice that encompass research and production: the member groups over the first two years have developed a variety of cutting-edge projects involving virtual reality and digital technology, critical discourse and publishing, civic issues and public spaces, urban regeneration, emergency response and more.

The member groups for the second year, from fall 2016 through summer 2017, were Animate Lot, Ashley Simone, Bika Rebek, : (Colon), Consortia, Dan Choi, f.architecture, Forrest Jessee, Marty Wood, Poché Arts, QSPACE, Untapped Cities, Xin Wang, and X-Lab.

Architecture, equipped with new storage, processing and study facilities for Avery's Drawings and Archives collection and for the University's art properties. Avery's ground floor reading room, designed in 1911 by William Mitchell Kendall of the McKim, Mead and White firm, was also renovated and re-named the Miriam and Ira D. Wallach Reading Room. It is linked to the Wallach Study Center by a 1970s underground extension designed by the late Professor Alexander Kouzmanoff. Avery is now working on Phase two renovations to the 1974 Kouzmanoff extension. Upgrades to technology offerings, seating, environmental controls and collection arrangements are introduced incrementally each year.

Carole Ann Fabian
Director
Anna Blok
Bibliographic Assistant
Vivien Boyle
Serials Assistant
Stephen Breski
Access Clerk
Pamela Casey
Archivist
Kitty Chibnik
Associate Director/
Head of Access Services
Roberto Ferrari
Curator of Art Properties
Paula Gabbard
Fine Arts Librarian
Ted Goodman
Avery Index/Communications
Coordinator
Teresa Harris

Curator of Classics
Shelley Hayreh
Archivist
Lena Newman
Classics Assistant
Anna Opryszko
Access Clerk
Nicole Richard
Drawings + Archives Assistant
Jeffrey Ross
Indexer/Reference Librarian
Eric Reisinger
Art Handler
Zak Rouse
Reserves/Access Supervisor
Chris Sala
Architecture Librarian
Margaret Smithglass
Registrar +
Digital Content Librarian
Abebe Tessema
Access Clerk
Lillian Vargas
Administrative Assistant,
Art Properties
Richard Walters
Access Clerk

Embodied Energy Project

In February of 2015, the Embodied Energy Pilot Project (EEPP) at Columbia University's Graduate School of Architecture, Planning and Preservation was launched with the premise that embodied energy is an important feature of architecture, but it is currently not well documented or easy to act on. The project was an open-ended research initiative that aimed to uncover the key questions, issues, and opportunities for architectural design in the context of embodied energy.

In the initial phase of the project, we explored the topic in a variety of ways. We reviewed the prior research and studied existing databases. We analyzed how and where embodied energy intersects the design process. We discussed this hidden yet essential layer of architecture and the city. Inevitably, we started to draw.

Our initial drawings of embodied energy included a zoomed-out map of buildings in New York City and a

2

1

Hudson Valley Initiaive

The Hudson Valley Initiative (HVI) facilitates applied research into the complex spatial, ecological, and economic opportunities of this vast region. Extending several hundred miles north from Manhattan Island, and touching five states, the region includes nine counties, 13 cities and over 200 villages and towns, and its watershed covers over 13,000 square miles. The status and future of this area deeply affects the lives of millions, from New York City to a broad swath of the American northeast. By serving as the GSAPP clearinghouse for urban design, architecture, landscape, preservation, and planning work, the HVI enables substantive contributions to the long-term health and viability of the region.

Kate Orff
David Smiley
Lee Altman
Jacob Moore
Michael Murphy
Erica Avrami

SITE 1: TACONITE MINE   SITE 4: STEEL FORMER

SITE 2: IRON ORE   SITE 3: BLAST FURNACE   SITE 6: TRUCKING

SITE 5: CONTAINER SHIP

SITE 7: STEEL YARD   SITE 8: STRUCTURE

zoomed-in view of the intersection of Houston Street and The Bowery. Next we created a set of physical models that compared the embodied energy in six historic and contemporary building types in Shanghai. We explored Washington, D.C. in a similar way. These quantitative drawings and models were interesting and helpful, but they didn't tell the whole story. We quickly recognized that data and its visualization were necessary but not sufficient. It became clear that any illuminating drawings would have to span both quantitative and qualitative representations—both metrics and narratives. At this point, we turned to drawing "material stories"—the narratives of how matter comes to be formed into construction materials and buildings, including the distributed locations where this happens and the diverse people who are directly involved and indirectly affected.

Over the course of 2016, we developed two different sets of drawings to further explore embodied energy. The first was a set of data visualizations that outlined different ways to quantify energy. These drawings were developed through cross-referencing multiple studies and databases, and using numbers to create a sequential argument that was legible to non-experts but not oversimplified. They were then crafted in collaboration with the visualization firm Accurat. The second set of drawings was a series of material stories, developed by piecing together a single immersive, multi-scalar frame with all of the steps that contribute

to the embodied energy of a material (such as steel, concrete, or wood), including extraction, transportation, factory production, and construction. They were then crafted and extended by Lindsey Wikstrom, originally one of the students from the EEPP and now part of a new generation of multi-dimensional designers.

The two sets of drawings are shown together in Embodied Energy and Design: Making Architecture between Metrics and Narratives (Lars Muller Publishers, 2017) as a starting point for a fresh discussion about embodied energy. Though the drawings use different strategies, they are complementary. They resonate. Each set fills in the gaps of the other. The drawings offer insights and they pose questions. Though neither set is finished, and though the pair is not comprehensive, together they point to a design territory we must explore.

David Benjamin
    Director
Carlo Bailey
Fancheng Fei
Jean Qin Gu
Bingyu Guan
Jonathan Alexandru Izen
Nishant Jacob
Sharon Leung
Nabila Morales Pérez
Jeffrey Montes
Catherine Qi
Alexander Rosenthal
Lorenzo Villaggi
Xiaoyu Wang
Thomas Wegener
Lindsey Wikstrom
Mike Che-Wei Yeh
Ronald Yeung

1   Hudson Valley Regional Map
2   Urban Design HDI Exhibit
3   Embodied Enrgey Case Study
4   Steel Material Story by Lindsey Wilkstrom
5   Site or Regrowth Forest by Lindsey Wilkstrom

DeathLAB

At Columbia GSAPP DeathLAB, we are critically re-imagining the city's relationship with death and designing new forms and civic space. DeathLAB is directed by architects in close dialogue with environmental engineers, philosophers, theologians, sociologists and sustainability experts. We are currently refining a process that transforms the biomass of the corpse into the energy that we literally embody. During the past year, DeathLAB's founder and director, Karla Rothstein, delivered the keynote address at the 7th International Conference on Latin American Death and Dying held at the University of São Paulo, Brazil, presented Green Cemeteries: A New Paradigm for Public Open Space at the American Association of Landscape Architects annual meeting in New Orleans, and published "DEATHLAB: Designing the Civic-Sacred" in PASAGES arquitectura diseño e innivación, No. 141. Rothstein was also invited to share DeathLAB's initiative at the MoMA R&D Salon on Modern Death, and at the San Francisco Asian Art Museum's "Reviving the Environment: Ways to Honor the Living and the Dead."

The lab's work was recognized as "an important contribution to the growing field of whole systems design"

Waste Initiative

The Waste Initiative is an applied research platform that aims to explore the possibilities—both real and speculative—of the role of waste in relationship to architecture and the city. At once ubiquitous and forgotten, waste is a growing and pressing area of inquiry that extends across scales and disciplinary expertise. Within the context of Columbia GSAPP, the platform will investigate three independent yet overlapping thematics dealing with waste and disposability: infrastructure, aesthetics, and materiality. Key questions will look at waste and value propositions, as well as waste material life cycles and those transformations over time. The work of the Waste Initiative operates in a range of formats including design studios, seminars, summer workshops, and continuous long-term projects concerned with material investigations and public design speculations.

Tei Carpenter
Director

1 Ryu Ahn and Yongwoo Park,
   Clingwrap Research
2 Jesse McCormick, Shuo Yang,
   Waste Meat Research
3 Death Lab plan perspective
4 Extraction Lab map of sites

244

by the Buckminster Fuller Institute and DeathLAB was invited into BFI's Catalyst Program. DeathLAB was also nominated for KATERVA's 2017 Accelerating the Future Award, and became a finalist in the category of Behavioral Change, "showing how innovation can be scaled for both business opportunities and global good... making dents in conventional ways of thinking to defy and fight for global change." The KATERVA competition has been described by Reuters as "the Nobel Prize for Sustainability."

Having won first place in the international Future Cemetery design competition, DeathLAB took up residence at Arnos Vale Cemetery in Bristol UK in the Summer of 2016. Collaborating with the University of Bath Center for Death and Society, an exhibition in the Non-Conformist Chapel and installation in the cemetery are currently being planned.

With support from the Earth Institute's Cross Cutting Initiative, Rothstein and co-PI Kartik Chandran's work on DeathLAB's Anaerobic Bio-Conversion Vessel (ABC-V) was filed in an Invention Report accepted by Columbia Tech Ventures, and a preliminary patent on this content is in place.

Inspired by DeathLAB's ongoing initiatives, Columbia J-school graduates produced "A New York Glow" video submission to the Mega-Cities short docs competition in the category "New York - Climate and Environment'" and DeathLAB's Constellation Park project was featured in New York Magazine's

4

parts of a new architectural practice. The laboratory is not so interested in the latest technological hype, but on using the latest technology in an off-label way to foster architectural understanding both inside and outside the discipline.

The laboratory produces arresting short films, documentary loops, architectural earworms, e-books, booklets, VR-pamphlets; all in collaboration generating sticky, intensely memorable, magnetic, even addictive architectural information. Virtual realities and physical analogues are parallel agents used to inspire, irritate, and ignite new dialogues and modes of creation.

annual "Reasons to Love NY" issue: "What began as a methodical winnowing process led DeathLAB to something new and sublime."

Karla Rothstein
   Director

Extraction Lab

Columbia GSAPP's Extraction Laboratory is a research team that extracts architecture from situations, rather than places.

The Extraction Laboratory is where architects go to remember whatever the hell is relevant, research-driven and worthy of dissemination on new platforms. Informational outreach, ideas exposition, technique prototyping... these cannot be left to external agents, they must be embedded as constituent

There are 7 Rules of Extraction:

0. State of Affairs: Futurity demands an architectural thinking that is situational, responding in real-time to conditional, urgent forces.

1. Logics: Objects are imperfect. They make an abstract idea one dimensional, incapable of processing dynamic patterns or implicating situational spatiality.

2. We focus on situations, as a dynamic set of conditions, or intensified systems.

3. We extract core samples of data; mediating overloaded sensorial inputs, fast-happening systems, troubleshooting to find what is relevant.

4. Mode: We operate in situ or in the reaction mixture.

5. We depart from a standard point of departure, seeking hyper-awareness, phenomena initiating state changes,

implicating scale, yet scale-less.
6. Repeat.: Create a feedback loop for architecture, response driven, yet limitless in implication and application.

The Laboratory's inaugural project, with the desert as a canvas, and Burning Man as a context, will create and build architecture for the desert through the design and fabrication of a roof to be deployed at the GSAPP Burning Man Camp.

There are three goals we will work towards achieving with our Installation:

1. Architecture and Politics: The roof will provide a common ground of discourse.

2. Architecture and Situations: The roof will extract what is the most absent in the Desert: WATER.

3. Architecture and Elements: The roof creates a habitable desert landscape.

Termination: The laboratory self-destructs on August 1, 2021.

Christoph a. Kumpusch
   Director
Alessandra Calaguire

Fabrication Lab

The Fabrication Lab provides material, technical, and conceptual support for all building, modeling, and physical production endeavors at GSAPP.

This includes: a continuum of manual, power, and digital tools ranging from super-fine to heavy duty; a machine shop with four CNC routers with various features and working envelopes; a computer lab with on-site expertise for technical and CAM software; an open shop floor with active work space; and a rotating roster of instructors providing tutorials, workshops, and guidance for all projects and ideas that come through the shop.

The Fab Lab also provides production support for GSAPP operations, exhibitions, and special events. Some projects in the past year included exhibition construction for "Liam Young: New Romance," highly-detailed physical replications of 3D scans of oil paintings (via Historical Preservation), and a solid-chocolate 1:100 scale model of the Seagram Building for Phyllis Lambert's 90th birthday celebration.

The Fab Lab's ongoing mission is to substantiate critical ideas with physical evidence, and to provide physical fabrications with critical meaning. This mission is supported daily by the stewardship of dozens of working student Fab Lab monitors, by the hundreds of students who use the shop regularly, and by the ongoing commitment of the GSAPP community toward questions of making.

Josh Jordan
Director

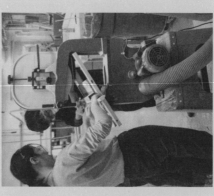

Global Africa Lab

With the research project "INTELLECTUAL MOBILITY: Data, Media, Race + Space," the lab continues to develop data spatializations as a study of the transportation and infrastructural networks in Cape Town, South Africa with respect to the quality and efficiency of access to college and other informal networks of education. The collaboration is undertaken with researchers in the Department of Information Systems at the University of the Western Cape in Cape Town. The research studies the relationships between urban mobility, physical access to education, and historically disadvantaged populations in both cities. The research will collect data and information relative to the following areas: travel route, cost, travel distance, travel time, modes of transport, student income level, and grades. GAL also organized with the New York AIA Center for Architecture a one day symposium African Modernism(s): Past/Present/Future that explored the legacy of architectural modernism featured in the exhibition Architecture of Independence—African Modernism. The event considered the complexity of modernism's political and social agendas and the influence of this body of modernism on contemporary and future building projects in various parts of Africa. The afternoon symposium brought together scholars and architects to critically examine the modernism built in the 1950s and 1960s in post-colonial nations around the African continent. Architects discussed recently built works, including schools and health facilities, and shared projects underway that address the future of architecture in African cities.

Mario Gooden
Co-Director
Mabel O. Wilson
Co-Director
Carson Smuts
Researcher
Jonathan Izen
Assistant

1 Fabrication Lab
2 Global Africa Lab, Routes Logged

Studio-X

Global

Malwina Łyś-Dobradin
Director,
Global Initiatives

Studio-X is GSAPP's global network of its most advanced laboratories for exploring the future of cities. The label conveys the sense that a new platform for research and debate is needed to address the array of urgent questions that will face the next generation of designers. Studio-X serves GSAPP's global mission by fostering open dialogue and cultural exchange, encouraging collaborative research addressing urgent topics of our time, and producing new knowledge.

Each Studio-X develops new lines of inquiry and fosters academic and professional exchanges and collaborations between people that might not normally come together. At the same time, Studio-X spaces are equipped with the latest technology to take advantage of Columbia's expertise in digital design and data visualization and to draw on the widest array of global resources and communicate ideas to the widest possible audience. The local director of each Studio-X acts as the curator of a continuous array of projects, workshops, lectures, seminars, symposia, exhibitions, and performances. In key moments, all the Studio-X spaces link together in single real-time global

workshops allowing unprecedented bursts of creativity.

During the 2016-2017 academic year, Studio-X continued to host GSAPP faculty and students from across disciplines throughout the academic year. Studio-X Istanbul facilitated Micro-Networks of Istanbul's Streets, a cross-disciplinary research and design summer workshop the examined the micro-scale urban networks of the Tophane neighborhood. Studio-X Amman collaborated with the Urban Design Program's comparative water urbanism studio, which investigated the critical role of water scarcity, abundance, and quality in determining the health and viability of global cities. Studio-X Rio worked with the Urban Planning spring studio Design Thinking for a Healthy Urban Environment. In addition, Studio-X sites in Istanbul and Johannesburg welcomed Advanced Architectural VI Studios and Studio-X sites in China and Rio de Janeiro participated in the Real Estate Development Program's International Regions courses.

This year Studio-X launched its next collective theme, Architecture Practice and the City. This Studio-X initiative engages design practices whose work addresses key debates taking place in their respective cities. The series probes how architects who practice in urban domains must contend with local and global conditions. Discourse on the city is explored through the comparative examination of specific projects. During the fall semester, GSAPP invited Heinrich Wolff and Ilze

1 Summer Workshop participants with local partners
   at the Rock Hewn Churches
   of Lalibela World Heritage
   Site, Ethiopia

Wolff of Wolff Architects from Cape Town, South Africa and Marta Moreira of MMBB from São Paulo, Brazil. Wolff Architects presented their Watershed Project, a business incubator and market on the Victoria and Alfred Waterfront that generated economic opportunities for small businesses through a new market. MMBB presented Jardim Edite, a social housing complex with three public facilities: a catering school, healthcare clinic, and daycare center. The discussion revealed ways in which architectural interventions developed in partnership with the community can generate socio-economic transformations. In the spring semester, Ammar Khammash of Khammash Architects from Amman, Jordan presented the Royal Academy for Nature Conservation and Mehmet Kütükçüio lu and Ertu Uçar, Partners of TEGET in Istanbul, Turkey, presented the Istanbul Maritime Museum. The discussion addressed the ways in which architects navigate the demands of the government and the public to develop projects for the public realm while also taking into consideration historical and cultural conservation and the geographical constraints of a site. The series will continue next year, furthering the School's commitment to thinking relationally across contexts and connecting the urban to the rural and the local to the global.

Ethiopia

HERITAGE, TOURISM, + URBANIZATION: UNDERSTANDING THE LANDSCAPE + DEVELOPMENT OF LALIBELA, ETHIOPIA • SUMMER 2016 • Erica Avrami and Will Raynolds, coordinators

The eleven Rock Hewn Churches of Lalibela have stood for more than eight hundred years. They are part of a sacred landscape that still welcomes tens of thousands of religious pilgrims during the holidays of the Ethiopian Orthodox Tewahedo Church. The churches were also one of the first sites to be designated as World Heritage by UNESCO. Work to conserve the churches has been accompanied by significant urban growth and tourism development in the past decade. In the summer of 2016, students from GSAPP and Addis Ababa University, in collaboration with World Monuments Fund, undertook a rapid field assessment and data collection to understand these changes, and identified key issues and questions that can inform future research and planning. The field work included the analysis of urban growth areas, mapping of significant elements of the heritage landscape, a user/visitor survey, a tourism infrastructure survey, and examination of the management structure of the site. The findings were summarized in a report that aims to support the sustainable development of Lalibela—while also preserving its tangible and intangible values—by providing a more robust, data-driven foundation for decision-making.

1

1 Rock Hewn Churches of Lalibela
  World Heritage Site, Ethiopia
2 Urban Design studio trip to
  Jordan River Valley
3 Urban Design studio trip to
  Jordan Desert
4 Studio-X Amman installation
  at Milan Design Week 2017

Amman

STUDIO-X AMMAN • Nora Akawi, Director

Studio-X Amman operates as a regional platform for conversations and research in architecture in the Arab region, with projects focused on the following:

• borderlands, territories, migration and citizenship
• housing speculation, excess, and abandonment
• preservation, erasures, and collective memory
• environmental histories, imaginaries, and injustice
• counter-narratives, archives, and representations

4

In Summer 2016, in partnership with Rasha Salti (independent curator and writer), Studio-X Amman curated a program of film screenings and discussions titled Like You've Never Been There: Cinema and the Memory of Cities. Over the course of a week during Ramadan, a program of film screenings, discussions, and conversations was held around cities, film, counter-narratives, and subjectivity. Speakers included Mona Assaad (independent filmmaker), Sarah Francis (independent filmmaker,), Omnia Khalil (participatory planner, urban anthropologist, and doctoral candidate at CUNY Graduate Center), Arya Lalloo (independent filmmaker), Khaled Malas (architect and doctoral candidate at NYU), Mpho Matsipa (curator of Studio-X Johannesburg), Elis Mendoza (doctoral candidate at Princeton University), and Rasha Salti (writer and independent film and arts curator). The second iteration of this program will be held in Fall 2017 in partnership with the Columbia Global Centers in Tunis.

In the prologue of *The Arab City* published by Columbia GSAPP in 2016, Lila Abu-Lughod (Professor of Anthropology and Women's Studies at Columbia University) introduces the personal library of her late mother, towering figure in urban studies and history Janet Abu-Lughod. The Janet Abu-Lughod Library was donated to Columbia University and is housed at Studio-X Amman. In partnership with Sijal Institute for Arabic Language and Culture in Amman, Studio-X Amman continues to develop the

Janet Abu-Lughod Library Seminar, a series of seminar discussions around readings selected from the library on questions of migration, racism, capitalization, and globalization in cities. The first iteration of the seminar led by Zachary Sheldon, doctoral candidate The University of Chicago, was presented at Sijal Institute in Summer 2016, and featured in Jadaliyya Cities in Spring 2017. This year the seminar "Before Before European Hegemony" will be led by Khaled Malas, doctoral candidate in Islamic Art History at New York University. Columbia GSAPP faculty members Hiba Bou Akar and Ziad Jamaleddine will also join the seminar for public lectures during the summer.

Mapping Borderlands, a project launched in August 2014 by Nora Akawi and Nina V. Kolowratnik continues to produce, through a Fall seminar course at Columbia GSAPP, new representations of border regions and new

definitions of territories that challenge static and exclusive understandings of geopolitical formations. In Fall 2016, seminar participants traveled to Jordan and Israel/Palestine, to conduct field visits and conversations supporting the mappings of borderlands. Seminar participants met with human rights activists in legal aid consultants in the Naqab desert, and in the Syrian town of Majdal Shams near Mount Hermon. They also worked closely with researcher, anthropologist, and doctoral candidate at Oxford University and former Janet Abu-Lughod Library Seminar participant, Allison Hartnett on the conditions of migrant workers and refugees along the Jordan Valley's agricultural communities. Mappings and essays produced so far through the seminar will culminate in an publication exhibition in 2017/2018.

Photographer and co-founder of Planar, Antonio Ottomanelli (photo-

2

3

grapher/Planar Gallery) and Jawad Dukhgan (Studio-X Amman) continue to develop Frozen Imaginaries, an initiative that investigates Amman's abandoned construction sites and speculative projects that were stopped or fell short of realizing their intended results. Architects, students, and participants took part in a third workshop in Fall 2016. The closing exhibition of the workshop took place in Turbo Gallery, downtown Amman, with critics and speakers including Javier Arpa (The Why Factory/Columbia GSAPP), Marco Ferrari and Elisa Pasqual (Studio Folder). The outcomes of this workshop were presented in an exhibition in Planar, Bari in February 2017. As part of the opening of this exhibition, a symposium was held also in Planar, with speakers including Columbia GSAPP faculty member Mark Wasiuta.

As part of the ongoing "Water Urbanism" project at the Architecture and Urban Design program at Columbia GSAPP, 27 students traveled to Amman in January 2017 for field research as part of the urban design studio course on water infrastructures and distribution inequalities in the Jordan Valley. Together with faculty members Kate Orff (director of the program), and Petra Kempf (Amman studio coordinator), as well as Ziad Jamaleddine, Laura Kurgan, and Nora Akawi, students visited farming community members, experts including anthropologists, hydrologists and geologists, government officials, and others. Throughout the Spring 2017 semester, students developed research mappings with the

guidance of Laura Kurgan and Grga Basic (Center for Spatial Research) which informed the design interventions addressing issues of migrants' and refugees' rights, sustainable tourism, borders and accessibility, cooperative economies. In addition to the program's exhibitions and publications, the projects will be exhibited at Studio-X Amman in 2017/2018.

During the Water Urbanism student travel in Spring 2017, and as part of the ongoing X-Talk series, Beth Stryker and Omar Nagati (founders of the Cairo Lab for Urban Studies, Training, and Environmental Research - CLUSTER) gave a lecture at Al Balad Theater to launch CLUSTER's year-long collaboration with the Center for Spatial Research and Studio-X Amman at Columbia GSAPP. To lead the project, Ali As'ad joined the CLUSTER team at Studio-X Amman, together with researchers Jomana Baddad, Razan Khalaf, Nadine Fattaleh, and Hani Qudah.

In Spring 2017, Studio-X also participated in Milan Design Week through a day-long symposium with a lecture by the design studio AAU Anastas from Bethlehem, and two roundtables. The first roundtable was titled "Days, Weeks, Biennials: Design in Unsettled Times" on the evolution of design events in the Middle East with the participation of Rana Beiruti (co-director of Amman Design Week), Deniz Ova (director of the Istanbul Design Biennial), Mohamed Elshahed (curator for Modern Egypt, British Museum), Karim Kattan (founder/director of El Atlal), and

Danah Abdulla (lecturer the University of Arts, London). The second roundtable was titled "Speculation, Excess, Abandonment: Beyond #RuinPorn, with the participation of Rene Boer (Failed Architecture), Jawad Dukhgan and Antonio Ottomanelli (Frozen Imaginaries), Ignacio Evangelista (photographer), Alison Hugill (Antiforum), and Eduardo Rega (lecturer at PennDesign, University of Pennsylvania).

1 Lebanon SW visit to Zaha Hadid's Issam Fares Institute for Public Policy and International Affairs at the American Univ. of Beirut
2 Lebanon Summer Workshop excursion to Baalbek

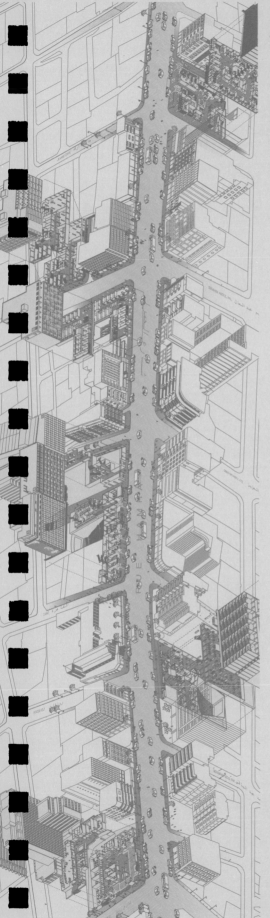

Lebanon

HAMRA STREET, A CASE OF URBAN RESILIENCE—BEIRUT, LEBANON • SUMMER 2016 • Ziad Jamaleddine and Makram el Kadi, coordinators, with Mayssa Jallad

The two-week workshop in Beirut, Lebanon culminated with the production of one continuous, (hybrid North/South) axonometric drawing of Rue Hamra. Along the one kilometer long area of study, eight 'modernist' structures neatly nested in the fabric are methodically surveyed and represented using an exploded axonometric drawing technique, uncovering their ground floor level(s) like an archeological site, and revealing their programmatic and architectural conversions and their relationships to the street.

The final product is a snapshot of the state of those buildings in one moment in time, precisely in August 2016. Few are mildly altered in commercial use, some are drastically transformed and dissected while preserving and mobilizing the spatial organization, or main architectural features (stairs, rails, pedestrian shortcuts through blocks...) others are frozen in time with no visible changes besides the aging quality of the finishes and cladding material.

All, with a lively and robust ground floor articulation uncovered through the drawing, demonstrate a high degree of resilience and a sense of purpose in serving and sustaining the health of a street in an ailing city.

August 5th – August 21st

Students: Kurtis Streich, Andrew Luy, Fancheng Fei, Xiaoxue Xiao, Zhuo Guo, Zhengyang Yue, Nabila Morales Pérez

Partner: historical documentation provided by the Arab Center for Architecture, Beirut

3   Axonometric Drawing of Rue Hamra in Beirut, Lebanon
4/5 Visit to unfinished Oscar Niemeyer project for Tripoli International Fair grounds
6   Group photo of workshop participants

3

4

5

6

Beijing

STUDIO-X BEIJING

Studio-X Beijing is setting up a research and knowledge exchange platform to investigate the most relevant issues of architecture and urbanism in contemporary China. There are three parallel lines of research, including urban regeneration, rural development and urban data science solutions. The goal behind these three continuous research topics is to explore novel strategies to tackle emerging urban issues. In 2016–2017, there were three pilot projects following such research topics.

China's urban development focus has been transformed from sprawling at the edge to densification at the center, from real estate driven megacities to ubiquitous rural construction, and from analog and physical urban space to the digital and online public sphere. Development interventions are no longer a service towards the powerful or the wealthy, nor the previous Chinese dream to become the next superpower to the globe. In order to be relevant in this age, we need to work closely with the local communities to explore a new participatory model for regeneration, to collaborate with multidisciplinary experts to create a holistic socio-spatial development model of the rural, and to develop new tools for us to handle complexity and generate insights.

Rural is the New Urban: Rural China Workshop

Rural China Workshop aimed to explore new possibilities in rural China. It is one of the earliest international academic endeavors to dive deep into the rural and village communities in China. The criticality of this issue is not about creating the next utopian, nostalgic, or post modern vision of rural lifestyle, but boldly confronting the most complex, urgent and neglected issues in current massive rural development, such as poverty, environment, and social inequality. GSAPP students and China's local partners spent one and half months, traveling to a dozen well selected villages in middle China, documenting their unique development models and reflections from the communities. Multidisciplinary knowledge has been plugged in to the research, from social science to economics and political science. This will set up a baseline of a long-term engagement of Studio-X Beijing to explore another territory of knowledge in rural China. The goal of the workshop is to redefine the practice model of architects and urbanists, co-creating values with local villagers.

Beijing Design Week: Data, Insight and Value-co-creation Workshop

Studio-X Beijing participates in Beijing Design Week, *Baitasi Remade*, in a hutong area in Beijing. Studio-X Beijing developed a two-way datafication system to create transparency of social impact generated from the event. In this workshop, local data agents collected data from the community while a real-time dashboard was broadcasting social impact during the event. The goal of this workshop is to experiment with how to go beyond the technocracy of data technology and explore new ways to empower the community through data technology.

1 Rural China
2 Beijing Design Week
3 Students conducting interviews in China

252

Shenzhen

HOUSING THE MAJORITY: BAISHIZHOU URBAN VILLAGE • SUMMER 2016 • Adam Frampton and Lindsey Wikstrom, coordinators

This workshop took on the question of Housing the Majority through the intense study and observation of Baishizhou, an urban village in Shenzhen. Embedded within the city, urban villages are contested territories of exceptional land ownership structures that have played an inextricable role in Shenzhen's rapid urban growth since 1980. With their incredible density and lack of zoning regulations, urban villages like Baishizhou have become not only a significant source of affordable housing for rural migrants, but also places with specialized economies and a vital street life absent elsewhere in the city. Increasingly, urban villages are seen not as slums or inferior forms of urbanism to be demolished, but rather valuable and unique components of the city to be preserved and maintained. The workshop framed the following questions: What is the future of Baishizhou, and more generally, the urban village? What value does the urban village provide to the city as a whole? How does the urban village challenge our thinking about both informal and formal modes of housing? How might the urban village be a prototype for new housing typologies?

In collaboration with Woods Bagot, Shenzhen Center for Design, Future + Academy, and Shenzhen University, Shenzhen, China

August 1 through August 30, 2016

Istanbul

STUDIO-X ISTANBUL

4

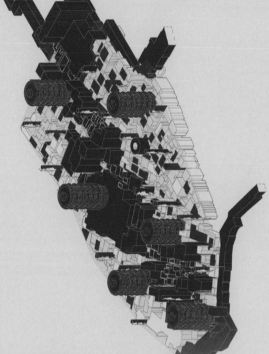

In 2016, Studio-X Istanbul was a key partner in the 3rd Istanbul Design Biennial, "ARE WE HUMAN? : The Design of the Species : 2 seconds, 2 days, 2 years, 200 years, 200,000 years", curated by Columbia GSAPP Professor and Dean Emeritus Mark Wigley and Princeton University Professor Beatriz Colomina. Opening on 22 October 2016, the Biennial included the work of many Columbia GSAPP faculty, students, and alumni, including Professor Andrés Jaque and his Office for Political Innovation as exhibition designer.

Studio-X Istanbul served as one of the five main venues for the Biennial, hosting one of the four "clouds" of overlapping projects called Designing Life. It featured experimental work on new forms of mechanical, electronic, and biological life—including projects by GSAPP professors Juan Herreros, Hilary Sample, and David Benjamin.

Columbia GSAPP faculty in the 3rd Istanbul Design Biennial:

- Mark Wigley, Professor and Dean Emeritus, biennial co-curator
- Andrés Jaque, Office for Political Innovation, exhibition designer
- Zeynep Celik Alexander: *Observer Affect / Observer Effect*, with Vanessa

6

4 Axon by Lindsey Wikstrom
5 Shenzhen
6 Workshop participants in Shenzhen

5

Heddle and Elliott Sturtevant
- David Benjamin, *The Living: Open Future*, with Sculpting Evolution Group, MIT Media Lab
- Juan Herreros, estudioHerreros: *The Designer Designed by the Humans*
- Laura Kurgan and the Center for Spatial Research: *Conflict Urbanism: Aleppo* and *1 Brain, 100 Billion Neurons, 100 Trillion Connections* with the Brown Institute for Media Innovation and the Zuckerman Institute at Columbia University
- Hilary Sample, MOS Architects: *An Unfinished Encyclopedia of Scale Figures Without Architecture / Model Furniture*
- Mark Wasiuta: *Detox USA* with Florencia Alvarez, and *Information Fall-Out: Buckminster Fuller's World Game* with Adam Bandler

Columbia GSAPP alumni:

- Urtzi Grau and Cristina Goberna Pesudo (Fake Industries Architectural Agonism): *Portable Indo Pacific*
- Mitch McEwen: *Glitter Disaster*
- Charles Renfro (Diller Scofidio + Renfro): *Unspoken*

Current students from the M.Arch and CCCP programs that participated in the Biennial included Becca R. Book, Ayesha S. Ghosh, Chia Hou, Jarrett D. Ley, Jesse L. McCormick, Iara Pimenta, Gizem Sivri, Miranda J. Shugars. Columbia alums Diana Cristobal, Jessica H. Ngan and Bart-Jan Polman also worked on the Biennial installations.

Superhumanity e-flux Architecture

GSAPP faculty Laura Kurgan, Felicity Scott, Mabel O. Wilson, Jorge Otero-Pailos, and Andrés Jaque also participated in the major SUPERHUMANITY e-flux architecture project accompanying the biennial. Visiting Professor Nikolaus Hirsch, who co-founded e-flux architecture, is co-editor of the series.

Design Chronology Turkey 1 Draft

Within the scope of the 3rd Istanbul Design Biennial, Studio-X Istanbul together with Pelin Dervi started a major research project: *Design Chronology Turkey 1 Draft*. The research focused on the 200 years of history of design in Turkey since the Ottoman reform of 1839 and brought together a group of more than 50 experts. The group playfully called itself the *Curious Assembly* and focused on topics such as packaging, lighting, graphics, communications and advertising, housing, furniture, music, toys, landscape, health, industrial buildings, ceramics and non-governmental organizations.

Archive of the Ephemeral

An open visual source was also initiated within the framework of the *Design Chronology Turkey 1 Draft* by Metehan Özcan through a collection of photographs. The archive is an invitation to revisit family photographs through a lens of design, trying to create new connections between people, places and objects.

X-Reads

In addition to operating as an active research platform during the biennial, Studio-X Istanbul also started an extensive collection of books and specialized reference material as resource and reading-room for designers and scholars interested in the history of design in Turkey.

MICRO-NETWORKS OF ISTANBUL'S STREETS • SUMMER 2016 • Phu Hoang, coordinator, with Nesli Naz Aksu

The "Micro-Networks of Istanbul's Streets" workshop researched and uncovered the urban identity of Tophane, a dynamic neighborhood in Istanbul that includes GSAPP's Studio-X facility. The neighborhood has historically had a diverse composition. Embedded within this mix are street-based micro-scale economic networks essential to Tophane's everyday life. These networks exist beneath the surface but are integral to the neighborhood's everyday life and identity, from corner shops (bakkal) that sell goods to residents using buckets lowered from above to semi-clandestine urban recycling networks to the extensive community of food cart hawkers. With support from Studio-X Istanbul, the workshop asked students to conduct "live research" of the micro-scale urban networks in Tophane through research, interviews, and drawings. Their research generated proposals for design interventions in the micro-networks, which were similarly small-scale while imagining possible futures as Tophane rapidly transforms with much of the city. The research and design proposals were exhibited in Studio-X Istanbul and became part of a series of workshop pamphlets.

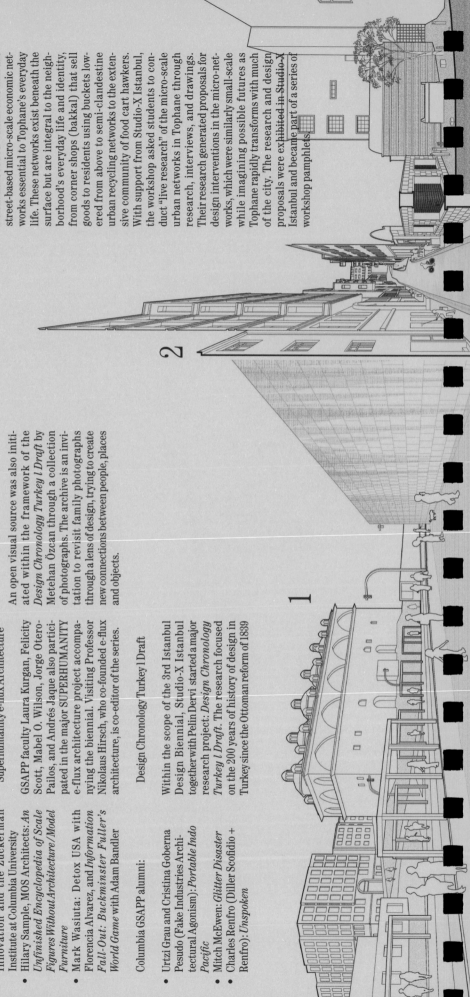

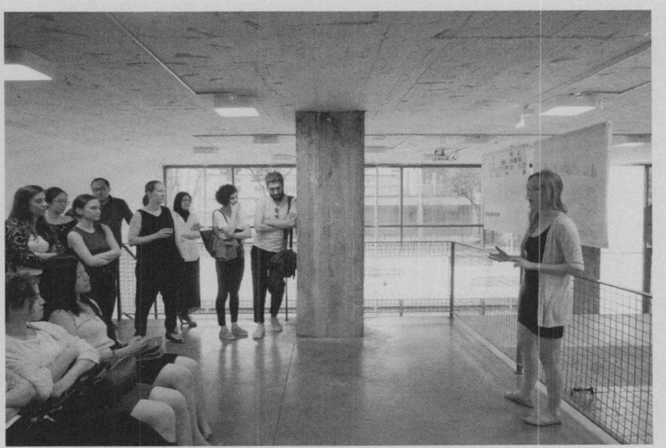

3

5

4

1/2 Micro-Networks of Istanbul's streets, drawing by Jean Gu
3 Istanbul Summer Workshop participants
4 Hilary Sample/MOS Architects installation at Poyraz Tutuncu at Istanbul Design Biennial
5 Mitch McEwen installation at Sahir Ugur Eren at Istanbul Design Biennial

Johannesburg

STUDIO-X JOHANNESBURG

Book Launches
November 19, 2016
Gallery MOMO, Parktown North, Johannesburg

Mabel O. Wilson's *Begin with the Past*, and Shatema Threadcraft's *Intimate Justice: The Black Female Body and Body Politic* were hosted by Gallery MOMO, Johannesburg.

Both books take into account debates on African American history, feminism and modern body politics. Both books confront difficult histories as a way to shed light onto what otherwise would have been forgotten.

In her opening remarks Mabel O. Wilson said that, "it is time to think critically about humanity and space," as a way to reflect on the implications of building a museum within a space that symbolises a violent and painful African American history. Wilson recounted how efforts to build the museum were thwarted by white racist Congressmen and how this did not stop activists and civil society from trying to get the museum built. They linked the struggle to build the museum to politics, labour movements, and civil rights work. The museum was signed into law in 2002 after a long and protracted battle through the 1990s, after which, an international competition was held to find suitable architects to build it. One of the main challenges was to find an appropriate site to build the museum. It was finally decided that it will be built on the prominent National Mall which is situated next to the White House in the US Capitol—for the public and for the world to see. The design work and building happened simultaneously to encompass different kinds of spatial and material strategies in order to tell the African American story. The museum illuminates like a lantern at different times of the day, particularly when it's dark. It is next to the Washington Monument which is in classic white, this represents an interesting juxtaposition of *light* and *darkness* given Washington DC's history with slavery. The Museum ties in with the history and iconography of the National Mall.

In Shatema Threadcraft's book titled, *Intimate Justice: The Black Female Body and Body Politic* she charts the long and incomplete path of female inequality as a path marked by sexual terrors, race, and violence. The book brings together the insights of black feminist thinkers as well as their critiques, and conceptions of modern body politics. Her objective is to locate the presence of the black female body in the past, present, and future in body politics. She writes about the disproportionate violence the black female body has had to endure. At the height of American racial oppression,

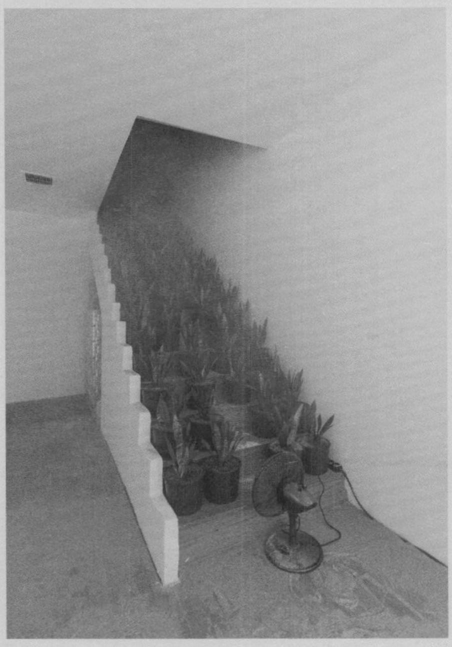

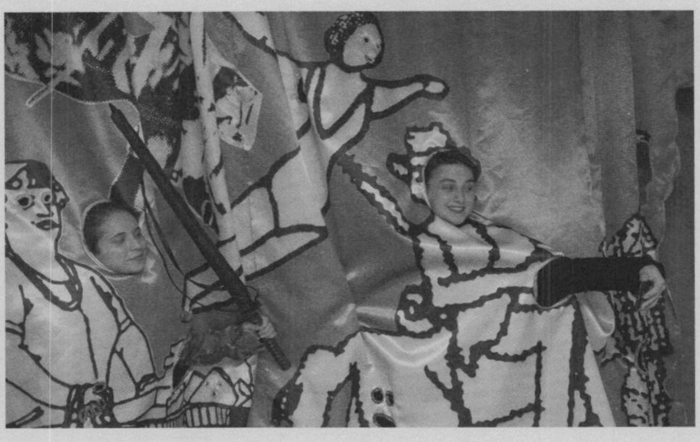

1

Threadcraft argues, black women were subject to systematic sexual assault and that rape never became as powerful a symbol of racial oppression as lynching.

Panel Discussion
December 9, 2016
Avery Hall

On the occasion of the lecture entitled: *Architecture Practice and the City: Cape Town and Sao Paulo*, on 9 December 2016, GSAPP, in collaboration with Studio-X Johannesburg and Studio-X Rio, co-hosted a panel discussion between two design firms: Marta Moreira of MMBB (São Paulo, Brazil) and Heinrich and Ilze Wolff of Wolff Architects (Cape Town, South Africa). The panel discussion explored whether design has transformative possibilities in urban contexts that are characterized by colonial legacies and ongoing socio-political inequality. Each firm briefly presented their respective projects followed by a conversation moderated by Mabel Wilson.

Wolff Architects, are a Cape Town-based design practice that is concerned with confronting socio-spatial inequality and the legacy of the apartheid landscape in post-apartheid South Africa. Their practice is not only transdisciplinary, but it also aims to disrupt strict distinctions between research and practice. In a context where architects constitute a minority, Wolff refocuses the value that citizens have to engage in the shaping of our/their own built environment. Wolff Architects presented their project: *The Watershed*—a market, incubator, and public street. It is located in Cape Town's Waterfront—prime real-estate site for high-end commercial and residential redevelopment, tourism, and leisure, that historically served as a site for prisoners and as a site for intense maritime activity. The Watershed proposed an aggregation of micro-economic enterprises whose scale and density was not only informed by the differentiated spatiality and relative programmatic porosity found in informal trading spaces of Du Noone. It also sought to challenge the traditional 'super-tenant' retail patterns, that characterizes the V&A Waterfront's model of re-development.

MMBB is a notable architecture practice in São Paulo with regard to design investigation and urban debates in São Paulo across multiple area: academia, research, large-scale infrastructure, and residential projects. Their project, *Jardim Edite*, is a social housing project, designed in collaboration with H+F. *Jardim Edite* is a 252 unit, high density social housing project, that includes various community facilities: a nursery, hospital, school and healthcare center, in the center of São Paulo.

Both MMBB and Wolff Architects reflected on the limits of utopian design visions for openness and integration when faced with power asymmetries, the logic of neo-liberal capitalist development, as well as pressing socio-economic insecurity. For example, in their discussion of community participation, Wolff revealed that because their imagined community for the market were marginalized urban traders and micro-enterprises, their client opted for a more carefully curated tenant profile that would be in keeping with their primary consumers. On the other hand, *Jardim Edite* stood as an example of community mobilization and the complementary advantages of a mixed income community the architects were ultimately unable to achieve their desired goals of openness and interconnectivity between the different design elements.

Nevertheless, the significance of these projects is that, unlike most other social housing projects or trading spaces, they are not built on the outskirts of a city. Both *Jardim Edite* and *The Watershed*, serve as examples of design projects that have emerged at the intersection of private and public sector interests, the strength (or weakness) of community mobilizations, complementary advantages of a diversified design programming, and strategies that subvert functionally and socially homogenous urban environments. Another question that this dialogue threw into sharp relief was not only the role of good design but also the extent to which the architect has the capacity to serve as both a spatial and political agent, within the context of increasingly privatized urban space?

1 Heinrich and Ilse Wolff present at Architecure Practice and the City: Rio de Jeneiro and Johannesburg

Copenhagen

CHER • SUMMER 2016 • Caitlin Blanchfield, Farzin Lotfi-Jam, Leah Meisterlin, coordinators

Cher is a digital platform that allows users to offer and reserve objects by the minute, whether in the home or public space. Community-driven and crowd-sourced, Cher identifies untapped opportunities within sharing-economy social platforms and the communities that comprise dynamic urban environments.

For the GSAPP summer workshop, students alphatested the app, amassing a photographic taxonomy of Copenhagen. As investigators of the city, they discovered unseen public spaces and novel interior objects through documentation-driven derives and voyeuristic explorations of their own accommodations and the city's public spaces. Through photo taking and annotating, students compiled the initial listings for Cher, to be used by focus group testers and ultimately for its launch at the Oslo Architecture Triennale. With the dominant narratives of Danish design culture and Copenhagen's public landscape in mind, they sought out the counter-narratives that captured the complex, the quirky, and the real sides of a heterogenous city. Meanwhile, in public workshops and conversations students joined an open debate about the nature of sharing in Copenhagen and the broader effects of the sharing economy on cities.

Rio de Janeiro

III

4:38 AM   Available Today

Architecture Tour

BIG's first main architecture project - the Mountain.

Offered by: Violet Whitney

Cost : It is free

Suggested Use : architecture tour

2 Wireframe of Cher app for the Oslo Architecture Triennial
3 Studio-X Rio exhibition for UN Habitat III in Quito, Peru
4 Studio-X Rio
5 Metrópole Expandida exhbition of Urban Design studio work at Studio-X Rio

STUDIO-X RIO • Pedro Rivera

Rio de Janeiro is one of the most emblematic cities in Latin America. Within the lush tropical forest and famous beaches, twelve million people face the challenge of living in an extremely unequal urban environment where precarious infrastructure, lack of housing and high violence rates severely affect one's opportunities. For a short period of time, when Brazil's economy was booming and the city being prepared for the 2016 Olympic Games, the flow of investments and major urban transformations produced a hope that things would change. Today, less than one year after the event, all the promises seem like a distant echo. The city—and the country—are overwhelmed by a complex economic and political crisis that will last well into the future. Within this context, the urban agenda became more urgent and more critical.

As part of its core mission, Studio-X Rio is permanently experimenting with new forms of exchanging knowledge by relying on continual collaboration with GSAPP faculty and students, other Columbia University initiatives such as the Global Center, and on outside institutions, academic partners, and companies. The network built over the years is Studio-X Rio's most important asset.

From 2011 to 2017 GSAPP had a privileged opportunity to deeply investigate Rio and other Brazilian cities. The agreement with the City of Rio was key to the implementation of Studio-X Rio and to place it as a leading institution in Brazil dedicated to a public program on architecture and cities, available through an intense set of exhibitions, workshops, and lectures. During the period, thirty GSAPP studios made Studio-X Rio their basecamp to explore the country challenges, dilemmas, and innovations and, more importantly, to promote knowledge exchange via academic research, case studies and open conversations.

Studio-X Rio's leading initiative followed the 2015 GSAPP conference *Housing the Majority*, and is exploring different relations and forms of low-income housing in Brazil. The first part of the investigation looked at squats and social movements, and was exhibited in Rio de Janeiro, Rotterdam, and in a condensed version at GSAPP. The second round, recently displayed at Studio-X Rio, looked at housing projects to raise the question "What makes good social housing?" The initiative has partnered with Urban Planning studios, led by Alejandro Castro Mazzarro/Clara Irazábal and Jose Luis Vallejo, as well as a M.Arch. studio led by Juan Herreros and Ignacio Galán, that was awarded by the American Institute of Architects.

257

New York

NYC UPPER WEST SIDE TECH CORRIDOR • SUMMER 2016 • Patrice Derrington, coordinator

The workshop investigated the potential emergence of a "technology corridor" (similar to Kendall Square, Cambridge, for example) which connects the existing Columbia University campuses, biotech research and other such facilities in the Harlem west neighborhood. Starting with a spatial-economic analysis of some existing nodes of tech research—NYC's F-train corridor (Flatiron district), Brooklyn's Tech Hub, and Cambridge's Kendall Square—and seeking key components of such successful incubator projects, and considering the history of the targeted urban area and the instances of emerging technology groupings, the possibilities and challenges for the evolution of this neighborhood will be evaluated.

As a site for this experiment, the workshop studied two sites in Lichtenberg, a district in the Eastern part of Berlin, set within the context of tower-in-the-park development, built in the second half of the 20th century. The neighborhood consists primarily of prefab concrete buildings ("Plattenbau"), which were developed by the socialist East German government using WBS70, a standardized offsite construction system. Site visits to experimental housing projects as well as visits to current emergency shelters provided input for negotiating a balance between shared and private spaces, between off-site and on-site construction, and for thinking of integration as interaction.

Berlin

BERLIN: IMMEDIATE SHELTER-SUSTAINABLE NEIGHBORHOOD • SUMMER 2016 • Kaja Kühl, coordinator

In 2015 Germany had taken in over 1 million "newcomers" primarily from Syria, Iraq, and Afghanistan. Berlin, already experiencing a housing shortage even without additional new arrivals, needs innovative models for temporary and permanent shelter to accommodate the newcomers quickly in decent housing, while also taking a long view on sustainable growth for future generations and societal groups. The workshop teamed up with students from Berlin and recent newcomers to develop convincing concepts for housing that can be built fast and become an integral part of the neighborhood in the long run.

1 Berlin: Immediate Shelter
  Sustainable Neighborhood
  workshop axon drawing by Lama
  Suleiman, Karol Stern, Lia
  Soorenian, Michael Nickerson
2 Site visit to existing
  refugee center
3 NYC Upper West Side Tech
  Corridor Summer Workshop,
  site map

Amsterdam Avenue

Broadway

CLIMATE CHANGE CHANGES EVERY- THING

Columbia GSAPP Design Mantras, 2017

Taken together, these statements can be read as a sort of time-sensitive mantra for the disciplines of the built environment, a set of pedagogical imperatives that have emerged from the school, and a statement of engagement as an institution. We understand these six statements, dispersed throughout this book, as an urgent call to action for Columbia GSAPP, and we recognize their relevance and implications for the larger global community of which the school is inextricably embedded within. They address issues of political engagement, social equity, representation, pursuing action on climate change, global perspectives, cultural diversity, and developing professional practice in all disciplines of the built environment in which we study and practice.

Urban Design
Kate Orff, Director

Urban Planning
Weiping Wu, Director

Historic Preservation
Jorge Otero-Pailos,
Director

Real Estate
Development
Patrice Derrington,
Director

Introduction to
Architecture
Danielle Smoller,
Director

New York / Paris
Danielle Smoller,
Director
Patrick O'Connor,
Paris Coordinator

Urban Design

Kate Orff, Director

The Urban Design Program is focused on the city as an agent of resilient change, and the role of design in redefining the 21st century urban landscape. The program advances new paradigms of research, practice, and pedagogy to meet the urgent challenges of rapid urbanization, increasing threats of climate change, and social inequality. Students and faculty in the program struggle with the venerable if necessarily shifting question: what is "the good city?"

Global shifts in the climate system require resetting the paradigms that have guided urban growth for centuries. The program frames the city not as a fixed, delineated territory—a modernist fixation on boundaries—but instead as a gradient of varied landscapes supported by networks of food, energy, resources, culture, transportation, and capital. In this light, the historical terms—urban, rural, or suburban are no longer sufficient to address the "wicked problems" of climate change and social justice. Program work stresses near and long-term threats to local, regional, and global ecosystems, framing urban design as both an inclusive, activist, tools-based project for specific sites and communities, and as a critical project examining urban form, knowledge and research.

Students and faculty work together over a series of three intensive semesters to weave a multi-scalar analysis of urban-regional fabrics and infrastructures with on-the ground, detailed studies of places and lived conditions. New York City's five boroughs serve as a primary initial case study for a design methodology; the scope expands in the second semester to regional research in New York's Hudson River Valley, and concludes in the final semester with investigations into urban design for climate adaptation and equity in emerging global agglomerations in the Middle East, Asia, Africa and South America.

1
2

URBAN DESIGN STUDIO 1: THE 5 BOROUGH STUDIO ¶ SUMMER 2016 ¶ KAJA KÜHL, JAMES KHAMSI, COORDINATORS; BRIAN BALDOR, DAVID BROWN, ELLEN NEISES, THAD PAWLOWSKI, BEN BRADY, CRITICS, WITH DESPO THOMA ¶ The 5 Borough Studio introduced students to an urban design process where site and program are not a given, but are treated as principal variables of urban design thinking. Working in multiple scales as well as multiple time frames was an integral part of this investigation to design an intervention that follows a speculative hypothesis for the future of the city. ¶ As the boundaries between the responsibility of the state to provide public space and public goods (such as transportation, education, water, power, etc.) and the degree to which private entities provide such goods blur, the idea of the "common" or the "collective" may offer a third alternative to "public" and "private," which does not mean closed off to all. The idea of land or services that are commonly owned and managed speaks to a 21st century sensibility of participative citizenship and peer-to-peer production. Five neighborhoods in New York City were used as the laboratory for experimenting with the idea of a collective city.

3
4
5
6
7

URBAN DESIGN STUDIO 2: JUSTICE IN PLACE: DESIGN FOR EQUITY AND REGIONAL CURRENTS, THE CASE OF POUGHKEEPSIE, NY, AND THE HUDSON VALLEY ¶ FALL 2016 ¶ LEE ALTMAN + MICHAEL MURPHY, COORDINATORS; PIPPA BRASHEAR, JAMES CARSE, CHRISTOPHER KRONER, SANDRO MARPILLERO, JUSTIN MOORE, AND DAVID SMILEY, CRITICS; WITH ELENI GKLINOU AND NANS

VORON ¶ The Fall Semester Studio was organized around the Hudson River Valley, a region defined by multiple systems, histories, and geographies that touch the lives of millions. "Region" was defined neither by political boundary nor physical area but as multiple non-contiguous territories delimited by specific temporal and spatial parameters, from income to sewage, from topography to zoning, from commuting to homelessness. In other words, the term "city" implicated a vast network of politically inflected relations, a concentration and particularization of densities, ecologies, and economies. ¶ Drawing from the evolving discourse of spatial justice brought to the fore by scholars like Edward Soja as well as groups like Black Lives Matter, and responding to the shifting political climate that dominated the public arena in the 2016 elections, studio projects identified various manifestations of injustice evidenced in, but not unique to, Poughkeepsie—social, economic, environmental, and others—and proposed design strategies to challenge them. Students also examined the functioning of various other American cities and regions, offering a basis for examination of the Hudson Valley as a larger system of mobility and production. ¶ Working with residents, local non-profits, and officials from the City of Poughkeepie and Dutchess County, students examined on-the-ground conditions, as well as spatial and policy debates about redevelopment and urban change. Each student team formulated specific research agendas, studied institutional actors, and proposed specific design interventions.

8
9
10
11
12

URBAN DESIGN STUDIO 3: WATER URBANISM ¶ SPRING 2017 ¶ KATE ORFF, STUDIO COORDINATOR, WITH NORA AKAWI, DILIP DACUNHA, ZIAD JAMALEDDINE, PETRA KEMPF, LAURA KURGAN, GEETA MEHTA, AND JULIA WATSON, CRITICS ¶ Water is constantly in motion, changing states, crossing borders, nourishing (and destroying) life. How can water

and urbanism be considered together as a generative frame for urban design practice, social life, and ecological regeneration? The spring semester urban design studio investigated urbanization challenges in two regions with robust ecological contexts, intense migration, resource conflicts, and urban growth trajectories: Amman and the Lower Jordan River Valley, and Kolkata, India and the Sundarbans mangrove forest. In both cases, the studio investigated the dynamics of water flux relative to migration and climate change, alongside the generation of new social infrastructure, public space, and urban design in an expanded rural-urban context. Students studied large-scale territorial independencies, operational landscapes, and simultaneously identified pilot sites of detailed investigation for design exploration, linking the material and particular with the geographical and generic. Students explored the operative potential of scale as a strategy and developed a multi-scalar, ecological framework for designing the architecture, cities, and landscapes of the future, and investigated the power and potential of ecology and urban design as a tool to a create a platform for exchange in these contested zones.

URBAN THEORY AND DESIGN IN THE POST-INDUSTRIAL AGE ¶ SUMMER 2016 ¶ NOAH CHASIN, INSTRUCTOR, WITH ANTHONY ACCIAVATTI ¶ This course was an introduction to the historiographical, theoretical, critical, and formal vocabularies of postwar urbanism throughout Europe, the U.S., and beyond. The class was arranged thematically and, in a larger context, chronologically. We discussed the deployment of new urban design strategies against the backdrop of rapidly proliferating discursive and technological advances. From modernization leading to urbanization, from suburban sprawl to New Urbanism, from techno-utopian Megastructures to participatory and informal urbanism, we measured the merits of various paradigms (and their critiques) against one another in an effort to understand the processes that provide the structures and infrastructures for the world's built environments. The course built toward the present with the aim of measuring the ever-increasing influence of ecological paradigms of globalization on both theory and design. As an extension of the history and theory component, the course provided an opportunity to demonstrate the importance of writing as a key tool for urban designers through research-oriented essays.

DIGITAL TECHNIQUES ¶ SUMMER 2016 ¶ PHU DUONG, COORDINATOR; ELIZABETH

BARRY, KYLE HOVENKOTTER, MICHAEL SZIVOS, INSTRUCTORS, WITH ZHOU WU ¶ This course introduced contemporary representational techniques for urban design. It brought meaning to questions which underlie the nature of how urban designers think, work, and communicate. By combining the conventions of static and moving drawings, students were offered opportunities to discover the value of spatial data exploration and analysis (ArcGIS); descriptive and generative 3d modeling (Rhino, Grasshopper), and storytelling with motion graphics compiled as video (After Effects) into new constructs for envisioning urban space. The multiple formats broadened possibilities for analysis and idea creation to support nonlinear processes. By virtue of provocation, content-rich techniques enabled students to navigate their individual agency across collaborative settings. ¶ This year lessons were guided by an investigation of public space in the city. New York City was the stage where the class explored the meaning of "public" today. A series of integrated exercises allowed students to learn software to visualize and understand urban systems—both visible and embedded relationships across urban space and time. By contemplating the physical makeup of the commons, students develop their digital skillsets and methodologies for urban design study and speculation.

CASE STUDIES IN URBAN WATERFRONT PLANNING & DESIGN: CONSTRUCTING COLLABORATIVE UNDERSTANDINGS ¶ FALL 2016 ¶ ANDREA KAHN, INSTRUCTOR ¶ Waterfront transformation projects involve many players, demand many forms of expertise, and have urban impacts that play out over many scales. Local municipal planning agencies, regional port authorities, design professionals, private developers, as well as preservationists, community actors, and engineers each bring value-laden assumptions to the table regarding project goals and desired outcomes. By applying a multi-disciplinary perspective to the study of cases from New York, metropolitan regions in Norway, Sweden, Denmark, France, Germany and the Netherlands, the seminar addressed the numerous, and often incommensurate, value systems at work in any large-scale, long-term urban transformation effort.

CLIMATE CHANGE AND GLOBAL CITIES ¶ SPRING 2017 ¶ MICHAEL KIMMELMAN, INSTRUCTOR ¶ Climate Change and Global Cities, an urban design seminar offered by New York Times Architecture critic Michael Kimmelman, asked a multidisciplinary group of students to consider the interrelated social and infrastructural threats that climate change poses to cities. The class looked at cases such as heat waves in Chicago, storm surges in New York, water scarcity in Mexico City, and flooding in Guangzhou, examining the myriad ways in which climate change stresses city systems. Throughout the semester, guest speakers brought their experiences confronting these challenges to the class: among others, Henk Ovink discussed bringing Dutch water management strategies to the international stage, Shaun Donovan explained how the Obama administration had approached climate resiliency, and Kai-Uwe Bergmann presented the Bjarke Ingels Group's work on the Rebuild by Design competition and the resulting Big U project. Students were asked to propose a design or policy intervention and grapple with its political and social ramifications in a particular city, making a case for action in the face of inevitable competing priorities.

URBAN DESIGN NOW: NEW PARADIGMS & NEW PRACTICES ¶ FALL 2016 ¶ KATE ORFF, INSTRUCTOR ¶ This seminar explored urban design practice through the lens of infrastructure and activism. Critical readings that conceptualize the contemporary city from 1960 through the present were interspersed with analyses of case studies of catalytic urban design projects and emergent forms of design practice. Our aim was to gain new perspectives on how to better transform knowledge into world-changing design practice. ¶ Students examined a range of modes of urban design practice today, from non-profits to global NGOs, to local, experimental research units based in academia to labs based within for-profit firms. We explored how research-driven design culture is moving beyond traditional notions of site- and service-driven practice to define interventions at multiple scales with social and environmental purpose. ¶ Faced with massive challenges of climate change, social inequity, and privatization, we tend towards inaction, bogged down by contrasting perceptions, overwhelmed by the scope and interrelated extents of the most pressing issues of our time. This seminar therefore aimed to arm the urban design student to thoughtfully engage these challenges with specific tools for research, analysis, decision making, and participation to reveal methods and means of transformative critical practice.

FABRICS AND TYPOLOGIES: NY/GLOBAL ¶ FALL 2016 ¶ RICHARD PLUNZ, INSTRUCTOR ¶

This course explored the meaning of urban building typology and fabric in the evolution of cities worldwide. It questioned the canons of architectural and urban historiography that tend to overemphasize the isolated monument rather than fabric. Students scrutinized the evolutionary history of anonymous urban fabric, often created by the uncelebrated architect or builder, which comprises the major building volume of this and all cities. The focus was on the culture of housing with the intent to grasp the political and tectonic devices that lead to specific fabrics in specific urban contexts. The city became a crucible to be understood both forwards and backwards in time, from extant present-day realities to underlying formational causes and vice versa. Beginning with New York City, this exercise in urban forensics was played back for other global cities. Seminar participants translated the technique and values learned from the New York case to case studies embedded in their own local knowledge, culminating in a final forum in which comparative projected architectural transformation of fabrics became the basis of critical discourse.

PUBLIC SPACE AND RECOMBINANT URBANISM ¶ SPRING 2017 ¶ DAVID GRAHAME SHANE, INSTRUCTOR ¶ This seminar examined how cities grow and develop over time. It employed a theory of urban actors and conceptual models as tools for the analysis of the city and its design ecologies. The course mapped transformations in these actors and models at various scales over time in specific locations. Actors use conceptual models to link to the larger forces shaping a city network. Students constructed a layered model of a city of their own choosing and employed models derived from the course to illustrate the structure and growth of that city, including its representative public spaces and urban fabrics. Groups this year made models of and studied multi-use spaces in Ahmadabad, Bangalore, Guangzhou, Johannesburg, Mumbai and Santiago.

READING NEW YORK URBANISMS ¶ SUMMER 2016 ¶ CASSIM SHEPARD, INSTRUCTOR; WITH NANS VORON AND GRACE MILLS ¶ This course introduced urban design students to New York City as a laboratory of historical experiments in both designing and understanding the urban environment. The goal was to arm students with the observational and representational tools to "read" the city and the multiple forces that influence its physical form and social experience. The class delved into specific places throughout the five boroughs of

New York and analyzed how different actors—writers, artists, designers, real estate developers, and government agencies—have interpreted, represented, or intervened in these sites over time.

NEW TOWN TO SMART CITY ¶ SPRING 2017 ¶ DAVID SMILEY, INSTRUCTOR ¶ This class examined the spatial management of populations as demonstrated in two paradigmatic instances: the "New Town" of the mid-20th century and the "Smart City" of the early 21st century. We explored how these would-be total urban forms have been theorized, represented, planned, designed, and sometimes built and experienced. ¶ The New Town was modernism's answer to the troubled metropolis. Embedded in both practical and utopian discourses of improvement, the mid-20th century New Town entailed the deployment of architecture to manage newly delineated territories. The interaction among people, goods, land, policies, and technologies was a singular event to be controlled. This goal reached across scales, economies, and experiences, from house plans, to streets, to regional infrastructures. This logic was adopted by professional organizations, government bodies, and international institutions, under varied and unequal conditions, and New Towns were built across the globe. ¶ In recent years, the discourse of totality and management continues in the Smart City and in the deployment of Information and Communication Technology (ICT). Smart Cities are sometimes fixed territories like their New Town cousins but increasingly, ICTs are embedded in existing patterns of urbanization. In either case, "Smart" entails the monitoring of resources, bodies, activities, spaces, and infrastructures via ubiquitous computing, sensing networks and widespread surveillance. All scales of life are measured as a promise of frictionless interaction, environmental balance and, unsaid or celebrated, economic development. Like New Towns, Smart Cities and ICTs have been deployed across the globe, the effects of which are in their infancy. ¶ The class asked how historical and contemporary forms of urban totalization can be charted, discussed and (con)tested.

1

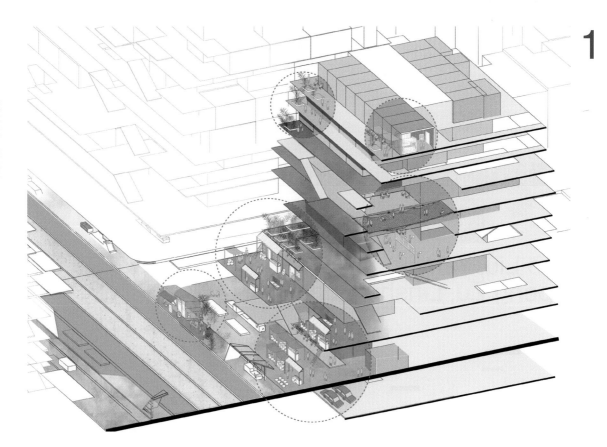

Deniz Onder, Evelina Kondel,
Mayra Mahmood, Vrinda Sharma

2

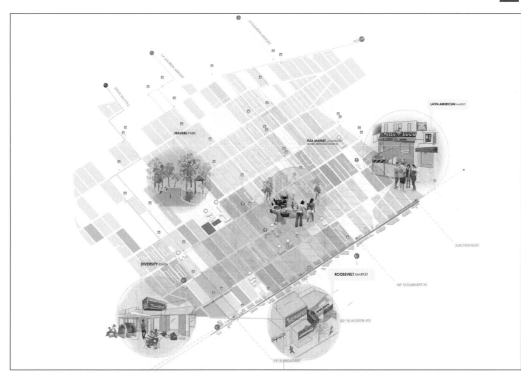

Evelina Kondel, Mario Andre, Ulloa Leon,
Vrinda Sharma, Yiran Hu

Jinbao Liu, Yanyan Xu,
Wanpeng Zu, Linshu Huang

4

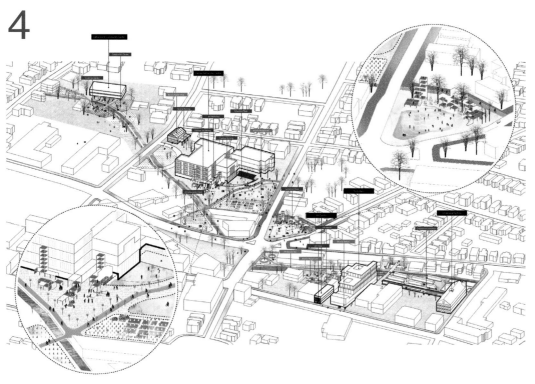

Daiyue Lyu, Haochen Yang,
Liwen Zhao, Zhaoyu Zhu

5

Paul Xiaopu Wang,
Zhen Quan, Tianyang
Xie, Grace Ng

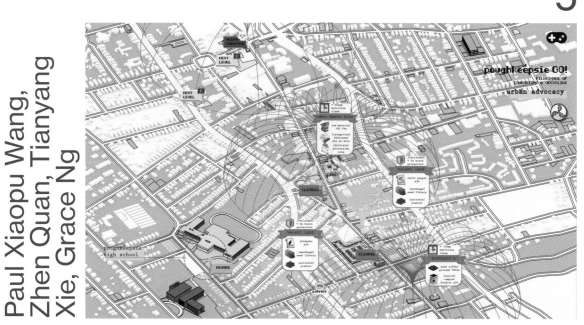

6

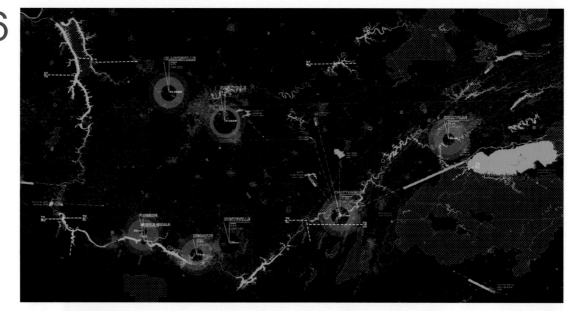

Carmelo Ignaccoio, Deniz Onder, Dissa
Pidanti Raras, Andrea Benavides Ward

7

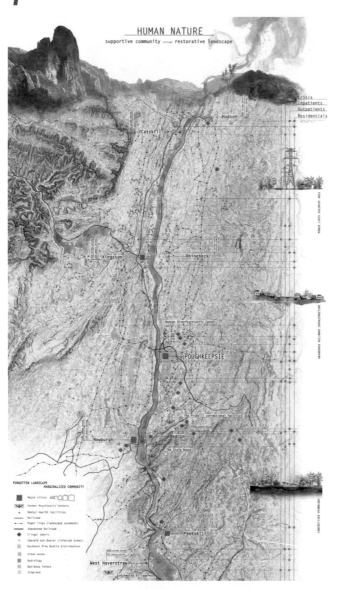

Carmelo Ignaccoio, Maria Isabel,
Carrasco Vintimilla, Mario Andres,
Ulloa Leon, Shuman Wu

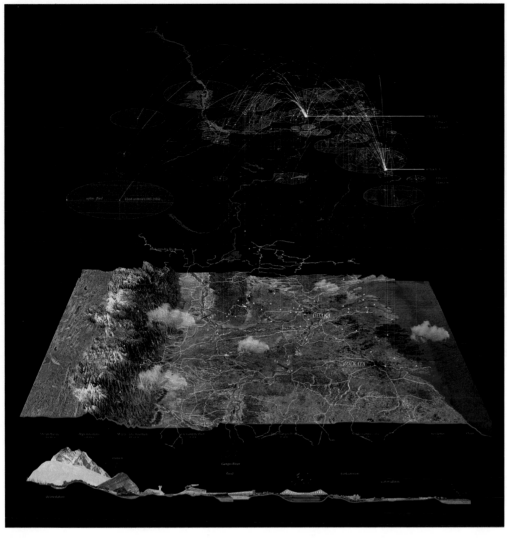

Carmelo Ignaccolo, Dissa
Raras, Deniz Onder

8
9

Chris Chiou, Kristen Reardon,
Mario Ulloa, Grace Ng

10

Majed Abdulsamad,
Isabel Carrasco, Jun Seong
Ahn, Haochen Yang

Bridgett Cruz, Shuman Wu,
Huai Kuan Chung, Jiahong Lu

11

12

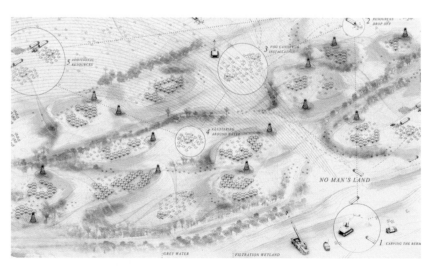

Gariela Fiorentino, Ahmed Jawdat, Zarith
Pineda, Yang Liao, Mayra Mahmood

The Columbia University Master of Science in Urban Planning is an accredited two-year program of professional education. Actively engaged in practice, our curriculum connects the study of the urban built environment with grounded analysis of socioeconomic and political conditions. We explore the tensions between market forces, civil society, and the goals of planning, paying special attention to the role of urban analytics and the quest for social justice. Students learn to evaluate and shape efforts to develop and enhance cities and their communities in ways that foster healthy and sustainable living.

Located in New York City, our program promotes a global outlook. We look to planning issues locally and internationally for studio projects, classroom case studies, and thesis research. By studying the impact of global linked processes (e.g. immigration and climate change) as well as local conditions on cities and communities, we think creatively about planning and policy approaches to improve processes and outcomes in cities around the world.

Our students connect challenges of urban development, sustainability and equity with the political and socioeconomic conditions that define them. They learn to engage and assess the increasing abundance and

Weiping Wu, Director

availability of data to address urban problems and inform planning efforts. Throughout the curriculum, the emphasis is on real-world problems and how planners can act to improve the lives of urban residents. Students are required to choose at least one concentration area among four options: Built Environment, Community and Economic Development, International Planning and Development, and Urban Analytics.

Built Environment

Planning of the built environment balances competing demands on the land and environment brought about by urban and rural growth. This concentration prepares students to work with stakeholders to guide public and private development processes in ways that ensure an adequate supply of land and resources to meet people's present and future needs, while complying with environmental and fiscal requirements.

Community & Economic Development

Planning education promotes the redistribution of resources and social justice in cities as much as the creation of wealth. This concentration prepares students to undertake community and neighborhood planning and decision-making,

local economic development, and/or housing and redevelopment activities. Students examine resource, institutional and socioeconomic issues at various spatial scales, paying particular attention to disadvantaged population and communities.

International Planning & Development

This concentration prepares students to work with governments, NGOs, consulting firms, and international development agencies around the world. Students receive multidisciplinary training to understand the impact of global flows as well as local conditions on cities and communities in various world regions and to think creatively about planning approaches in developing countries.

Urban Analytics

This concentration prepares students to engage and assess the increasing abundance and availability of data to address urban problems, collaborate on design projects for the built environment, and inform planning efforts within a variety of contexts and practices. Students acquire skills in data science and visualization, spatial and statistical analysis, and research design with stakeholder engagement, in addition to the planning skills taught in the core curriculum.

URBAN PLANNING STUDIO 1 ¶ REDEVELOPMENT OF BROOK-LYN WHOLESALE MARKET ¶ SPRING 2017 ¶ ELDAD GOTHELF, INSTRUCTOR ¶ The central question asked of the Brooklyn Wholesale Meat Market Studio was, "How can we add value to a fully operational wholesale market located along Sunset Park's waterfront?" The client, the New York City Economic Development Corporation, had two goals: maximizing the financial gains from this property as well as generating positive social impact. To meet the client's needs, studio members developed a comprehensive understanding of the site. Demographics, zoning and land use, transportation, and economic trends were researched. Studio members also engaged with community stakeholders such as the Community Board 7, Sunset Park Business Improvement District, and Carlos Menchaca City Council Office. The final product was a holistic plan to redevelop the site into a food distribution and manufacturing ecosystem, which includes co-packing space, a food incubator, step-up spaces, and a workforce training center. The plan included the site programming and architectural renderings, environmental sustainability policies and programs, and economic development strategies. At the end, studio members were given the opportunity to exhaustively explore urban planning issues in a practical setting.

URBAN PLANNING STUDIO 1 ¶ IMPROVING AIRPORT ACCESS AND ENVIRONMENTAL CONDITIONS ¶ SPRING 2017 ¶ FLOYD LAPP, INSTRUCTOR ¶ The New York City metropolitan area's airports are vital to the transportation and economy of the region. The future operations of some of these airports are vulnerable due to unsustainable planning decisions of the past. Two of the main challenges our airports face are risks associated with the effects of climate change and limited ground connections between the central business district and the airports. These issues will continue to worsen as climate change progresses and traffic congestion increases due to population growth and greater tourist demand. While some visionary proposals for resolving these challenges have been put forth, there have been few, if any, practicable actions taken toward improving the main resiliency and connectivity challenges the airports face. This studio explored realistic strategies to adapt to the dynamic transportation landscape of a 21st century city. We proposed context-appropriate solutions for climate change adaptation at LaGuardia and Teterboro Airports and innovative ground access improvements for John

F. Kennedy Airport. We consulted with professionals from relevant agencies such as the Port Authority of New York and New Jersey and the New York City Department of Transportation, and drew on the research of a number of primary and secondary sources to inform our decision-making.

URBAN PLANNING STUDIO 1 ¶ RIO: DESIGN THINKING FOR HEALTHY URBAN ENVIRONMENTS ¶ SPRING 2017 ¶ JOSE LUIS VALLEJO AND BELINDA TATO, INSTRUCTOR ¶ This studio centered around using urban planning and design to improve residential health conditions for those living in the Rio de Janeiro social housing complex formally known as Conjunto Residencial Prefeito Mendes de Moraes (Pedregulho). This project aimed to explore multiple options that activate underutilized public spaces within the building through design and ethnographic studies. The proposals illuminated both the opportunities for growth and the methods to which implementation could be achieved through facilitated toolkit processes. These interventions intended to spur grassroots actions for the improvement and maintenance of Pedregulho's culture, built environment, and community involvement.

URBAN PLANNING STUDIO 1 ¶ BELFAST, IRELAND: CITY CENTER IN DEVELOPMENT CONTEXT ¶ SPRING 2017 ¶ RICHARD PLUNZ, INSTRUCTOR ¶ This studio comprised both architecture and urban planning students in a joint project tasked with exploring scenarios for redevelopment of the City Centre of Belfast, Northern Ireland, including its reintegration with the surrounding city. The client and sponsor was the Belfast City Council and its Office of City Centre Development. Beginning in 1969 as a consequence of the sectarian conflicts in Belfast, strategies were implemented for partitioning the city, including a "ring of steel" around the City Centre that drastically reduced accessibility during daytime and effectively closed it to the public at night. The Centre was deliberately maintained as a "neutral" (i.e. uninhabited) zone. While the "ring of steel" no longer functions, the cumulative negative effects of this long period of isolation is evident. This studio was tasked with investigating the reintegration and renewal of the City Centre in concert with the de-partitioning process for the entire city. Proposals for the City Centre included heightened pedestrian linkages; investment in renewed transportation networks; rebuilding of "shatter zones;" and options for next generation cultural production. Both

spatial and economic redevelopment of the City Centre was considered, in the context of future economic potentials for Northern Ireland and with particular reference to options for new global investments in a post-Brexit era.

URBAN PLANNING STUDIO 1 ¶ DESIGNING A NEW MASTER PLAN FOR CHINATOWN ¶ SPRING 2017 ¶ ETHEL SHEFFER AND DOUGLAS WOODWARD, INSTRUCTORS ¶ The focus of the Reimagining Chinatown studio was to develop a framework to promote, preserve, and protect the historic singularity and cultural uniqueness of Manhattan's Chinatown by focusing on preventing resident displacement, supporting the area's economic vitality, and safeguarding neighborhood character. Primary research dealt with cultural identity and urban design, affordability and housing, economic development, and sanitation. At the urging of the studio's clients—Manhattan Borough President Gale Brewer and Councilmember Margaret Chin—the analysis led to the development of action plans in the form of six major initiatives: enhancing wayfinding, preserving community identity, promoting efficient circulation, improving living and street conditions, and securing housing tenure.

ADVANCED URBAN PLANNING STUDIO ¶ IMPROVING GROUND ACCESS TO JFK ¶ FALL 2016 ¶ FLOYD LAPP, INSTRUCTOR ¶ Many world cities have a one-seat transit ride to their major airports. This infrastructure does not exist in the New York metropolitan area. This condition is especially critical for JFK, the region's aviation hub with the potential to increase capacity by up to 50%. The subject has a history going back half a century and includes: reactivating the Rockaway Beach Branch of the Long Island Rail Road, a subway to bus at Howard Beach to JFK terminals, subway service from lower Manhattan and finally the opening of an automated guideway system known as Air Train in 2003. However, these services do not provide a one-seat ride from the central business district. With this background, what can be done to improve access to JFK? How will JFK be able to handle increased automobile traffic given the aging highway and parkway infrastructure? Are there other modal options that should also be explored? Based on the inventory of experiences, a preferred set of options was advanced.

ECONOMICS FOR PLANNERS ¶ FALL 2016 ¶ MOSHE ADLER, INSTRUCTOR ¶ This required course reviewed the basic concepts and methods of urban economics with a major emphasis on location and land-use economics. The course provided an examination of both equilibrium-based models and the new critical models derived from analyses of the production process and spatial organization. In addition to the lectures, students attended one of three weekly recitation sessions, which were assigned at the start of the semester.

PRIVATE PARTNERSHIPS, PRIVATIZATION, AND THE NEW CITY GOVERNMENT ❡ FALL 2016 ❡ MOSHE ADLER, INSTRUCTOR ❡ Public/private partnerships and privatization raise questions both about the proper role of government on the one hand, and about who governs on the other. They also raise the practical question of how best to manage them, given that the criteria for "best" must involve not only considerations of financial costs but also access and control. The integration of private contractors and not-for-profit organizations into the government has reached such a level that managing them is now a requirement of planning practice. The course examined when public/private partnerships and privatization make sense as well as the structure of the new government and the tools available for its governance.

TECHNIQUES OF PROJECT EVALUATION ❡ SPRING 2017 ❡ MOSHE ADLER, INSTRUCTOR ❡ The course had two parts: cost benefit analysis and economic development. Cost benefit analysis deals with the taxpayer as a consumer while economic development, which is fast emerging as an important function of government, deals with the taxpayer as a worker in need of employment and with businesses as a source of tax revenues.

CITIES, BUILDINGS AND MATERIALITY ❡ FALL 2016 ❡ ROBERT BEAUREGARD, INSTRUCTOR ❡ The purpose of this course was to set cities, and the buildings that comprise them, into a framework that views them as heterogeneous assemblages of people, material forms, technologies, and nature. Students were introduced to a less human-centered perspective on planning, architecture, and historic preservation. Instead, the course emphasized how humans and their various organizations collaborate with nature and technologies to make and unmake cities and buildings.

ON SPATIAL EXCLUSION AND PLANNING ❡ SPRING 2017 ❡ HIBA BOU AKAR, INSTRUCTOR ❡ This course investigated the idea of geographies of exclusion through a multidisciplinary inquiry which located spatial production and planning practice at its center. The course crossed issues of spatial exclusion and social justice across cities in the Global North and the Global South. What are geographies of exclusion? Who gets excluded, why, by whom, and how? What are some of the legal, spatial, socio-economical, moral, and political apparatuses that get articulated in producing segregated spaces of poverty and lavishness, violence and fear, connectedness and confinement? What are the roles of state agencies and "experts" such as planners, architects, and policy makers in producing such geographies, and how are these practices reproduced in the everyday?

PLANNING HISTORY & THEORY ❡ SPRING 2017 ❡ HIBA BOU AKAR, INSTRUCTOR ❡ This course addressed the history and planning profession in the United States with its intellectual evolution, while focusing on planning functions and planning roles. The course considered multiple rationales and alternative means of understanding and practicing planning. Particular attention was paid to the interplay of power and knowledge, ethics and social responsibility and issues of race, gender, class, and identity. Consideration to some aspects of history and theory of planning in other parts of the world was included in comparative perspective.

INTRODUCTION TO GEOGRAPHIC INFORMATION SYSTEMS ❡ FALL 2016 ❡ JESSICA BRADEN, JEREMY WHITE, INSTRUCTORS ❡ This course introduced spatial concepts and GIS technical skills using ESRI's ArcGIS software. Students learned spatial analysis and visualization techniques as well as data acquisition, cartographic principles, and management approaches through a combination of lecture and lab sessions.

FUNDAMENTALS OF URBAN DIGITAL DESIGN ❡ SPRING 2017 ❡ ALEJANDRO DE CASTRO MAZARRO, INSTRUCTOR ❡ This course provided conceptual and practical tools to enhance the visual literacy of urban planners, and taught how to understand and communicate projects that range from the scale of the building to that of the city. Classes observed and discussed techniques of effective visual communication and taught the methods and details of realizing such work using Adobe InDesign, Illustrator and Photoshop; AutoCAD; and SketchUp. The seminar departed from the premise that images are a form of language, thus during the semester students developed an urban argument through the design of visual instances: photos, series, maps, plans, sections, diagrams, charts, renderings, and video.

HISTORICAL DEVELOPMENT OF URBAN INFORMALITY ❡ FALL 2016 ❡ ALEJANDRO DE CASTRO MAZARRO, INSTRUCTOR ❡ This seminar exposed, explored and questioned contemporary, acknowledged urban planning programs and urban design strategies dealing with informality. To this end, it showcased related texts and projects that can be understood as historical paradigms and paradoxes of current programs developing urban informality. These international case studies included, among others, examples from Indonesia, Hong-Kong, Thailand, Kenya, Peru, Brazil, Chile, Colombia, Mexico, Nicaragua, India, the UK, and Argentina.

PRACTICUM: RESIDENTIAL PLANNING IN GLOBAL CITIES ❡ SPRING 2017 ❡ KATE DUNHAM, INSTRUCTOR ❡ As the world's urban population grows towards six and a half billion by 2050, cities all over the world are resorting to the mass-production of residential super-blocks to address new urban housing demands. But is this model appropriate for all cities, regardless of their environmental, social, political and economic differences? This seminar provided students with a hands-on opportunity to understand how planning code regulations—specifically residential codes—can shape the design and functioning of future urban neighborhoods. Through lectures, readings and projects, students were exposed to an array of different residential zoning systems from around the world. Students worked in teams to document case studies of existing regulatory systems from a selection of global cities chosen for their distinctive residential developments. Based on what they learned in the seminar, students also had a chance to explore their own ideas about how regulatory codes can address the new challenges ahead that come with unprecedented urban expansion.

COMMUNITY DEVELOPMENT PLANNING ❡ FALL 2016 ❡ LANCE FREEMAN, INSTRUCTOR ❡ The objective of this course was to prepare students to develop strategies for revitalizing forlorn inner city neighborhoods. By the end of the course, students were able to understand the various theories of neighborhood change, were able to use these theories to inform the development of revitalization strategies, and were familiar with techniques for analyzing and diagnosing neighborhood trends relevant to community development.

INTRODUCTION TO HOUSING ❡ SPRING 2017 ❡ LANCE FREEMAN, INSTRUCTOR ❡ This course addressed many of the housing issues that have vexed planners and policy makers for decades. Examples of such questions include: Why is there a shortage of affordable housing? Should everyone be guaranteed a right to decent housing? When, if ever, should the government intervene in the provision of housing? This course provided students with the analytical skills to address the questions listed above. In addition, students learned to take advantage of the plethora of housing data available so as to be able to assess housing market conditions in a particular locality. With these skills, students were better prepared to formulate effective housing policies.

QUANTITATIVE METHODS ¶ FALL 2016 ¶ LANCE FREEMAN, INSTRUCTOR ¶ This course introduced students to the concepts, techniques and reasoning skills necessary to understand and undertake quantitative research. Students honed their skills through a combination of attending weekly class meetings, participating in weekly labs, completing written assignments, and writing a research paper that tested a hypothesis using quantitative techniques. In addition to the lecture, students attended a weekly two-hour lab session.

PUBLIC FINANCING OF URBAN DEVELOPMENT ¶ SPRING 2017 ¶ RICHARD FROEHLICH, INSTRUCTOR ¶ This course was an introduction to how public entities (cities, states, public benefit corporations) finance urban development on a pay-as-you-go budget basis and by issuing public securities. We started with an examination of how public entities leverage limited capital resources through the issuance of debt, including a review of statutory and political considerations as well as limitations put on such debt. We discussed how the current economic conditions, debates about federal programs/debt and credit market disruptions effect investment in development and the funding of governmental activities in procuring capital goods and funding infrastructure improvements. We explored the limitations of tax-exempt financing and the kinds of development that can qualify for such financing. By examining different kinds of financial tools we reviewed how investment is made in mass transit, health care facilities, schools, public utilities, airports, and housing. The class also delved into rating agency requirements, security disclosure rules, current market dynamics, and the mechanics of offering bonds for public sale.

NYC LAND USE APPROVALS ¶ FALL 2016 ¶ ELDAD GOTHELF, INSTRUCTOR ¶ The course took a real-world approach in examining the various land use approval processes in New York City. Students reviewed the ULURP public review process, the Board of Standards and Appeals variance process, the Landmarks Preservation Commission procedures, and other elements of governmental approval processes. Students attended public hearings, reviewed past cases, and critically analyzed what gets approved, what does not, and why. By following current and past development projects through these processes, students gained an understanding of the interplay between planning and politics.

ADVANCED GIS ¶ FALL 2016 ¶ NICK KLEIN, INSTRUCTOR ¶ This research seminar covered a variety of advanced techniques in geographic information systems analysis, for both practice and research. The course operated with a two-fold mission: to critically discuss the theories, concepts, and research methods involved in spatial analysis and to learn the techniques necessary for engaging those theories and deploying those methods. The class worked to meet this mission with a dedicated focus on the urban environment and the spatial particularities and relationships that arise from the urban context.

COMPLETE STREETS SEMINAR ¶ SPRING 2017 ¶ NICK KLEIN, INSTRUCTOR ¶ This seminar focused on contemporary planning for transit, bicycles and pedestrians. Throughout the world, cities are redesigning their streets. Planners are taking back street space from automobiles and reallocating the space for transit vehicles, bicycles and pedestrians. We began by studying the history of urban streets and transportation in the United States in order to understand how the current automobile dominated urban landscape developed. We then transitioned to studying contemporary planning approaches that planners are using to encourage more sustainable travel. The course covered topics including Complete Streets, bus rapid transit, bike sharing, and bike and pedestrian planning topics. The class included a combination of lectures and in-class discussions, guest lectures from local planners, field trips and tours to study innovative transit, bicycle and pedestrian planning projects in New York City, and a final term paper.

PLANNING METHODS ¶ FALL 2016 ¶ NICK KLEIN, INSTRUCTOR ¶ This was an introductory course designed to help prepare students for common analysis methods used in planning practice. Common methods of analysis were covered using publicly available data sets and data collected through assignments. Through weekly readings, lectures and lab sessions, students were able to gain a basic understanding of the tools and skills required in planning practice. In addition to the lectures, students attended weekly lab sections.

INTRODUCTION TO TRANSPORTATION PLANNING ¶ FALL 2016 ¶ FLOYD LAPP, INSTRUCTOR ¶ This course provided an introduction and overview of transportation modes, characteristics of transportation planning policies and procedures, the impact of location, economic development of urban places and related land use patterns. The growing dilemma in moving goods and freight were introduced as both components continue to increase their share of overall trips. The role of the environmental impact statement and the increasing interest in environmental justice were discussed. The governance of transportation as it has evolved for more than half a century with the federal mandated metropolitan transportation planning organization (MPO) was also evaluated.

INTRODUCTION TO ENVIRONMENTAL PLANNING ¶ FALL 2016 ¶ PETER MARCOTULLIO, INSTRUCTOR ¶ This course provided an introduction to the background of the practice of urban environmental planning. Students in this class had a basic foundation in environmental studies, although the first portion of the class was spent reviewing human impact on the environment. The class was run in seminar fashion, meaning that there was a heavy reading load and participation in discussion was vital. Through texts, articles and chapters, students were introduced to a variety of recently published documents that focus on urban environmental planning issues both in the developed and developing world.

PLANNING FOR URBAN ENERGY SYSTEMS ¶ SPRING 2017 ¶ PETER MARCOTULLIO, INSTRUCTOR ¶ This class explored planning for urban energy systems. The course was divided into four sections. The first section examined the history of energy use in cities. The second section examined the components of contemporary urban energy systems from primary energy supply to end use. The third section examined the consequences of urban energy use in cities including local to global environmental and health impacts as well as vulnerabilities. In the final section, we examined the politics and planning of these systems, paying particular attention to mitigation efforts.

LAND USE PLANNING ¶ SPRING 2017 ¶ JONATHAN MARTIN, INSTRUCTOR ¶ This course presented the nuts and bolts of land use planning as practiced in the US today and gave students the opportunity to develop/design a land use plan for a small hypothetical city. Through lectures and readings students were exposed to contemporary land use planning issues (including urbanization and urban growth trends, ethics, quality of life indicators, ecological land use planning, and inner city revitalization).

SUSTAINABLE ZONING & LAND USE REGULATIONS ¶ FALL 2016 ¶ JONATHAN MARTIN, INSTRUCTOR ¶ This course introduced the basic techniques of land use control as practiced in the United States today with an emphasis on regulations that support green building practices and promote sustainable development patterns. Attention was given to the history, development and incidence of a variety of land use regulations, from the general or comprehensive plan to the advanced, including growth management and recent sustainable zoning practices. Of interest to the student was a focus on the practical questions of what works, what doesn't, and why.

DIGITAL RESTRUCTURING OF URBAN SPACE ¶ SPRING 2017 ¶ LEAH MEISTERLIN, INSTRUCTOR ¶ This seminar investigated the extent to which digital technologies are producing structural changes in urban environments, processes, and practices. Through a series of case studies, we questioned the nature of those changes—their effects on the material condition and organization of cities, their benefits and costs, their promises and their failures. Ultimately, we asked whether, and how, this potential restructuring carries with it a concomitant re-imagining of "the city" itself and the ways in which we plan for its future.

INTRODUCTION TO GIS ¶ SPRING 2017 ¶ LEAH MEISTERLIN, INSTRUCTOR ¶ This course introduced spatial concepts and GIS technical skills using ESRI's ArcGIS software. Students learned spatial analysis and visualization techniques as well as data acquisition, cartographic principles and management approaches through a combination of lecture and lab sessions. The course focused on GIS for the planning field.

NEGOTIATIONS FOR PLANNERS ¶ SPRING 2017 ¶ LEE MILLER, INSTRUCTOR ¶ This course introducesd students to the art of negotiating and influencing. Planners spend much of their time negotiating and influencing; yet generally devote little time thinking about how to negotiate and exert influence. They tend to focus only on the outcomes achieved, and fail to explore how the processes or tactics on which they relied could have been varied to attain even better results. Our goal was to explore both the theoretical and practical aspects of negotiating and influencing. In this seminar, we reviewed the literature dealing with negotiating and influencing, engaged in influencing and negotiating in a variety of settings and studied the negotiating and influencing process.

URBAN DESIGN FOR PLANNERS ¶ SPRING 2017 ¶ JUSTIN MOORE, INSTRUCTOR ¶ This course was an introduction to urban design through weekly discussions and design workshops. The discussions focused on the history, theory, and analysis of urban forms, spaces, landscapes, and systems through presentations and case studies. The workshops developed a project-based exchange and application of the interdisciplinary ideas and techniques—from art and architecture to landscape architecture and environmental engineering—that designers use in developing projects in the urban context. This work used a site in the greater New York and Hudson Valley region as a context for exploring the complex interactions between users, program, buildings, public spaces, infrastructure, and environmental systems in the definition and performance of urban spaces and landscapes.

DESIGN AND PLANNING FOR RISK, CRISIS, AND DISASTER ¶ SPRING 2017 ¶ THADDEUS PAWLOWSKI, INSTRUCTOR ¶ Students in this seminar explored concepts of risk, resilience, adaptation, disaster prevention, and disaster recovery. Through weekly lectures, readings, short writing assignments, and class discussion, this seminar was intended to allow students to explore the practices and ethics of planning, urban design, and real estate development in a world that is increasingly defined by instability and uncertainty. Throughout the semester, students used tools of scenario planning to advance resilience strategies—modelling and testing actions that work across systems, scales and time frames—for alleviating these stresses over time. There was also a strong emphasis on developing communication strategies, especially using written and visual narratives to engage with multiple stakeholders. Students conducted guided individual research while collectively learning together about how New York City has begun to address crises in its physical environment, particularly growing economic inequality, exposure to flooding and extreme heat, and aging and poorly maintained infrastructure.

REAL ESTATE FINANCE AND DEVELOPMENT ¶ SPRING 2017 ¶ STEPHEN PEARLMAN, INSTRUCTOR ¶ The course was intended for planners and others in GSAPP who are interested in real estate development and financing, but who need an introductory explanation of concepts and valuation techniques. Topics within the course included: introduction to real estate markets and cycles; real estate cash flows and valuations; financing income-producing real estate properties financing real estate development; construction liquidity risk and the benefits of diversification; important entities in the real estate industry; evaluating the financial performance and strength of real estate entities; and important real estate transactions.

EXPLORING URBAN DATA WITH MACHINE LEARNING ¶ SPRING 2017 ¶ KAZ SAKAMOTO, INSTRUCTOR ¶ Urban planning decisions are inherently difficult, as cities comprise systems of immense complexity. While planners aren't new to qualitative and quantitative tools to model such decisions, this course engaged the role of technologies in the planning process by focusing on challenges and advantages gained from two new skills in particular: data munging and basic machine learning. Students learned munging and machine learning (with R) while studying their implications within the history and theory behind technocracy and urban planning.

PLANNING LAW ¶ FALL 2016 & SPRING 2017 ¶ ANDREW SCHERER, INSTRUCTOR ¶ This was a core course exploring the legal foundations of planning in the United States. Case studies and legal readings provided the foundations to understanding fundamental constitutional issues, as well as zoning, environmental law, aesthetic regulations, related human rights issues, and housing policies.

PUBLIC SPACE IN THE PRIVATE REALM ¶ FALL 2016 ¶ ETHEL SHEFFER, INSTRUCTOR ¶ One basic planning and civic standard for dense cities to work well is the provision of attractive, usable public spaces that can foster a variety of urban experiences and activities. This course focused on physical public space in its many forms: public parks, streets, sidewalks, and a New York City zoning-created hybrid known as privately owned public spaces. We also examined public spaces established above ground such as the High Line and others that are now being developed below elevated structures. Students analyzed major issues of design, theory and practice, uses, financing, management, zoning, government regulation, enforcement, democracy and public expression, and competing claims on contested space. The course combined extensive reading together with field observations and analysis. There was significant direct interaction with planning officials, designers, and civic groups during the semester as students investigated and developed the criteria for well-planned public spaces.

INTRODUCTION TO INTERNATIONAL DEVELOPMENT ¶ FALL 2016 ¶ MARCELA TOVAR, ALEJANDRO DE CASTRO MAZARRO, INSTRUCTORS ¶ This course was designed to provide theoretical and methodological tools for planners in non-Western contexts. Planners are agents that must mediate between global political and economic pressures, and local socio-cultural and institutional conditions. This course examined planning processes through the lenses of key actors, multi-lateral development agencies, and approaches, with a special focus on planning challenges in the international arena. Applied theory including South/Eastern perspectives, were used to illuminate planning case studies around the world. Case studies addressed questions about "who" plans for "whom," and "why" and "how" planners act and intervene in different contexts. The students were expected to critically compare and discuss the nuanced differences across planning environments, assess the level of effectiveness and results of planning approaches, and envision better planning practices in the attainment of more just cities.

CLIMATE CHANGE AND CITIES: OUR NEW NORMAL ¶ FALL 2016 ¶ MARCELA TOVAR-RESTREPO, INSTRUCTOR ¶ This course explored the vulnerability of urban populations with emphasis on context-specific impacts in low- and middle-income nations. Using case studies, students analyzed how climate change impacts different social groups in our cities and identified adaptation and mitigation strategies currently being implemented. Students were provided tools to draw on climate change scientific data and the uncertainty inherent in future projections. Students also had the opportunity to study and engage climate change and international development processes.

ENVIRONMENTAL IMPACT ASSESSMENT ¶ SPRING 2017 ¶ GRAHAM TRELSTAD, INSTRUCTOR ¶ This course explored the key procedural elements of NEPA, SEQRA, and CEQR; the key analytic techniques used in impact assessment; and investigated how application of environmental impact assessment affects project outcomes. Lectures introduced students to the statutory requirements of the laws, important judicial decisions interpreting the laws, and standard methodologies for conducting environmental assessments. Case studies were used to illustrate the effect of the environmental impact assessment on design and implementation of projects or governmental actions. Practical assignments gave students an introduction to the state of practice and the range of analytic techniques used in environmental impact assessment.

SITE PLANNING AND SUPPORT SYSTEMS FOR DEVELOPMENT ¶ FALL 2016 ¶ GRAHAM TRELSTAD, INSTRUCTOR ¶ Human settlements are created and communities structured mostly by private individuals or firms constructing buildings on parcels—as long as the sites are accessible, somehow related to nodes of other urban activity, and equipped with support services. In the United States, this practice has been called "site planning" or "subdivision" and has created millions of houses and thousands of commercial centers around all American metropolitan areas and cities since World War II. The results have been roundly criticized from an urbanistic point of view; however, the public preference is still strongly in favor of this type of development. We should be able to do this job well, and seek methods through which a better environment, at affordable costs, can be built. Within this course, the specific techniques that planners and developers can employ toward achieving good site development were discussed. To take specific physical actions alone is not enough—they also need to be understood in terms of their effectiveness and sustainability.

SOCIAL ENTREPRENEURSHIP AND THE URBAN BUILT ENVIRONMENT ¶ SPRING 2017 ¶ LAURA WOLF-POWERS, KAIROS SHEN, INSTRUCTORS ¶ Increasingly, the financial, institutional, legal, political and conceptual boundaries between public and private have become less distinct, with public and private roles in urban development and governance overlapping. Developers and public authorities alike think of their work as social (i.e. mission-driven) and entrepreneurial. Meanwhile, companies like Uber, Air BnB and Etsy have disrupted established economic and socio-spatial patterns, influencing the choices that people have and make in the realms of housing, work, consumption, and travel. Finally, entities in the so-called "third sector" – consisting of benefit corporations, civic organizations, cooperatives, and non-profits – have proliferated, assuming a large role in shaping urban built and social worlds. This course relied on a series of cases to illustrate and explore the ways in which cities—and planning—have changed with the deployment of "smart" technology and the acceleration of entrepreneurial activity across sectors in recent decades. Students were exposed to both thinking on important questions of ownership and public responsibility and best practices in planning and policy designed to confront these challenges.

ADVANCED RESEARCH AND INDEPENDENT STUDY ¶ SPRING 2017 ¶ WEIPING WU, INSTRUCTOR ¶ In this course, students planned a course of self-study and inquiry, along with an advisor who reviewed and graded the work. Advanced research could involve library research, lab work, fieldwork, or other research methods, and the final product could be a paper, digital design, map, or some other format.

CHINESE URBANISM IN GLOBAL CONTEXT ¶ FALL 2016 ¶ WEIPING WU, INSTRUCTOR ¶ While urbanizing China is undergoing socioeconomic and spatial transformation resembling patterns seen elsewhere in the world, parts of its trajectory clearly push the limits of contemporary urban and planning theories and experience. This course situated Chinese urbanism in the global context, exploring the institutional settings, policy interventions, and urban realities. We focused on four broad topic clusters and explicitly compared them with practices in other countries: China's urbanization path and formation of urban regions, migration and increasingly bifurcated urban landscapes, land management and effect on urban finance, and the reshaping of urban space and livability. Course materials were drawn from academic publications, policy documents and analyses, and mass media.

THESIS I WORKSHOP ¶ FALL 2016 ¶ ROBERT BEAUREGARD, INSTRUCTOR ¶ The six-credit two-semester thesis is an essential part of the planning curriculum. It is an individual study or investigation of the student's own choice, but it is closely supervised by a full-time faculty member of the Urban Planning Program. The thesis demonstrates the student's ability to structure an argument surrounding an issue or problem significant to planning practice, planning theory, and/or the profession itself. Students were assigned to one of several sections for the duration of the semester.

URBAN PLANNING THESIS II ¶ SPRING 2017 ¶ ROBERT BEAU-GUARD, INSTRUCTOR ¶ The second semester of a six-credit two-semester thesis is an essential part of the planning curriculum. It is an individual study or investigation of the student's own choice, but it is closely supervised by a full-time faculty member of the Urban Planning Program. Students wrote and defended their thesis research during the term and submitted a digital copy of their final thesis.

Jahnavi Aluri

SHIFTING FROM DRIVING TO RIDING: A STUDY OF THE IMPACTS OF ON-DEMAND CAB SERVICES ON PUBLIC TRANSIT RIDERSHIP AND VEHICLE OWNERSHIP IN HYDERABAD, INDIA ¶ LEAH MEISTERLIN, ADVISOR ¶ This thesis explores the effects of on-demand cab services, Uber and Ola, on public transit ridership and vehicle ownership in Hyderabad, India. India has grown to be Uber's third largest market in the world but still lacks any comprehensive policies at the federal level to regulate on-demand cab services. These services have risen in popularity and have led to the evolution of new ownership and financial models to help populations afford a car to "drive to work." This research examines the spatial effects of this rising popularity on public transit ridership and vehicle ownership in Hyderabad. This research found that there has been a shift in the proportion of on-demand cabs and cars to all vehicles from 2010 to 2016. This research also found that annual occupancy ratio along bus routes in the city has decreased from 2014 to 2016. This research found that these relationships are localized in the city. This thesis concludes by recommending further studies be carried out to understand the full extent of these effects to effectively incorporate these technologies and plan for the future mobility of city residents.

Vicente Arellano

IS THERE A MUNICIPAL ROLE IN IMMIGRATION POLICY? EXAMINING CASE STUDIES IN FOUR CITIES IN THE UNITED STATES TO BUILD A TYPOLOGY OF "IMMIGRATION LOCALISM" ¶ KIAN TAJBAKHSH, ADVISOR ¶ This research seeks to understand the landscape of local immigration policies in the United States and asks, what role do municipalities have in immigration policy? To what extent can municipalities be involved in the cooperation or noncooperation with national immigration laws? Specifically, what kind of municipal actions or inactions are associated with the classification of certain immigration policy responses and is this generalizable? The aim of this thesis is to establish a typology of municipal responses culminating in the production of a static four quadrant – matrix model within which cities can be located. It is the intention of this work, that a more comprehensive and multi-dimensional approach to municipal policy analysis can create the circumstances for a new evaluation of immigration policy localism in a global governance perspective.

THE GEOGRAPHY OF RESETTLEMENT: HOUSING AND EMPLOYMENT TRAJECTORIES IN DIVERSE URBAN DESTINATIONS ❡ WEIPING WU, ADVISOR ❡ Previous research has demonstrated that urban context significantly affects refugees' access to suitable housing and jobs, however little research has been done into how sites for resettlement are selected. Through interviews with refugee resettlement professionals and analysis of American Community Survey data, I will describe the way in which actors interact to determine the location and type of housing provided to a refugee upon their arrival to the United States. This story varies significantly based on the type of city in which a family is placed. These different environments offer distinctly different pathways to finding housing and becoming an economically self-sufficient member of American society.

Rebecca Book

IMPACT OF ZHENGZHOU SUBWAY SYSTEM ON ADJACENT MIGRANT NEIGHBORHOODS ❡ WEIPING WU, ADVISOR ❡ The subway has advantages of large capacity, fast speed, punctuality, less pollution, low energy consumption and so on. It has become a chief means of public transportation and an important approach to solve the traffic problems in big cities. The purpose of this research is to investigate the impacts of the new subway lines (Line 1 and Line 2) in Zhengzhou on adjacent migrant neighborhoods. To study the impacts of Zhengzhou subway system, door-to-door surveys and interviews on household level in the two target communities (West Guanhutun and Yanzhuang) were conducted. The major findings of this research reveal the negative impact of the subway system on migrant neighborhoods, and the importance of taking minority groups' voice into the policy-making process for future development of metro system in the city.

Mingda Chen

SITUATING URBAN AGRICULTURE: WHAT, WHERE, AND WHY IN NEW YORK CITY ❡ LEAH MEISTERLIN, ADVISOR ❡ Urban agriculture has the potential to address multiple concerns simultaneously in dense urban spaces. Where and how urban agricultural interventions are sited within cities are critical questions to ask as governments, municipalities, and urban planners address the need for healthy and resilient food systems as well as environmental resiliency. This thesis explores the potential for planners to utilize digital mapping methodologies and multi-criteria decision making analysis (MCDA) in a way in which socio-economically vulnerable neighborhoods and neighborhoods facing environmental vulnerability can be addressed simultaneously. This research demonstrates this process by utilizing a geospatial mapping model that incorporates multiple layers of information on the current state of food access, rates of health, economic need, and water and heat risk that New York City currently exhibits. The results of this model, run multiple times, are applied to each of the tax lots in New York City, thus identifying exactly where the greatest socio-economic need and environmental vulnerability exists.

Elizabeth Cohn-Martin

IMPACT OF GANG VIOLENCE ON "TRANSPORTE COLECTIVO PÚBLICO URBANO" IN GUATEMALA CITY ❡ WEIPING WU, ADVISOR ❡ A key aspect of growing sustainably, efficiently, and equitably, for metropolitan areas in Guatemala, specifically Guatemala City, is the improvement of the public transportation network. In recent years, residents of Guatemala City have increased their use of private vehicles, and decreased their usage of public transportation, in efforts to improve their safety against gang violence. In addition, the lack of enforcement of the public private partnership supplying transit in the city, risks the lives of individuals who are most dependent on the system. Between 2010 and January 2017, 1,138 passengers, drivers, and bus assistants were killed throughout the country. The deaths are attributed to increased gang violence, and the targeting of drivers and bus assistants by gang members. As Guatemala continues to move towards a majority urban population, eliminating the barriers to mobility and accessibility of the transportation networks is crucial to ensuring economic growth and decreased rates of inequality.

Jessica Cruz

AN EMPIRICAL STUDY ON THE RELATIONSHIP BETWEEN FISCAL AUTONOMY AND ECONOMIC GROWTH—THE CASE OF CHINA ❡ WEIPING WU, ADVISOR ❡ There is a close relationship between the revenue and expenditure assignment system and economic growth. Based on a literature review of the relationship between fiscal autonomy and economic growth, which shows that scholars have not made a consensus conclusion, this paper introduces the historical process of fiscal decentralization in China since 1978, particularly as related to the establishment of the Tax Sharing System (TSS) in 1994. By studying the dataset of 30 provincial units, this paper finds that the degree of fiscal autonomy remains at a relatively lower level after the TSS reform. There are significant variations in the level of fiscal autonomy across regions and provinces. Through the pooled OLS regression analysis, it is found that a higher level of fiscal autonomy is positively related to economic growth.

Yixiao Fang

GETTING THE WHEELS TURNING: ASSESSING STRATEGIES FOR FINANCING AND ADVANCING MASS TRANSIT INFRASTRUCTURE IN THE 21ST-CENTURY ❡ KIAN TAJBAKHSH, ADVISOR ❡ This thesis explores several strategies for advancing the growth of mass transit infrastructure in the United States. This thesis finds that public-private partnerships (P3), design-build delivery systems, and value capture tools like tax-increment financing (TIF) all have potential for improving the feasibility of financing and constructing transportation infrastructure. However, they do carry some drawbacks and must be utilized in an appropriate context. While the three tools may address different components of a project and are not necessarily applicable in the same situation, this thesis finds that design-build carries the least risk and should be incorporated more broadly.

James A. Gerken

276

THERE GOES THE BARRIO: MEASURING GENTRIFICATION IN BOYLE HEIGHTS, LOS ANGELES ¶ LEAH MEISTERLIN, ADVISOR ¶ This thesis develops a methodological approach to gentrification that reveals the extent to which gentrification of Latinos by Latinos—otherwise known as "gentrification"—has occurred in the neighborhood of Boyle Heights in downtown Los Angeles, California. This thesis adapts existing quantitative methodological frameworks in order to confirm through spatial analysis that middle class, educated Latinos are a gentrifying force in Boyle Heights. It does so by arguing that in order to identify self-gentrifying communities, socio-economic indicators used to determine gentrification must be racially relative. By exploring gentrification as a process through four methods, each comparing Latino-specific data at the census tract and city level in different ways, this thesis concludes that Boyle Heights is being gentrified by Latinos with varying capacities to gentrify. Finally, the thesis explores the implications that this type of gentrification has for urban planning and economic development in Latino communities like Boyle Heights.

Ubaldo Escalante

SPATIAL ETHNO-GEOGRAPHIES OF 'SUBCULTURES' IN URBAN SPACE: SKATEBOARDERS, APPROPRIATIVE PERFORMANCE, AND SPATIAL EXCLUSION IN LOS ANGELES ¶ ROBERT BEAUREGARD, ADVISOR ¶ Today, street skateboarding has transformed from a subcultural pursuit to a mainstream urban endeavor, as more than 50 million people partake in the activity globally. Cities respond to skateboarders' spatial movements by imposing contradictory legal prescriptions and physical design barriers in public and private spaces. The point of departure for this thesis is that planning reactions provide subpar public skate spaces while imposing regulations that ban/stigmatize skateboarding outside of these sanctioned skate spots. A sizable population is denied their full right to the city, proscribed from partaking in the everyday organicism of democratic spatial experience and life. These exclusionary planning/design practices/regulations warrant further investigation. The purpose of this research was to undertake an ethno-geographic inquiry into skateboarders' performances and transgressions in two public skate parks and two privately-owned plazas in Los Angeles, CA. Using traditional planning tools (i.e., zoning incentives, engagement workshops, programming), this paper recommend four policies for cities to plan, design, and celebrate equitable, vibrant spaces where diverse publics can produce social space, create spectacles for cultural consumption, and represent themselves as legitimate actors in everyday urban life.

Christopher Giamarino

EXAMINING THE EXTENT TO WHICH AFFORDABLE HOUSING DEVELOPMENT ACTS AS A CATALYST FOR NEIGHBORHOOD ECONOMIC DEVELOPMENT ¶ LEAH MEISTERLIN, ADVISOR ¶ This study examines the effect of affordable housing construction with regulatory agreement on neighborhood economic development and housing indicators. It attempts to disprove the myth that the construction of affordable housing leads to neighborhood decline. Overall, this study shows that subsidized affordable housing units are not equal in creating or preserving neighborhood economic and housing conditions, but rather are distinct in their actual effects based on a multitude of factors. This is in contrast to the overall negative perception of all subsidized housing units leading to neighborhood decline, destabilization, and sinking property values.

Steven Getz

SATELLITE CITIES OF THE TWENTIETH CENTURY: A SUSTAINABILITY ANALYSIS OF MILTON KEYNES AND RESTON ¶ WEIPING WU, ADVISOR ¶ The population residing in urban areas has been rapidly increasing, especially in the developing world, giving rise to the need for cities and urban establishments to adapt and grow with the change. Satellite cities were developed in the 20th century to shift the population from congested urban areas to new developments established nearby. Milton Keynes in the United Kingdom and Reston in the United States are two New Towns of the 20th century developed to decongest a larger urban center. The paper assesses these two towns against sustainability standards of today, to explore the potential of this form of development as a sustainable tool for planners in the 21st century. It finds that while both towns are somewhat economically sustainable (self-contained with a high median household income), they are not sustainable environmentally (highly auto-dependent with poor air quality), and only slightly sustainable socially.

Shahneez Haseeb

EVALUATING PUBLIC HOUSING FOR MIGRANTS IN CHINA: A CASE STUDY OF PUBLIC RENTAL HOUSING IN DONGGUAN ¶ ROBERT BEAUREGARD, ADVISOR ¶ This thesis evaluates the affordability and accessibility of public rental housing for migrants by taking Dongguan as a case study. It includes six sections. Section one is the introduction, and the background of affordable housing policy in China. Section two offers a literature review of studies about public rental housing and migrant housing in China. Section three provides the methodology of the research, including theoretical framework of affordability and accessibility, methods, and data sources. Section four and five give a specific background of public rental housing in Dongguan. Section six analyzes the public housing affordability and accessibility for migrants and explains the findings. Section seven gives a conclusion and suggestions on how to offer affordable housing to migrants such as public rental housing based on previous results.

Ying Huang

COOL ROOFS AS A MUNICIPAL STRATEGY IN ZONE 5 CLIMATE CITIES ¶ KIAN Y. TAJBAKHSH, ADVISOR ¶ The central purpose of this thesis is to evaluate the effectiveness of the City of Pittsburgh's 2013 Cool Roofs Program, of which the author of this thesis was one of the administrators. The original stated goal of the program, according to mission statement and grant agreements, was to engage volunteers, reduce greenhouse gas emissions & lessen the heat island effect, and save the City of Pittsburgh operating costs due to a reduced cooling load. The realization of volunteer engagement occurred after the project's implementation, but the other two key metrics for project success required several years of data collection and observation to determine if the project had achieved its stated goals. It has been 3 years since the implementation period of the Cool Roofs Project and the following thesis evaluates whether or not the two remaining goals were achieved and whether this is a viable strategy for other cities in the same climate zone with comparable municipal building assets.

Jon Tristan Jackson

EFFECT OF LOCAL CONTEXT ON FLOOD VULNERABILITY IDENTIFICATION: A COMPARISON BETWEEN NEW ORLEANS' FLOOD VULNERABILITY ASSESSMENT TOOLS AND GLOBALLY APPLICABLE VULNERABILITY INDICES ¶ LEAH MEISTERLIN, ADVISOR ¶ Flood occurrences are on the increase all over the world and large numbers of people are constantly exposed to the risk associated with these disasters. Vulnerability assessment is integral to flood risk management. It helps identify areas with high flood risk and guides resilience policies. Vulnerability, being an intangible notion, is difficult to assess. Many municipalities resort to field-survey and community outreach based assessment processes. Another widely used assessment method is indicator-based, which involves developing Flood Vulnerability Indices (FVIs) by using available data to provide a logical image of a region's vulnerability to disaster. This study aims to investigate the effectiveness of FVIs and find out if their quantitative nature, by ignoring the intangible local characteristics of society, compromises the credibility of outcomes derived. The research concludes with recommendations to statistically improve FVIs and, when necessary, use a combination of local knowledge based qualitative techniques and FVIs to get adequate results, in turn making better informed decisions when devising flood resilience policies.

Maira Khan

PLANNING TO GROW: PROGRESS & CHALLENGES TO IMPLEMENTING BALTIMORE'S GROW LOCAL URBAN AGRICULTURE PLAN ¶ KIAN TAJBAKHSH, ADVISOR ¶ Urban agriculture is transitioning from a predominantly fringe activity into a land classification with increasingly mainstream appeal for achieving neighborhood improvements. Cities around the world have reversed earlier positions prohibiting agricultural uses on urban land. Some, such as Baltimore, MD have gone even further into a full embrace of urban agriculture in hopes of reaping the social, economic and environmental benefits touted by urban agriculture advocates. This study takes a qualitative look at Baltimore's plan to expand and support urban agriculture through a formal plan: Grow Local. The plan was written with the intent to help Baltimore create an environment that facilitates urban agricultural practice. This study examines and challenges the robustness of the Grow Local plan, and attempts to identify critical barriers to implementation to date. The research attempts to answer the question of whether planning for urban agriculture is relevant and if so, how can other cities learn from the implementation challenges facing the city of Baltimore.

Androniki Lagos

CREATIVE SMALL BUSINESSES AND THEIR ECONOMIC IMPACT ON NEW YORK CITY'S NEIGHBORHOODS ¶ LEAH MEISTERLIN, ADVISOR ¶ Richard Florida's idea on "creative class" in the year 2002 led many researchers from diverse disciplines to seek the value of "creativity" as a potential engine for metropolitan economic growth. This thesis is founded on this earlier concept and investigates the extent to which the growth of creative small businesses can impact the economic conditions of neighborhoods in New York City. Rather than assessing the issue from a metropolitan scale, however, this study zooms in and focuses on the neighborhood level in order to detect impacts at a micro level. Through the mapping of creative small businesses (CSB) in New York City neighborhoods over time, this study found that there was a strong growth of creative small businesses in Brooklyn from 2000 to 2012. Decreases in unemployment rates and increases in median rent values were evaluated through mapping and statistical analyses to find that CSB might affect the decline of unemployment rates at the neighborhood boundary level. Also, median rent changes studied at the borough level showed an inverse relationship between creative small business growth and increase in rent values in Brooklyn, while the opposite was found for the Bronx and Queens. Since original property characteristics and rent values are distinct in each borough and yield divergent results from the analysis, this thesis found that it is important to understand the relationship between CSB growth and rent values in the boroughs separately.

Hyunseung Lee

ASSESSING INCLUSIONARY HOUSING POLICY IN SANTIAGO, CHILE: RESIDENTIAL SEGREGATION BY INCOME, 2006-2016 ¶ KIAN TAJBAKHSH, ADVISOR ¶ In 2006, residential integration based on income was included for first time as a main goal in Chile's national housing policy. In 2015, the National Council for Urban Development (Consejo Nacional de Desarrollo Urbano, CNDU) challenged the homeownership voucher program employed to achieve this goal and recognized the inexistence of any official instrument to measure segregation in Chile. This thesis responds to these concerns and i) provides an index to measure residential segregation of subsidized low-income households; ii) analyzes the index's change during the last decade; and iii) uses these findings to evaluate whether the new policies introduced in 2006 have reduced the levels of residential segregation in the Region of Santiago (RS). The study demonstrates that new housing policies have not reduced the levels of residential segregation affecting subsidized low-income households in Santiago. The thesis analyzes the relation between spatial clusters of government assistance with poverty rates, overcrowded conditions, physical deficiencies, infrastructure and social problems, to demonstrate the persistence of negative urban conditions associated with the location of subsidized stock.

José Gabriel Lemaître

THE POLITICS AND POLICIES OF NEW YORK CITY'S MANUFACTURING INDUSTRY ¶ ROBERT BEAUREGARD, ADVISOR ¶ The proliferation of the manufacturing industry and creation of manufacturing jobs has been a lasting part of economic development policy for American cities at both the State and local level. The study of economic development policies and changes in manufacturing compare changes among cities or regions and are most often inconclusive or offer mixed results, begging a more localized understanding of the industry. This thesis explores how economic development policy specific to the manufacturing sector is created and implemented in New York City. Understanding the state of manufacturing-related policy and its effectiveness requires understanding and influences over a significant time period. The analysis of the research and the findings is developed in three parts in the following sections, a compilation of statistics related to the manufacturing industry and the labor in New York, a survey of legislation and policies enacted in New York City meant to impact industrial activity in New York City, and results of interviews conducted with experts involved in creating or working with policy related to the manufacturing industry in New York City. Findings from the research are then developed into recommendations for future policy and research.

Melissa Loomis Bindra

RESIDENTIAL DEVELOPMENT AND ITS IMPACT ON SCHOOL ACCESS IN NEW YORK CITY ¶ LEAH MEISTERLIN, ADVISOR ¶ Residential development in New York City has been increasing since 2010. This increase is due to both private and public players in the built urban environment, as developers try to push the limits of the luxury market, while the city has plans to increase and preserve the stock of affordable housing throughout the city. Such increases in residential development, however, have negative impacts on public amenities by adding pressure in the form of overcrowding, noise pollution, or traffic. This study seeks to explore such consequences of residential development, specifically its impact on access to schools in New York City. By looking at access as spatial accessibility, consulting publicly available data, and proposing a methodology adapted from others established in academic literature, this study reaffirms the notion that residential development has a negative impact on access to schools. The results of this study also shed light on the appropriateness of research methodologies to understand urban phenomena, as not a single method is deemed to be the best in revealing a relationship between residential development and spatial accessibility to schools.

Patrick Li

EXPORTING EXPERTISE? ROTTERDAM'S PLANNERS AND THE FLOOD ADAPTATION INDUSTRY ¶ LEAH MEISTERLIN, ADVISOR ¶ The effects of climate change and its implications for flood-vulnerable cities have incentivized systematic knowledge exchanges among urban planning professionals globally. Rotterdam, a delta city with an extensive water-management background and an innovative urban design culture, has emerged as a leader in water-related planning and has shared its strategies with cities such as New Orleans and New York. This research investigates the ways in which the City of Rotterdam has positioned itself as a leader in climate adaptation planning and a center of knowledge exchange. The research seeks to identify whether and to what extent Rotterdam benefits from its enhanced international profile. Upon review of existing theory and interviews with Dutch and American planners, this research concludes that the City of Rotterdam's brand is strengthened by Dutch planners' international activities, but that any direct economic impact on the city has been negligible. Finally, it suggests that further investment into Rotterdam's local knowledge institutions and adaptation infrastructure could more efficiently serve the city's economy while maintaining its international profile.

Dorothy MacAusland

UNCOVERING THE EFFECTIVENESS OF POST-SANDY HOUSING RECOVERY EFFORTS IN NEW YORK CITY ❡ BOB BEAUREGARD, ADVISOR ❡ This thesis seeks to examine the effectiveness of post-Sandy CDBG-DR-funded housing recovery efforts in New York City. Using historical precedents to understand federal disaster policy and to identify its common limitations, this research then attempts to analyze the progress of NYC's existing housing recovery programs. In order to identify the challenges and limitations of these programs, this thesis utilized information gathered from an inspection of available housing recovery data as well as interviews with representatives of various city, state and federal agencies. By combining the quantified progress of NYC's housing recovery with the varied perspectives of individuals implementing and guiding these efforts, this research attempted to distill the broad successes and failures of different recovery programs. Taking these lessons, several recommendations are provided with the goal of improving the effectiveness of future CDBG-DR-housing recovery efforts.

Richard Martoglio

RIOT: COMMUNITY ORGANIZATIONS AND PUBLIC COMMUNICATION FOLLOWING CROWN HEIGHTS AND TOMPKINS SQUARE ❡ LEAH MEISTERLIN, ADVISOR ❡ This is a qualitative study of the extent to which community organizations reclaimed public space in the face of community conflict and the mechanisms by which they did so, in the case of the Crown Heights and Tompkins Square Park riots. Six community organizers, activists and residents took part in semi-structured interviews regarding safety, ownership, public space and community organizations in their neighborhoods. Media in the form of newspaper articles and op-eds were also utilized to gauge the public discourse surrounding the riots and how the communities were able to represent themselves. The research uses a communicative planning theory approach to the issues of conflict and community organizing, and exposes opportunities planners can take advantage of in order to assist communities in representing themselves and minimizing conflict.

Madeleine McGrory

RESILIENCE PLANNING IN A COASTAL URBAN ENVIRONMENT: AN ANALYSIS OF CLIMATE CHANGE PLANNING POLICY AND PROCEDURE IN CHARLESTON, SOUTH CAROLINA ❡ KIAN TAJBAKHSH, ADVISOR ❡ The purpose of this thesis was to understand the roles of shared learning and cooperation among local and regional levels of governance in building or enhancing resilience to disturbances of climate change. In seeking to understand the roles shared learning and cooperation have in resilience building, this thesis analyzes planning strategies being promoted or taken in the Charleston, South Carolina region. Specifically, this research examines seven planning documents put forth by local and regional jurisdictions and interviewed five planning professionals working at local and regional levels to gauge the degree to which shared learning and cooperation operate in building and enhancing this region's resilience.

Joseph McKenzie

URBAN CONSERVATION IN CHINA: THE REASONS AND CONFLICTS OF HISTORICAL NEIGHBORHOOD PRESERVATION ❡ KIAN Y. TAJBAKHSH, ADVISOR ❡ Historical neighborhood conservation plays an important part in the inner-city redevelopment in China. The purpose of this thesis is to identify and understand the complexity of stakeholders' incentives and their responsibilities in historical neighborhood conservation in Chinese urban contexts by analyzing two cases in Beijing and Shanghai. The two research questions are: 1) who are the stakeholders and what are their incentives in an urban conservation project? 2) What social, political, and economic factors affect decisions to preserve neighborhoods in Chinese cities? From the analysis, political implications are drawn that: 1) The governments should encourage and solicit original residents' participation on a historical neighborhood conservation project. 2) The governments should introduce the private capital into the neighborhood conservation project.

Mengyao Wang

VYING FOR FIBER: A COMPARATIVE ANALYSIS ON LOCAL GOVERNMENT DECISION-MAKING FOR FIBER INTERNET ❡ LEAH MEISTERLIN, ADVISOR ❡ High-speed internet access is becoming increasingly important to people's daily lives and futures. In an effort to provide broadband services, cities have been investing in fiber optic infrastructure which can achieve transmittal speeds at almost 100 times faster than traditional Digital Subscriber Line (DSL) internet. This thesis assesses three cities that have attained fiber internet infrastructure and operations in three radically different ways and will identify relevant themes when planning for fiber. Chattanooga, TN, Kansas City, MO and Provo, UT are cities that have expressed their understanding of the implications of high-speed internet for their communities. Uncovering the planning processes that led to these infrastructures as well as assessing the outcomes of them are vital to the pursuit of fiber in other localities. Through an evaluation consisting of comprehensive document review, city contracts, as well as interviews with related city officials, this study found that infrastructure planning processes for fiber-optic internet vary based on level of state regulation, degree of private sector involvement, and perceived notions of economic development. The study also found that intra-city technological upgrades may have been the initial reasoning for public fiber infrastructure ventures; however, when deciding whether to connect fiber internet to homes, economic development was the main driver.

Sahra Mirbabaee

MAINSTREAMING DISASTER RISK REDUCTION INTO URBAN PLANNING—MUMBAI'S DISASTER MANAGEMENT PLAN IN A GLOBAL CONTEXT ¶ WEIPING WU, ADVISOR ¶

Neha Krishnan

The risk of disasters in urban areas due to natural hazards is increasing in frequency and intensity worldwide, and it is now widely recognized that extreme weather events that will become a regular part of life in the future. The United Nations and other international agencies have developed several extensive frameworks to understand and reduce disaster risk. Disaster Risk Reduction remains however, largely the prerogative of national governments, even though the effects of disaster are felt at an urban scale. Solutions must come from cities themselves, and international frameworks must be integrated into urban planning policies and practice. This thesis is a study of Disaster Risk Reduction as it is practiced in Mumbai, India; and examines the extent to which it is "mainstreamed" into urban planning.

CUTTING BACK THE CAR—LESSONS ON REDUCING SUBURBAN AUTOMOBILE DEPENDENCE FROM THE US & GERMANY ¶ WEIPING WU, ADVISOR ¶

Matthias Neill

This thesis attempts to answer the research question: "How have suburbs reduced car dependence?" It looks specifically at two suburbs, one in the US and one in Germany, that have had success in reducing automobile dependence and creating new paradigms of suburban development and transportation planning. These case studies, the Rosslyn-Ballston Corridor in Virginia and Rieselfeld and Vauban in Germany, are different but provide valuable lessons on how suburbs can reduce automobile dependence. Information on the case studies and their strategies to reduce car dependence was gathered primarily through secondary sources and through interviews with experts. Findings indicate that the Rosslyn-Ballston corridor has reduced car dependence by coordinating transportation and land use planning, incentivizing a shift away from driving, and by securing community consensus in favor of densification and transit provision. Ultimately this thesis finds that a range of strategies can work to reduce car dependence in suburbs but that the success of both case locations in reducing car dependence is context dependent.

POLICY APPROACHES TO ENERGY USE REDUCTION IN TENANT SPACES ¶ ROBERT BEAUREGARD, ADVISOR ¶

Lauren Ossey

The aim of this research was to understand the approaches that local governments have used to influence energy use in tenant spaces through both mandatory policies and voluntary programs. Additionally, this research aimed to understand the impetus and barriers to policy creation and implementation regarding private tenant spaces. This study utilized two research methods: 1) review of policy documents and 2) interviews with selected city officials and industry experts. The research focused on cities participating in the C40 program, specifically within the Private Building Efficiency Network.

FIVE YEARS LATER: ARE WE LEARNING FROM THE STORM? THE IMPORTANCE OF INSTITUTIONAL LEARNING AND COMMUNITY-CENTRIC APPROACHES TO BUILDING LOCAL RESILIENCE ¶ KIAN TAJBAKSH, ADVISOR ¶

Krithika Prabhakaran

In the case of Hurricane Sandy, critical lessons demonstrate that underlying issues of lack of trust and the absence of sustainable engagement with community-based organizations create significant disparities in resilient outcomes following emergencies and disasters. Recognizing this, over the past five years since Hurricane Sandy, New York City policymakers, researchers, and planners have been exploring ways in which top-down resiliency policy along with innovative community-driven projects can be integrated to foster social bonds, community networks, and local resilience within struggling communities. This study aims to narrate how City and local agencies have restructured their priorities to focus on resilience since Sandy, and understand the importance of community-based organizations and community-centric approaches in facilitating recovery efforts and strengthening local communities for long-term sustainability.

ARTS & CULTURAL DISTRICTS AND PRESERVATION POLICY: A NEIGHBORHOOD ANALYSIS OF THE RIVER NORTH (RINO) ART DISTRICT ¶ ERICA AVRAMI AND ROBERT BEAUREGARD, ADVISORS ¶

Cameron Maureen Robertson

Though cultural planning is a relatively recent concept its contribution to urban planning and historic preservation is paramount. Many states, cities and smaller communities within the United States have turned to cultural planning and programming to aid revitalization and development, including arts and cultural districts, which serve as models of place-based ingenuity. These places serve as points of community engagement and economic development as well as support the cultural identities that strengthen business and tourism. Moreover, they are designed to encourage artists, entrepreneurs, institutions and potential developers to build upon and organize around existing arts and culture-based resources. This research aims to understand the role that historic built environments play in the vitality of arts and cultural districts. The study undergoes an intensive examination of a singular case study, the River North (RiNo) Art District in Denver, Colorado, through qualitative and quantitative analyses. This thesis proves the economic value and visual appeal that these historic buildings have on the RiNo Art District, and provides recommendations that help to expand the preservation toolbox and facilitate an intersection between arts and cultural districts and the preservation field.

GREEN JOBS, GREEN SKILLS, AND THE GREEN ECONOMY: A SURVEY OF NEW YORK, WITH BROADER IMPLICATIONS ❡ ROBERT BEAUREGARD, ADVISOR ❡ To borrow from Van Jones's book on the green economy, we have a "dual problem" on our hands. First, that we continue to damage the environment by our destructive practices; and second, that we have a large group of people that were laid off during the last economic regime, because of the supposed insufficiency of their skillsets. There exists a solution to both these problems, and it comes in the form of green jobs. This thesis was undertaken, in part, because of a lack of clarity in the scholarly literature about the nature of green jobs: which jobs are they? and what do they require in the way of skills? The aim of this paper is to restart the conversation surrounding green jobs by showing evidence of a broad-based economic transformation that is primed for the previously maligned, and their likely level of skills. This thesis offers a look, through a broad lens, at the occupations that are being affected by greener industry practices, and the skills that are needed to be included in this oncoming economic paradigm.

Brandon Robinson

LAND USE AND SEA LEVEL RISE VULNERABILITY IN NEW YORK CITY: ADDRESSING ENVIRONMENTAL JUSTICE THROUGH ZONING ❡ WEIPING WU, ADVISOR ❡ Sea level rise is becoming more of a relevant topic within urban planning as projections for climate change solidify. In addition to these findings, environmental justice literature demonstrates that not all populations will be affected equally: communities of color and lower socioeconomic backgrounds are exposed to greater risks. While urban planners are proposing initiatives ranging from resiliency reports to design solutions, there is little attention towards land use regulations as a way to reduce vulnerability. The purpose of this paper is to analyze how land use affects the social vulnerability of neighborhoods in New York City towards sea level rise. The findings of the quantitative analysis suggest that residential use and industrial use pose a strong relationship with vulnerability towards sea level rise. Through the use of qualitative methods, my research provides policy recommendations that incorporate environmental justice to address risk of those who are most vulnerable. These include considering inequitable zoning in industrial use areas and incorporating sea level rise into different types of residential densities. This framework provides the tools for addressing mitigation strategies through an equitable and long-term perspective.

Lia Soorenian

OPERATIONALIZING THE SOHO EFFECT: AN ANALYSIS OF AFFORDABLE ARTIST HOUSING IN BRIDGEPORT, CONNECTICUT ❡ ROBERT BEAUREGARD, ADVISOR ❡ Artists have historically clustered in neighborhoods that offer cheap rent and a prevalence of physical space. Their presence often resulted in some form of cultural commodification, rising rent, and the eventual displacement of the artists themselves. Affordable artist housing protects artists from displacement while simultaneously engendering economic development and cultural identity. It accomplishes these outcomes through public funding for affordable housing and often historic preservation. This thesis seeks to understand the impacts and limitations of affordable artist housing by analyzing the Read's Artspace building in Bridgeport, Connecticut. It examines issues of gentrification, identity, economic development, and affordable housing through the lens of a city that has experienced decades of population loss and economic decline. Through case studies, a review of economic development, artist housing, and affordable housing literature, and interviews with stakeholders in the Bridgeport community, this thesis identifies the impacts of affordable artist housing and offers a critique of the enterprise itself, hopefully challenging our conventional wisdom and contributing to this emerging field of study.

Charlie Stewart

AGING POPULATION AND SLUM RESETTLEMENT IN GURYONG VILLAGE, SEOUL, SOUTH KOREA ❡ ROBERT BEAUREGARD, ADVISOR ❡ The purpose of this thesis is to evaluate if the elderly population of Guryong Village is receiving adequate provision of services to mitigate their resettlement process. Located in Seoul, South Korea, Guryong Village is the last illegal shantytown in the city that has survived a tumultuous history of aggressive urbanization policies. Although the squatter community has been under development pressure ever since the turn of the 21st century, the Seoul Metropolitan Government finally made a public announcement of its proposal for redevelopment in 2011. The issue at hand, however, is not only the threat of displacement for current residents, but also that the majority of the Guryong population are senior citizens of low socioeconomic status. Recognizing that persons of older age require more proactive and committed policy interventions, this thesis highlights: first, if the elderly population of Guryong Village is receiving adequate provision of services, and second, if the government has communicated and provided additional services to facilitate their relocation process.

Jacquelyne D. Sunwoo

EVALUATING STATE BASED ECONOMIC DEVELOPMENT POLICY: LEARNING FROM ATLANTIC CITY ¶ ROBERT BEAUREGARD, ADVISOR ¶ Economic development planning has increasingly become a primary function of state governments. Atlantic City, New Jersey serves as a unique case study for this form of economic development. Since the legalization of casino gaming in the city in 1976, the State of New Jersey has been heavily involved in the development of the city's economy and has engaged in large-scale urban renewal programming as a form of economic development. Through a variety of agencies, including the Casino Reinvestment Development Authority and New Jersey Economic Development Authority, the State has utilized a variety of economic development practices including eminent domain, tax credits and incentives to go about the redevelopment of Atlantic City. Through the exploration of three specific development programs undertaken by the state: eminent domain, financial incentives, and public-private partnerships, this thesis critically evaluates the economic policies of the State of New Jersey in order to provide detailed analysis of the impacts and outcomes of these policies, including those traditionally overlooked by economic development practitioners. Ultimately, concluding that the state's use of economic development planning has been inadequate and at times run contrary to a holistic economic development strategy intended to uplift a very depressed and economically disadvantaged Atlantic City.

Evan Sweet

POLICIES AND INNOVATION HUBS: EVALUATING POLICIES THAT SUPPORT AND SUSTAIN THE TECH INDUSTRY IN NEW YORK CITY ¶ ROBERT BEAUREGARD, ADVISOR ¶ Cities around the world are seeking to accommodate the needs of a new generation of technology based industries and firms, whose innovation model depends on proximity and whose talent pool prefers urban locations and lifestyles. Such cities are motivated to host a larger portion of this innovation economy in order to grow a new base of jobs, adjust to the process of industrial change, or leverage technology for the challenges of sustainability, resilience, and social cohesion. Many are trying to raise their innovation profile by focusing investment and promotion on new 'innovation hubs or districts', locations within their city where the innovation economy might cluster and concentrate. The innovation economy is proving to be a disruptor and opportunity for cities, businesses and the real estate sector. Consequently, this thesis focuses on the effectiveness of governmental policies in promoting and sustaining the tech industry and its spatial manifestation, innovation districts, in New York City.

Maryam Yaghoub

ANALYSIS OF URBAN EXPANSION AND TRANSPORTATION CHARACTERISTICS ¶ KIAN Y. TAJBAKHSH, ADVISOR ¶ Urban expansion and transportation are actually interrelated. Shanghai's rapid urban expansion was caused by the inflow of people and the relocation of employment, which increased people's travel demand, particularly for long-distance and motorized travel, greatly from 1990s onward. People are working to increase transportation supply to fulfill travel demand by constructing more roads and promoting a well-designed public transportation system. However, the growth in demand has outpaced the increase in supply, as indicated by more congested roads, trains, and buses despite the significant increase in subway ridership. The demand management strategy needs to be involved in the policy making process to manage not only the growth of motorization, but also the growth of urban spaces and population. More supply still induces new demand, and the demand will continue to grow unless it is managed.

Lina Yin

EFFECT OF COMPLETE STREETS INFRASTRUCTURE AND DESIGN ON STREET LIFE ¶ WEIPING WU, ADVISOR ¶ "Complete streets" policies are spreading throughout the United States, and this thesis provides greater understanding of how "complete streets" style designs impact street life. Research for the thesis includes observations of street life at four locations with "complete streets" designs as well as interviews with residents, community advocates, municipal planners, and other project stakeholders. Observational research provides examples of how people interact in a "complete streets" environment, compared with control sites within the same neighborhood. This thesis found that "complete streets" style infrastructure affects street life through improved street safety, creating a welcoming environment and sense of place, and through economic development. The study of four street redesigns and interviews with project designers reveal implementation patterns and which parts of the street redesign were most effective in achieving their goals. The thesis concludes with a critique of "complete streets" design and implementation, yet proposes that they should be created where possible due to their positive impacts on safety for the most vulnerable street users.

Taylor Young

IMPACTS OF PUBLIC ART PROJECTS ON UNDERUTILIZED URBAN SPACES IN NYC ❡ KIAN TAJBAKHSH, ADVISOR ❡ As more people move to cities and become urban population, active and dynamic urban spaces will become more desirable. Public art has the ability to beautify, attract attention, stir up discussion, and involve various parties. All the above contribute to a dynamic and inviting urban space. But often, there are doubts about the value of public art its contribution to urban spaces and urban life. As a result, for my thesis, I want to explore the impacts public art could have on underutilized urban spaces throughout NYC. The approach adopted for this study is a comparative case study method. I have selected three underutilized locations around New York City with public art work installations. I will compare the impact public art has created or failed to create in these three different spaces. Overall, public art installations encourage us to reflect on our physical and cultural surroundings, and our place within this complex landscape.

Amy Zhou

SUPERBLOCKS IN BEIJING: A SURVEY CENTRIC STUDY FOR THE FEASIBILITY OF OPENING UP SUPERBLOCKS AND OTHER POTENTIAL SOLUTIONS TO ALLEVIATE THEIR PROBLEMS ❡ KIAN TAJBAKHSH, ADVISOR ❡ This thesis examines the goals of opening up existing Superblock Developments, and also focuses on residents' perception by performing survey data analysis. The thesis asks the following questions: is opening up superblocks a feasible solution in the residents' perspectives? What are their preferences toward superblocks? What other measures can be taken in order to alleviate the problems cause by superblocks? The thesis starts by analyzing the reasons behind superblocks' formation. A survey was conducted in Beijing in January 2017 to collect information and opinions from residents of superblocks. The survey results were compiled into a dataset for research and analysis. In the end, using data and the results obtained through the analysis, a set of recommendations were presented, focusing on measures of alleviating the problems in the existing superblock neighborhoods.

Huitian Zhou

The Historic Preservation program at Columbia GSAPP is unique in its focus on architectural heritage, emphasis on creative expression, critical thinking, and experimental research. It educates architects, as well as related professionals such as historians, planners, engineers, artists, anthropologists, archeologists, developers, and others, in the art and science of preserving the world's architectural heritage. Our student-centric curriculum is designed to support individuals in pursuing their own research interests in depth, and culminates in a year-long master's thesis, on which students work one-on-one with a faculty advisor. The core sequence of three studios provides students with real-world hands-on experience in projects both in New York and internationally. In the studios students critically apply and test the theories and ideas learned in a rich array of lectures, intimate seminars and laboratory classes. Students study the architectural and archival riches of New York City, and learn how preservation is practiced in the United States and abroad. Students graduate with a solid foundation in the humanistic, scientific and technical knowledge necessary for being the professionals in charge of preservation projects. Interested students may pursue dual degrees with the Master of Architecture, Master in Urban Planning, or Master in Real Estate Development programs at Columbia GSAPP—each requires a separate application. Columbia University's program boasts a world-class faculty that has set the standard in the dynamic profession of historic preservation since James Marston Fitch founded it in 1964 as the first such program in the United States.

1

HISTORIC PRESERVATION STUDIO 1 ¶ FALL 2016 ¶ EMILIE EVANS, CLAUDIA KAVENAGH, KIM YAO, INSTRUCTORS, WITH MAYSSA JALLAD, ALEX RAY ¶ Studio 1 was a foundational course for a three-studio sequence within the Historic Preservation program. It was simultaneously broad in reach and narrow in focus. Studio 1 was the space for engaging overarching historical and contemporary issues of preservation, urbanism, planning, and architectural design. The goal for Studio 1 was to equip students with skills, techniques, and critical thinking—the means to engage practice and research—in order to engender leadership, interpretation, and advocacy—the ability to exercise judgment and propose solutions. Studio 1 engaged students in questions of preservation and its role in a larger context of environmental, social, cultural, historical, and physical built environments of New York, while also contemplating preservation's role beyond high-growth, hot-market cities. It encouraged students to think about non-traditional partnerships to explore, existing preservation tools and tools to create, and diverse potential outcomes. Studio 1 explored two distinct sites in New York City—one vacant, touristic, and disconnected; the other full, developing, and integrated into urban fabric. The studio offered models for approaching preservation, planning, and design questions and the role of the preservationist, planner, architect, conservator, advocate, and historian in contemporary practice.

2

HISTORIC PRESERVATION STUDIO 2 ¶ SPRING 2017 ¶ ERICA AVRAMI, INSTRUCTOR ¶ A core aim of this studio was to engage students in evidenced-based preservation planning and project development at a scale beyond the individual building or site, so as to understand the role heritage and plays within larger community, urban, and regional dynamics, and to ensure that preservation generates positive long-term outcomes for populations and environments. This studio focused on the downtown ("middle Main") area of Poughkeepsie. Once a thriving, mixed-use hub of the city, it has declined significantly, having been cut off from the waterfront and other areas, in part due to past urban renewal efforts and the construction of arterial highways as well as the loss of industry in the region.

3
4
5

HISTORIC PRESERVATION STUDIO 2 ¶ PRESERVATION DESIGN PROPOSALS FOR THE ANDREW FREEDMAN HOME ¶ SPRING 2017 ¶ BELMONT FREEMAN, INSTRUCTOR ¶ This studio focused on the enlightened development of the Andrew Freedman Home, in the Bronx, as a strategy for the long-term preservation of the historic property. The Andrew Freedman Home is a grand renaissance revival palazzo on the Grand Concourse, built in 1924 as a retirement home for formerly-affluent people. Owned today by the Mid-Bronx Senior Citizens Council, the Freedman Home supports a variety of social service, educational and cultural activities. However, maintaining the large building, much of which is vacant, and its extensive grounds remains a constant challenge. The Andrew Freedman Home (by the architects Friedlander and Jacobs) is an individual NYC Landmark as well as being included in the Grand Concourse Historic District. Once called "the Champs Élysées of the Bronx," the Concourse and its environs slid into decay in the latter part of the 20th century. Today the neighborhood is in vibrant flux, with a resurgent economy, demand for affordable housing, and a lively cultural scene. The Freedman Home occupies a full city block with, by current zoning, tremendous unrealized development rights. Private developers have approached the MBSCC with schemes for the development of the property, but the Council has thus far kept the site remarkably intact.

6

HISTORIC PRESERVATION STUDIO 2 ¶ HARLEM IN TRANSITION ¶ SPRING 2017 ¶ BRYONY ROBERTS, INSTRUCTOR, WITH ALLISON SEMRAD ¶ Focusing on churches in central Harlem, this studio foregrounded questions of social value in historic preservation. The course looked at monumental churches, such as St. Luke's Episcopal Church and St. Martin's Episcopal Church, which are recognized for their architectural value but suffer from declines in use and economic resources. Through processes of community involvement, students documented the social histories of these churches and strategized methods of re-purposing them for contemporary users. The studio also connected analysis to design experimentation. Students developed proposals for the future use and transformation of the sites, including conservation, programming and design. This studio encouraged a broad range of design thinking beyond standard architectural solutions, including possibilities for multimedia, ephemeral and performative design ideas.

HISTORIC PRESERVATION STUDIO 3 ¶ JOINT HP / UP STUDIO ¶ FALL 2016 ¶ ERICA AVRAMI, WILL RAYNOLDS, INSTRUCTORS ¶ This joint HP/UP studio sought to develop skills in mapping, assessing, and integrating cultural heritage within broader planning efforts, tourism development, and urbanization. As a project-based studio, students worked collaboratively to research, analyze, and propose recommendations, compiling findings in a collective final report. The studio studied the 800 year-old Rock Hewn Churches of Lalibela, which are part of a thriving landscape of religious worship and pilgrimage. Lalibela was one of the first sites designated as UNESCO World Heritage and is now a top tourism destination in Ethiopia. Work to conserve the churches themselves has been accompanied by extensive urban growth, tourism development plans, infrastructural upgrades, and resettlement of local residents to areas outside of the heritage site's buffer zone. Managing these dynamics to preserve the living and physical heritage of the site, while also allowing for community and economic development, presents numerous challenges that were explored by the studio.

7
8
9
10
11

HISTORIC PRESERVATION STUDIO 3 ¶ HP TECHNOLOGY STUDIO ¶ FALL 2016 ¶ CARLOS BAYOD, ADAM LOWE, INSTRUCTORS ¶ This project-based studio explored advanced applications of digital preservation technology through international real-world fieldwork. Drawing on previous knowledge of architectural structures systems and materials, students employed cutting edge digitalization, 3D scanning, photogrammetry and printing technologies to devise an experimental preservation treatment for a historic building. Students carried out high-resolution 3D and color scans of the San Baudelio murals at the MET, and of the building in Spain. We then experimented with how to reassemble the pieces digitally, and envisioned ways in which the construction of a replica could re-unite the scattered fragments in the building. Students considered technology in a broader cultural, political and aesthetic context. They informed their solutions with archival research, materials science research and other relevant research in order to address the range of issues that opened up throughout the course.

12
13
14
15

HISTORIC PRESERVATION STUDIO 3 ¶ JOINT HP/ADVANCED ARCHITECTURE STUDIO ¶ FALL 2016 ¶ JORGE OTERO-PAILOS, MARK RAKATANSKY, INSTRUCTORS ¶ This was an architecture studio offered for both historic preservation students with a design degree and Masters of Architecture students in their final year of study. The problem for the studio was a major addition to an existing building that required an understanding of the meaning of the old building—all of the ways its form and materials express the values it sought to represent and serve at the time—and the ways that meaning might or might not be extended, enriched and brought forward by the addition. This year we focused on the United Nations campus in Geneva, Switzerland, the second largest UN site after New York. We visited the UN Headquarters in New York, and later traveled from October 1-9, first to Geneva to document the buildings and activities of the complex (along with a day trip to Lausanne contemporary architecture of the École Polytechnique including Sanaa's Rolex Center), and subsequently to Paris to visit the World Heritage Center, the 1958 UNESCO Headquarters (designed by Marcel Breuer, Pier Luigi Nervi, and Bernard Zehrfuss), and related contemporary cultural facilities.

SUSTAINABLE RETROFITS ¶ FALL 2016 ¶ MICHAEL ADLERSTEIN, INSTRUCTOR ¶ Historic preservation and sustainable design are considerations generated by ethical obligations to the future. The public has generally accepted the wisdom of historic preservation. The acceptance of sustainable design within the preservation field has also made progress. However, climate change events are moving fast and have created a shared sense of urgency. The tens of thousands of refugees moving away from the politics and deserts of the Middle East brought the issue to Europe's door. The weather and the refugees helped create unusual cooperation in the UN climate conference in Paris in December 2015. After 20 years of discussion, agreement was reached, for the first time, on climate change. The design and construction industry is responsible for a large share of the ongoing carbon production. We have convinced ourselves that our contribution to save the planet is a strong commitment to greener buildings. This course explored whether building greener is the best we can do. Building greener is helpful, but building less might be necessary. This course discussed the concepts of preservation/retrofit versus new green construction on a conceptual basis, and looked at the renovation/retrofit of the United Nations as a case study.

INTERNATIONAL ISSUES IN PRESERVATION ¶ SPRING 2017 ¶ ERICA AVRAMI, INSTRUCTOR ¶ This course examined international policies and processes in the preservation of cultural heritage, as well as their theoretical underpinnings. A primary aim of the course was to promote critical thinking about the various approaches to preservation and the cultural values that inform them, with an eye toward better understanding the diversity of global practices. The initial part of the course focused on the infrastructure of the international conservation arena, including programs, entities/institutions, and the World Heritage system. The remainder of the course explored cross-cutting issues, such as tourism, social justice and human rights, postcolonial dynamics, urbanization and sustainable development, the role of experts and disciplines, preserving vernacular practices and constructive cultures, etc., and the ways in which heritage and its conservation factor into these issues across varying geocultural contexts. The course had a hybrid lecture-seminar structure, and utilized cases, readings, student projects, and robust discussion to examine philosophies, policies, and professional praxis.

PRESERVATION PLANNING AND POLICY ¶ FALL 2016 ¶ ERICA AVRAMI, INSTRUCTOR ¶ This course was a comprehensive introduction to preservation planning that examined the history, theory, methodologies, and practices of historic preservation as a form of land use planning and public policy. The curriculum included the development of international conventions and charters, US federal legislation and programs, as well as municipal level regulations and practices, so as to analyze the institutional and professional development of preservation within a broader context of urban policy and governance. The course emphasized a critical understanding of the field's history and evolution to form a robust foundation from which to examine current policy tools and planning methods and their application to various heritage typologies, and also explored emerging trends in the field.

PRESERVATION COLLOQUIUM ¶ FALL 2016 ¶ PAUL BENTEL, CHRIS NEVILLE, INSTRUCTORS ¶ This colloquium was structured as a collective inquiry into preservation practice and theory, and as an opportunity for participants to reflect not only on preservation's role in the world, but also on their own roles within preservation. To that end, subject matter was drawn from each student's independent work, which provided focal points for an unfolding discussion about the potentials and limitations of contemporary practice. This course was offered in conjunction with Thesis 1.

OLD BUILDINGS—NEW FORMS: SURVEY AND ANALYSIS OF CONTEMPORARY WORK ¶ SPRING 2017 ¶ FRANÇOISE BOLLACK, INSTRUCTOR ¶ Old Buildings – New Forms examined the subject of architectural additions and transformations, from a design perspective, from the Renaissance to the present time, with an emphasis on international contemporary work. The seminar started with lectures providing an overview of additions and transformations from a historical perspective and progressed to the study of contemporary built projects in New York and worldwide: the seminar was intended to introduce preservation, architecture and planning students to the architectural questions posed by architectural additions and transformations to significant old buildings and to help them develop a method and an intellectual framework for evaluating the effect of the New Forms on our built heritage. The emphasis was on the physical reality of the works and their relationship to the architectural and artistic culture of their time.

NEIGHBORHOOD PRESERVATION AND ZONING ❡ SPRING 2017 ❡ CAROL CLARK, INSTRUCTOR ❡ This course provided an introduction to the ways in which neighborhood preservation goals are being achieved in several American cities. The use of neighborhood conservation district ordinances was a principal focus. Other mechanisms that seek to protect neighborhood character or regulate community appearance were also be explored. The class included an overview of the development of zoning in New York City to illustrate its role in local neighborhood preservation efforts. Contextual zoning, form-based codes, and the preparation of preservation plans were also discussed. Students were asked to debate the effectiveness of a variety of approaches to sustaining the integrity of neighborhoods.

DIGITAL VISUALIZATION TECHNIQUES FOR HISTORIC PRESERVATION ❡ FALL 2016 ❡ BRIGITTE COOK, INSTRUCTOR ❡ This workshop helped students develop dexterity in architectural representation in order to conceptualize and materialize the environmental, spatial and social aspects of an individual piece of architecture. Students built a three-dimensional computer massing model, which could be effectively manipulated and reproduced. A set of graphic images was produced to address a series of questions with shifting scales and topics. These images were examined critically for their ability to foster an understanding of the meaning of buildings.

LAW FOR PRESERVATIONISTS ❡ FALL 2016 ❡ WILLIAM COOK, INSTRUCTOR ❡ This course was designed to provide students with answers to questions all preservationists need to know about the law, concerning government regulation, private property, and historic resources. In the process of learning the answers to these questions, students developed an understanding of preservation law, its application, the legal system, and the interface between preservationists and lawyers.

PREMODERN AMERICAN ARCHITECTURE ❡ FALL 2016 ❡ JANET FOSTER, INSTRUCTOR ❡ This course examined the development of American architecture beginning with the earliest European settlements and culminating in the work of Henry Hobson Richardson and his peers in the late 19th century. Beginning with the earliest Spanish, French, Dutch, and English colonial architecture, the course explored the American adaptation of European forms and ideas and the development of a distinctly American architecture. The course lectures and readings examined high style and vernacular architecture in rural and urban environments throughout the settled parts of the United States.

BUILDING DIAGNOSTICS AND CONDITION SURVEY ❡ SPRING 2017 ❡ DON FRIEDMAN, WILLIAM RAYNOLDS, INSTRUCTORS ❡ This was a project-based course centered around ongoing restoration work at St. Bartholomew's Episcopal Church. Through lectures and field study, students gained exposure to techniques of condition survey and diagnosing typical problems that occur on ornamental facades. The assessment of the portal included a summary of its history and previous interventions, identification of materials of construction and description of current conditions, analysis of materials and their deterioration products, analysis of structural stability, and recommendations for future interventions. Students gained exposure to contemporary techniques in documentation including: using poles, lifts and a drone to capture visual information not available from the ground; creating 3D representations and orthophotographs of the portal using photogrammetry; using an AutoCAD workflow to generate measured drawings from photogrammetric results. Students also gained familiarity with diagnostic and analytical techniques including: vibration monitoring, ground-penetrating radar, and XRD/XRF. Information about previous interventions relied on field analyses and significant extant archival material held by the church. Laboratory analysis was performed using facilities at Columbia University, the Metropolitan Museum of Art, the Conservation Center at the Institute of Fine Arts of New York University, and field instrumentation provided by advising experts. The collective results were compiled into a report that models an Historic Structures Report typically provided for a project such as this. Students also communicated these processes clearly to the St. Bartholomew's Conservancy in a final presentation.

THE SOCIAL CONSTRUCTION OF TECHNOLOGY ❡ FALL 2016 ❡ DONALD FRIEDMAN, INSTRUCTOR ❡ Buildings are technological objects that reflect the practices of their builders, which in turn reflect their social context. Discussions of the history of technology have not dealt with building materials and systems in detail, particularly in the era of industrialized construction, leaving constructive technology as an adjunct to architectural history. This class examined the development of the technology of buildings in the context of the society that produced them: its style, its economy, its tools, and its expectations.

THE RIGHTS OF MONUMENTS ❡ FALL 2016 ❡ DAVID GISSEN, INSTRUCTOR ❡ Do monuments have international rights? And if monuments have such legal rights and protections, what might they be? How do they address protections from iconoclastic violence and combat, historical interpretation and misinterpretation, copyright and reproduction, aesthetic transformations, among other issues? This course examined these questions and those historical documents that called for the rights of monuments during times of war, revolution, environmental degradation, and social and political upheavals. The ultimate goal was to draft a provisional list of ten rights of the monument and that can provide axioms for future considerations of architectural heritage.

AMERICAN ARCHITECTURE SINCE 1876 ❡ SPRING 2017 ❡ JENNIFER GRAY, INSTRUCTOR ❡ This course surveyed architecture built in the United States from the first centennial in 1876 to the present. During these years, industrialization, urbanization, and mass migrations, all fueled by an expanding market economy, transformed the built environment. We learned about exceptional architects and iconic buildings, of course, but also about everyday spaces, such as shopping malls, suburbs, and highways. We also engaged topics in critical preservation, such as ecological conservation and curatorial practices. Questions related to race, gender, economic inequality, and militarism were explored, particularly as we unpacked the meanings of terms such as progressive, democracy, and American and considered them in a global context. The goal is to develop competence in identifying, understanding, and analyzing historic structures, their significance, and types. We gained proficiency in the use of methodological, historiographic, visual, and intellectual tools necessary to interpret historic buildings in their various contexts.

ARCHITECTURAL FINISHES ❡ SPRING 2017 ❡ MARY JABLONSKI, INSTRUCTOR ❡ Every building has architectural finishes. These finishes tell the stories of how people saw themselves and expressed themselves in their homes and any building they used. Architectural Finishes introduced students to how finishes convey meaning and style while they are also indicators of economics and technology. We focused on paint and wallpaper, examining how they were used as decoration, ornamentation, instruction, and protection. The course was a mix of lectures, site visits, and investigative work. As part of this course, the class worked on a field project.

PROFESSIONAL PRACTICE AND PROJECT MANAGEMENT ¶ SPRING 2017 ¶ CLAUDIA KAVENAGH, INSTRUCTOR ¶ Professional Practice and Project Management helped prepare students for what comes next, after graduation. Whether as a designer, a conservator, or a preservationist and whether in private practice or working for a non-profit or the government, how does it all come together to make a project happen, and what is your role in the process? Using completed and current projects as examples, including site visits to projects in construction and discussions with guest lecturers about their project work, we explored the many aspects of professional life that students don't learn about in their other academic coursework. The class included an examination of the principles as well as the practical application of project management. We study the typical sequence of activities that various types of projects follow, learning how a project manager shapes and guides a project. To accomplish this, the syllabus followed a "real world" process that preservation and restoration projects utilize, from responding to a Request for Proposals to the various phases of the design process and required governmental regulatory procedures, and including a review of the different kinds of work products that result from all these activities.

EXPERIMENTAL PRESERVATION ¶ SPRING 2017 ¶ JORGE OTERO-PAILOS, INSTRUCTOR ¶ This seminar explored how heritage is used and abused politically, and how recent experimental preservation practices are working on heritage to engage, resist, alter or influence cultural and political processes. The class was structured around discussions of readings and case studies. Readings included Koolhaas, Derrida, Deleuze, Agamben, Latour, Harman, Chakrabarti, Gadamer, Foucault, Lefebvre, Young and others. Case studies focused on practices that are crossing disciplinary boundaries, especially between art, architecture and preservation. We examined projects by Rachel Whiteread, Theaster Gates, José Damasceno, Jeremy Deller, Howard Giles, SVESMI, Andreas Angelidakis, David Gissen, Ines Weizman, Adam Lowe/Factum Arte, Santiago Borja, Johanna Blakley, Alex Lehnerer, Anya Sirota, Thomas Demand, Krzysztof Wodiczko, Tacita Dean, OMA, FAT, Luftwerk, Jakob Tigges, Numen/ForUse, Fujiko Nakaya, and others.

HISTORIC PRESERVATION THEORY & PRACTICE ¶ FALL 2016 ¶ JORGE OTERO-PAILOS, INSTRUCTOR ¶ This lecture course was an introduction to historic preservation theory and practice, as it developed in the West, from the Enlightenment to the present moment of globalization. The course focused especially on how preservation theories and experimental practices helped to redefine and advance new conceptions of architecture, cities and landscapes. The course asked questions about how theory and practice relate to one another, and how a solid grasp of the discipline's history can help preservationists articulate new ways of thinking and doing historic preservation.

ARCHITECTURAL METALS ¶ FALL 2016 ¶ RICHARD PIEPER, INSTRUCTOR ¶ This course reviewed the structural and decorative uses of metals in buildings and monuments. The metals covered include iron and steel; copper and copper alloys including bronze and brass; lead; tin; zinc; aluminum; nickel and chromium. The seminar examined the history of manufacture and use; mechanisms of deterioration and corrosion; and cleaning, repair, and conservation.

PRESERVING MODERN ARCHITECTURE ¶ FALL 2016 ¶ THEODORE PRUDON, INSTRUCTOR ¶ Most of our built environment dates from Post-WWII and is part of our collective cultural heritage. However, to what extent these sites deserve preservation and how this should be accomplished remains the subject of much discussion. This course addressed philosophical issues, building typologies, design, technology, architectural details, color, and art in the context of modern architecture and postmodernism.

READING BUILDINGS, WRITING BUILDINGS ¶ SPRING 2017 ¶ MARK RAKATANSKY, INSTRUCTOR ¶ This seminar explored a variety of visualization and written techniques in the close-reading of buildings, contemporary as well as those of prior centuries, that have been engaged to investigate the significance of the built environment. The building that students chose to develop their own forms of close-reading for the course could be from anytime and any place, chosen by the student because they found it particularly engaging. Readings included short texts and excerpts from the writings of Daniel Abramson, Reyner Banham, Giovanni Careri, Beatriz Colomina, Peter Eisenman, Robin Evans, Michel Foucault, Kenneth Frampton, Jeffrey Kipnis, Rem Koolhaas, Irving Lavin, Sylvia Lavin,

Greg Lynn, Colin Rowe, Bernhard Siegert, Manfredo Tafuri, Bernard Tschumi, Robert Venturi, and Rudolf Wittkower. As writing is itself an act of design, one can track how these writings are constructed so that an intended argument is proposed, developed, and articulated through the narrative and rhetorical attentions in its design as it tracks the attentions of the building under investigation.

DRAWING IDEOLOGY ¶ SPRING 2017 ¶ BRYONY ROBERTS, INSTRUCTOR ¶ This seminar looked at the visual culture of preservation—how different drawing techniques convey radically different approaches to historical architecture. Moving chronologically from the Italian Renaissance to contemporary 3D scanning, the course looked at drawings that express major transitions in preservation thinking, such as John Ruskin's romantic watercolors, Viollet-le-Duc's analytical axonometrics, and virtual 3D models. The course examined drawings alongside written treatises on preservation to understand the relationship between visual and textual polemics. Students were encouraged to think critically about the visual tools they often use, by understanding their historical lineages. Students had the option of developing visual or written assignments for the course, and were encouraged to experiment with different forms of representation.

BASIC CONSERVATION SCIENCE ¶ SPRING 2017 ¶ NORMAN WEISS, GEORGE WHEELER, INSTRUCTORS ¶ This course presented the basic principles of conservation science of architectural materials and served as the foundation for subsequent material-based conservation courses such as: 1. Architectural Metals, 2. Concrete, Cast Stone and Mortar, 3. Brick, Terra Cotta and Stone, 4. Architectural Finishes in America, and, 5. Wood. The first two lectures focused on developing the fundamental scientific language for the study of inorganic materials that were explored in the following weeks through lectures, demonstrations, and laboratory sessions. The pattern was repeated for organic materials later in the semester: two lectures on fundamental scientific language followed by lectures, demonstrations and laboratories on paint, clear finishes, and wood.

BRICK TERRA COTTA & STONE ¶ SPRING 2017 ¶ NORMAN WEISS, DAN ALLEN, GEORGE WHEELER, INSTRUCTORS ¶ This course explored the group of traditional masonry materials—brick, terra cotta and stone. The format included lectures, demonstrations, field and laboratory exercises and field trips. The goals of the course were to provide: 1) an historical overview of their manufacturing and sourcing as architectural materials with a focus on the 18th century to the present; 2) an understanding of their fundamental material properties in relation to their use and deterioration in a range of masonry construction systems; and 3) an exploration of the means and methods of their repair, maintenance, and conservation.

CONCRETE, CAST STONE AND MORTAR ¶ FALL 2016 ¶ NORMAN WEISS, JOHN WALSH, INSTRUCTORS ¶ This course discussed the growing importance of concrete, cast stone and mortar—and the associated construction techniques developed during the Industrial Revolution, reviewing discoveries that led to the development of lime and cement-based compositions from the late 18th century to the present. By the 20th century, advances in technology transformed concrete and precast from functional engineering media into the most expressive and sculptural substances of modernism. The visual simplicity of these materials belies the complexity of their curing and aging mechanisms. Materials science is the fundamental tool used to examine history, and to define suitable repair, replication and maintenance methods for masonry and concrete structures. Key topics in this course were binder types and curing mechanisms; the role of aggregates and admixtures; performance criteria; construction/manufacturing methods; and field and laboratory evaluation. The format of this course was a lively combination of lectures (including guest speakers), hands-on exercises, and field trips.

BUILDING SYSTEMS, AND MATERIALS ¶ FALL 2016 ¶ GEORGE WHEELER, INSTRUCTOR ¶ This course surveyed historic building systems and materials. The first part focused on traditional building materials such as stone, brick, terra cotta, metal, concrete, cast stone, mortar, and wood. It also explored sourcing, identification and production of the materials, their use in the fabrication of architectural elements, and basic properties that limit or allow their use and performance as architectural materials. The second part surveyed historic building systems and approached the building not from its constituent materials and their properties but as an assembly of particular materials and building elements. This course also explored the design, detailing and material together to understand how materials interact and to assess their collective performance beginning with building technologies as they began to emerge by the middle of the 19th century.

INTERPRETATION AND ARCHITECTURE ¶ SPRING 2017 ¶ JESSICA WILLIAMS, INSTRUCTOR ¶ This course introduced students to the theory and practice of interpretation, a process of revealing the meanings of cultural resources to an audience. Through readings, class discussion, case studies and exercises, students explored such topics as philosophies of interpretation, methods of interpretation and current issues and challenges in interpretation. The course emphasizes the importance of storytelling and narrative development, as well as the various tools—traditional and 21st century—that interpreters employ. The first part of the course introduced interpretation as a process and a practice, while the second part looked closely at current problems in interpretation. Course readings were interdisciplinary, drawing upon literature from historic preservation, museum studies, public history, and related disciplines.

THESIS 1 ¶ FALL 2016 ¶ PAUL BENTEL, CHRISTOPHER NEVILLE, INSTRUCTORS ¶ Students began work on their thesis in the fall semester. They articulated and refined their thesis topic, decided on a faculty advisor, and began research to answer the thesis question.

1

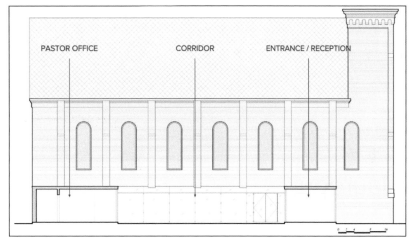

NEW ADDITION

PASTOR OFFICE   CORRIDOR   ENTRANCE / RECEPTION

Siri Olson, Halley Ramon, Armon M. White, Travis Kennedy

2

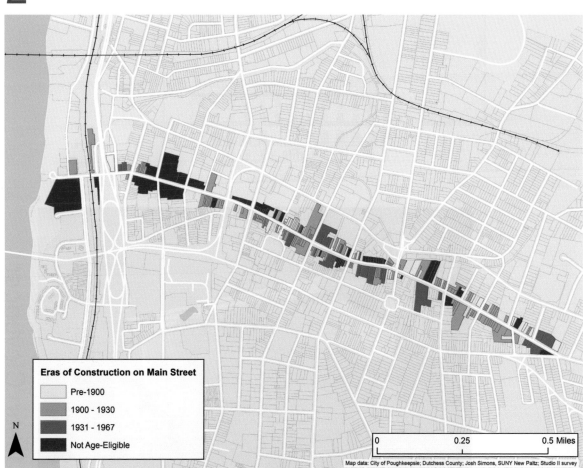

Eras of Construction on Main Street

Pre-1900

1900 - 1930

1931 - 1967

Not Age-Eligible

0   0.25   0.5 Miles

Map data: City of Poughkeepsie; Dutchess County; Josh Simons, SUNY New Paltz; Studio II survey

N

Andre Jauregui

3

Armon White

4

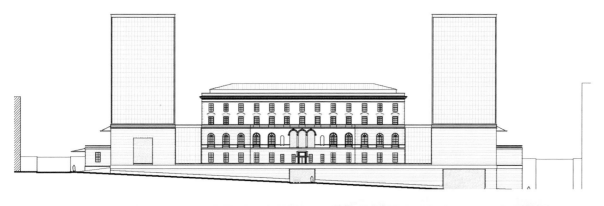

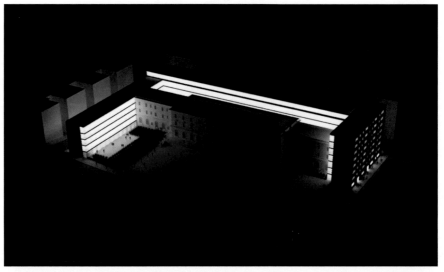

5

6

7

8

Alex P. Ray, Fei Teng,
Teresa A. Spears

9

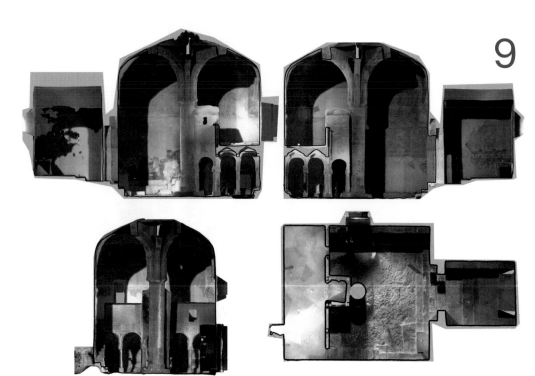

Nicole M. Mezydlo,
Andrea N. Sforza

10

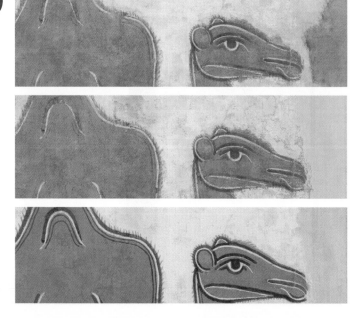

Jessica E. Betz,
Katrina L. Virbitsky,
Yuanyi Zhang

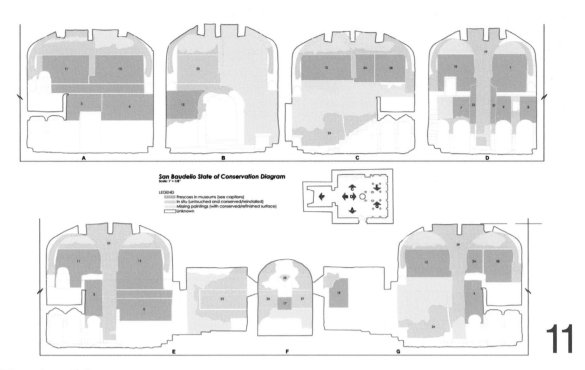

11

Tania Alam,
Allison L. Semrad

12

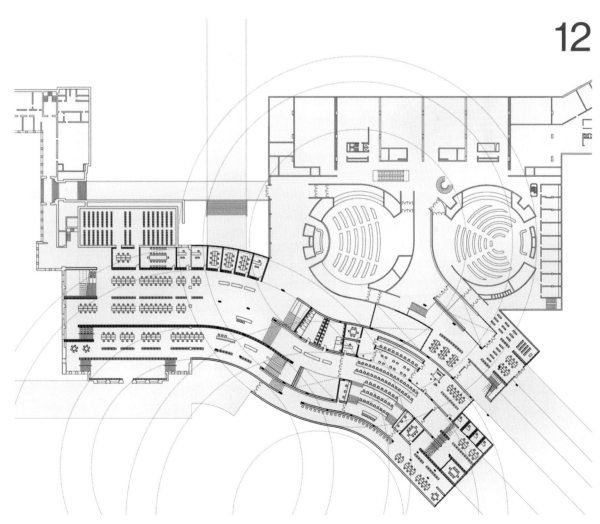

Andrew M. Luy

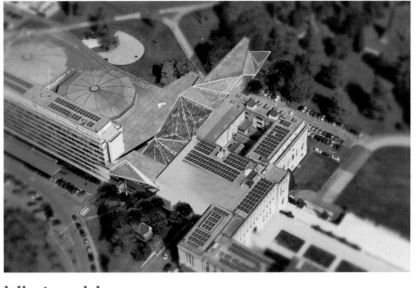

Victor Hugo

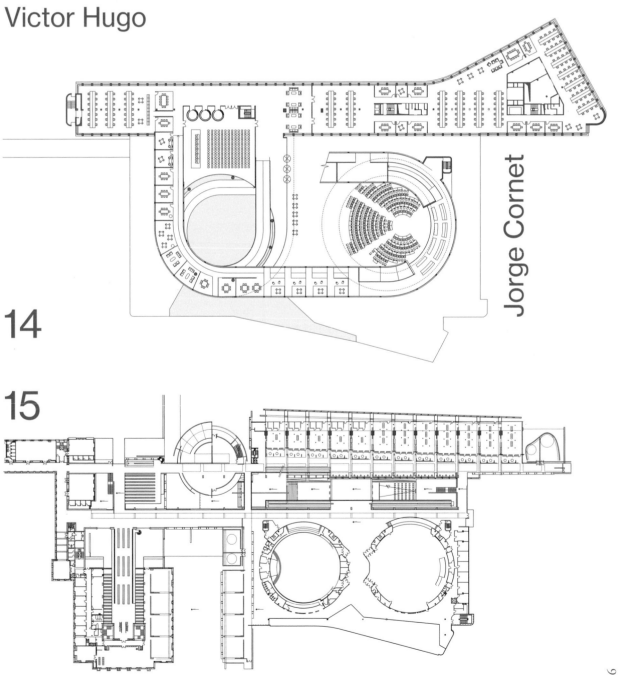

14

Jorge Cornet

15

Miguel F. Castaneda

THE EVOLUTION OF AMERICAN "HISTORIC COLOR PALETTES" ¶ MARY JABLONSKI, ADVISOR ¶

Tania Alam

"Historic Color Palette" is a group of paint colors that are supposed to have a historic connection to architecture. This thesis is a look at how these color palettes came into existence and how they have developed over time. The concept of linking certain color groups to particular time periods and places is an intriguing one. It first emerged in the United States as a descriptor of historic colors discovered at Colonial Williamsburg. With time the palettes have extended beyond the Colonial period and now include even the mid-century modern. These palettes have grown over time to become a popular means of creating visual connections to the past. But what do these colors represent? Representing specific regions and time-periods in history, the "historic color palette" is an important means of telling the story of the nation.

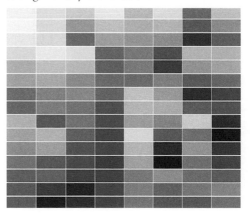

THE INFLUENCE OF GLASS TRANSITION TEMPERATURE ON THE PERFORMANCE OF ACRYLIC THERMOPLASTIC ADHESIVES ¶ GEORGE WHEELER, ADVISOR ¶

Jessica Betz

Acrylic thermoplastic resins are commonly used in conservation for consolidation and as adhesives. They are popular with conservators due to their reversibility and their considerable strength in moderately temperate environments; however, when used in an environment that exceeds their glass transition temperature (Tg), the adhesives will soften and flow, causing the adhered objects to slump or fall apart. The research presented in this thesis examines the performance of acrylic adhesives in environments with high heat exposure.

ENGLISH ANTECEDENTS OF THE QUEEN ANNE IN AMERICA: A STUDY OF ANGLO-AMERICAN DOMESTIC ARCHITECTURE ¶ JANET W. FOSTER, ADVISOR ¶ There is a significant English influence on the development of the American domestic architectural style known as "Queen Anne." Beginning in the 1870s American architects used both "Old English" and "Queen Anne Revival" elements as a way for Anglophiles to express their values in their houses. These clients and their houses enabled a few American architects to transform into practice what they absorbed from English architectural journals. This architectural style is visually distinct from American Queen Anne buildings that developed after 1876 and thus constitutes an exploration of a previously undiscussed chapter of American Architecture.

Elizabeth Lawrence Canon

THE COLORS OF CULTURE: A FINISHES STUDY OF THE DUTCH-AMERICAN STONE HOUSES OF BERGEN COUNTY, NEW JERSEY ¶ JANET W. FOSTER, ADVISOR ¶ The Dutch-American Stone Houses of Bergen County, New Jersey represent a distinctive form within the American vernacular architectural tradition. Built from the early eighteenth to the middle of the nineteenth century, these houses are commonly characterized by the employment of structural members based upon H-bent frame construction, red sandstone elevations, and steep gable or gambrel-shaped roofs. Although a large body of research has been undertaken concerning this vernacular house type, including research on those stylistic traits just mentioned, little if any research has been published concerning the architectural finishes of these distinct structures. This thesis aims to identify if a palette of distinctively Dutch paint colors for interior and exterior paints existed and was employed in the Dutch-American Stone Houses of Bergen County from 1740 to 1776; or, if the paint colors employed within these houses were part of a larger colonial trend.

Kimberly DeMuro

BEIRUT'S CIVIL WAR HOTEL DISTRICT: PRESERVING THE WORLD'S FIRST HIGH-RISE URBAN BATTLEFIELD ¶ JORGE OTERO-PAILOS, ADVISOR ¶ This thesis aims to preserve a historic event in Beirut through the proposal of a historic district. The event in question is the Battle of the Hotels, a 5-month urban battle that took place within and around the historic luxury hotel district in the Minet El Husn neighborhood of Beirut at the beginning of the 15-year Lebanese Civil War (1975–1990). The battle opposed the left-wing pro-Palestinian Lebanese National Movement against the right-wing Christian-nationalist Phalanges Party. The battle is worth commemorating, and therefore preserving, for its instrumental role in shaping the urban rift that divided the city of Beirut during the Lebanese civil war, violently affecting the lives of all Lebanese citizens for a period of 13 years. Lebanese society shares a violent history that could, if considered a common heritage, be part of its postwar nation-building identity and inspire socio-political reform. The Battle of the Hotels' significance also lies in its status as the first high-rise urban battle in the world. As a global historic event, the battle deserves to be commemorated as a peace-building historic district, protesting urban warfare and civil war as the current most common methods for conducting war.

Mayssa Jallad

THE DRAFT RIOTS RECONSIDERED: INTERPRETING NEW YORK'S SITES OF RACIAL CONFLICT ⁊ JESSICA WILLIAMS, ADVISOR ⁊ The 1863 New York Draft Riots were the largest civil insurrection in American history—it is estimated that hundreds perished in the violence of the week of July 13–18, 1863, triggered principally by the imposition of the Union Army's Federal Conscription Act. Motivated additionally by the passage of the Emancipation Proclamation earlier that year, mobs viciously targeted the City's African-American population, brutally beating and lynching black New Yorkers in the streets. While New York's identity has traditionally been understood as that of a great melting pot, a haven for diversity, the violence of the Draft Riots perhaps serves as the singular, representative event in the City's history to counter such a notion. This thesis involves a proposal for the design and implementation of a series of experimental, site-based, public history interpretation efforts related to the racial and social implications of the 1863 New York Draft Riots. The initiatives formulated throughout seek to interpret the contemporary social significance and relevance of the Draft Riots, and the most effective means of place-based education of the events, which thus far have remained largely obscured in the public conscience.

Nicholas Kazmierski

RETHINKING THE VERNACULAR IN CHINA: UNDERSTANDING THE DYNAMICS OF SOCIAL TRANSFORMATION AND THE EVOLUTION OF RURAL ARCHITECTURE ⁊ ERICA C. AVRAMI, ADVISOR ⁊ The physical forms of vernacular architecture and spatial use reflect the social systems and ideologies of the rural environment. This thesis seeks to rethink the preservation of vernacular architecture by analyzing the physical manifestations of three eras and their respective architectural layers, characterized by social identities in the history of China. In this sense, this thesis does not necessarily follow past practices of studying vernacular architecture, which prioritize formal, structural, and material analyses. It instead recognizes a paradigmatic shift in heritage theory and policy that seeks to understand and valorize the relationships between populations and their environment.

Cheng Liao

DIGITAL PHOTOGRAMMETRY FOR LONG-TERM MONITORING ⁊ WILLIAM RAYNOLDS, ADVISOR ⁊ Digital photogrammetry has established itself as an effective tool for documenting cultural heritage in the twenty-first century. With portable equipment and a relatively short amount of time, an incredible amount of surface data can be captured for an object and stored as point clouds. This richness of data raises questions of whether it should be used for analytical purposes in addition to documentation. This thesis uses close-range, digital photogrammetry to describe physical change over time. The image sets were captured, point clouds created in Agisoft, and analyzed using CloudCompare to identify any dislocations. The speed, ease, and relatively low cost of photogrammetry makes it very effective at homing in on areas of concern.

Nicole Mezydlo

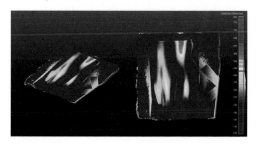

REINTERPRETING PIONEER DEEP SPACE STATION ¶ JESSICA WILLIAMS, ADVISOR ¶ This project argues for the interpretation of NASA's historic space probes. Robotic space exploration programs have permanently transformed humans' understanding of Earth, but the probes at the center of NASA's first pioneering missions to deep space in the 1960s and 1970s will never return to their origin. Today, the historical significance of these objects is embodied in a network of resources that reflect triumphs of human curiosity, not just advancements in technology. The widely unrecognized contributions that women and men made to the history of "unmanned" space exploration reveal themselves on Earth through the enduring infrastructure that humans built and the data that humans rendered in their pursuit to understand the Solar System.

Alex Ray

EVALUATING THE SUCCESS OF UNESCO WORLD HERITAGE SITES ¶ ERICA AVRAMI, ADVISOR ¶ The UNESCO World Heritage Convention was signed in 1972 with the purpose of protecting cultural and natural heritage on a global level for all the peoples of the world. Since the signing of the Convention, there have been hundreds of books, articles, and media reports written about the effects of World Heritage designation. A large number of these critiques focus on the negative impacts on the local communities at the heritage sites. While the World Heritage system has helped protect hundreds of heritage sites, these criticisms related to the local communities suggest that there is a disconnect between local communities and the global stakeholders. The primary aim of this thesis is to examine how the success of World Heritage Sites is currently evaluated, and how the measures used for evaluation may need to evolve. Now that the World Heritage system has been in place for nearly 50 years, an improved understanding of global-local dynamics and the effects of designation on communities can inform new indicators of success that better respond to today's societal conditions.

Sarah Reddan

ARTS & CULTURAL DISTRICTS AND PRESERVATION POLICY: A NEIGHBORHOOD ANALYSIS OF THE RIVER NORTH (RINO) ART DISTRICT ¶ ERICA AVRAMI AND ROBERT BEAUREGARD, ADVISORS ¶ Though cultural planning is a relatively recent concept its contribution to urban planning and historic preservation is paramount. Many states, cities and smaller communities within the United States have turned to cultural planning and programming to aid revitalization and development, including arts and cultural districts, which serve as models of place-based ingenuity. These places serve as points of community engagement and economic development as well as support the cultural identities that strengthen business and tourism. Moreover, they are designed to encourage artists, entrepreneurs, institutions, and potential developers to build upon and organize around existing arts and culture-based resources. This research aims to understand the role that historic built environments play in the vitality of arts and cultural districts. The study undergoes an intensive examination of a singular case study: the River North (RiNo) Art District in Denver, Colorado, through qualitative and quantitative analyses. This thesis proves the economic value and visual appeal that these historic buildings have on the RiNo Art District, and provides recommendations that help to expand the preservation toolbox and facilitate an intersection between arts and cultural districts and the preservation field.

Cameron Maureen Robertson

INHERENTLY FLAWED: CARBONATION-INDUCED CRACKING IN REINFORCED CONCRETE STRUCTURES ¶ Concrete was considered an everlasting, permanent material from its expanding use at the end of the 19th century until the early 1900s. In the 1910s and 20s scientific research on concrete failure began, a response to the inevitable cracks and deterioration that began to plague concrete structures. Today cracks are recognized as an inevitable symptom of the deterioration of concrete structures. Early-age cracking is often due to improper rebar cover and carbonation-induced corrosion. This thesis explores some aspects of the cracking of reinforced concrete structures caused by carbonation-induced corrosion, and historical approaches to conservation repair and treatment, from the use of early cementitious patching and crack stitching in the 1950s to modern conservation materials, such as injectable crack fillers, sealers, and penetrating silane water repellents. This thesis has attempted to clarify the understanding of conservation treatments for reinforced concrete structures.

Katrina Lee Virbitsky

PRESERVATION, MANAGEMENT, AND STABILIZATION APPROACHES AT FRANK LLOYD WRIGHT'S TALIESIN: AN ANALYSIS OF THE EVOLUTION OF INTERVENTION STRATEGIES ¶ THEODORE PRUDON, ADVISOR ¶ Taliesin, Frank Lloyd Wright's home and studio in Wisconsin, is an eight-hundred acre estate situated in a rural, rolling landscape. The site is significant because of its architectural character, as a collection of representative works spanning Wright's entire career, as well as for its association with the Taliesin Fellowship, Wright's elaborate and well-documented model for teaching and living. Taliesin is currently open for tours and also houses a resident community made up of students, their faculty, interns, and a few older members of the Fellowship, often referred to as Legacy Fellows. For preservationists and the site's caretakers, Taliesin's buildings pose a particularly thorny problem. Students and apprentices were responsible for much of Taliesin's construction, and Wisconsin's harsh climate often accelerates the material deterioration of wood details, structural elements, plaster, stucco, and cedar-shingle roofs. The research presented in this thesis lays out a chronology detailing how Taliesin has been managed and preserved since Frank Lloyd Wright's death in 1959. The second half of the thesis details three case studies—areas that shed light on specific structural interventions, as a way to understand how these physical projects reflect the values of Taliesin's residents and caretakers.

Allison Semrad

AN EFFECTIVE FRAMEWORK OF PUBLIC-PRIVATE PARTNERSHIPS: CREATING AN ECONOMICALLY VIABLE PLAN FOR CONSERVING AND MANAGING BEIJING'S URBAN HERITAGE SITES ¶ CAROL CLARK, ADVISOR ¶ In the ongoing process of urbanization, China is experiencing budgetary constraints on heritage conservation, as well as the inappropriate reuse of buildings, have together exerted a negative impact on urban heritage sites in China's cities, like Beijing. Despite these problems, public-private partnerships (PPPs), may serve as an effective tool which can not only address these problems, but also achieve a balance between heritage conservation and economic development. The primary aim of this work is to build more understanding about key factors for developing an effective framework of heritage PPPs to create an economically viable plan for conserving and managing Beijing's urban heritage sites.

Fei Teng

VISUALIZING VALUE: A GEOSPATIAL LOOK AT COMPARATIVE APPROACHES TO LOCAL VALUATION OF CULTURAL HERITAGE ¶ WILLIAM RAYNOLDS, ADVISOR ¶ This study researches the viability and effectiveness of using Twitter data as a research tool for assessing local valuation of cultural resources. It looks at Twitter as a tool that can be used alongside other more tested community value assessment techniques. The study's subject population is the LGBTQ community in New York City's five boroughs, but these or similar tools could potentially be used for other populations that use Twitter around the country and world.

Stacy Lynn Tomczyk

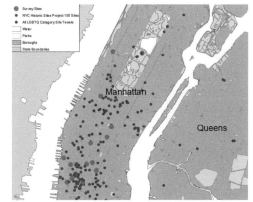

BERTRAND GOLDBERG: PRESERVING A VISION OF CONCRETE ❡ THEODORE PRUDON, ADVISOR ❡ This thesis seeks to evaluate how an architect's intentions play a role in preservation and conservation work on the exterior surface of modern concrete structures; more specifically, the impact coating has on exposed concrete structures. To do this, the body of work of architect Bertrand Goldberg is analyzed. Bertrand Goldberg's architecture, characterized by monumental curvilinear concrete forms, has been the subject of both praise and scorn in recent years. Goldberg is among a generation of architects who designed their work in reinforced concrete for both the freedom of form and the economy that it provided. Because the aesthetic of exposed concrete has generally been either dismissed or entirely despised, many of these buildings, including Goldberg's, have been subject to coating treatments which completely transforming the character of the building. These repairs or restorations are often inconsistent with, and insensitive to, the intentions of the original architects who prioritized the surface of the concrete exterior as part of the overall expression of the architectural work.

Andrea N. Sforza

THE PROGRESSION OF HISTORIC PRESERVATION IN MIAMI BEACH AND THE CHALLENGES OF SEA LEVEL RISE ❡ CAROL CLARK, ADVISOR ❡ Climate-based disasters caused $46 billion in damage and killed at least 138 in the 48 contiguous United States last year, with inland flooding emerging as the costliest weather event for the first time since 1997. The number of billion-dollar occurrences in 2016 was the second highest since 1980. Combined with increasing sea levels on prone low-lying coastal areas, disaster mitigation has been a top concern of municipalities. Miami Beach currently averages just four feet above sea level, and has already begun to rigorously experiment with resiliency infrastructure. This is especially concerning as experts estimate beachfront property in Miami-Dade County to be valued at $15 billion, with over $3.5 trillion in losses by 2070. This thesis examines a chronological progression of historic preservation in Miami Beach as a case study for understanding and applying past lessons learned for future integration within citywide resiliency planning and adaptation.

Laura Weinstein-Berman

URBAN PRESERVATION IN CHINA: THE SURVIVAL OF AN IDEA DESPITE POLITICAL REPRESSION, 1950-1982 ❡ JORGE OTERO-PAILOS, ADVISOR ❡ This thesis is an intellectual history of the idea of urban preservation in China from its origins in the 1950s, through its survival despite political repression during the 1960s and 1970s, to its becoming official policy in the 1980s. This thesis addresses a history that has been overlooked, as the period between the 1950s and 1980s is generally skipped over in textbooks and articles about Chinese urban preservation. This thesis unveils the social, academic, and professional histories that covertly nurtured and carried forward the idea of urban preservation. This work tells the story of individuals who fought for preservation, often at great personal risk.

Qi Zhang

Real Estate Development

Patrice Derrington, Director

The Masters of Science in Real Estate Development (M.S.RED) degree program is a one-year, full-time, immersive learning environment for the technical training, intellectual advancement and practical formation of the most accomplished and prepared professional for the real estate industry.

The M.S.RED program is uniquely resourced to provide the various theoretical explorations and technical skills needed for the real estate sector, in addition to effective training in the synthesis of decision-making through development projects and pertinent industry case studies, achieved as follows:

(1) The conceptual construct of this amalgamated learning is immediately referenced to the fundamental theories of urban planning and architectural design at GSAPP.

(2) The necessary technical knowledge from various disciplines—such as finance, market analysis, construction methods, law, data science, and project management—to perform in the industry are provided by excellent instructors who practice at the top levels of their respective professions in New York City.

(3) The application of the theory and skills to resolving various real estate challenges and issues are given rich, complex and exciting examples in New York that also connect and have implications globally.

Furthermore, with the growing entrepreneurial and technologically advanced environment of Columbia University, the program includes training and proficiency in real estate databases and the digital tools of analysis, with the opportunity to explore emerging applications being investigated in the Center for Urban Real Estate, the affiliated research laboratory. It is anticipated that within this rich, innovative environment, the program's curriculum development will continue to produce further synthesized forms of teaching and research to produce the most effective, intellectually progressive and multi-faceted real estate profession.

REAL ESTATE FINANCE I ❡ SUMMER 2016 ❡ PATRICE DERRINGTON, INSTRUCTOR, WITH JOHNNY DIN ❡ The objective of this course was for the student to develop a robust working competency with the tools and methods of financial analysis used by real estate developers, lenders, and investors. Students solidified and expanded their knowledge of the various concepts inherent in the financial analysis of real estate investments, applied these concepts to making critical analyses of various real estate investment proposals, and built upon these tools in formulating the capital structure of debt and equity for real estate transactions. In parallel with the lectures, students attended a Modeling Tutorial to develop their facility with Excel and also strengthened their understanding and utilization of the analytical processes learned in the lectures.

REAL ESTATE FINANCE II ❡ FALL 2016 ❡ PATRICE DERRINGTON, MARIA KASTANIS, AND STEVEN BLOOM, INSTRUCTORS ❡ Building on the fundamental analytical tools and methods of Real Estate Finance 1, this course extended the investigation to the financial aspects of the development and construction phase, and to the equity investment structures and returns for real estate deals. The development and construction phase comprises the following analytical processes: quick back-of-the-envelope analysis, evaluating highest & best use, establishing sources and uses for the project, formulating the construction loan and repayment, valuation of completed project, and project returns. These tools and methods were learned and applied to example situations and case studies. Real estate investors can choose among many vehicles through which to gain equity exposure, and the structuring of the deal's capital stack to achieve maximized returns, the alignment of interests, liquidity, operator incentives, and tax-efficiency provides added complexity. Specifying the format and timing of the investors' returns on the deal requires advanced cash flow modeling. Various equity structures were reviewed to determine the associated cash flow patterns and tax implications, paying particular attention to limited partnership promotes and waterfall distributions. Additionally, the utilization of the REIT and UPREIT structures to finance acquisitions was introduced.

REAL ESTATE FINANCE III: CAPITAL MARKETS ❡ SPRING 2017 ❡ LISA BEESON, INSTRUCTOR ❡ Building upon the fundamental analysis of real estate investments, this course

provided an understanding of complex equity investment strategies, structured finance, and various capitalization formats including direct and securitized equity. The creation and management of investment funds was proposed and evaluated for optimal return performance. Students were required to model and propose a unique and compelling capitalization structure.

REAL ESTATE FINANCE III: CAPITAL MARKETS ❡ SPRING 2017 ❡ MERRIE FRANKEL, INSTRUCTOR ❡ The course touched on all facets of public and private capital providers, as well as investors, with particular focus on commercial real estate in the public markets: the recent history of securitized real estate debt and equity; the structure of CMBS and roles of the major participants; the growth, structure, valuation and performance measurements of real estate investment trusts (REITS); and other deal formats. Current events permeated all classes as capital markets is a fluid subject. The general topics included: Real Estate Industry Trends—past and present; Overview of Real Estate Capital Markets and Participants; Alternative Investments (CMBS, REITs, high yield, syndications); Financial and Ownership Structures; Rating Methodology; Bankruptcy; Capital Markets Instruments.

THE DEALMAKING PROCESS: DEBT, EQUITY AND THE ART OF NEGOTIATION ❡ SUMMER 2016 ❡ MITCHELL ADELSTEIN, INSTRUCTOR ❡ This elective taught practical methods and techniques used by investors, lenders, and equity investors: (i) how to underwrite value-add opportunistic income-producing real estate, (ii) finance positions in real estate using various debt facilities and/or equity vehicles, and (iii) understand the transaction process through group participation in a mock transaction case study. The class was split up into "Deal Teams" that were responsible to underwrite and negotiate a deal to purchase, finance and close the transaction. The Deal Teams were encouraged to make a deal—in other words—the Buyers want to buy, the Lenders want to lend, the Sellers want to sell and Equity Investors want to invest. Each group presented their analysis and discussed the transaction process during the final session.

CAPITAL MARKETS: DEBT ❡ SPRING 2017 ❡ ED ADLER, INSTRUCTOR ❡ This course covered the various CRE debt instruments and financing techniques: balance sheet direct lending, syndications, bridge and mezzanine structures, and the

process of underwriting for CMBS, warehouse, and Repo financing. In parallel, the students took a course Capital Markets: Equity Transactions in which they examined M&A, REITs, Private Equity, and Sponsor Waterfalls. Each class was case based and gave the student an understanding of the lender's point of view regarding the application and use of various capital market's based debt products to finance commercial real estate.

DEVELOPMENT ANALYSIS: URBAN PLANNING ❡ SUMMER 2016 ❡ KATE ASCHER, ETHEL SHEFFER, INSTRUCTORS ❡ Real estate development is largely an urban phenomenon. Understanding the fundamental urban planning issues, opportunities and risks associated with a given project is critical to successful development. These include a range of government regulations, powers and incentives, including those associated with land use, zoning, sustainability, building safety, historic preservation and the environment. They also include broader issues associated with gentrification, public space and community participation. This half-semester introduction to urban planning used New York as the canvas to introduce these topics to students through relevant readings and case studies.

HISTORY OF REAL ESTATE DEVELOPMENT IN NEW YORK CITY ❡ FALL 2016 ❡ KATE ASCHER, INSTRUCTOR ❡ This course offered a historical survey of the last four centuries of real estate development in New York City, with a primary focus on Manhattan. It relied not only on existing sources held by Columbia libraries and others, but also on material from the collection of Seymour Durst—a patriarch of one of New York's foremost real estate families and a passionate collector of the city's historical memorabilia. The course was organized chronologically, and covered the period from the original Dutch settlement of New Amsterdam through the present time. However, each presentation also contained thematic elements, using real estate developments to examine social and economic forces of the period. In the first half of the course, these topics ranged from the earliest systems of landholding and the evolution of the Manhattan street grid through the development of the nation's first public housing projects and the construction of the world's tallest skyscrapers. The latter part of the course touched specifically on modern themes that continue to shape the real estate environment of the city today. These include the continued regeneration of a once-industrial waterfront, the ever-evolving nature of public-private partnerships in development, and the seminal connection between civic places, like transportation hubs and parks, and real estate.

REINVENTING RESIDENTIAL ZONING FOR THE URBAN AGE ¶ FALL 2016 ¶ KATE ASCHER, KATE DUNHAM, INSTRUCTORS ¶ Cities all over the world are facing new challenges regarding rising housing demands as the majority of the world's population becomes urbanized. In many cases, cities are resorting to the "quick and easy" mass-production of residential super-blocks to address the increasing housing demands. But is this model appropriate for all cities, regardless of their environmental, social, political and economic differences? In this seminar students developed their own responses to this question based on international case study research and analysis. The seminar provided students with a hands-on opportunity to understand how planning code regulations—specifically residential codes—can shape the design and functioning of future urban neighborhoods.

REAL ESTATE ENTREPRENEUR-IALISM FOR ARCHITECTS, BUILDERS, DEVELOPERS, BUY-ERS & SELLERS ¶ FALL 2016 ¶ HANK BELL, INSTRUCTOR ¶ This course was led by the one of the first practitioner academics to define the independent discipline of development. The lectures were designed to fill in the gaps with practical knowledge and hard lessons learned from generations of practitioners. Students were provided with the know-how of materializing their visions at the entrepreneurial scale.

REAL ESTATE DEBT SECU-RITIZATION ¶ SPRING 2017 ¶ STEVEN BLOOM, INSTRUCTOR ¶ In this course, students investigated the process of real estate debt securitization including underwriting, issuance templates, debt tranches, and ratings. The analysis and modeling of portfolios of commercial real estate loans for securitization was undertaken with students performing individual securitization structuring. The securitization of residential mortgages was briefly discussed.

DEVELOPMENT FINANCIAL ANALYSIS AND MODELING ¶ FALL 2016 ¶ RIDGE CHEW, INSTRUCTOR ¶ This course advanced students' knowledge and technical skills with Excel financial modeling, and covered the more complex construction of the DCF Proforma around various capital structures of partnership equity waterfalls, preferred equity, mezzanine debt and securitized debt. By comple-

tion, the course required students to build complex financial models from scratch. In this course, students learned the technical concepts and analytical methods utilized in determining the financial feasibility, the debt funding, and investment returns of real estate development projects and the inter-linking with investment returns of the stabilized income-producing asset. Competence with the applicable financial modeling tools was gained; and the details of decision-making in the various stages of the development and construction process were covered.

ADVANCED CASE STUDIES IN REAL ESTATE ANALYSIS ¶ SPRING 2017 ¶ PATRICE DER-RINGTON, CHRIS MUNSELL, INSTRUCTORS ¶ Building upon the concepts, models and tools previously studied, in this course students learned to analyze, capitalize and negotiate various types of real estate transactions, including in the more complex partnership, family company, and funds management situations. The course required critical thinking and analysis, deep investigation and resolution of case studies, and active engagement in discussion and debate.

CAPSTONE: DEVELOPMENT CASE STUDIES ¶ SPRING 2017 ¶ PATRICE DERRINGTON, KATE ASCHER, RICK LELAND, SHAWN AMSLER, INSTRUCTORS ¶ The class utilized various real estate development and investment case studies, in conjunction with outside real estate developers and investors within the industry. The cases reached across a broad array of product types, situational decision making, and business styles. This course utilized selected real estate development and investment case studies, in conjunction with guest presentations by external real estate developers and investors within the industry. In reviewing the cases, determining alternative actions, and debating the decisions made, students honed their rapid and effective decision-making and management skills while working in a team-based process where all aspects of the real estate business proved to be critical success factors. Each student then formulated an individual development or investment proposal, as a Deal Book, in which the comprehensive and compelling proposition was made. Each student also made a verbal "pitch" for their proposal to an audience of faculty and industry professionals.

INTERNATIONAL REAL ES-TATE REGIONS ¶ SPRING 2017 ¶ SECTION 1: CHINA ¶ PATRICE DERRINGTON, JOHNNY DIN, INSTRUCTORS ¶ SECTION 2:

BRAZIL ¶ SHAWN AMSLER, INSTRUCTOR ¶ SECTION 3: LONDON ¶ KATE ASCHER, IN-STRUCTOR ¶ The classroom sessions preceding these international trips comprised research, analysis, and discussions regarding the destination countries—the details of the macroeconomic conditions, the real estate markets, the opportunities for attractive investment returns, the challenges of investing cross-border into the country, and the identification of a specific investment. Students in small groups prepared an investment proposal, or Deal Book, for a cross-border investment in the target country; and in addition to producing the e-copy and hard copy of the Deal Book, each group made a presentation "pitch" for the proposal.

REAL ESTATE FINANCE MODEL-ING TUTORIAL 2 ¶ FALL 2016 ¶ JOHNNY DIN, INSTRUCTOR ¶ In parallel with the lectures, students attended a Real Estate Finance Tutorial to develop their facility with Excel and also strengthen their understanding and utilization of the analytical processes learnt in the lectures.

IT AND THE REAL ESTATE ENTERPRISE ¶ SPRING 2017 ¶ ROBERT ENTIN, INSTRUCTOR ¶ This course dealt with a variety of IT issues and real estate business activities. It is a large topic, spanning from the hardware infrastructure that supports the organization to the applications that drive the content and property transactions. The course examined specific applications and the underlying transactions they support, attempting to show the relationship between data points within the organization, the multitude of people whose jobs are affected by the data, and the financial outcomes. Additionally, the definition of the smart building continues to evolve: tomorrow's smart building will have integrated network, communication, and control systems that allow the building to operate more efficiently and profitably.

HOTEL DEVELOPMENT AND INVESTMENT ANALYSIS ¶ FALL 2016 ¶ ADAM FEIL, INSTRUCTOR ¶ This course covered the complete financial cycle of hotel investment analysis including development; lending; operations; investment analysis; renovation decisions; and acquisition or disposition. Real estate valuation principles and procedures were explored with emphasis on the replacement cost, sales comparison, and income capitalization approaches. The role and function of the asset manager was discussed as well with emphasis on investment under-writing, operations analysis, portfolio management, strategic investment analysis, market strategy, management contracts, franchises and involvement with the property management team.

RETAIL REAL ESTATE AND DEVELOPMENT ¶ SPRING 2017 ¶ GARY FOGG, INSTRUCTOR ¶ The success of the shopping center is driven by a combination of the strength of the real estate and the retailer. In the case of retail real estate, the success of the retailer is arguably more correlated to the fundamentals of the underlying real estate than the tenants of other asset classes such as office and industrial. The course discussed retail real estate from the perspective of both the retailer and the landlord/developer. A thorough understanding of the retailer's business model increased the likelihood of success for retail real estate investors and developers. At the same time, the class reviewed the primary considerations of the retail developer and owner, including tenant mix, shopping center design, leasing, and valuation. A strong emphasis was placed on leasing and financial valuation. The lease not only outlines the economics of rent and expenses; it also establishes various rights and restrictions of both the landlord and that tenant.

FUNDAMENTALS OF CONSTRUCTION MANAGEMENT ¶ SUMMER 2016 ¶ DENNIS FREED, INSTRUCTOR ¶ For students pursuing a concentration in real estate development, this course provided an immersion in the processes and procedures of the construction of buildings particularly in urban environments. Fundamental tools for management of the construction project were learned and applied to problem exercises.

AFFORDABLE HOUSING FINANCE TECHNIQUES ¶ FALL 2016 ¶ RICHARD FROEHLICH, CHUCK BRASS, INSTRUCTORS ¶ This course presented a detailed review of the techniques for financing affordable housing. In combination with the focus on financing techniques, the course also looked at the development issues associated with this complex area and the policy focus of governmental programs. Incentives, public-private partnerships, the use of tax exempt bonds, the securitization of debt are all techniques initially developed for use in residential finance and in the financing of affordable housing. The crisis in credit and mortgage markets is impacting every segment of the real estate finance industry, including affordable housing. The residential finance system that has evolved in the US over the past 50 years is in the process of breaking down and being

remade. Housing policy and the federal role in making residential mortgage markets function, as well as serving the affordable housing needs of the country, is in flux. Although the course was focused on finance and financing techniques, it also considered the role of the public sector in regulating and creating incentives for the development and financing of housing in particular. The public sector's role ranges from the establishment and regulation of the capital markets, to the creation of tax incentives and specialized treatment for real estate enterprises and to the offering of particular subsidies for the development of affordable housing. An understanding of the public sector's financial and regulatory role is essential for understanding real estate financial markets in general and housing markets in particular. Every real estate project, and especially affordable housing projects, has a hidden partner: the federal government. The course was primarily taught through the case method. Each class had a case, a finance problem and reading assignment.

REAL ESTATE INVESTMENT ANALYSIS ¶ SUMMER 2016 ¶ FRANK GALLINELLI, INSTRUCTOR ¶ This course was intended specifically to benefit those students who have a somewhat limited background in finance by offering an "applied finance" approach to mastering key real estate investment concepts. Using several different property types as examples, the course evaluated various scenarios of potential acquisition, cash flow, financing, resale, and partnership. The course analyzed specific metrics to identify what appears to be favorable about each investment, what is problematic, and what might be missing from the scenario as presented. The course objective was for students to learn to recognize and understand key concepts and metrics through an inductive approach. By examining the specifics of each property and the market it is in, they apprehended the relevant financial concepts using this inferential method.

IN THE FIELD ¶ SUMMER 2016 ¶ ROBERT GARNEAU, INSTRUCTOR ¶ The course gave an introduction to development through individual exposure to prominent local real estate professionals that will include: developer, architect, financier, contractor and broker, in order to better understand the multifaceted field of real estate development. These hosts not only presented their views and experience on the topic at hand but also interacted in a Question and Answer format. Course topics include partnership, acquisition, zoning, financing, designing, construc-

tion, selling and other challenges of building developments. All classes met off-campus except for the first session.

PRIVATE EQUITY DEVELOPMENT: HOSPITALITY FOCUS ¶ SPRING 2017 ¶ RANI GHARBIE, INSTRUCTOR ¶ This course discussed the rapidly evolving real estate investment and development industry and addressed various approaches with capital markets. The course primarily covered major facets of creating a private equity development business while focusing on the hospitality industry. The course also discussed the rise of independent lifestyle hotels, the shifting development strategies of large lodging players and the growing movement around the next generation of travellers. There was also a focus on key industry disruptors that have been triggered by the rise of technology and the shared economy—Airbnb, Online Travel Agency's (Hotel Tonight, hipmunk...) and others.

COMMERCIAL LEASING ¶ SPRING 2017 ¶ MARTY GOLD, MITCHELL NELSON, INSTRUCTORS ¶ This course looked at commercial leasing from both a landlord and tenant perspective, and contained both legal and business analysis of the most important provisions and issues in leasing today. It provided a firm basis for understanding space leases as the revenue stream behind building operations, financing and profits. Allocation of risks related to the provision of space in a building was a consistent thread in the conversation. The readings included clauses from standard leases and articles about the subject matter, as well as some court decisions that illuminated the complexities and conflicts.

REAL ESTATE ECONOMICS AND MARKET METRICS ¶ SUMMER 2016 ¶ PAMELA HANNIGAN, INSTRUCTOR ¶ This course examined connections between the national and global economies and real estate markets from both theoretical and an empirical perspectives. It explored the performance of specific property types under different macroeconomic business and growth cycles and changing monetary conditions. The course explored key policy issues, their economic impact on real-estate decision-making, and identified indicators used to track economic and real estate performance. The course also examined the economic structure of major metropolitan areas, the impact of local governments on urban economic growth, the impact of urban economic growth on supply and demand identification for specific property types, and conditions under which certain regions thrive while other decline. Building upon the concepts and tools of economic analysis, this course introduced appropriate data sources and techniques useful in analyzing and forecasting real estate demand and supply in different markets for specific property types at specific locations. Class assignments also followed current economic news and potential impacts for real estate markets.

COMPARATIVE GLOBAL REAL ESTATE ¶ FALL 2016 ¶ WILLIAM HEISHMAN, INSTRUCTOR ¶ This course was designed to provide students with a comparative and critical approach to undertaking international real estate development projects, transactions and investments. It aimed to cultivate a general understanding of the dynamics of real estate developments and investments internationally as a foundation for the specific analysis of unique contexts and conditions for real estate activities within selected countries. The course was a prerequisite for participating in the study trips offered to students in the winter or spring break. In this course, the Study Trip destinations were analyzed with respect to their investment return potential and possible challenges, thereby preparing students for an intensive and detailed study trip whereby they supplemented their classroom understanding with "on-the- ground" details of real estate investing with the purpose of proposing a cross-border financial transaction in the country visited.

CONSTRUCTION LAW: NEGOTIATION AND MANAGEMENT ¶ SPRING 2017 ¶ LISA K. HOWLETT, INSTRUCTOR ¶ This class surveyed construction law to establish a practical understanding of legal issues that arise in construction. Using standard industry forms (owner-architect, owner-contractor, contractor-subcontractor, etc.), students developed the knowledge and skills necessary to successfully navigate the relationships that are governed by these agreements. Key principles including fees, project delivery, completion, defects, delays, warranties and liens were explored as well as how these issued are handled in the field.

RESIDENTIAL INVESTMENT AND DEVELOPMENT ¶ FALL 2016 ¶ JOSH KAHR, INSTRUCTOR ¶ This course focused on residential investment and development. Topics included: finance, investment, development, affordable housing subsidies and programs, REITs and public markets, environmental remediation/"brownfields," and partnership structures.

GLOBAL REAL ESTATE INVESTING ¶ FALL 2016 ¶ SONNY KALSI, JOHNNY DIN, INSTRUCTORS ¶ The class focused on investment themes, risks, opportunities, and real life case studies of global real estate investing. The case studies covered the global investment strategy of GreenOak Real Estate, and included office visits and site tours of NYC investments. The goals of this course included strategy, financial analysis, and "making the case" for investing.

ENVIRONMENTAL DESIGN AND SUSTAINABILITY ¶ SUMMER 2016 ¶ JESSE KEENAN, INSTRUCTOR ¶ This survey course covered the following modules: (i) basic environmental regulation and permitting; (ii) introduction to site planning and urban design; (iii) sustainability and high performance building systems; (iv) resilient engineering; (v) adaptive design and development; and, (vi) adaptive planning and decision making. Each module considered physical phenomena such as water and heat, and how these environmental elements relate to the financing, design and engineering of the built environment. The course surveyed each of the principal paradigms ranging from environmental protection to climate change. Students developed a set of tools which allowed for a greater understanding and analytical capacity for evaluating, managing and underwriting environmental risks and systems.

HOTEL TRANSACTIONS ¶ SPRING 2017 ¶ RICK KIRKBRIDE, TODD FIELDSTON, INSTRUCTORS ¶ This course integrated market and transactional perspectives in advancing a practical understanding of the global hospitality industry. At the heart of the industry is a unique accounting and transactional process that requires specialized training in the management agreements, operating agreements, design (FFE) and development agreements and flag agreements that define not just real estate development but day-to-day operations. Students were exposed to a variety of special topics ranging from boutique hotels to distressed repositioning of legacy assets.

CAPITAL MARKETS: REIT ANALYSIS ¶ FALL 2016 ¶ DAVID KRUTH, INSTRUCTOR ¶ This course commenced with the history, description and benefits of the REIT corporate structure particularly as it relates to the publicly listed vehicles. It then covered in detail the determination of the specific stock valuation of companies utilizing various methodologies such as Net Asset Value , price to FFO

and Price to Cash Flow. The various property sectors were evaluated and compared in terms of economic cycles, revenue structures, capital structure, risk profiles and valuation. Students were required to perform in-depth financial analyses of publicly traded REIT including comparative analysis and buy/sell decisions.

INTERNATIONAL REITS ¶ SPRING 2017 ¶ DAVID KRUTH, INSTRUCTOR ¶ Building on the fundamental REIT analytical methods, in this course the international variations of REIT structures were investigated: the history of the emergence of REITs in various countries, the respective structural differences, and the proportional presence of this corporate form in the local real estate investment markets. Students were required to perform in-depth financial analyses of publicly traded REIT in the various countries and proposed a cross-border merger/acquisition opportunity.

ADVANCED EXCEL SKILLS ¶ SPRING 2017 ¶ JIHO LEE, MATTHEW CHOI, INSTRUCTORS ¶ This course advanced the student's knowledge and technical skill with Excel financial modeling, and covered the more complex construction of the DCF Proforma around various capital structures of partnership equity waterfalls, preferred equity, mezzanine debt and securitized debt. By completion, the course required students to build complex financial models from scratch.

REAL ESTATE LAW ¶ FALL 2016 ¶ RICHARD LELAND, INSTRUCTOR ¶ This course examined development and investment issues as they interface with property, zoning, contract, securities, and tax law. The course provided students the opportunity to actively engage legal professionals in mitigating and resolving contractual and regulatory risk.

MARKET ANALYSIS ¶ SUMMER 2016 ¶ RYAN LEVASSEUR, SHUPROTIM BHAUMIK, INSTRUCTORS ¶ This course introduced students to the methods used in analyzing real estate markets, considering the perspective of decision-makers who are considering potential development, investment, or financing decisions. The course focused on the thought processes and mechanics of producing a market analysis report and were framed around the various methodologies of performing a market analysis for each real estate asset class: residential, commercial office, retail, industrial and hospitality. Students were expected to participate in a combination of class lectures, in-class discussions, independent readings, analytic assignments, and a group project focusing on a real site in New York City. By the end of the semester, each student had learned the skills required to frame a thoughtful real estate market analysis.

STUDIO: THE ART OF THE RFP RESPONSE ¶ SUMMER 2016 ¶ BRIAN LOUGHLIN, INSTRUCTOR ¶ Thousands of public bids are released each quarter throughout New York City, many of which include tremendous opportunities for creative developers with a clear vision to transform the urban landscape, impact the real estate market, and affect meaningful change in our city. The gateway to these opportunities is the Request for Proposals, or RFP, and there is often a little difference between a successful response and a disastrous one. This studio class introduced students to the art of preparing a successful RFP Response. Using an RFP recently released by the New York Department of Housing Preservation and Development, the class evaluated the scope of work called for by the RFP; analyzed the possibilities within the RFP given current trends in the market, make-up of the neighborhood, and interests in the community; and identified dormant opportunities and avoided hidden pitfalls. By working primarily in teams across the six weeks, students utilized various strategies and techniques to create a clear vision for the project; outline a strategic and competitive response to the RFP; developed a compelling initial design, massing, program, and pro-forma; and presented a winning proposal. Class requirements included preparation and presentation of weekly deliverables, and the class culminated with a presentation of final proposals to a (mock) jury comprised of various community members, city officials, and related professionals.

THE ARCHITECTURE OF DEVELOPMENT, PART 1 ¶ SUMMER 2016 ¶ BROOKS MCDANIEL, INSTRUCTOR ¶ The real estate development process is rife with potential complications and pitfalls. By understanding the distinct phases of the process and the decisions that are required in each phase, a developer can minimize risk and increase the potential value of a development. Additionally, a developer orchestrates the efforts of a team of consultants and city agencies to move a project towards completion, so an understanding of the roles and responsibilities of the various members of the project team will contribute to the efficiency of the decision making process. This course explored the development process with respect to site selection, design, construction,

value, and risk. The objective of The Architecture of Development was to gain an understanding of the role of the full development team, expose the students to a variety of case studies, and provide a framework for decision making during the development process.

UNDERWRITING ¶ FALL 2016 ¶ ROGER NUSSENBLATT, INSTRUCTOR ¶ The course covered all major facets of underwriting income-producing commercial real estate from a lending perspective. Students learned how to effectively underwrite stabilized office, retail, industrial, multifamily and hotel properties. Emphasis was placed on credit evaluation, cash flow analysis, break-even analysis, market analysis, sponsorship and loan structure. Exit strategies including securitization and loan sales were also examined.

UNDERWRITING II ¶ SPRING 2017 ¶ ROGER NUSSENBLATT, INSTRUCTOR ¶ The course covered all major facets of underwriting the repositioning of income-producing commercial real estate from a lending perspective. Students learned how to effectively underwrite transitional office, retail, industrial, multifamily and hotel properties. Emphasis was placed on loan structure, interest reserve analysis, LIBOR caps, reposition timing, credit evaluation, market analysis and sponsorship. Exit strategies including permanent takeout financing and loan sales were also discussed.

TAX ISSUES IN ACQUISITIONS AND DEVELOPMENTS ¶ SPRING 2017 ¶ RICHARD O'TOOLE, INSTRUCTOR ¶ This course was an overview of federal income tax and local tax issues that affect the planning and execution of urban real estate developments. Topics addressed included income tax treatment for sellers (and alternatives to cash acquisitions), transfer and mortgage recording tax concerns, issues with equity partners, and distinctions between condominium and rental developments.

ZONING AND ITS IMPACT ON ARCHITECTURE, REAL ESTATE AND THE COMMUNITY ¶ SUMMER 2016 ¶ ROY PACHECANO, INSTRUCTOR ¶ This elective course helped train future real estate developers how to author, defend and present a sound zoning analysis. The fast-paced six-week summer session aimed to offer the student not only the practical application of this important skill for the next generation developer, but went further to convey the underlining power of land use controls. This course aimed to provide a foundation of knowledge in understanding zon-

ing as an art form in providing both the basis (theoretical) and application (practice) of zoning techniques. The higher aim of the course was to successfully impart the essence of zoning through a unique teaching experience that involved classroom lectures and 6 zoning problems.

PUBLIC-PRIVATE PARTNERSHIPS IN REAL ESTATE DEVELOPMENT ¶ FALL 2016 ¶ ROBERT PALEY, INSTRUCTOR ¶ This course explored public sector involvement in real estate development, and was designed to impart a set of skills necessary to manage the complex medley of governmental actors with conflicting goals and agendas in public/private development. Case studies were drawn from a variety of projects, primarily in the New York City metropolitan region. These case studies provided an opportunity to examine the motivations, powers and constraints of public agencies, as well as the approaches to planning projects, soliciting support, sustaining momentum and structuring public/private partnerships.

TECHNOLOGICAL INNOVATION IN REAL ESTATE ¶ SPRING 2017 ¶ JOSH PANKNIN, INSTRUCTOR ¶ This class demonstrated the ongoing and increasing disruption of the real estate industry through the use of bigger data and more sophisticated technology applications. The use of technology is fast becoming an integral part of the real estate and finance industry. With the number of real estate technology firms growing exponentially and the amount of venture capital funding being poured into the development of more sophisticated technology for real estate, understanding the technology trend is an essential part of a real estate career. The class covered a brief history of how technology applications to real estate have changed in the past 10-20 years and where they might be going in the future; introduction to coding and database management; a test-driven and modular approach to modeling/programming that makes analysis cleaner and more efficient; and demonstrations of analysis integration to get more out of the students' models.

REAL ESTATE MANAGERIAL FINANCE AND ACCOUNTING ¶ SUMMER 2016 ¶ STEPHEN PEARLMAN, INSTRUCTOR ¶ The course offered an introduction to topics in the managing of businesses with emphasis on the methods and sources of financing a business. Topics included corporate finance analysis and how it works for real estate, financial planning procedures, present value and security valuation, capital budgeting, optimal capital structure and approaches to raising capital. The course also covered securities markets, factors and models explaining security returns and the concept of market efficiency.

WORKOUTS AND RESTRUC-TURING ¶ FALL 2016 ¶ STEPHEN PEARLMAN, INSTRUCTOR ¶ This half-term course introduced students to the legal and financial fundamentals of the workout and restructuring of real estate development and investment properties. It explored exit strategies and workout issues from restructuring through liquidation or reorganization—including out-of-court settlements versus bankruptcy—as well as pre-packaged bankruptcy. The course examined the relevant skill-sets and underlying framework utilizing examples of actual workouts during 2008-2012 and the causes that contributed to this volatile time in the history of real estate investments. Given current projections of approximately $1.2 trillion of loans maturing over the next four years, this curriculum provided students with the foundation to deal with the potential workout and restructuring problems that may arise over this period of time.

AFFORDABLE HOUSING, DEVELOPMENT AND POLICY ¶ SPRING 2017 ¶ ED POTEAT, INSTRUCTOR ¶ This course used the affordable housing techniques discussed in previous semesters to design and plan an actual affordable housing development. Besides utilizing affordable housing techniques such as tax credit and tax exempt bond financing, the course also looked at the other aspects of affordable housing development such as design and constructability elements, community involvement and political considerations. Developers must be a "jack of all trades" to successfully execute a new project. Although a keen understanding of affordable housing finance is a necessity for any successful developer, development requires an understanding of several disciplines. Political considerations have stymied many feasible affordable housing developments. Design and constructability issues have severely delayed or bankrupted a financially feasible project. Finally, this course also discussed the role of intermediaries and government agencies in the creation of affordable housing.

ASSET MANAGEMENT ¶ SPRING 2017 ¶ SARA QUEEN, INSTRUCTOR ¶ This course studied the issues that impact an asset from initial investment through disposition, with a particular focus on leasing, repositioning strategies, hold-sell analysis, and operations. The focus was to demonstrate how effective asset management works with property management, leasing, construction/ development and accounting to maximize financial performance. Overall, the class emphasized real-world issues and examples through the life cycle of an asset.

CREATIVE NYC ZONING ¶ FALL 2016 ¶ RAQUEL RAMATI, INSTRUCTOR ¶ The course covered NYC Zoning from its inception in 1916 until today. It covered the basics of zoning, from residential, commercial, manufacturing districts, use regulation, density, special purpose districts to privately owned public space and the use of air rights. The students were guided step-by-step through the maze of the NYC zoning resolution and learn about "as of right" and special permits. Emphasis was made on how to use zoning tools and incentive zoning to maximize the floor area of a development. The course covered the new zoning sections such as the mandatory inclusionary housing and zoning for quality and affordability, and analyzed the impact of zoning in real estate development.

URBAN DEVELOPMENT PROJECT ¶ SPRING 2017 ¶ RAQUEL RAMATI, INSTRUCTOR ¶ In this course, students pursued the detailed planning of a complex urban development project: commencing with an intensive site analysis incorporating evaluation of progressive responses to zoning and legislative requirements, proceeding through programmatic objectives and market conditions, and reviewing massing and building envelope possibilities. Each student presented a physical plan combined with financial feasibility analysis for the development project.

THE ARCHITECTURE OF DEVELOPMENT, PART 2 ¶ SUMMER 2016 ¶ EDUARD SANCHO POU, DAN CHOI, INSTRUCTORS ¶ This course taught the methods used by developers to secure deals, sell projects and erect buildings. This course examined real estate development from the point of view of which strategies work in our complex economic, political and social global-environment we operate in today. The course broke down the process into 6 major paired themes: 1. Marketing/Branding; 2. Icon/Design; 3. Politics/Government; 4. Masses/Construction; 5. Entrepreneurship/Due Diligence; 6. Leadership/ Networks. Each lecture reviewed one theme, starting with the conceptual idea, referencing one past and one present case study, and then ending with the practical knowledge of the actual development process.

CONSTRUCTION MANAGEMENT & TECHNOLOGY ¶ SUMMER 2016 ¶ BOB SANNA, INSTRUCTOR ¶ This course bridged the physical disciplines with the regulation and financial complexities of modern development. The course provided an overview of construction technologies, the construction process, and construction management. Course topics included cost estimating; value engineering; scheduling and management methods; contract documentation and administration (AIA); RFP/bidding; insurance; labor relations; civil and mechanical engineering; and, delivery systems design and implementation.

THE BUSINESS OF DEVELOPMENT ¶ SUMMER 2016 ¶ SHAI SHAMIR, INSTRUCTOR ¶ This course provided an immersive understanding of the development world from the point of view of a real estate developer. The students learned the fundamentals of development theory using basic analytical tools, and how to develop a successful business plan.

ALTERNATIVE & DISTRESSED INVESTMENT STRATEGIES ¶ FALL 2016 ¶ DONALD SHEETS, INSTRUCTOR ¶ This course introduced students to the basic framework of commercial real estate investment through a lens of distressed and distorted assets and markets. Basic elements of bankruptcy procedure and valuation were discussed, along with a specific concentration on those issues most pertinent to workout situations. Common characteristics and factors that lead to distress were also addressed. Students were exposed to cases and experts that bring forth legal, valuation, strategic, and other key considerations typical in commercial workouts—with maximum recovery from a lender, borrower, and joint-venture partner perspective.

PROJECT MANAGEMENT ¶ SPRING 2017 ¶ LEEZA SPRINGER, INSTRUCTOR ¶ The tools and techniques of project management were taught with respect to the overarching management of development projects including during the phases of envisioning, planning approvals, design, construction documentation, building, and delivery of the completed project on time and within budget. Taking into account the disparate objectives of the many constituents in the process, a rigorous method for optimizing decision-making and resolving challenges was learned. The general theory and methods of project management were tailored to the complex area of real estate such that the developer retains control and management of the process to achieve the most successful outcome.

RESIDENTIAL DEVELOPMENT AND ASSET STRATEGY ❡ FALL 2016 ❡ MARGARET STREICKER PORRES, INSTRUCTOR ❡ Multifamily real estate is a much-favored investment for a wide range of investors ranging from institutions to small, individual owners. However, managing these assets strategically, and in terms of every day activities, requires a combination of diligence, planning, and creativity. Drawing on extensive experience and the current management of a very large portfolio of assets, this course taught students the details of the asset management/value maximization proposition for multifamily assets and portfolios.

VALUE OF DESIGN ❡ FALL 2016 ❡ JAMIE VON KLEMPERER, GENE KOHN, INSTRUCTORS ❡ Addressing the financial objectives of the developer, this course presented an understanding of the importance of design in optimizing those objectives. Reviewing case studies of significant development projects by the renowned architectural firm KPF, the design process, and the timing of critical and collaborative decision-making was investigated. Students were challenged to formulate the value proposition of design alternatives and seek to estimate the financial consequences of design decisions.

PRIVATE EQUITY & CAPITAL RAISING ❡ FALL 2016 ❡ MARC WEIDNER, MICHAEL CLARK, INSTRUCTORS ❡ This course exposed students to the fundamentals of real estate private equity, basic terms, players in the industry, various roles of professionals, legal and financial aspects of real estate private equity in today's environment. The course also taught a broad base of understanding in private equity real estate to prepare students in the concepts, terms, and fundamentals that govern the real estate private equity markets. The course was taught from the perspective of the General Partner in managing funds and the Limited Partner in investing in funds. Additionally, outside industry experts guest spoke on their real estate private equity experience. These leading industry professionals included intermediaries and prominent LPs and GPs. The class focused in particular on current fundraising issues as well as on the structuring of private equity transactions. The course was of particular interest to students who wanted exposure to real estate private equity in the future, either as a General Partner, Limited Partner, or Local Operating Partner domestically or internationally.

REAL ESTATE TRANSACTIONS LAW ❡ SPRING 2017 ❡ ROBERT WERTHEIMER, NATHALIA BERNARDO, INSTRUCTORS ❡ This course provided students with a practical knowledge and critical skill set for understanding how real estate transactions proceed from deal making to closure. Taught within the context of real estate and contract law, this course surveyed a variety of instruments and provisions that are both standardized and the subject of negotiation. The format of the course followed the timeline of a series of exemplar transactions, as manifested in a variety of instruments including land and building purchase and sale agreements, equipment contracts and leases, mortgages and UCC-1 security agreements, loan agreements, partnership agreements, and development agreements.

Danielle Smoller, Director

Critics
Emanuel Admassu
Gisela Baurmann
Babak Bryan
Sarah Carpenter
Diana Cristobal
Esteban de Backer
Sheryl Kasak
Jane Kim
Daniel Talesnik
Ray Wang

with
Yujia Bian
Jesse Catalano
Aranzazu Gayosso
Nishant Jacob
Britt Johnson
Chad Karty
Nabila Morales Perez
Michael Nickerson
Kurtis Streich
Alexander Van Odom

This five-week intensive design studio, comprising studio and lecture formats, presented a comprehensive experience in architectural design. Using New York City as a laboratory, the morning sessions developed an awareness of the relationships between the history, theory, practice and design of architecture; Lectures and workshops along with field trips to professional offices, museums, and sites focused on these issues. The afternoon or evening sessions took place in the architecture studio.

This summer, each studio took a different approach to a design problem posed around several sites, all featuring outcroppings of Manhattan schist. Using these neighborhood sites to develop critical questions, base analyses and design techniques, studios were able to reflect on the existing conditions and design briefs and propose thoughtful interventions. Students worked with studio critics on a series of projects developed by the studio director and individual critics and presented their individual designs to juries comprised of faculty members and practitioners. Students used various materials along with spatial/formal operations to explore different aspects of drawing, mapping and modeling while producing a proposal for the assigned site. A final exhibition of work demonstrated the diversity of work produced as well as the significant improvement each studio and student made over the fast-paced semester.

Diana Cristobal, Matthew Ninivaggi

1

2

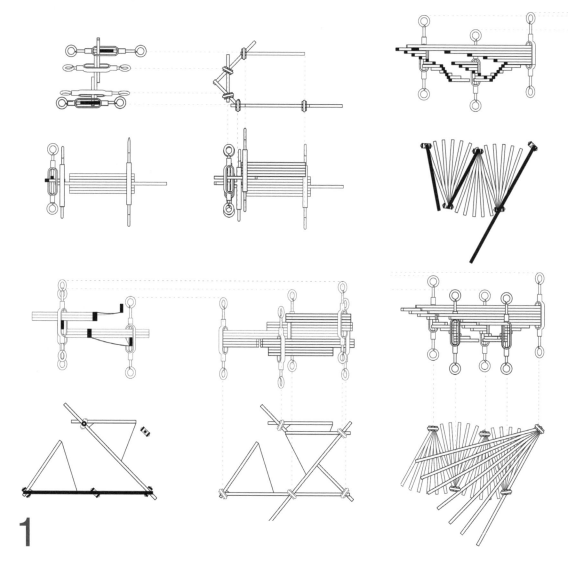

Esteban DeBacker,
Michelle Silwester

Ray Wang, Ceara Donnelley

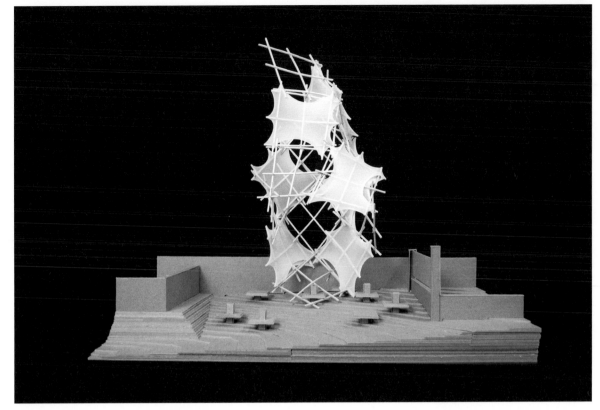

3

4

Jane Kim, Delaney McCraney

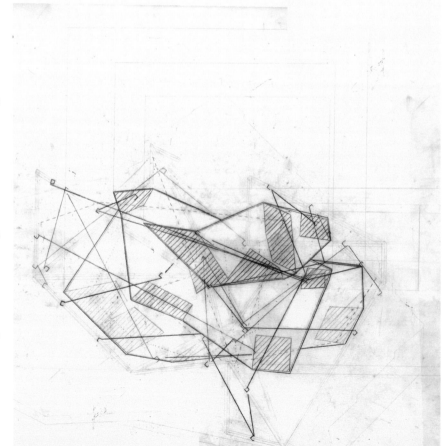

The Shape of Two Cities: New York/Paris Program

Danielle Smoller, Program Director
Patrick O'Connor, Coordinator (Paris)

The Shape of Two Cities: New York-Paris Program is designed to develop a student's critical appreciation of urban forms, their genesis and the role of architecture, preservation, and planning in the creation of the contemporary urban environment. As a one-year intensive liberal arts program with a strong studio component, the curriculum focuses on design issues and the urban history and theory of these two cities. In addition, the program provides an introduction to the disciplines of architecture, urban studies and planning for highly motivated undergraduates who have completed at least two years of study at their home institutions or for post-baccalaureate students interested in preparing for graduate studies. Previous study in these disciplines is not required for admission to the program, allowing students from a broad range of academic and professional backgrounds to participate. The program's curriculum is designed to provide students with a better understanding of the design and urban studies disciplines as they are practiced in New York and Paris.

New York and Paris are important global cities, each representative of its unique cultures. For students, these cities offer an ideal opportunity to explore the historical, social and political development of urban form and to clarify the roles of architects, planners, and preservationists. During the first semester, students are enrolled at the Graduate School of Architecture, Planning and Preservation in New York and enjoy the resources of the GSAPP and Columbia University. The following semester students are based at Reid Hall, Columbia University's center for French cultural studies, located in the Montparnasse district of Paris. Reid Hall offers reading rooms, lounges, a library, and a network of activities to help students bridge the culture gap.

The Shape of Two Cities offers postgraduates twenty four credits applicable toward the NY/Paris Certificate and offers undergraduates credits towards the Bachelor of Arts or Bachelor of Architecture degrees granted by participating institutions. The program provides an excellent preparation for graduate and professional study and for postgraduates the fall curriculum can be tailored to satisfy pre-graduate school requirements. Upon completion, many students are admitted to graduate programs in architecture, urban planning and historic preservation at universities including Columbia, Harvard, Princeton, M.I.T., Pennsylvania and Yale.

1
2
3

STUDIO 1: NEW YORK STUDIO: (A)DRESSING THE CITY ¶ FALL 2016 ¶ DANIELLE SMOLLER, DIRECTOR ¶ BABAK BRYAN, SARAH CARPENTER, JANE KIM, THOMAS DE MONCHAUX, CRITICS, WITH MATTHEW DAVIS, KENNETH AMOAH, YUJIA BIAN, STEPHAN VAN EEDEN, AND CHAD KARTY ¶ The New York/Paris Program approached two cities as sites and strategies for studying architecture and urbanism. Each assignment was sourced from, and sited through, two simultaneous urban sites: an actual condition physically located in New York and a virtual condition conceptually located in Paris. In New York, the sequence of physical locations provided a source and site for each project loosely tracing a hundred year timeline of the history of the manufacture, design and commerce of clothing, from the late nineteenth century to the present day: Orchard Street, Ladies Mile, Seventh Avenue/"Fashion District," Bryant Park/former site for the tents of New York's Fall Fashion Week. ¶ One thematic focus was the idea of scale in architecture and urbanism: the absolute and relative dimensions and operations of these phenomena and of their components. Another thematic focus was the idea of staging a continuous encounter between conditions and operations at the scale of the body—clothing—and conditions and operations at the scale of the city—New York and Paris—thereby surrounding, critiquing and creating work at the scale precisely in between these two: the alleged scale of the architectural practice, the building.

4
5
6

STUDIO 2: PARIS, LIFT-ME UP: HIGH-RAISED CULTURAL EMBASSIES ¶ SPRING 2017 ¶ MARCOS GARCIA ROJO, ANTOINE SANTIARD, TSUYOSHI TANE, INSTRUCTORS, WITH COLLIN ANDERSON ¶ The vertical extension of the existing buildings (surelevation

in French) is a major subject nowadays and one of the main strategies that the municipality envisions (and encourages) for the future development of Paris. This mode of densification offers great potential to a highly consolidated city with a high number of patrimonial assets that would be too constrained otherwise. The advantages of these kind of interventions are multiple. The students were asked to speculate on the possibilities for a "surelevation" in three canonical places of the city in order to construct a "Cultural Embassy": the Haussmannian, historical city (Avenue de l'Observatoire), the 70s urban fabric (Rue Didot), and an ongoing industrial site (Exacompta). The program had to be designed and defined by the students but would necessarily imply the creation of a series of temporary programs and spaces with a combination of housing/in residence programs and other cultural/public spaces that could evolve with time. The goal of this cultural embassy was to provide the city of Paris with a new infrastructural array of spaces that can absorb, fulfill and trigger a more flexible functioning of the city.

ARCHITECTURE, PLANNING, AND PRESERVATION: NEW YORK (APP) ¶ FALL 2016 ¶ CAROL WILLIS, INSTRUCTOR ¶ Architecture, Planning, and Preservation: New York (APP), a core course for the New York session of The Shape of Two Cities program, was designed to introduce students to the professional and theoretical issues in the three disciplines. The lectures and readings focused on history, theory, and public policy, examining the interplay of forces that have shaped New York's built environment in the past and that influence it today. Field trips to professional offices, public hearings, and development projects as well as guest lecturers exposed students to the dynamics of design, planning, and policy decisions. ¶ This year's APP applied its general overview and critical analysis to a special focus on Density and Public Space—especially in New York City, but also beyond—by studying both current examples and historical texts. We pursued a close reading of classic texts—Jane Jacobs, Kevin Lynch, and William H. Whyte, etc.—which we studied for both their evergreen empirical approaches, as well as their historical contexts. Our field trips, guest speakers, and class discussions highlighted the contrasts and tensions between planning on a large scale and listening to and learning from community concerns. ¶ Group projects and individual research papers prepared students for an informed classroom debate near the end of the semester.

WORKSHOP IN URBAN STUDIES ¶ FALL 2016 ¶ MICHELLE YOUNG, INSTRUCTOR, WITH SREYASH DASGUPTA ¶ The Urban Studies Workshop engaged students with a studio-based approach to the issues and discourse of the contemporary city by exploring a variety of conceptual, analytical and design tools for understanding and operating within urban contexts through focused individual or collective research and design projects. ¶ The studio studied the potential futures of Rikers Island, currently home to New York City's largest incarceration facility. The studio worked in partnership with Just Leadership USA, an advocacy group in the movement to close Rikers Island. ¶ The studio first looked at the history of Rikers Island and surrounding communities, the history of incarceration in New York City, and best practices from all around the world. Current site conditions and edge conditions were observed, mapped and uncovered. On-site interviews and surveys supplemented analytical research. From this background research phase, analyses were performed to assess the scope of the city's current proposals in serving the detainees at Rikers Island and the surrounding neighborhoods. ¶ In the third phase, students choose specific sites both within and outside Rikers Island to propose design and policy solutions, addressing challenges specific to their site. ¶ In the project shown here, the student proposed that through a multi-step process, Rikers Island could cease to function as a jail, be progressively remediated and dismantled and then transformed into a network of flood resiliency projects with recreational programming to offer new green spaces to the underserved communities of Queens and the Bronx.

THE DEVELOPMENT OF PARIS ¶ SPRING 2017 ¶ ANDREW AYERS, INSTRUCTOR ¶ Of the three history courses offered on the NY/P program, this course was in a sense the most traditional, since it consisted of a (more or less) chronological survey of Paris's growth and architecture from Gallo-Roman times to the present day—essential for understanding the historical context of the city in which students were asked to propose an architectural intervention. But of DoP's twelve classes, only one (the first) took place in the classroom—all the others took place out in the field, in direct contact with the city's architecture so that students could see and experience it for themselves. The sites we visited were very varied, from historic churches (e.g. Notre-Dame, the Dôme des Invalides), palaces (the Louvre) and mansions, to parks and gardens (the Tuileries, the Buttes-Chaumont, La Villette), to 19th-century railway stations and the Paris Opera, to seminal works of Modernism (e.g. Le Corbusier's Villa La Roche), to more recent urban developments such as the La Défense business district or the two new neighborhoods on reclaimed riverside industrial land in eastern Paris. Since history is to a large extent a literary discipline, an extensive reader accompanied the visits.

FRENCH CONVERSATION ¶ SPRING 2017 ¶ PASCALE BEN-HAIM, INSTRUCTOR ¶ In this class, students engaged in both individual and group work designed to give them grammatical and conversational abilities at an intermediate to advanced level. Outside of class, students completed independent work and exercises on a regular basis from the Grammaire Progressive du Français (GP), in order to strengthen skills acquired in class. Students were placed in "real life" situations in which they had to converse with French people and were asked to write an evaluation of the experience. In addition, students were required to visit museum exhibitions, films and gallery openings and write a review of the work.

IMAGINATIVE TRANSFORMA-TIONS: BETWEEN WORLDS ¶ SPRING 2017 ¶ CLAUDE BOUCHA-RD, INSTRUCTOR ¶ The purpose of this course was to help students begin to develop an individual formal vocabulary of their own. The way in which you communicate your creativity is essential. Developing your own distinctive vocabulary to represent your ideas and illustrate your projects is the foundation on which you will build–it is the tool through which you will communicate your ideas. ¶ The methodology employed in this course was designed to force students to abandon their naturally rational and logical approach and to embark on an intuitive process of discovery, to work with their intuition and emotions in order to access their imagination directly and without the censorship of reason. ¶ The course is divided into 4 stages. Each step with its hidden purpose was essential to the next. We worked with photos, 3-dimensional models and drawings. We constantly moved between the 2-dimensional and the 3-dimensional world as well as the 2-dimensional representation of the 3-dimensional world. Students were encouraged to modify and free up their perspective, to develop a new way of looking at the world around them, one in which their imagination can guide their hand and transform their vision.

MANUFACTURING CONCEP-TUAL INTERPRETATIONS ¶

SPRING 2017 ¶ MARCOS GARCIA ROJO, INSTRUCTOR ¶ Inherently unpredictable and never linear, the process of design rarely moves straight forward from point A to B. Rather; it oscillates between a broad field of influences ranging from purely abstract concepts and ideas to detailed rules and techniques profoundly rooted in the discipline. Yet this process varies in its formulation seeming on occasions random or accidental—sometimes even deliberately—it follows patterns that can be studied, analyzed, and categorized. The scope of this class was to precisely study the design process through its different stages, forms or patterns, named here as conceptual interpretations. These processes (and the ideas involved) constituted a valuable set of tools used by all design professionals that engage in the creative process. ¶ The objective of the course was not to create a set of design process recipes for any situation—that would be impossible—but to develop a method in which we precisely analyze the process. This rigorous investigation allowed us to understand the logic behind the designer's creative process and provided insight into the ideas that lie within the project itself. ¶ Through specific case studies this course deepened the understanding of the design process to develop individual tools that can be utilized in students' design work. Each session required weekly readings, research, and presentations as well as an open discussion between students, the instructor, and invited professionals.

ILLUSORY PARIS—BLOCK-BUSTER ARCHITECTURE AND URBANISM: HOW THE IMAGININGS OF CINEMA AND OTHER MEDIA RESHAPE URBAN REALITY IN PARIS ¶ SPRING 2017 ¶ MICHAEL HERMAN, IN-STRUCTOR ¶ Cinema, advertisements, and other forms of media can not only influence perceptions of the cities they portray, but in union with other forces, media's power can induce physical transformations of cities. In an increasingly media-infused world, an understanding of this perceptual and physical transformative power is essential to the future of architecture and urbanism. ¶ This course explores how Paris's representation in numerous forms of media, in conjunction with unprecedented numbers of visitors, has altered both the perception and physical form of the city. As one of the urban environments most represented in media, as well as one of the world's most visited cities—receiving annually more than 30 million visitors—Paris hosts a fascinating and powerful collision of media-influenced preconceptions with urban reality. As a result, the

city is the ideal laboratory in which to understand the effects of these forces on the future of architecture, planning and preservation. ¶ Predictions about the power that these forces can have range from the inconsequential to the extreme; an example of the latter is French urban anthropologist Marc Augé's late-20th century prediction that by the year 2040 the city of Paris will be an amusement park divided into immaculately maintained historically themed zones, organized around selected monuments and attractions, with no permanent inhabitants, its streets used solely by pedestrians and horse-drawn carriages, and its former resident population displaced to the periphery of the city. ¶ Through seminar discussions, site visits of both completed projects and construction sites, analyses of film and other forms of representation, and design work, this course explored and questioned the relationship among media, tourism, and the physical form of cities, and in the process attempted to predict the future of not only Paris, but the numerous cities increasingly subjected to the combined power of media and tourism.

PHOTOGRAPHY AND ARCHI-TECTURE ¶ SPRING 2017 ¶ MARK LYON, INSTRUCTOR ¶ Students were introduced to architectural photography using either color or black and white materials, and with the camera format of their choice, be it digital or analog based. They learned how to make aesthetic decisions based upon where they place themselves in the field of vision and how their lens and its focal length affect their final composition. ¶ Technical issues such as exposure, depth of field, and the use of a tripod were addressed, as was the utilization of shift lenses and the view camera to correct for perspective. The importance of light and its source (be it daylight or artificial, centralized or diffuse) was examined in relation to its direct impact upon structuring space, volumes and contour. ¶ An emphasis was placed upon each student developing a personal vision in their approach to photographing architecture and interiors. They printed the images resulting from several assignments with digital media available in the studio. The viewing of historical antecedents as well as work by contemporary photographers provided a context in which student work was discussed. The culmination of their efforts was a group exhibition, curated by themselves in a collaborative spirit to summarize the semester's discoveries and accomplishments.

RE-DRAW ¶ SPRING 2017 ¶ PETER OBRIEN, INSTRUCTOR ¶ We simultaneously make many choices when drawing in regard to composition, framing a placement. The demands we make on our own formal drawing choices take on equal importance to the imperatives of the "real" observed subject. Draw I focused on expanding these choices while maintaining a connection with the observed world by addressing light and shade. Consistent with the first session, we approached light and shade as observation of relations. In the first sessions, "Classic" drawing subjects were proposed in the studio: Life drawing sessions as well as work on still life. As the weather became nicer during the second part of the semester, outdoor drawing was favored, permitting more drawing of architecture and urban spaces. In addition to traditional drawing materials, ink and ink wash, as well as collage, were explored.

FRENCH INTENSIVE ¶ SPRING 2017 ¶ PASCALE BENHAIM AND CATHERINE PIECE, INSTRUCTORS ¶ In this course students learned the basic structure of French language and how to manage everyday situations in their Parisian life. The varied class activities and exercises, such as oral presentations, in-class and outside readings, written compositions, and traditional tests, required students to use those four skills to constantly hone their French. To achieve the goals of this class, students needed to actively participate in all of the scheduled activities and to take care in preparing the given assignments

HISTORY OF THE EUROPEAN CITY ¶ SPRING 2017 ¶ JACOB SIMPSON, INSTRUCTOR ¶ The European continent was first to see the majority of its population concentrate in cities, the result of long-run economic growth beginning in the 12th Century. As the urban trend continues worldwide, this course sought to define the particular character of the European city as a product of history and human creativity. Case studies focused on drivers of urban development, highlighting noteworthy territorial specializations during the second millennium, from international finance in Venice to shipbuilding in Glasgow. Students had the opportunity to build upon their understanding of the history of American cities and the built forms to which they gave rise. ¶ To encourage an understanding of the value and viability of existing urban fabric, often centuries-old, students were asked to design marketing tools to attract hypothetical design and development projects to contemporary European cities. This exercise, ongoing throughout the term, coincided with the class's structure in examining several key sectors including agriculture and food

production, government, transportation, housing, education, religion, trade and commerce, manufacturing, culture and recreation, each with relation to the built forms they generate. Special attention was given to matching past and present place-based expertise to address the challenge of selling European cities for future development. ¶ With a myriad of publications by architectural historians, urban theorists, economic geographers, etc. at their disposal, students had extensive resources to corroborate and complement lectures, group work and field trips.

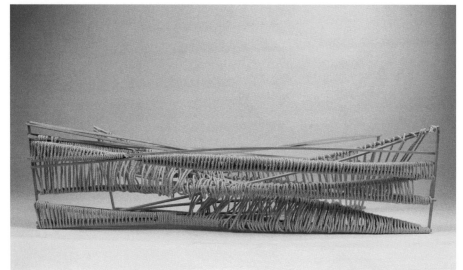

Maggie Musante

1

2

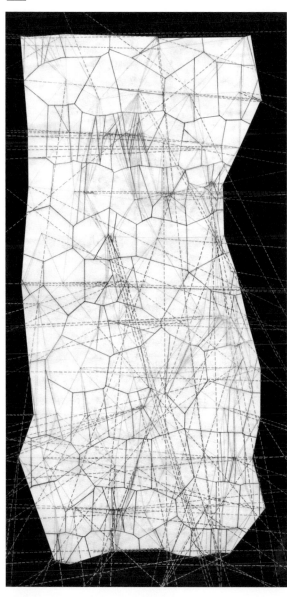

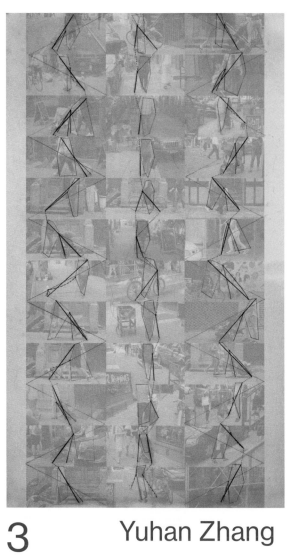

3

Yuhan Zhang

Oliver Oglesby

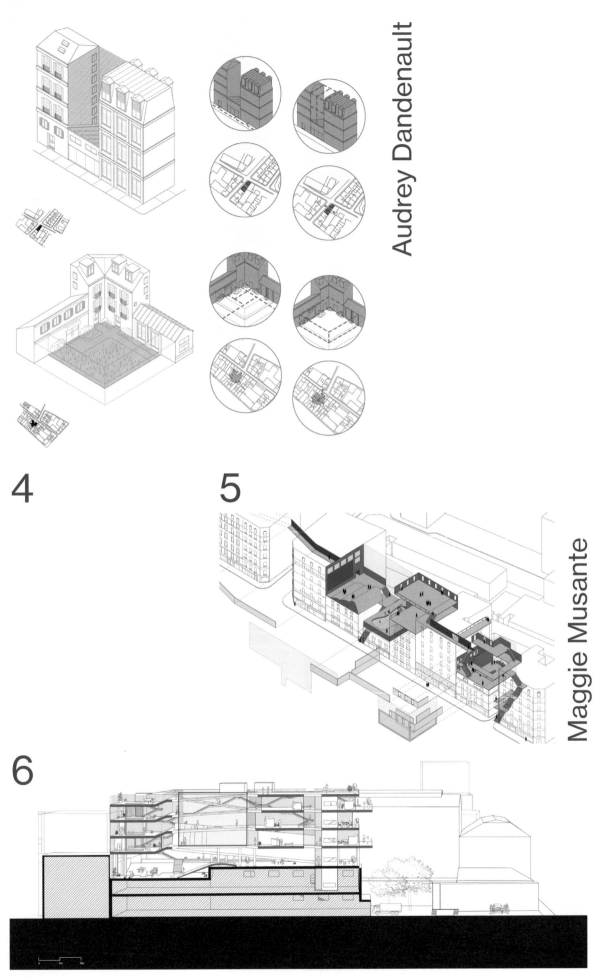

4

5

6

Audrey Dandenault

Maggie Musante

Yuhan Zhang

PRACTICE
IDEAS

Columbia GSAPP Design Mantras, 2017

Taken together, these statements can be read as a sort of
time-sensitive mantra for the disciplines of the built
environment, a set of pedagogical imperatives that have
emerged from the school, and a statement of engagement
as an institution. We understand these six statements,
dispersed throughout this book, as an urgent call to action
for Columbia GSAPP, and we recognize their relevance
and implications for the larger global community of
which the school is inextricably embedded within. They
address issues of political engagement, social equity,
representation, pursuing action on climate change,
global perspectives, cultural diversity, and developing
professional practice in all disciplines of the built
environment in which we study and practice.

Architecture Ph.D.
Felicity D. Scott, Director

Urban Planning Ph.D.
Robert Beauregard,
Director

Critical, Curatorial
& Conceptual Practices
in Architecture
Felicity D. Scott,
Mark Wasiuta, Directors

Architecture Ph.D. Program

Felicity Scott, Director

Ph.D. Committee:
Barry Bergdoll
Kenneth Frampton
Mary McLeod
Reinhold Martin
Jorge Otero-Pailos
Mark Wigley
Mabel O. Wilson
Gwendolyn Wright

The Ph.D. program in architecture is oriented toward the training of scholars in the field of architectural history and theory. Its structure reflects a dual understanding of the scholar's role in the academy: as a teacher and as a researcher making an original contribution to the field, with an emphasis on expanding and reinterpreting disciplinary knowledge in a broad intellectual arena. Course requirements give entering students a solid foundation in historical knowledge and theoretical discourse, with sufficient flexibility to allow the initiation and pursuit of individual research agendas. The program's focus is on the history and theory of modern and contemporary architecture and urbanism in an international and cross-cultural context, from the mid-eighteenth century to the present. Within this, a wide range of research is supported through the expertise of the faculty and through strong relationships with other departments throughout the University and beyond.

PH.D. COLLOQUIUM: THEORIZING MODERNISM AND AVANT-GARDE: MODERN ARCHITECTURE AND THEORY IN THE NETHERLANDS, FRANCE, AND GERMANY, 1917–27 ¶ SPRING 2017 ¶ MARY MCLEOD ¶ Modernism, the most significant aesthetic movement of the twentieth century, found expression across a range of forms, including architecture. While participants and critics associated the movement with innovation and the disruption of traditional aesthetic conventions, there is considerable dispute today about what modernism was. For example, did it focus on internal formal qualities or did it explore and disrupt the boundaries of disciplines, calling for the dissolution of art itself? Was it involved with fragmentation or pastiche (qualities now often associated with postmodernism), or did it seek to attain a new form of aesthetic unity or order, which in turn imposed new compositional constraints? Was it concerned with "truth" and "essence" or rather with multiple realities and appearances? Was it elitist in its formal abstraction and experimentation, or was it democratic and populist in its engagement with everyday life and mass culture? ¶ This seminar addressed some of these questions by investigating the theoretical and ideological positions of several movements in modern architecture, during the years immediately following World War I. These included De Stijl in the Netherlands; Purism and L'Esprit Nouveau in France; and Elementarism, the Bauhaus, and New Objectivity in Germany. The intention was not only to gain a deeper knowledge of these developments, but also to explore more broadly theoretical issues surrounding the concepts of "modernism" and "avant-garde" as they apply to architecture. In particular, the seminar examined the tensions between formal autonomy and the role of technology and mass culture in architecture.

PH.D. SEMINAR: HISTORIES AND MODERNITIES ¶ FALL 2016 ¶ FELICITY D. SCOTT, INSTRUCTOR ¶ This seminar addressed the question of what other (or alternatively cast) histories of architectural modernism or historical representations of the discipline's encounters with the forces of modernity might be told. The ambition was not to refuse the importance of extant narratives and their conceptual terms—standardization and industrialized mass production, capitalist rationalization, nationalism, secularism, urbanization, circumscribed social, class and gender relations, labor and leisure, health and hygiene, media and the public sphere, Kantian aesthetics, abstraction, Enlightenment notions of progress,

technological invention, environmental control, utopianism, revolution, public programs, regionalism, etc. Rather, taking them as an important discursive and disciplinary archive, the ambition of the seminar was to ask how, why, and to what ends might additional historical materials and foci as well as critical and conceptual frameworks be introduced to complicate such already variegated narratives. What happens, for instance, when modernity is no longer equated with Enlightenment notions of progress or rationality, or when it is no longer understood simply to have emanated from a Western metropolitan context? What happens when other archives supplement existing histories, or when other stories are told, including those addressed, for instance, to questions of gender, social injustice, colonization and anti-colonial struggles, geopolitical transformation, the persistence of mysticism, or the discipline's relation to new techniques of power? The ambition of the course was thus to raise questions regarding how, as an architectural historian, one constructs or demarcates an archive for the discipline and its historiography, deciding what is included, what is excluded, and how to address that which has previously been cast as other to it. How, that is, to take responsibility for articulating critical and political stakes within architectural history, stakes that attempt to account for architecture's imbrication within a transforming and disjunctive modernity.

THINKING RACE, READING ARCHITECTURE ¶ SPRING 2017 ¶ MABEL WILSON, INSTRUCTOR ¶ This doctoral colloquium examined the topic of the racial in architecture. The doctoral colloquium closely read primary treatises and manifestos, scholarly essays and books, along with reviewing drawings, models, buildings, and urban plans to trace a genealogy of how concepts of human and racial difference shaped modern architectural discourse and practices. Critical for the seminar was to understand how and why the racial evolves in western philosophy. These concepts are found in the writings Kant, Hegel, and others from which architectural theory and history derives its conceptual frameworks. The course charted a history of the racial in order to understand its presence in the writings and projects of various architects, theorists, and historians, including Thomas Jefferson, Viollet-le-Duc, Gottfried Semper, Adolf Loos, Le Corbusier, and others. One key objective of the seminar was to understand why the discipline and profession of architecture has been resistant to recognize how the racial has been part of its discursive genealogy.

RATIONALIZING GLOBAL GROWTH: STEEL ARCHITECTURES, PART-TO-WHOLE SYSTEMS, AND THE INFRA-STRUCTURES OF FINANCIAL MODERNITY, 1890–1970 ¶ "Steel" is a synecdoche, a figurative part that stands for a number of different wholes: a construction material, a major productive industry, corporate and labor power, military might, or strength and modularity. Since the dawn of corporate capitalist modernity, "steel" has been closely associated with the "whole" known as "economic growth": nationally before World War II, and internationally thereafter. As the physical material around which the corporate form consolidated, steel underpinned global financialization since the late 19th century. Discursively, steel was a key sector for the theorization of abstract metrics of economic growth like Gross National Product, disciplinary fields like macroeconomics, and labor processes like Taylorization. This dissertation seeks to examine how the architectural history of steel systems mediated the construction of competing frameworks for rationalizing and implementing economic growth, addressing it as part of the shift in global hegemony—both financial and architectural—from the British Empire in the 19th century to the United States in the 20th. Crucially, this shift in power—gathered here under the general rubric of "financial modernity"—could not have occurred without an architectural expertise for managing projects in far-flung territories, whether in the informal colonies of Latin America, or at the edges of the US's own national frontiers. The technical and discursive tools of different political-economic models for "growth"—from free trade, to national growth, to the more recent discourses of international development and environmental limits to growth—can thus be examined in relation to the logistical, managerial, financial, and cultural technologies that enabled steel systems to be increasingly designed and built at a distance.

Manuel Schvartzberg Carrió

THE CANTONMENTS OF NORTHERN INDIA: ARCHITECTURAL SECURITY AND BRITISH RULE (1765–1889) ¶ Military architecture and urbanism have played a significant yet overlooked role in the expansion and maintenance of British colonial rule within India, not least during its turbulent first century while under the private government of the East India Company (1757–1858). This dissertation traces the development over this period of the Company's singular military formation—the cantonment—exploring how this permanent camp was conceived, developed, and spread in large numbers, especially across the subcontinent's northern hinterlands or mufassil, those vast provincial, rural, and frontier areas of India. ¶ This dissertation argues that there was a strategic reluctance within these spaces for these entities to appear fully crafted, fully completed. This not only enabled both their planning and function to adapt to countless situations, but also allowed for a degree of stealth in their deployment, producing a slow, psychic violence through an ambiguity of intent entirely consistent with the means and ideology of territorial extension by the British, and in the securing of this territory. Such "lack of completion" could be described as preserving the effect of a diagram or a plan in its realization, bypassing the normal requirements of translation into an architecture of open representation. This almost-aesthetic gave it a peculiar power; and this type sits distinct from the ideologies of "progress" subsequently embraced by the Raj. ¶ A key theoretical thrust of the research, therefore, is to explore the colonial cognitive dissonance between permanence and impermanence, and lived experience and abstraction, through the operation of the cantonment system across several phases in the ideological development of Indian colonialism. It is to determine if and what were the causal relations between the two (the system and the ideology), joining the varying scales of design and construction, internal social economy, border security, tax and revenue collection, logistics and infrastructure, and wider political and conflict strategies.

Christopher Cowell

Anon., View of Deolali Cantonment near Nasik, Bombay Presidency, 1870. British Library, Temple Collection, 125/1(10).

IN SEARCH OF A SOFTER PATH: COUN-
TERCULTURAL VISION, ENERGY POLI-
TICS, AND THE AMERICAN APPROPRI-
ATE TECHNOLOGY MOVEMENT ¶ In the
late-1960s, a handful of young, countercultural
Americans, inspired by E.F. Schumacher's concept
of "intermediate technology," initiated the Appropriate Technology, or AT, movement in the United
States. Although Schumacher's project focused
on the ways in which technologically sustainable
methods could gently and prudently support the
modernization of underdeveloped nations, American
proponents of AT recognized, in this approach, an
opportunity to check the overdevelopment of the
Western world. By advocating, promoting, and
effecting sustainable techniques from a grassroots
to governmental level, practitioners of appropriate
technology sought to prevent the further environmental, economic, and social degradation of
American communities. ¶ The mission of AT was
holistic; under its aegis were "appropriate" methods
of energy production, building design, education,
health, communications, and activism, among
others. This conceptual inclusivity encouraged
the organization of a diversity of AT proponents
into cooperative, multifunctional groups which
acted both from within government bureaucracy,
in the case of California's Office of Appropriate
Technology and the National Center for Appropriate Technology, and outside the Establishment, in
the case of the New Alchemy Institute and RAIN
collective. This dissertation centers upon these four
groups—in particular, their realized projects and
numerous publications—emphasizing the ways in
which the initial philosophy, politics, and focus of
AT evolved as the movement transitioned from a
countercultural pipe dream to a widely supported
solution for America's energy problems in the wake
of the 1973 Oil Crisis.

Meredith Gaglio

*Diane Schatz, "Urban Renewal," in RAIN: Journal
of Appropriate Technology (April, 1976).*

ARCHITECTURE AS INFRASTRUCTUR-
AL INTERFACE IN URBAN AMERICA,
1954–1996 ¶ This dissertation explores the role of
architectural building types as critical components
of four infrastructural systems, built or rebuilt in
New York City in the decades after World War
II. These buildings, treated here as socially co-
constitutive technologies, occupy unique roles
as points of interface with large technological
systems. The case studies (food distribution,
telephone service, the police and prison network,
and sewage treatment) reveal different spatial
techniques of managing, revealing, and obscuring commodities, information, bodies, and waste.
Reading each project both through the lens of the
social history of technology and the disciplinary tools of architectural history, brings to light
unique aspects of architecture's participation in
the political, social, and technological landscapes
of the contemporary city. By working through
infrastructural buildings, this study contributes
to urban studies and the history of the American
city. Well-studied phenomena such as white flight
and "urban crisis," often examined through studies
of housing and transportation networks, take on
different casts. This study forces a reconsideration
of the period's mid-tier American architectural
practices and how they understood their work as
well. Evidently enmeshed in regional and global
networks far beyond the administrative bounds
of the five boroughs, contemporary infrastructure
is inescapably local when considered in terms of
material effects such as air pollution and political struggles surrounding the siting, design, and
construction of buildings. Today, these same
infrastructures continue to affect the formation
and transformation of an ostensibly postindustrial
city, organized around the perceived desires of elite
groups and the "creative class."

Addison Godel

THE PSYCHOTECHNICAL ARCHITECT: PERCEPTION, VOCATION AND THE LABORATORY CULTURES OF MODERNISM, 1914–1945 ¶ Technological rationalization has often been held as one of the defining characteristics of architectural modernism, as the engine of industrial modernity was fueled by a quantitative sense of Arbeitskraft through which labor power was rendered knowable, abstract, and exchangeable. But this caloric understanding of the urban worker was frequently shadowed by an interest in perceptual rationalization as well. If Taylorist empiricism implied an architecture of efficient work, where did that leave the figure of the architect? Could design and experience be rethought as kinds of work, and rendered similarly empirical? Such was the promise of Hugo Münsterberg's invention of "psychotechnics" in 1914—a parascientific discipline that blended industrial management with perceptual psychology, creating data from phenomena and human capacities that had previously resisted quantification. Psychotechnics promised a vocational bureaucracy through which to judge not just architecture, but architects (with aspiring students finding themselves on both sides of the scientific apparatus, as researchers and as subjects of inquiry). ¶ From its naming in 1914 through the close of the Second World War, a number of architects took interest in this since forgotten field, which held the significant possibilities for new directions in design pedagogy, architectural practice, urban planning, and more generally understanding the interface between human subjects and the spaces and systems of the industrialized city (whether communist or capitalist). In the search for a modernism beyond the formal precepts of the "modern movement," the architectural laboratory became the central scene of action, grounding architectural production in new models of research that redefined architecture's status as a discipline. Following a number of attempts at psychotechnical architectures through the United States, Germany, and the Soviet Union—by figures such as Hugo Münsterberg, Hanns Riedel, Hannes Meyer, Walter Moede, Nikolai Ladovsky, Pavel Rudik, Frank Gilbreth, and László Moholy-Nagy—my research traces the contours of an evolving discourse of expertise, aptitude, and spatial sensibility as the discipline of architecture remade itself on simultaneously aesthetic and political grounds.

James D. Graham

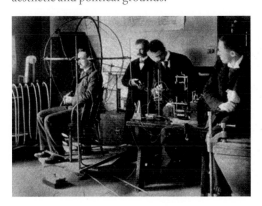

WELT BILDEND: ARCHITECTURES OF SECURITY AND INFRASTRUCTURAL MODERNISM IN GERMANY AND BEYOND, 1848–1952 ¶ This dissertation follows several generations of German architects, engineers, planners, and scientists across Central Europe and German colonial Africa whose work gave shape to new forms of technical expertise through involvement in internal and external colonization projects and housing programs. Borrowing a pivotal concept from Timothy Mitchell, this study argues that a new and enduring 'rule of experts' developed within the circuitry of certain infrastructural technologies—colonial camps, settlement commissions, housing estates, and transnational power networks—that gave rise to a modern image of the architect as an intervention-oriented planner. It explores the spatial politics of the social reform movement of the 1880s and its legislative legacy—from coercive tenancy laws, to the development of colonial infrastructure, and land-use policies—and tracks its influence on the cultural logic of avant-garde housing estates, energy substructures, and interventionist development programs. In drawing such an arc, this study demonstrates how architectural technologies helped to form an infrastructural network of European power, and reframed the relationship between the body and the state.

Hollyamber Kennedy

CONCRETE COLONIALISM: ARCHITECTURE, URBANISM AND THE AMERICAN COLONIZATION OF THE PHILIPPINES ¶ This dissertation focuses on two different though interconnected uses of the word concrete, both of which were central to a largely overlooked chapter of American history—the American colonization of the Philippines (1898–1945). Originally a logician's term meaning "actual and solid," the word concrete only came to refer to the building material in the mid-nineteenth century, a popular usage emerging co-incident with the industrial production of Portland cement—a material that American producers and promoters argued would enable the construction of an era of durable American greatness. The dawn of an American "concrete age"—an era otherwise referred to as the Progressive Era was also a time that saw the emergence of a language of "concrete" values; of actual, specific and measurable results. This period in history saw the apparent focus of American governance shift from the abstract and foundational principles of liberty towards more tangible values of investments and returns, i.e. on "development." This dissertation examines Daniel Burnham's City Beautiful plan for Manila in addition to the construction of the colonial institutional and infrastructural projects (government buildings, ports, forts, bridges, roads, housing and prisons) through the analysis of five of concrete's (and sometimes Portland cement's) qualities; portability, stability, salubrity, strength, and plasticity. These examples demonstrate that concrete was not only a material used widely across America's new possession in the Far East, but also played a role in shaping new forms of global governance.

Diana Martinez

Frontispiece to William Cameron Forbes' "The Romance of Business". The caption reads "A few huddled, half naked creatures in crazy shelters of grass, mud and leaves."

FEMINISM IN AMERICAN ARCHITECTURE, 1968–2000 ¶ This project—an examination of the impact of feminism on American architecture from the late 1960s through the 1990s—explores the ferment that shook architecture during these pivotal decades. Second-wave feminism emerged out of the turmoil of the late 1950s and early 1960s, and was well established as a movement by the time women in architecture began organizing associations and conferences in the early 1970s. From early concerns about improving their numbers and status in the profession, feminist architects and architecture scholars expanded the knowledge of women's involvement in the built environment, and challenged the boundaries of the discipline. The 1990s saw a proliferation of scholarship and academic conferences that, reflecting a broader shift towards theory in architecture and feminism, took up gender and discourse analysis. Through careful archival work, supported by extensive interviews, This research seeks to uncover the history of the feminist movement in architecture and assess its present-day legacies.

Andrea Merrett

Women's School of Planning and Architecture participants, 1975. Courtesy of the Women's School of Planning and Architecture Records, Sophia Smith Collection, Smith College (Northampton, Massachusetts).

THE INCOMMENSURABILITY OF MODERNITY: ARCHITECTURE AND THE ANARCHIC FROM ENLIGHTENMENT REVOLUTIONS TO LIBERAL RECONSTRUCTIONS

Peter Minosh

¶ This dissertation examines the architecture of the French, American, and Haitian revolutions as well as the French 1848 Revolution and the Paris Commune. The traditional historiography of neoclassical and Beaux-Arts architecture considers it as coextensive with the establishment of the nation-state, culminating in the institution building of the French Second Empire and post-bellum United States under the banner of liberal nationalism. This interpretation is complicated by highlighting its slippages and crises through examining moments of insurrection against the state and spaces outside of the conventional construal of the nation. The hypothesis is that democracy, as a form of social and political life, is intrinsically anarchic and paradigmatically revolutionary, and that architecture cultivates the aims and paradoxes of revolution. Revolutionary conditions render this radical capacity of architecture salient, showing the ultimate incommensurability between architecture and the regimes that determine and delimit it.

Rainsford – View of a Temple

THE AESTHETICS OF PRECISION: RESEARCH AND TECHNIQUE IN THE ARCHITECTURE OF SEALED SPACE, 1946–1986

Alexandra Quantrill

¶ This dissertation addresses a critical technical and architectural problem of post-war building: how to achieve the tightly modulated environment implied by the regulated lines and taut materiality of the window wall. Through case studies of facade details it examines how modernist ideals of transparency, technical precision, and environmental containment were translated in the development of smooth glazed skins. Central to this process was an attempt to resolve dissonant research, design, and engineering strategies—a tangle of subjectivity and objectivity—within discrete, precise techniques. The dissertation traces the emergence of a discourse on precision in interactions between the architects, engineers, scientists and manufacturers who collaborated on the production of increasingly complex glazed envelopes. This pursuit of precision manifested the period's general cacophony of technical, aesthetic, and economic tendencies, engaging oppositions between interior and exterior, universal and specific, custom and standard, expert and amateur, and nature and artifice. The fragments studied, drawn from buildings for the United Nations, a major corporate enterprise, an insurance broker, and an international bank, depict a shift in techniques of enclosure from the mid- to late-20th century, which, together with systems of energy regulation and spatial management, created contained worlds reflecting a changing global order.

Model of the Hong Kong and Shanghai Banking Corporation (HSBC) headquarters being tested by lighting engineers Bartenbach and Wagner under their "artificial sun" in Innsbruck, Austria, c. 1983. Image courtesy of Foster+Partners.

Pollyanna Rhee

DESIGNING NATURAL ADVANTAGES: COMMUNITY, CIVIC DESIGN, AND THE CONSERVATIVE FOUNDATIONS OF ENVIRONMENTALISM, 1920–1970 ¶ My dissertation charts the growth of a grassroots, conservative environmental movement, through changes in the built environment, and asks what those efforts reflect about the relationship between the built and natural environments and how those ideas behind that relationship helped shape social and political visions of American life. By using Santa Barbara, California as a central case study, this dissertation examines how local civic leaders with the cooperation of political officials, architects, and planners worked to transform the built environment in ways that produced and normalized new understandings of community life and environmental consciousness. Working at multiple scales from interior designs in the home to the coastline, these generally affluent, well-educated, and white activists saw little contradiction in their commitments to conservative politics and concern for their natural surroundings. Controlling aesthetic features of Santa Barbara's architecture to reflect its Spanish and Mexican pasts, advocating for "native" plants in gardens, and attempting to ban offshore oil rigs were seen as common sense rather than radical ideas.

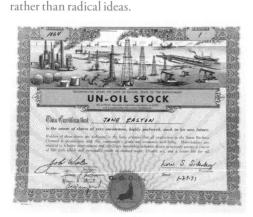

Jonah Rowen

ARCHITECTURE'S INVENTION OF ATMOSPHERE: BUILDING FOR THE THREAT OF FIRE ACROSS THE NINETEENTH-CENTURY BRITISH ATLANTIC ¶ By the early 19th century, processes of industrialization were well underway in the British Empire. Architecture, though, began to orient and to participate in those processes through new forms of planning, production, and organization. This project focuses on the ways in which the practices of architecture and construction in the British territories of the Caribbean, Canada, and the British Isles took into account hypothetical and actual threats to buildings, particularly fire, in architectural production. If modernity may be characterized by attempts to control for an uncertain future, emerging capabilities of measurement and technologies for preempting or responding to threats to property damage suggest means of evaluating architecture that collapse quantification onto aesthetics, and which blur the line between technical knowledge and talent or skill in architectural design. Requisite to the processes of professionalization for architects, builders, and engineers were new forms of expertise aimed at hedging against unpredictability, in which architects chose materials and devices less for their representational or symbolic values than for their properties in resisting newly analyzable threats. ¶ Historians have studied modern architecture using the notions of space and time as constitutive elements; this project seeks to redefine space in terms of atmosphere, and time in terms of material resistance (e.g., heat), thereby arriving at an alternative conception of architectural modernism. This project seeks to demonstrate architecture's role in ushering in a modernity whose primary goal was an ability to control for hypothetical but fundamentally uncertain futures.

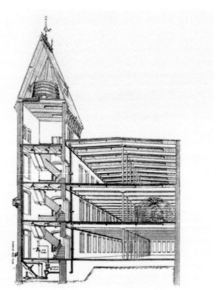

Insurers Automatic Fire Extinguisher Company, Automatic Sprinklers for Extinguishing Fires, 1891 from Cecil D. Elliott, Technics and Architecture (Cambridge, MA: The MIT Press, 1992), 374

RICE AND COAL: FOX LORE IN JAPAN'S INDUSTRIAL LANDSCAPE, 1863–1932 ¶ Dating back to the Edo Period (1603–1868) in Japan wherein Mitsui was a powerful merchant, their devotion to the agricultural-commercial deity—Inari and its emissary, the fox—continued after their transformation into the business conglomerate, Mitsui Zaibatsu, that established a bank, trading company and mining company in the late nineteenth century. This dissertation investigates how the architecture of the conglomerate mediated their folk-religiosity and valorized its respective sites, while also internalizing other forms of folk-religiosity, often in conflicting ways. Those sites include Mitsui's tutelage shrine, business headquarters in Tokyo and, in particular, coal mines in Fukuoka. The dissertation intends to demonstrate that fox-related folk practices, such as Inari worship, of coal miners and corresponding structures, rooted in their previous social relations, were synchronized into capitalist processes. While Mitsui received a "gift" from the processes in the form of coal, the miners did not earn the blessing, experiencing instead a shortage of rice—the metonym of their life force. As Inari was originated in an agricultural deity, it remains profoundly ironic that Mitsui's Inari worship did not provide enough rice for its workforce. My research deciphers this vulpine exchange at work in the making of the capitalist landscape in Japan.

Norihiko Tsuneishi

ENGLISH ARCHITECTURE IN THE AGE OF COLONIZATION, 1585–1642 ¶ This dissertation examines relations between English colonization efforts in the early seventeenth century and the cultural production arising in and around the courts of James I (1603–25) and Charles I (1625–49). While both phenomena have long been acknowledged as indispensable to an understanding of 17th century England, relations between the two have gone largely unexamined. Historians of empire and colonization have viewed this period as one in which England turned its attention outward, seeking colonies in hope of competing with its rival, Spain. In much the same way, architectural historians have viewed the period as one in which England turned away from a medieval (even a neo-medieval) past and towards the classicism of the Italian Renaissance. This dissertation seeks to relate these two watershed events, arguing that England's relation to its colonies was not unlike its relation to the Italian Renaissance. Both were known at a distance—through books, images, and travel accounts rather than first-hand; artists played crucial roles in the "discovery" of both; and each served to define an "Englishness" made newly urgent by both discoveries. Drawing from the fields of art history, archaeology, ethnography, and media studies, this dissertation construes the built environment as a realm of contestation that served as a medium through which English civility was differentiated from its colonial other.

Aaron White

Unknown Artist, The Execution of King Charles I, circa 1649

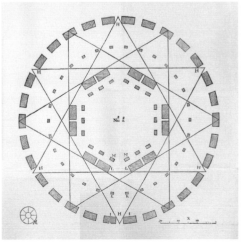

Inigo Jones, Plan of Stonehenge Reconstruction, 1655

THE GROWTH OF THE FIRM: THE TRANS-
FORMATION OF THE PRACTICE OF
ARCHITECTURE IN NEW YORK CITY,
1865–1930 ¶ This dissertation traces the changing role, status, and definition of architects, the
transformation of design, drawing, and practice,
and the emergence of the modern architecture
firm in the United States from the end of the Civil
War to the 1930s. It shows how a small elite shaped
the profession in their image, elevated the art of
design, the culture of drafting, and the ethos of
expertise into the centerpiece of their practice,
and developed large, specialized, and hierarchical
firms that were aligned with the most advanced
sectors of the modern building industry. The
study of the firms of Richard M. Hunt, George
B. Post, McKim, Mead, and White, Cass Gilbert,
and Ely Jacques Kahn, trace the development of a
stratified, hierarchical, and collaborative culture
of work. This dissertation argues that such firms
represented a new vision of the profession, created by
architects to take advantage of a rapidly expanding
market for their services, to meet the challenges
of a new scale, complexity, and sophistication of
buildings, and to assert their authority over the
process of construction in the complex commercial
environment of the modern American metropolis.

Alexander Hilton Wood

The Office of Carrère and Hastings, New York, 1901

WINDOWS AT THE TOP, BLOOD ON THE
FLOOR: THE ARCHITECTURE OF POLI-
TICS AND RIGHTS IN BRAZIL, 1964–1985 ¶
This research seeks to unpack the deep contradiction
that troubles attempts by architectural historians to
assess the consequence and legacies of architectural
projects realized in Brazil during the period of
autocratic military rule, from 1964 to 1985. How
does one understand and discern the design merit
of buildings whose undertaking was sponsored
by an apparatus of state-institutionalized attacks
on civil society? ¶ The dissertation aims to offer a
possible answer by investigating the architecture
from a time and place where the crisis conditions of
politics were stark and unambiguous. The investigation will proceed by revisiting several prominent,
iconic projects and events from Brazil in the 1960s
to the mid-1980s: the Brazilian Pavilion for the
Osaka World Expo of 1970 by Paulo Mendes da
Rocha, FAU-USP by Vilanova Artigas, the social
housing experiments of Grupo Arquitetura Nova in
the 1960s, the ludic designs of Lina Bo Bardi, etc.
¶ The movements and activities of architecture in
Brazil during the military regime might contribute
towards understanding architecture's relationship to
politics; untethered from the economic dependency
theory dialectic through whose aporia the case for
their disconnect has been made, the projects under
examination begin to offer themselves as sites of
more expansive conflicts and contestations than
previously perceived. The central hypothesis of
this dissertation is that the claims which emerge
from these enriched scenes are comprehensively
rights claims, and that architecture differentiates
the politics of these rights.

Amy Zhang

Urban Planning Ph.D. Program

Robert Beauregard, Director

The intent of the Ph.D. Program in Urban Planning is to educate and train scholars and researchers in the field of urban and regional planning. Substantive areas of study include: affordable housing, infrastructure planning, energy policy, environmental planning, and transportation, among others. These substantive concerns are approached both theoretically and methodologically. In the former instance, students draw, for example, from neo-classical economics, participatory democracy, regulatory policy and planning theory. In the latter, they utilize key informant interviews, statistical analysis of secondary data, mixed methods, and case study design. Emphasis within the program is given to the role of space and of collective action on the part of governments and civic organizations. Of particular concern are issues of social justice and democracy.

DOCTORAL COLLOQUIUM: UR-
BAN THEORY ¶ FALL 2016 ¶ KIAN
TAJBAKHSH, INSTRUCTOR ¶
This doctoral colloquium surveyed and
critically assessed some of the major
strands in the study of urbanism and
cities as it has developed since the 1960s
up until today. We explored claims for
the so-called fracturing of the urban and
assessed recent attempts to reassert new
forms of coherence to the understanding
of human and ecological habitats, as
well as the implications for the practices
of design, policy and planning. These
include theoretical innovations such
as "new materialism"; concepts such
as infrastructures, landscape and ecological urbanism; phenomenological
attention to place-making, locality and
identity; the new urbanism; the role of
religion and the sacred in ecological
sustainability; as well as the potential
of criteria such as justice, authenticity
and existential meaning as indicators
of what is important in urban experience. The colloquium was structured
around two main frames. First we
contrasted the three main competing
ideological paradigms in this field
(liberal, conservative, radical). Second,
we examined a perennial conundrum
of urban theory, namely the question
of whether by the term "urban" we
are referring to an independent aspect
of society; or whether the urban has
today lost its conceptual, even spatial,
specificity. The colloquium explored
cities and city life in regions including
Africa, South Asia, the United States
and the Middle East.

ADVANCED PLANNING HIS-
TORY ¶ SPRING 2017 ¶ ELLIOTT
SCLAR, INSTRUCTOR ¶ Planning
history examined the intersection of
ideas about spatiality, physicality and
social organization; "the planning intersection." The passage of time changes
both the literal and figurative physical
reality of urban space and our conceptions and articulations of it. Via the
study of the historic narratives that
other scholars constructed about the
planning intersection we sought to
gain insight into the future directions
of the urban condition and the ability
of planning to effectively address the
equity and sustainability concerns that
are now urgent global imperatives. ¶
The questions around which the critical
work of this course revolved included:
how did ideas about planning and the
narratives of its history develop? How
did they intersect with one another?
In what ways do they influence our
contemporary understanding of the
planning intersection? What methods
did the writers use to reach the conclusions they reached? What concerns did
they make background for their work
and what did they choose to display

in the foreground? Which ideological
positions were the writers promoting
and which were they discouraging?

DOCTORAL COLLOQUIUM II
& IV: APPLIED QUALITATIVE
METHODS ¶ SPRING 2017 ¶
WEIPING WU, INSTRUCTOR ¶
This seminar introduced commonly
used approaches to conducting and
analyzing qualitative research, including participant observation, in-depth
interviewing, ethnography, case studies,
action research, interpretive analysis,
and more. We also addressed issues that
arise when using qualitative methods,
paying special attention to theory building, reliability and validity, research
ethics, and the degree to which evidence
from qualitative research can be presented convincingly. Students advanced
and deepened skills in managing the
design, data collection, analysis, and
reporting strategies for select methods
of qualitative research.

CCCP

Felicity D. Scott & Mark Wasiuta, Co-Directors

The Masters of Science in Critical, Curatorial, and Conceptual Practices in Architecture (CCCP) offers advanced training in the fields of architectural criticism, publishing, curating, exhibiting, writing and research through a two-year, full-time course of intensive academic study and independent research. The program recognizes that architectural production is multi-faceted and diverse and that careers in architecture often extend beyond traditional modes of professional practice and academic scholarship, while at the same time reflecting and building upon them.

The CCCP program is structured to reflect this heterogeneity and the multiple sites and formats of exchange through which the field of architecture operates while at the same time sponsoring the ongoing critical development and interaction of such a matrix of practices and institutions. The program's emphasis is thus on forging new critical, theoretical and historical tools, and producing new and rigorous concepts and strategies for researching, presenting, displaying and disseminating modern and contemporary architecture and closely related fields. The program is aimed primarily (but not exclusively) at those with a background in architecture who wish to advance and expand their critical and research skills in order to pursue professional and leadership careers as architectural critics, theorists, journalists, historians, editors, publishers, curators, gallerists, institute staff and directors, teachers, and research-based practitioners. Students might be seeking further academic training or specialization after a professional degree or years of teaching, or even at mid-career. They might also have worked in a related field and be seeking an academic forum to develop additional specializations in architecture. The program also provides the highest level of preparatory training for application to Ph.D. programs in architectural history and theory.

This year the CCCP program hosted: a day long symposium at e-flux entitled *Interpretations: Destabilizing Ground(s)*; a public lecture by Martin Beck entitled "Program: An Organized System of Instructions"; a workshop by Eva Franch, Chief Curator of Storefront for Art and Architecture entitled "Office*US (and Them)*"; and a collaborative visualization workshop with the Tohono O'odham Community College in southern Arizona led by Caitlin Blanchfield and Nina Kolowratnik entitled "Borderlands, Conservation and Ecology," for which students traveled to the Tohono O'odham nation.

CCCP COLLOQUIUM: OPER-
ATING PLATFORMS: PUBLI-
CATIONS, EXHIBITIONS,
RESEARCH ¶ SPRING 2017 ¶ FE-
LICITY D. SCOTT, INSTRUCTOR
¶ The core colloquium for the Critical,
Curatorial, and Conceptual Practices
in Architecture program (CCCP) focused on three interrelated "operating"
platforms: (1) publications including
magazines, reports, newspapers, and
books and the architects, critics, writers,
and publishers associated with them; (2)
exhibitions in galleries, museums, world
fairs, expos, biennales, and triennales
and the architects, curators, and institutions involved, and; (3) experimental
formats of research and the collaborative
arrangements and institutions through
which they function. Recognizing that
the domain of architectural work is
multi-faceted—as are the multiple forms
of practice and knowledge that reflect
back upon it—the course investigated
what role these platforms have played
in the conceptualization and transformation of architecture over the past
century, identifying their contribution
to seminal debates, to transformations
in architecture's technical and aesthetic
characteristics, to the sponsoring of
critical experimentation, as well as to
the careers of many architects. We asked,
in turn, what scope there is for pushing
new formats, developing new critical
concepts, opening new trajectories of
investigation, and expanding the very
territories of the discipline.

CCCP COLLOQUIUM: DOCU-
MENTS AND DISCOURSE ¶
FALL 2016 ¶ MARK WASIUTA,
INSTRUCTOR ¶ This CCCP colloquium approached contemporary
critical discourse through the filter
of documents and documentation.
It argued that architectural practice
is inflected by the status, history, and
ontology of the document and that
the informational, classificatory, and
discursive parameters of various forms
of practice are delineated and organized
by contracts, drawings, manuscripts and
photographs. The course traced how
the genre of document has expanded
almost boundlessly to include memos,
receipts, email files, audio recordings,
films, tapes, notes and computer code
and studied how documents' legal,
institutional, social, and political identities cut across diverse architectural,
academic, popular, and administrative
cultural registers. In specific historical
examples, the status, definition, use, and
authority of documents for architecture,
architectural history, architectural
exhibitions, and architecture's other
media practices were examined and
assessed.

CCCP THESIS ¶ FALL 2016 &
SPRING 2017 ¶ ADAM BANDLER,
INSTRUCTOR AND COORDINA-
TOR ¶ In addition to regular meetings
with their primary advisors, students
were required to attend four thesis
seminar meetings per semester with the
thesis coordinator. These sessions were
an important forum for reviewing the
requirements and expectations of the
CCCP thesis, for discussing individual
projects and clarifying research agendas,
for strategizing representational strategies, and for developing and refining
approaches to jury presentations.

SACRED LAND ¶ ADVISOR: REINHOLD MARTIN ¶ In the wake of the war in Vietnam and the subsequent economic fallout tens of thousands of people left Vietnam on boats headed to ports around the South China and Celebes Seas. In 1978 the first boat landed in Hong Kong carrying some 200 people. Migrants continued to arrive and while some were resettled in Hong Kong, the majority remained in refugee camps throughout the territory. Over the course of the next two decades nearly 100,000 migrants arrived in the colony. Many went abroad to host nations but the majority remained on the island, some for as long as fifteen years, entirely within the walls of semi-permanent internment camps. ¶ This thesis focuses on the camps as a means of unfolding the colonial government's management of the land's scarcity and population. The internment camps continued the government's development of social housing and focused their efforts by becoming a laboratory for using hygiene as a means of governance. This thesis examines how the camps were caught up in management projects while also being a pointed means to understand the agency of architecture principally as a site where architecture was most conspicuously inadequate. The refugees were kept in little more than rapidly recommissioned factory and industrial buildings, detention centers, and military barracks turned ad hoc camps. Issues arising from the longevity of contingent relationships, a result of the surprising number of refugees arriving over so long a period of time, help shed light on colonial architectural practices articulated principally through land management and hygiene. A focus on these threads and the latter in particular help unfold the stakes raised by this thesis. ¶ Focusing on the camps has led to in-depth research at the collections at the Public Records Office in Hong Kong where inter-agency discussions about the inadequacy of architecture of the camps is brought to light by The Housing Authority, the primary managers of housing conditions for the refugees. Material found in the collection there shows proposals to use the Vietnamese as promoters of hygiene at the same moment that The Urban Council developed a well-known campaign to use posters and graphic means to spread the word on the value of hygiene in the city at large.

Daniel Cooper

WALLED / OFF BEIJING: RESTORE THE ANCIENT WALL BRICK BY BRICK ¶ ADVISOR: FELICITY D. SCOTT ¶ This thesis traces the ancient inner city wall of Beijing and its ruination, survival remnants, and recent reincarnation—the Ming Dynasty City Wall Relics Park, through documentation and visualization. The research interrogates how the wall, with the public's wholehearted participation, was saved from obsolescence both physical and social and appeared relevant as it is framed and reframed by preservation as culturally significant. The scattered bricks donated by local communities engaged and created a mode of displacement within Beijing in the name of preservation, becoming enmeshed in the nexus of social relations, media representations, and political agendas. The bulk of the thesis is structured in two major sections, providing different lenses that inspect the inner city wall's transformations at two distinct scales: one micro scale of bricks and the other spectrum of cityscape. The aesthetics of the wall became part of political spectacles that both local community and the Chinese government contributed to, creating an unprecedented understanding of cultural heritage at the moment Beijing was experiencing an endless metamorphosis of its urban landscape, a metamorphosis geared towards staging itself as an "event-city" with high international prestige. Preservation redefines architecture, presents a novel comprehension, a philosophy, of the city. This is especially intriguing in the context of modern China, where preservation practice coincides with the development of modern architecture, in a sense, they are both arenas subjected to the external influences from technologies, economy, national sentiments, and international recognitions. The research destabilizes the rhetorics of preservation; it argues that the wall has been multiply appropriated, mobilized, and transplanted. With a capacity to renew itself, the ancient wall reappears as a picturesque reminder of a continuous urban history among residents.

Ruishi Ge

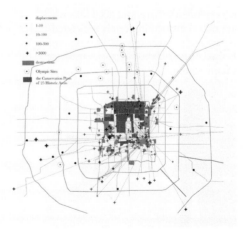

MIXED REALITIES AND ARCHITECTURE ¶ ADVISORS: STEVE FEINER, TED KRUEGER ¶ Institutions of architectural education have a call-and-response relationship to architectural discourse and practice. It is both the incubator for experimentation and replies to changes in the world beyond the walls of the university. This thesis proposes a new two-year master's of science degree program within GSAPP that responds to developments in computer science, electrical engineering, and developments in human behaviour that operate in the digital and virtual realm. This program is designed as a place for experimentation in designing interfaces for perceiving, orienting, and functioning within virtuality with an architectural approach and design perspective. ¶ This program posits that digital and virtual information and data is a kind of hostile environment, in much the same way as extraterrestrial space and the Antarctic tundra are extreme spaces for inhabitants. As it is true that architecture is a kind of interface that mediates hostile environments into habitable environments, this program is built upon the idea that digital interfaces are at their core architectural, and provide the framework to spatialise and temporalise virtuality such that users can perceive and interact with data. Interfaces are an architectural strategy to transform virtuality from the unfavourable to the agreeable. ¶ The master's program core consists of studio, technical, history, and theory courses that provide the opportunities to develop a framework through which to understand architecture's relationship to computational virtuality so as to design hybrid environments that blend the virtual and digital realms, but also to comfortably incorporate and even participate in the development of future technologies. Situated within a broader context, the aim of this program is to create a pathway for greater architectural perspective within the user experience (UX) field of computer science and to increase the incorporation of digital and hybrid interface design into the space of architectural practice. ¶ This thesis consists of a written component—which explores the basis and need for such a masters program—and the materials associated with the program itself: a website with the program details, as well as course syllabi and course readers for the core requirements.

Chloe English

NEW GAMES: COUNTERCULTURAL SPACES OF PLAY, 1973–1985 ¶ ADVISOR: FELICITY D. SCOTT ¶ *New Games: Countercultural Spaces of Play, 1973–1985* investigates play as a cultural vehicle, a means of community-building and of restructuring space, by exhibiting media artifacts propagating the ideas, politics, and social agenda of the New Games Foundation, an organization established in 1974 to promote New Games. The foundation attempted to "bring people in harmony with their environment and to eliminate the barriers of age, sex, race, and economics from leisure time activities." ¶ *New Games: Countercultural Spaces of Play, 1973–1985* immerses itself in the formats used by the foundation and explores the periodical as an exhibition format. However, it is neither a topical magazine, nor a traveling exhibition, rather it takes the form of a predefined number of issues of a newsletter-like display—an exhibition on demand—with built-in obsolescence. By incorporating aspects of the New Games movement's media and communication strategy, the mail order exhibition operates as a decentralized communitarian experiment. ¶ The main body of the exhibition consists of six sections, each discussing New Games within a different scope. These sections are materialized as individually curated box sets—each accompanied by a critical essay putting the specific documents in relation to a broader realm. While discussing historic precedents and paradigms as well as the movement's contemporaneous tendencies in education, land-use, and game theory, the spotlight stays on countercultural spaces of play, the tools used and marketed by the foundation, as well as the New Game Movement's implications and reverberations.

Joachim Hackl

ARCHITECTURE, NATIONALISM, AND INTERNATIONALISM IN INDONESIA, 1960–1965 ¶ ADVISOR: FELICITY D. SCOTT ¶ This study suggests an alternative way of reading the architecture of nationalism. It attempts to identify and theorize different modes through which architecture, in cultivating the collective subjectivities of a certain nation, manifests nexuses between the national and the international. Understanding this reciprocity requires an intensive examination of the international geopolitics that situates any national, architectural production. It involves reading architecture as diplomatic apparatuses, sites of negotiations, currencies of exchanges, exhibiting devices, and other manifestations of international relations that, conversely, helped foster the collective subjectivities of a certain nation. ¶ To undertake such a project, my research investigates two building projects in Indonesia that were built between 1960 and 1965, when attempts toward producing the architecture of nationalism in Indonesia were actualized at full-scale while Indonesia's links to the world and its nationhood were vigorously negotiated on wide cultural and political fronts. The first project, the Asian Games Stadium (1960–1962) in Jakarta, is emblematic of President Sukarno's recognition of sports as a prominent platform for producing national pride as well as cultivating anti-imperialist sentiment. The second project, the Indonesia Pavilion (1963–1965) at the 1964–65 New York World's Fair, was devised to position the nation-state strategically within the geopolitics of the Cold War by exhibiting neutrality. Both contrasting projects—one dealing with Indonesia hosting an international event, the other addressing the nation as an international guest—show that the architecture of nationalism hardly constitutes an isolated terrain.

Robin Hartanto Honggare

WOVEN: MANUFACTURED SOCIAL TEXTURE OF TEXTILE FACTORY IN TAIWAN ¶ ADVISOR: REINHOLD MARTIN ¶ This thesis expands upon a series of persistent labor movements in Taiwan initiated by workers who lost their jobs due to fraudulent bankrupt and relocated textile and clothing factories since 1996. The vast constellation of instances compelled the interrogation of the backdrop of the incidents—the factory. ¶ Taiwan does not have the climate for cotton production. Cotton textile is neither native nor does it grow well in Taiwan's geographical conditions. In spite of all the evidence that dissuaded the industry's development, it was implemented by the colonial regime and sustained from a global trading network. The industry itself was production; it produced the environment within the existing socio-geographical context. To build physical architecture is far less a concern than the construction of an operational network. ¶ This thesis investigates the role the textile factory served throughout different political stages in Taiwan, from the planned "ideal" factory model in the early 1950s which served government control purposes, to the full-blown development of capitalist factories in the free market era. Yet the focuses on the manufacturing territories and the formulated network within the consolidated geographical, national or economical entity can neither extend beyond the delineated organization, nor answer why the incidents happened at that very moment. ¶ As the example of the Taiwanese textile and clothing industry has shown, the accumulation of capital by manufacturing operations led not to the well-being of the participating parties but to the industry's own decay. Hence, the last presentation seeks to dismantle the focus on the consolidated entity, to zoom out to the macro scale, and to retrace the development of the industry along with post-WWII global economic development, in order to understand beyond the movement of raw material and products, to the movement of capital.

Chi-Chia Hou

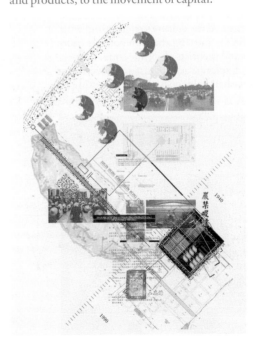

EXPLORING ABANDUM: BEHIND THE SCENES ⁋ ADVISOR: JAMES GRAHAM ⁋ The late 20th century saw a culture of exploration grow up around ever-expanding post-industrial landscapes rife with freshly abandoned places. This culture once operated underground as a secretive counter-culture, but with advancements in image producing and sharing technologies, it has grown in numbers and in the public eye, becoming a decidedly 21st century media culture. New ranks of urban explorers have found new ways not only of utilizing sites, but also of broadcasting their exploits. Whether seeking thrills, fame, truth, or history, these explorers inhabit a temporal space and capture a moment in its transformation. They report back on their findings, not only to a community of their peers, but also to an eager public, which feeds on the stream of imagery, living vicariously through the explorer. Explorers become producers, feeding a media economy in image and narrative commodities. The explorer curates a persona through what they produce, marketing themselves as a brand. ⁋ With or without a pseudonym, the explorer fashions an alter-ego through what they publish, dramatize, romanticize, and through selling themselves, the sites they visit, and the culture of exploration, before returning to their day-jobs as photographers, writers, or software engineers. ⁋ The culture of exploring abandum operates in modes similar to those used by architecture and film: each explores alternative worlds as a method of understanding our own. This thesis utilizes media forms in a similar fashion to explorers, pulling images and text out of context and splicing them into a dialogue with each other. Taking on the format of a screenplay, this thesis explores the culture's entanglement with media and spectacle from within the framework this discourse operates in. It utilizes the online forum, the chat room, and social media as sources documenting the psyche of the explorer and trends in the culture at large. It challenges explorers to examine the construction of their personas, to question media's influence on the culture and the culture's relationship with architecture, by putting them in conversation with critics and theorists of architecture, history, and media. Explorers act not just as subjects, but as experts in their field, questioning the future of this alternative culture as it slips into the norm.

Sara McGillivray

INSTITUTIONAL MEDIATIONS BE-TWEEN ARCHITECTURE AND THE PUBLIC SPHERE: THE CASE OF ART NET (1974–1979) ⁋ ADVISOR: MARK WASIUTA ⁋ Concerned with the conditions of architecture dissemination and debate, and considering that institutions have a large influence on the formulation of discourses and an impact on redefinitions of practice, this thesis investigates the case of architecture centers. Based on their primary focus on communication through exhibitions, talks, and publications, as well as their role as network agencies, architecture centers are studied here as relevant mediating agents between architecture and its different audiences and with other types of institutions such as museums, professional associations, and foundations. Reflecting on the challenge of pedagogical models and the consequent creation of new projects and institutions in the 1960s and 1970s, this thesis examines the case of Art Net, a non-commercial gallery for art and architecture conceived by Peter Cook. Operating in London from 1974 to 1979, Art Net promoted an environment for discussion and for the formulation of architectural ideas and experiments. This research studies Art Net's structure, activities, and forms of communication. It seeks to comprehend the conception, composition, and effects of Art Net's programs as well as the role the institution played in both its London and international contexts.

Iara Pimenta

STAGING THE AGENDA: KYONG PARK AND STOREFRONT FOR ART AND ARCHITECTURE, 1982–1998 ¶ ADVISOR: FELICITY D. SCOTT ¶ The thesis sets out to investigate curatorial practices at the end of the twentieth century (1980–2000), as an attempt to map or construct alternative pathways or narratives of the period—an exercise in historical revision and critical interpretation—bringing to the fore understudied disciplinary debates that contest the well-known theoretical depictions of these decades. Focusing on the case of Kyong Park and Storefront for Art and Architecture (1982–), the thesis attempts to produce a series of critical readings of Park's curatorial practice by studying the institution and the specificities of its production through particular exhibitions, publications, forums, and related events. Positioning each case within a certain context and mobilizing its milieu to its further extents, the thesis intends to probe the different historical projects of our recent past, and thus construct a method of 'measuring' their impact in architectural discourse.

Camila Reyes Alé

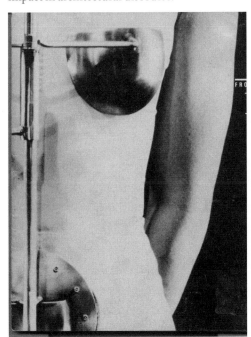

GOVERNMENTALITY EXPOSED: TURKEY'S EARLY REPUBLICAN VILLAGE INSTITUTES IN 6 OPERATIONS ¶ ADVISOR: FELICITY D. SCOTT ¶ During the early Republican period in Turkey, the national agenda included the development of rural lands in addition to building the nation's new capital. Advancement in these underdeveloped areas would contribute to the national economy and thus to the "nation building" itself, as the country was highly agrarian and most of the population lived in villages. This thesis proposes to trace an infrastructural experiment that operated within these agricultural landscapes. Implementations of this experiment as part of modernization attempts constituted the institutionalization and systematization of individual bodies and vast territories. ¶ Through the analysis of Village Institutes (1940–1954), this thesis aims to question the issue of territory in rural contexts, biopolitics, and its spatial implications within the geopolitical apparatus of an emerging nation. While reading the pedagogical/institutional technologies embedded in their logic and their inscriptions in mediascapes, it proposes that this experiment can be read as site for subject formation. It exposes the oscillation between modernity with all of its ideals, and instrumentalization of control and management. Village Institutes' operative field simultaneously juxtaposes the scale of the body with the scale of the territory, revealing the pieces of a bigger governmental apparatus. At the nexus of these two scales lies the architecture, as an infrastructural and territorial discourse, exposing the traces of the apparatus in its physical form. This thesis argues that this network operates in a two-fold manner: Through the creation of an infrastructure for the formation of subjects, it also works as a catalyst for the development of otherwise leftover countryside. Concurrently, while explicating rural modernization, the primary outputs—government published journals, maps, curriculums, reports, architectural competitions, and architectures, etc.—act also as propaganda vehicles in the formation of an urban psyche. By analyzing these primary sources, this thesis proposes alternative, non-chronological, readings of these projects through six operations, with each revealing a different aspect and agency of the apparatus, building up to an overarching complexity of an encompassing modernization project. The operations that are represented as stand-alone chapters are: Act of Propaganda, Act of Translation, Act of Mediation, Act of Imposition and Resistance, and Act of Collecting.

Gizem Sivri

OUR
ONLY
CONSTANT
IS
CHANGE

Columbia GSAPP Design Mantras, 2017

Taken together, these statements can be read as a sort of time-sensitive mantra for the disciplines of the built environment, a set of pedagogical imperatives that have emerged from the school, and a statement of engagement as an institution. We understand these six statements, dispersed throughout this book, as an urgent call to action for Columbia GSAPP, and we recognize their relevance and implications for the larger global community of which the school is inextricably embedded within. They address issues of political engagement, social equity, representation, pursuing action on climate change, global perspectives, cultural diversity, and developing professional practice in all disciplines of the built environment in which we study and practice.

Elizabeth Alicea
Director of
Administration &
Finance

Kevin T. Allen
Audio Visual
Assistant

Paul Amitai
Co-Director of
Events & Public
Programs

Rebecca
Andersen
Polimeda
Associate
Director, Career
Services
Real Estate
Development
Program

Adam Bandler
Assistant Director,
Exhibitions

Jillian Barsalou
Kincaid
Director of
Major Gifts

Carlito Bayne
Assistant Director,
Output Systems

Steffen Boddeker
Senior Director of
Communications
& Events

Dare Brawley
Program
Administrator,
Center for Spatial
Research

Leigh Brown
Secretary,
Historic
Preservation &
Urban Planning
Programs

Carla Maria Call
Assistant Director,
Finance

Kristina Camaj
Program Manager,
Finance Office

Lyla Catellier
Co-Director of
Events & Public
Programs

Rosana Chang
Audio Visual
Coordinator

Stephanie
Cha-Ramos
Administrative
Assistant,
Architecture
Programs

David Cohen
Administrative
Assistant, Urban
Design Program

Leah Cohen
Associate Dean
for Development
& Alumni
Relations

Matthew Colunga
Administrative
Assistant, Office
of the Dean

Jesse Connuck
Managing Editor,
Publications

Jaime Darrow
Executive
Assistant, Office
of the Dean

Iben Falconer
Director of
Strategic
Initiatives, Office
of the Dean

Francesca Fanelli
Career Services
Officer,
Architecture
Programs

Alvaro Gamboa
Systems
Coordinator,
Information
Technology Office

Benjamin Goldie
Director of
Information
Technology

James Graham
Director, Print
Publications

Jochen Hartmann
Exhibition
Designer, Center
for Spatial
Research

Kayla C. Heisler
Administrative
Assistant,
Student Affairs

Michael Higgins
Systems
Coordinator,
Information
Technology Office

David Hinkle
Special Advisor

Ashley Hoefly
Associate
Director of
Administration &
Finance

Marcelle James
Program Manager,
Finance Office

Aiste Jankauskaite
Audio Visual
Manager

Joshua C. Jordan
Manager, Digital
Fabrication

Jessica
Stockton King
Associate
Director of
Academic Affairs,
Real Estate
Development
Program

Isabelle C.
Kirkham-Lewitt
Associate Editor,
Publications

Claire Lachow
Information
Technology
Specialist,
Student Affairs

Malwina
Lys-Dobradin
Director of Global
Networks &
Special Projects

Sonya Marshall
Assistant Dean
of Faculty Affairs,
Office of the Dean

Hakiel McQueen
Program Manager,
Finance Office

Jacob Moore
Assistant Director,
Buell Center

Alexander C.
Muetzel
Manager of
Alumni Relations
and Annual Giving

Patrick O'Connor
Program
Coordinator,
New York Paris
Program

Yesenia Ozoria-
Urena
Assistant Director
of Administration
& Finance

Melissa I.
Parsowith
Program
Manager, Historic
Preservation
Office

Janet Reyes
Associate Dean of
Administration &
Finance

Nicholas Roberts
Manager,
Office of the Dean

Agustin Schang
Manager, GSAPP
Incubator

Jesse Seegers
Digital Editor,
Communications
Office

Danielle Smoller
Associate Dean
of Students,
Admissions &
Financial Aid

Jordan Steingard
Program Manager,
Buell Center

JD Stogdill
Administrative
Assistant,
Admissions Office

Irene Sunwoo
Director of
Exhibitions

Jeremy Tavera
Program Manager,
Finance Office

Mark Taylor
Director of
Operations

Edwin Torres
Senior Systems
Coordinator,
Information
Technology Office

Esther Turay
Office Manager,
Development
Office

Hannette Un
Manager,
Information
Technology Office

George Wheeler
Director of
Conservation
Research

Margaret
Wiryaman
Program Manager,
Urban Planning
Office

Mohamed Zamdin
Systems
Coordinator,
Information
Technology Office

FULL TIME

Amale Andraos
Dean

Kate Ascher
Paul Milstein
Associate
Professor of
Professional
Practice,
Real Estate
Development

Erica Avrami
Assistant
Professor,
Historic
Preservation

Robert
Beauregard
Professor,
Urban Planning

Michael Bell
Professor,
Architecture

David Benjamin
Assistant
Professor,
Architecture

Hiba Bou Akar
Assistant
Professor, Urban
Planning

Vishaan
Chakrabarti
Associate
Professor of
Professional
Practice,
Architecture
& Real Estate
Development

Lise Anne
Couture
Associate
Professor of
Professional
Practice,
Architecture

Patrice Derrington
Holliday
Associate
Professor,
Real Estate
Development

Andrew Dolkart
Professor,
Historic
Preservation

Kenneth
Frampton
Ware Professor,
Architecture

Lance Freeman
Professor,
Urban Planning

Mario Gooden
Associate
Professor of
Professional
Practice,
Architecture

Laurie Hawkinson
Professor,
Architecture

Juan Herreros
Professor of
Professional
Practice,
Architecture

Steven Holl
Professor,
Architecture

Nicholas Klein
Assistant
Professor, Urban
Planning

Laura Kurgan
Associate
Professor,
Architecture

Reinhold Martin
Professor,
Architecture

Mary McLeod
Professor,
Architecture

Leah Meisterlin
Assistant
Professor, Urban
Planning

Kate Orff
Associate
Professor,
Architecture &
Urban Design

Jorge Otero-
Pailos
Professor,
Historic
Preservation

Richard Plunz
Professor,
Architecture &
Urban Design

Hilary Sample
Associate
Professor,
Architecture

Craig Schwitter
Associate
Professor of
Professional
Practice,
Architecture

Felicity Scott
Associate
Professor,
Architecture &
Critical Curatorial
Conceptual
Practices

Galia Solomonoff
Associate
Professor of
Professional
Practice,
Architecture

Kian Tajbakhsh
Visiting Professor,
Urban Planning

Bernard Tschumi
Professor,
Architecture

Enrique Walker
Associate
Professor,
Architecture

Mark Wigley
Professor,
Architecture

Mabel O. Wilson
Professor,
Architecture

Gwendolyn
Wright
Professor,
Architecture

Weiping Wu
Professor, Urban
Planning

PART TIME

Ashraf Abdalla
Teaching Fellow

Anthony
Acciavatti
Adjunct Assistant
Professor

Mitchell Adelstein
Adjunct Assistant
Professor

Moshe Adler
Adjunct Associate
Professor

Edward Adler
Adjunct Assistant
Professor

Michael Adlerstein
Adjunct Professor

Emanuel Admassu
Adjunct Assistant
Professor

Nora Akawi
Adjunct Assistant
Professor

Nesli Naz Aksu
Associate

Daniel Allen
Adjunct Assistant
Professor

Lee Altman
Adjunct Assistant
Professor

Gabriela Álvarez
Hernández
Adjunct Assistant
Professor

Shawn Amsler
Adjunct Assistant
Professor

Juan Cristóbal
Amunátegui
Adjunct Assistant
Professor

José Araguez
Escobar
Adjunct Assistant
Professor

William Arbizu
Adjunct Assistant
Professor

John Pat Arnett
Adjunct Professor

Oskar Arnorsson
Teaching Fellow

Javier Arpa
Fernandez
Adjunct Assistant
Professor

Erieta Attali
Adjunct Assistant
Professor

Brian Baldor
Adjunct Assistant
Professor

Adam Bandler
Adjunct Assistant
Professor

Theodoros
Barbagianis
Adjunct Assistant
Professor

Sabrina Barker
Associate

Anne Barrett
Adjunct Assistant
Professor

Elizabeth Barry
Adjunct Assistant
Professor

Grga Basic
Adjunct Assistant
Professor

Gisela Baurmann
Adjunct Assistant
Professor

Jessie Baxa
Associate

Carlos Bayod
Lucini
Adjunct Assistant
Professor

Mark Bearak
Adjunct Assistant
Professor

Joseph Bedford
Adjunct Assistant
Professor

Lisa Beeson
Adjunct Assistant
Professor

Harold Bell
Special Lecturer

Zabe Bent
Adjunct Assistant
Professor

Paul Bentel
Adjunct Professor

Aaron Berman
Adjunct Assistant
Professor

Nathalia Bernardo
Adjunct Assistant
Professor

Stella Betts
Adjunct Assistant
Professor

Supratim Bhaumik
Adjunct Assistant
Professor

Maurizio Bianchi
Mattioli
Adjunct Assistant
Professor

Tatiana Bilbao
Spamer
Adjunct Associate
Professor

Skylar Bisom-
Rapp
Associate

Caitlin Blanchfield
Adjunct Assistant
Professor

Ezio Blasetti
Adjunct Assistant
Professor

Steven Bloom
Adjunct Assistant
Professor

Biayna Bogosian
Adjunct Assistant
Professor

Joshua Bolchover
Visiting Associate
Professor

Francoise Bollack
Adjunct Associate
Professor

Brigette Borders
Adjunct Assistant
Professor

Maite Borjabad
Lopez Pastor
Adjunct Assistant
Professor

Christopher
Botham
Associate

Jessica Braden
Adjunct Assistant
Professor

Ben Brady
Adjunct Assistant
Professor

Philippa Brashear
Adjunct Assistant
Professor

Charles Brass
Adjunct Assistant
Professor

Dare Anne
Brawley
Adjunct Assistant
Professor

Joseph Brennan
Adjunct Assistant
Professor

David Brown
Adjunct Assistant
Professor

Babak Bryan
Adjunct Assistant
Professor

Laura Buck
Adjunct Assistant
Professor

Eric Bunge
Adjunct Assistant
Professor

Benjamin Cadena
Adjunct Assistant
Professor

Matthew
Carmody
Adjunct Assistant
Professor

Sarah Carpenter
Adjunct Assistant
Professor

Zak Kostura
Adjunct Associate Professor

David Christopher Kroner
Adjunct Assistant Professor

David Kruth
Adjunct Assistant Professor

Kaja Kuehl
Adjunct Associate Professor

Christoph Kumpusch
Adjunct Associate Professor

Yen Chi Lai
Adjunct Assistant Professor

Richard Lambeck
Adjunct Associate Professor

Erik Langdalen
Visiting Professor

Jonathas Lanna Valle Filho
Adjunct Assistant Professor

Floyd Lapp
Adjunct Professor

Choonghyo Lee
Associate

Seo Hee Lee
Associate

Brian Lee
Adjunct Assistant Professor

John Lee
Adjunct Assistant Professor

Daniel Taeyoung Lee
Adjunct Assistant Professor

Jiho Lee
Adjunct Assistant Professor

Richard Leland
Adjunct Professor

Amy Lelyveld
Adjunct Assistant Professor

Dominic Leong
Adjunct Assistant Professor

Christopher Leong
Adjunct Assistant Professor

Robert Lerner
Adjunct Assistant Professor

Ryan LeVasseur
Adjunct Assistant Professor

Julia Lewis
Adjunct Assistant Professor

Giuseppe Lignano
Adjunct Assistant Professor

John Lin
Visiting Associate Professor

Jing Liu
Adjunct Assistant Professor

Bo Liu
Adjunct Assistant Professor

Maider Llaguno Municha
Adjunct Assistant Professor

John Locke
Adjunct Assistant Professor

Farzin Lotfijam
Adjunct Assistant Professor

Brian Loughlin
Adjunct Assistant Professor

George Louras
Associate

Jeffrey Lovshin
Associate

Adam Lowe
Adjunct Professor

Liam Lowry
Associate

Wilhelmus Maas
Adjunct Professor

Peter Marcotullio
Adjunct Professor

Robert Marino
Adjunct Associate Professor

Sandro Marpillero
Adjunct Associate Professor

Jonathan Martin
Adjunct Associate Professor

Nicole Mater
Associate

Giancarlo Mazzanti
Adjunct Professor

William Brooks McDaniel
Adjunct Assistant Professor

Brendan McLaughlin
Associate

Carlos Mauricio Medellín Sanchez
Adjunct Assistant Professor

Jordan Meerdink
Associate Nishant

Samir Mehta
Associate

Geeta Mehta
Adjunct Professor

Florian Mewes
Adjunct Assistant Professor

Kimberli Meyer
Adjunct Assistant Professor

Maxwell Miller
Associate

Lee Miller
Adjunct Professor

Grace Mills
Associate

Talene Montgomery
Adjunct Assistant Professor

David Moon
Adjunct Assistant Professor

Justin Moore
Adjunct Associate Professor

Tracie Morris
Adjunct Professor

Olivia Moss
Associate

Jennifer Most
Adjunct Assistant Professor

Christopher Munsell
Associate

Michael Murphy
Adjunct Associate Professor

Danil Nagy
Adjunct Assistant Professor

Junko Nakagawa
Adjunct Assistant Professor

Umberto Napolitano
Adjunct Assistant Professor

Haig Nazarian
Associate

Ellen Neises
Adjunct Associate Professor

Anton Nelson
Adjunct Assistant Professor

Mitchell Nelson
Adjunct Assistant Professor

Christopher Neville
Adjunct Associate Professor

Xintong Nie
Associate

Carrie Norman
Adjunct Assistant Professor

Davidson Norris
Adjunct Associate Professor

Roger Nussenblatt
Adjunct Assistant Professor

Enrica Oliva
Adjunct Assistant Professor

Erik Olsen
Adjunct Assistant Professor

Rory O'Neill
Adjunct Associate Professor

Richard O'Toole
Adjunct Assistant Professor

Ning Ou
Adjunct Assistant Professor

Nicolai Ouroussoff
Adjunct Associate Professor

Anna Oursler
Adjunct Assistant Professor

Roy Pachecano
Adjunct Assistant Professor

Robert Paley
Adjunct Assistant Professor

Philip Palmgren
Adjunct Assistant Professor

Josh Panknin
Adjunct Assistant Professor

Ilias Papageorgiou
Adjunct Assistant Professor

Galen Pardee
Associate

Pankti Parikh
Adjunct Assistant Professor

Gregg Pasquarelli
Adjunct Associate Professor

Rajesh Patel
Adjunct Assistant Professor

Amelia Patt
Associate

Edwin Thaddeus Pawlowski
Adjunct Assistant Professor

Stephen Pearlman
Adjunct Professor

Richard Pieper
Adjunct Associate Professor

Edward Poteat
Adjunct Assistant Professor

Silvia Prandelli
Adjunct Assistant Professor

Theodore Prudon
Adjunct Professor

Sara Queen
Adjunct Assistant Professor

James Quick
Associate

Clarence Radin
Associate

Philippe Rahm
Adjunct Associate Professor

Mark Rakatansky
Adjunct Associate Professor

Raquel Ramati
Adjunct Professor

Nina Rappaport
Adjunct Professor

Harrison Ratcliff-Bush
Associate

Adrien Ravon
Adjunct Assistant Professor

William Raynolds
Adjunct Assistant Professor

Bika Rebek
Adjunct Assistant Professor

Thomas Reiner
Adjunct Assistant Professor

Chae-Young Rhee
Preceptor

Garrett Ricciardi
Adjunct Assistant Professor

Loren Lynwood Rice
Adjunct Assistant Professor

JiEun Rim
Adjunct Assistant Professor

Felipe Robayo Rojas
Associate

Nicholas Roberts
Associate

Bryony Roberts
Adjunct Assistant Professor

Yan Roche
Adjunct Assistant Professor

Michael Rock
Adjunct Professor

Julian Rose
Adjunct Assistant Professor

Karla Rothstein
Adjunct Associate Professor

Jonah Rowen
Teaching Fellow

Clementina Ruggieri
Adjunct Assistant Professor

Yehuda Safran
Adjunct Associate Professor

Kazuki Sakamoto
Adjunct Assistant Professor

Juan Saldarriaga Chaux
Adjunct Assistant Professor

Eduard Sancho Pou
Adjunct Professor

Diana Sandoval Martinez
Preceptor

Victoria Sanger
Adjunct Assistant Professor

Robert Sanna
Adjunct Assistant Professor

Andrew Scherer
Adjunct Professor

Michael Schissel
Associate

April Schneider
Adjunct Assistant Professor

Eva Schreiner
Teaching Fellow

Holger Schulze Ehring
Adjunct Assistant Professor

Elliott Sclar
Special Lecturer

Paul Segal
Adjunct Professor

Shai Shamir
Adjunct Assistant Professor

David Grahame Shane
Adjunct Professor

Donald Sheets
Adjunct Assistant Professor

Ethel Sheffer
Adjunct Associate Professor

MASTER OF ARCHITECTURE

Saphiya Abu Al-Maati
Kenneth Amoah
Adriana Barcenas
William Edward Bodell
Rebecca Rand Book
Kimberlee Boonbanjerdsri
Mark Alden Borreliz
Christopher Michael Brockhoft
Eugene Chia-Yu Chang
Diandra Arielle Cohen
Elizabeth Leah Cohn-Martin
Jorge Juan Cornet
Roderick Cruz
Yujing Cui
Victor Hugo De Souza Azevedo
Boer Deng
Adele Fishbein Druck
Shu Du
Reza Durrani
Clara Celeste Dobiesz Dykstra
Jennifer C Fang
Fancheng Fei
Richard Frederick Fudge
Ayesha Saveri Ghosh
Stephanie Elaine Hamilton
Yujing (Mandy) Han
Amanda Kathryn Hibbs
Benjamin Alexander Hochberg
Michael Stephen Howard
A.L. Hu
Styliani Ioannidou
Jonathan Alexandru Izen
Nishant Chacko Jacob
Chantal Marie Jahn
Agnieszka Wanda Janusz
David Yukio Kagawa
Laura Michelle Kahan
Chad Paul Karty
Nicholas Anderson Kazmierski
Mustafa Hasan Khan
Konuk Kim
Chi Yin Kwok
Troy Matthew Lacombe
Eric Haoxing Li
Alex Waihoe Loh
Matthew Robert Lohry
Melissa Ivette Loyola
Brigitte Kathleen Lucey
Andrew Mitchell Luy
Kevin Paul MacNichol
Grant Edward Duncan McCracken
Nicholas Mark Mingrone
Emily Elizabeth Mohr
Nabila Gloria Morales Perez
Harrison Cole Nesbitt
Michael Gregory Snider Nickerson
Shoni Mizutani Oey
Julia Ellen Pedtke
Brendan William Pettersen
Britta Isobel Ritter-Armour
Lok Man Melody Siu
Thomas Louis Smith
Ilijana Soldan
Michael James Storm
Kurtis Robert Streich
Meng Chan Tang
Renyuan Wang
Ruomeng Wang

Andrew Joseph Weber
Violet Whitney
Ning Xiao
Pei Pei Yang
Zhengyang Yue
Mengjiao Zhang
Wen Zhou
Xiaomin Zhuang

MASTER OF SCIENCE IN ADVANCED ARCHITECTURAL DESIGN

Zahid Nawaz Ajam
Abubakr Hayder Ali
Amenah Ali Alkendi
Ankisha George Anto George
Vanessa Marie Arriagada
Jae Han Bae
Keren Bao
Jil Bentz
Karen Berberyan
Kalliopi Karolina Bourou
Zhe Cao
Jiangjing Chen
Kavyashri Cherala
Sebastian Cilloniz
Alejandro Ciudad-Casafranca
Giovanni Cozzani
Sebastian Cruz
Yi Ding
Zhengmeng Dong
Ruosen Du
Ruoqi Fan
Ali Fouladi
Mao Gai
Nusrat Gazi
Yun Gong
Yundi Gu
Rui Guan
Jong Yun Han
Yifang Hou
Chia-Shan Hsu
Qiyue Hu
Erin Justine Huang
Junyan Huang
Wei-lun Huang
Xiaoyu Huang
Xinyue Huang
Yang Huang
Zhiyun Huang
Tahsin X. Inanici
Chi Keung Ip
Sanghoon Jang
Yang Jie
Qiu Jin
Colin Robert Joyce
Sara Karim Mahmud
Beomkyu Kim
MinSun Kim
Tigran Kostandyan
Alexandra Noel Kurek
Su Jeong Lee
Hong Li
Tianji Liang
Nila Muliawati Liem
Chung-Yi Lin
Chunhui Liu
Naifei Liu
Michelle Karen Lozano
Shuying Mi
Jacobo Mingorance Arranz
Rawan Jaber Muqaddas
Sara Rad
Tharunya Ramesh
Jugal Atul Rana
Matthew Alexander Ransom
Sunaina Snehal Shah
Stephen Charles Smith
Ran Song
Yi Sun
Stephanie Alexis Tager
Charles Vincent Thornton

Marios Sotirios Triantafyllou
Chin-Yu Tsai
Wang Yuen Leroy Tung
Prasansiri Kig Veerasunthorn
Jiang Wang
Jue Wang
Ruizhi Wang
Yijun Wang
Yuyang Wang
Corina Sheri Wright
Jingxuan Wu
Kyle Jianghao Wu
Lin Wu
Shuni Wu
Yifei Wu
Zhida Wu
Wantong Xu
Yihan Xu
Yini Xu
Zhan Xu
Junchao Yang
Jiayi Yi
Yin Yin
Ye Yuan
Ines Elvira Yupanqui Anthony Louis Zampolin
Chi Zhang
Qi Zhang
Sen Zhang
Shuo Zhang
Siyu Zhang
Wenzhao Zhang
Siyu Zhao
Yuhao Zheng
Wenmei Zhi
Zhenwei Zhong
Chuhan Zhou
Fengyi Zhou
Pei Zhou
Yana Zhou

MASTER OF SCIENCE IN ARCHITECTURE & URBAN DESIGN

Majed Abdulsamad
Jessica Adiwijaya
Nishchal Agarwal
Nabi Agzamov
Jun Seong Ahn
Andrea Benavides Ward
Maria Isabel Carrasco Vintimilla
Christopher Chiou
Huai-Kuan Chung
Bridgett Ivanova Cruz
Sreyash Dasgupta
Gabriela Angelissa Fiorentino Cedeno
Marwah Atef Labib Garib
Yiran Hu
Linshu Huang
Carmelo Ignaccolo
Ahmed Saeed Jawdat
Jesfae Mariam John
Chu Li
Yang Liao
Jinbao Liu
Jiahong Lu
Daiyue Lyu
Mayra Imtiaz Mahmood
Grace Ning Sing Ng
Deniz Onder
Yuting Pan
Dongfang Pang
Yan Pang
Zarith Itzel Pineda
Kun Qian
Zhen Quan
Dissa Pidanti Raras
Kristen Elizabeth Reardon
Vrinda Sharma
Jiaqi Sun
Mario Andres Ulloa-Leon
Elif Merve Unsal
Fu Wang
Xiaopu Wang

Huaxia Wu
Mengke Wu
Shuman Wu
Tianyang Xie
Yanyan Xu
Zichang Yan
Haochen Yang
Ping Yin
Xuanchen Zhang
Ge Zhao
Liwen Zhao
Zhaoyu Zhu
Daniel Ziss
Wanpeng Zu

MASTER OF SCIENCE IN CRITICAL, CURATORIAL & CONCEPTUAL PRACTICES IN ARCHITECTURE

Daniel Maurice Cooper
Chloe Elisabeth English
Ruishi Ge
Joachim Hackl
Robin Hartanto Honggare
Chi-Chia Hou
Sara Elizabeth McGillivray
Iara Caroline Pimenta de Mello
Camila Paz Reyes Ale
Gizem Sivri

MASTER OF SCIENCE IN HISTORIC PRESERVATION

Tania Alam
Jessica Elizabeth Betz
Elizabeth Lawrence Canon
Kimberly Michele DeMuro
Mayssa Jallad
Nicholas Anderson Kazmierski
Cheng Liao
Nicole Marie Mezydlo
Alexander Paul Ray
Sarah Reddan
Cameron Maureen Robertson
Allison Leah Semrad
Andrea Nicole Sforza
Fei Teng
Stacy Lynn Tomczyk
Katrina Lee Virbitsky
Qi Zhang

MASTER OF SCIENCE IN URBAN PLANNING

Jahnavi Aluri
Vicente Oswaldo Arellano
Rebecca Rand Book
Mingda Chen
Elizabeth Leah Cohn-Martin
Jessica Joanna Cruz
Ubaldo Escalante
Yixiao Fang
James Asher Gerken
Steven Getz
Christopher Daniel Giamarino
Shahneez Haseeb
Ying Huang
Jon Tristan Sherbeck Jackson
Maira Khan
Neha Krishnan
Androniki Mei Lagos
Hyun Seung Lee
Jose Gabriel Lemaitre Palma
Dorothy Brayton MacAusland
Richard Charles Martoglio

Madeleine McGrory
Joseph Byron
 McKenzie
Sahra Mirbabaee
Matthias Kelsey
Atticus Neill
Lauren Raeya Ossey
Krithika
 Prabhakaran
Cameron Maureen
 Robertson
Brandon Neal
 Robinson
Lia Soorenian
Charles Carroll
 Stewart
Lu Sun
Jacquelyne Danielle
 Sunwoo
Evan Renek Sweet
Mengyao Wang
Mingze Wang
Lina Yin
Taylor Charles
 Young
Maryam Zargar
 Yaghoubi
Huitian Zhou
Yingzhi Zhou

MASTER OF
SCIENCE IN
REAL ESTATE
DEVELOPMENT

Vidhi Govind Advani
Joonbae Ahn
Rodal Ajami
Mert Aktas
Martin Alvero
Supanat
 Angsuwarangsi
Ben Selorm Avor
Michael Thomas Bea
Alastair George
 Boucaut
Joseph Vuong Bui
Edward Christopher
 Byrns
Alexis Jennifer
 Campbell
Seyma Ayse Cevahir
Victor Wing-Lun Chan
Upasana Chandra
Kevin Cheng Wei
 Chang
Christina Chao
Ravida Charntanawet
Xiao Chen
Yaqi Cheng
Ying Cheng
Michael Garn Clark
Jonathan Christopher
 Cobb
Brandon Scott Cook
Joseph Dabbah
Bruno De Los Reyes
 Teran
Maria Beatriz Diaz
Benjamin Adam
 Epstein
Richard Esquivel
Ryan Fateh
Andrew Trucksess
 Fitzpatrick
Gabriel Bernard Fort
Robert Daniel
 Franco-Tayar
Ashita Mahendra Gala
Somer Mahmoud
 Galal
Nicole Catherine
 Gayda
Adrianne Glascock
Chea Choong Goh
Leichen Gou
Thomas Matthew
 Graves
Disha Grover
Nicholas Russell Gruy
Yanpei Guo
Madeleine Marie
 Mallovy Hicks
Aalekh Pravin Hirani
Edward Harrison
 Horowitz
James Roth Horton
Haoran Hu

Patrick Cole Hutson
Aniruddh Jain
Mark L James
Myungsoo Jamie Jang
Jeongsoo Jeon
Yi Jin
Shivam Prem Jumani
Ioanna Karavelaki
Siddharth Sandeep
 Karnavat
Sungheon Kim
Ari Shaun
 Kirshenblatt
William Christopher
 Kurniawan
Haymen Law
Erica Lee
Min-Jae Lee
Qiuchen Li
Wenxi Li
Xiaofei Li
Yang Li
Yuxie Li
Edison Jeh-Wein Lin
Antong Liu
Lanxuan Liu
Leining Lu
Ying Luo
John William Lyons
Terence Richard
 Mallon
Abdullah A M R H
 Marafi
Amanda Jane Moses
Alexis Muller
 Pellerin
Alexander Noah
 Nachum
Akiko Nakatani
Jason Nik
Samuel Michael
 Oketcho
Emerick Paul
 Patterson
Brett Victor Price
Mathew Allan Propst
Tuomas Aukusti
 Raikamo
George Louis
 Ricciardelli
Samantha Kaitlin
 Richens
Drew Harris Rifkin
Maibi Carolina Rojas
Maria Rozenfeld
Hussein Tarek
 Ahmed Said
Eduardo Santos
Paul Shevchuk
Pratik Singhi
Yuqi Sun
Hengyi Tan
Mert Munir Tatari
Patrick Hamilton
 Taylor
Siyu Tong
Chia-sen Jerry Yuki
 Tsang
Ben Edmond
 Ulvevadet
Chanavudh
 Vanachaivong
Daniel Vega
Carl William Walker
Shuo Wang
Yueting Wang
Zhanbin Wang
Andrew Graham
 Watson
Bridget Browning
 Wilcox
Andrew David Wright
Yingzi Wuwei
Wanjing Xiao
Kaiqi Yao
Wanting Ye
DaeJung Yoon
Xiaomin Zheng
Xuelin Zhou
Qizheng Zhu
Amir Zwickel

ALI JAWAD MALIK
MEMORIAL
HISTORY/THEORY
HONOR AWARD
In recognition of
high quality of work
in the history/theory
sequence:
Nicholas Kazmierski
(MArch/HP)

GSAPP WRITING
PRIZE
For an outstanding
essay, paper, or thesis
on the history or
theory of architecture
written for a class
during their time at
GSAPP:
Robin Hartanto
Honggare (CCCP)
Uncornering
Speakers: On Political
Speech in Singapore

VISUALIZATION
AWARD
For innovative use of
computing media in
architectural or urban
research, design, and
fabrication:
Violet Whitney
(MArch)
Huai Kuan Chung (UD)

SCHOOL SERVICE
AWARD
Awarded to recognize
the student who
has performed
willing service to
the School, and who
gives promise of real
professional merit
through attitude and
character.
A.L. Hu (MArch)
Cameron Robertson
(HP/UP)

CAMPBELL AWARD
The University
Trustees and the
Board of the Columbia
Alumni Association—
the CAA—established
The Campbell
Award, presented
by the CAA to a
graduating student
at each School who
shows exceptional
leadership and
Columbia spirit as
exemplified by the late
Bill Campbell, Chair
Emeritus, University
Trustees, outstanding
alumnus, and CAA
co-founder.
Jorge Cornet (MArch)

WILLIAM KINNE
FELLOWS
TRAVELING PRIZE
These awards are
granted on the
merit of proposals
submitted for travel
abroad incorporating
the study of archi-
tecture, including
planning and other
specialized aspects
of architecture.

1,000 Libraries of
Ancient Manuscripts
in Timbuktu
Kenneth Amoah
(MArch)

Decoding Japan's Address System
Vanessa Arriagada (AAD)
Michelle Lozano (AAD)

Preservation & Legacy: Reconstructing the Irving J. Gill Archive
Adriana Barcenas (MArch)

Embracing a Warmer Planet: A Search for Heat Adaptation Design
Yujing Cui (MArch)
Xiaomin Zhuang (MArch)

The Right to Livelihood: Housing and Under Housing in India
Ubaldo Escalante (UP)
Jon Tristan Jackson (UP)

The Valence of Technological Sublime
Ruishi Ge (CCCP)

Surveillance Soundscapes, 1928-1937
Joachim Hackl (CCCP)

Narratives Beyond Borders
Stephanie Hamilton (MArch)
Andrew Luy (MArch)

The World of Disney: Mapping Control Apparatus of Neoliberal Dystopia
Chi Chia Hou (CCCP)

Spaces of the Third Gender
A.L. Hu (MArch)
Michael Storm (MArch)

Research of the Structure-Space Relationship in Works of Vilanova Artigas in Brazil
Yang Huang (AAD)

Visualizing Oral Histories of the Naqab
Stella Ioannidou (MArch)

Social Modernism in Brazil: The Social Dimension of Lele's Architecture
Nishant Jacob (MArch)
Nabila Morales (MArch)

Conflict Urbanism: Mozambique
Jonathan Izen (MArch)

The Commemorative Landscape of the Golan Heights
Nicholas Kazmierski (MArch/HP)

When Drones are flying: future of urban infrastructure and real estate value
Min-Jae Lee (RED)
Jeongsoo Jeon (RED)

Counternarrative spaces: An ethnographic study of Bajos de Mena
Jose Lemaitre (UP)

Modern Adaptations of Vernacular Architecture: Case Study of Architects and Non-Architects Practices in Vietnam
Cheng Liao (HP)

Hybrid Models in Collective Architecture
Matthew Lohry (MArch)

No Ma(n)d's Land
Mayra Mahmood (UD)

Something There Is That Doesn't Love A Wall: A Timely Documentation of the Border Architecture and Urbanism of Mexico's Programa Nacional Fronterizo (ProNaF)
Grant McCracken (MArch)

Main Street: An American Frontispiece
Sahra Mirbabaee (UP)

Houses that Move(d): America's Misunderstood Vernacular Vehicles for Living
Michael Nickerson (MArch)

This Land is Our Land: The Case for Collective Ownership Along the Rust Belt
Julie Pedtke (MArch)

Presence in Absence: A Hidden War's Persistent Impact on Lao Architecture & Landscapes
Brendan Pettersen (MArch)

The Northern Transition: Linking Hokkaido to Tokyo with Shinkansen
Tuomas Raikamo (RED)
Jamie Horton (RED)

Rethinking Territories of Extraction
Dissa Raras (UD)

Under the Radar
Gizem Sivri (CCCP)

The Afterlife of Soviet Palaces in Vilnius, Lithuania
Kurtis Streich (MArch)

Wonderlands: Architecturally Crafting Fictional Landscapes to Foster Creativity & Imagination in Spaces of Learning
Stephanie Tager (AAD)

What do we do after shopping?
Charles Thornton (AAD)

10 WORKS 10 PLACES, YOUNG

BELGIAN ARCHITECTS' OFFICE
Kig Veerasunthorn (AAD)
Yini Xu (AAD)

The conservation and management of the Berlin Wall concrete panels
Katrina Virbitsky (HP)

Artifacts of Relief
Anthony Zampolin (AAD)
Abubakr Ali (AAD)

Architecture of Commonality: Terunobu Fujimori and the Alternative Mode of Contemporary Japan Architecture
Mengjiao Zhang (MArch)

LUCILLE SMYSER LOWENFISH MEMORIAL PRIZE
The most outstanding student in the final semester design studio section selected by each critic (open to M.Arch, AAD, UD)

Nabi Agzamov (UD)
Water Urbanism Studio: Kate Orff (Studio Coordinator), Nora Akawi, Dilip DaCunha, Ziad Jamaleddine, Petra Kempf, Laura Kurgan, Geeta Mehta, Julia Watson, Critics

Kenneth Amoah (MArch)
Mario Gooden, Critic

Jacobo Mingorance Arranz (AAD)
Steven Holl, Critic

Victor Hugo De Souza Azevedo (MArch)
Umberto Napolitano, Critic

Jil Bentz (AAD)
Kersten Geers, Critic

Kimberlee Boonbanjerdsri (MArch)
Jing Liu, Critic

Eugene Chang (MArch)
Galia Solomonoff, Critic

Clara Dykstra (MArch)
Joshua Bolchover and John Lin, Critics

Fancheng Fei (MArch)
Juan Herreros, Critic

Nishant Jacob (MArch)
Ada Tolla, Giuseppe Lignano and Thomas DeMonchaux, Critics

Evelina Knodel (UD)
Water Urbanism Studio: Kate Orff (Studio Coordinator), Nora Akawi, Dilip DaCunha, Ziad Jamaleddine, Petra Kempf, Laura Kurgan, Geeta Mehta, Julia Watson, Critics

Troy Lacombe (MArch)
Cristina Goberna Pesudo, Critic

Brigitte Lucey Stephen Cassell and Annie Barrett, Critics

Emily Mohr (MArch)
Hilary Sample, Critic

Harrison Nesbitt (MArch)
Garrett Ricciardi and Julian Rose, Critics

Michael Nickerson (MArch)
Laurie Hawkinson, Critic

Deniz Onder (UD)
Water Urbanism Studio: Kate Orff (Studio Coordinator), Nora Akawi, Dilip DaCunha, Ziad Jamaleddine, Petra Kempf, Laura Kurgan, Geeta Mehta, Julia Watson, Critics

Brendan Pettersen (MArch)
Mark Wasiuta, Critic

Zarith Pineda (UD)
Water Urbanism Studio: Kate Orff (Studio Coordinator), Nora Akawi, Dilip DaCunha, Ziad Jamaleddine, Petra Kempf, Laura Kurgan, Geeta Mehta, Julia Watson, Critics

Kristen Reardon (UD)
Water Urbanism Studio: Kate Orff (Studio Coordinator), Nora Akawi, Dilip DaCunha, Ziad Jamaleddine, Petra Kempf, Laura Kurgan, Geeta Mehta, Julia Watson, Critics

Vrinda Sharma (UD)
Water Urbanism Studio: Kate Orff (Studio Coordinator), Nora Akawi, Dilip DaCunha, Ziad Jamaleddine, Petra Kempf, Laura Kurgan, Geeta Mehta, Julia Watson, Critics

Chuxue Wang (MArch)
Momoyo Kaijima and Yoshiharu Tsukamoto, Critics

Shuman Wu (UD)
Water Urbanism Studio: Kate Orff (Studio Coordinator), Nora Akawi, Dilip DaCunha, Ziad Jamaleddine, Petra Kempf, Laura Kurgan, Geeta Mehta, Julia Watson, Critics

PERCIVAL AND NAOMI GOODMAN FELLOWSHIP
The Percival & Naomi Goodman Fellowship is made possible through the generosity of Raymond Lifchez, M. Arch. '57, GSAPP Faculty 1961-70, in honor of his former teacher, colleague, and friend Percival Goodman. The purpose of the Fellowship is to enable the recipient to carry out a project of social significance related to the interests of Percival Goodman.

Violet Whitney (MArch) and Julie Pedtke (MArch)
Rebuilding Trust: Collective Ownership and the Changing Economic Infrastructures of Detroit

CURE AWARD
To graduates who have excelled in the advancement of transdisciplinary research in urban development.
James Horton (RED)
Patrick Hutson (RED)

—

M.ARCH PROGRAM AWARDS

CHARLES McKIM PRIZE FOR EXCELLENCE IN DESIGN / SAUL KAPLAN TRAVELING FELLOWSHIP
This prize is recognizes the student whose work throughout the studios has been outstanding and is funded by a bequest from Saul Kaplan (M.Arch '57).
Troy Lacombe

AIA HENRY ADAMS MEDAL
This prize is awarded to the student who has maintained the best general standard in all sequences during the professional course over the past 2-3 years in the School.
Emily Mohr

AWARD FOR EXCELLENCE IN TOTAL DESIGN
This prize is for excellence in total design.
Harrison Nesbitt

ALPHA RHO CHI MEDAL
This prize is for the student who has shown ability in leadership over the past 2-3 years in the School and who gives promise of professional merit through his/her attitude and personality.
Andrew Luy

HONOR AWARDS FOR EXCELLENCE IN DESIGN
The prize is for high quality of work in the design studios during the student's

program of studies at Columbia.
Brigitte Lucey
Nabila Morales Perez
Violet Whitney
Wen Zhou

BUILDING TECH-NOLOGIES HONOR AWARD
This award is awarded to the student who most demonstrates an ability to incorporate building science and technologies into the issues of architectural design. Selection is based on students' academic record in Building Technology coursework and the portfolio review. Applying students' end of year portfolios should include work from advanced Building Science and Technologies courses.
Jorge Cornet

M.ARCH STUDENT NOMINATED 'AVERY 6' AWARD
This student-nominated prize is awarded to the graduating M.Arch student Whose work questions the standards of architecture and promises to change the profession.
Julie Pedtke

Whose commitment within studio and the school at large has earned the respect of the student body.
A.L. Hu

—

M.S. AUD PROGRAM AWARDS

HONOR AWARD FOR EXCELLENCE IN DESIGN
The prize is for high quality of work in the design studios during the student's program of studies at Columbia.
Andrea Benavides Ward

GSAPP PRIZE FOR EXCELLENCE
This prize is intended to recognize the student whose work in the Urban Design Program has been most outstanding.
Carmelo Ignaccolo

—

M.S. AAD PROGRAM AWARDS

WILLIAM WARE PRIZE FOR EXCELLENCE IN DESIGN / SAUL KAPLAN TRAVELING FELLOWSHIP
This prize is awarded to recognize the student whose work in the studios has been outstanding and is funded by a

bequest from Saul Kaplan (M.Arch '57). The prize is for travel and study following graduation.
Jil Benz

HONOR AWARDS FOR EXCELLENCE IN DESIGN
The prize is for high quality of work in the design studios during the student's program of studies at Columbia.
Giovanni Cozzani
Qiu Jin
Chung-Yi Lin
Stephanie Tager
(Ella) Yini Xu
Ines Yupanqui

ARGUMENTS HONOR AWARD
Abubakr Ali

—

M.S. CCCP PROGRAM AWARDS

CCCP THESIS AWARDS

For the thesis exhibiting the most rigorous conceptual development and the most complementary format or medium.

Joachim Hackl
New Games: Countercultural Spaces of Plan, 1973–1985
Advisor: Felicity Scott

For the thesis making the most significant contribution to considerations of the public sphere and which includes a realized component.

Robin Hartanto Honggare
Architecture, Nationalism & Internationalism in Indonesia, 1959–1965
Advisor: Felicity Scott

CCCP PROGRAM AWARD
This prize is for high academic attainment in the CCCP Program.
Camila Reyes Alé

—

M.S. HP PROGRAM AWARDS

FACULTY AWARDS FOR OUTSTANDING THESIS

Tania Alam
The Evolution of American Historic Color Palettes
Advisor: Mary Jablonski

Jessica Betz
The Influence of Glass Transition Temperatures on the Performance of Acrylic Thermoplastic Adhesives
Advisor: George Wheeler

Mayssa Jallad
Beirut's Civil War Hotel District: Preserving the World's First High-Rise Urban Battlefield
Advisor: Jorge Otero-Pailos

Laura Weinstein-Berman
The Progression of Historic Preservation in Miami Beach and the Challenges of Sea Level Rise
Advisor: Carol Clark

Qi Zhang
Urban Preservation in China: The Survival of an Idea Despite Political Repression, 1950–1982
Advisor: Jorge Otero-Pailos

PEER TO PEER AWARD
This award is given in recognition of outstanding service to classmates, faculty, and school.
Mayssa Jallad

—

M.S. UP PROGRAM AWARDS

AMERICAN INSTITUTE OF CERTIFIED PLANNERS OUTSTANDING STUDENT AWARD
This prize is for outstanding attainment in the study of Urban Planning.
Patrick Li

NEW YORK CHAPTER OF THE AMERICAN PLANNING ASSOCIATION'S AWARD
This award is for academic excellence and leadership in Urban Planning.
Dorothy MacAusland

CHARLES ABRAMS THESIS AWARD
For a thesis that best exemplifies a commitment to social justice.
Lia Soorenian
Land Use and Sea Level Rise Vulnerability in New York City: Addressing Environmental Justice Through Zoning
Advisor: Weiping Wu

URBAN PLANNING PROGRAM AWARD
This prize is for high academic attainment.
Jose Gabriel Lemaitre Palma

PLANNING PRACTICE AWARD
For a Masters' thesis that directly engages the practice of planning
Dorothy MacAusland
Exploring Expertise: Rotterdam's Planners and the

Flood Adaptation Industry
Advisor: Leah Meisterlin

PLANNING METHODOLOGY AWARD
For a Masters' thesis that best applies a critical planning methodology
Jon Tristan Jackson
Cool Roofs Program as Municipal Policy in ASHRAE Zone 5 Climates
Advisor: Kian Tajbakhsh

PEER TO PEER AWARD
This award is given in recognition of outstanding service to classmates, faculty, and school.
Sahra Mirbabaee

—

M.S. RED PROGRAM AWARDS

HANK BELL ENTRE-PRENEURIAL AWARD
This award is for the student that best embodies Professor Emeritus Hank Bell's entrepreneurial spirit.
Rodal Ajami

SERVICE AWARD
This award is for student participation and leadership within the RED Program.
Edward Chris Byrns
(Kevin) Cheng-Wei Chang
Christina Chao
Amir Zwickel

SCHOLASTIC PERFORMANCE
This award is for high academic attainment.
Jonathan Cobb
Ravida Charntanawet
Abdullah Marafi

Professional Portfolio Review, Kamilla Csegzi '15 MSAAD

Working In Public and Private Sectors moderated by
Urban Planning Director Weiping Wu, Feb 17, 2017

Career Services office tour of Foster and Partners,
Feb 3, 2017

Internship Career Fair, Feb 14, 2017

RED Developer's Den Competition hosted by
York University, Toronto

Social Justice Career Fair at the GSAPP Incubator,
May 1, 2017, Quilian Riano, DSGN AGNC

Real Estate Director Patrice Derrington with students at MIPIM Hong Kong, Nov 30, 2016

Alumni Networking event, Mar 28, 2017

Social Justice Career Fair, May 1, 2017, Rasu Jilani, NEW INC.

Dean Amale Andraos, Felix Burrichter '04 MSAAD, Gregg Pasquarelli '94 M.Arch and Galia Solomonoff '94 M.Arch at Design Miami: GSAPP Alumni Discussion and Reception, Dec 1, 2016

Reception in Shanghai for alumni Hu Fei (Siza) '12 AAD, Gus Chan '10 AAD, I-Shin Chow '03 M.Arch, Yong He '14 AAD, Xintong Lee '14 AAD, Apr 7, 2017

Pantea Tehrani '11 MSAAD, Julie Perrone '18 M.Arch, Mouna Lawrence '18 MSAAD and Seda Oznal '18 MSAAD at the Architecture and Urban Design Mentorship Cocktail Party, Oct 2017

Beijing Alumni with Historic Preservation Director Jorge Otero-Pailos, Apr 10, 2017

Urban Planning Career Fair, Feb 17, 2017

Alumni Networking Event, Mar 28, 2017

GSAPP Incubator class of 2016–17 farewell party, Aug 2017

Janki Shah '18 MSAUD and her mentor Ankita Chachra '13 MSAUD at the AUD Mentorship Cocktail Party, Oct 2017

Betsy Daniels '18 MSAUD and her mentor Jonie Fu '86 MSAUD at the AUD Mentorship Cocktail Party, Oct 2017

Bay Area Alumni tour of SFMOMA, Oct 2017

Bay Area Alumni tour of SFMOMA, Oct 2017

ALUMNI OFFICE

CAREER SERVICES

DEVELOPMENT & ALUMNI RELATIONS

Leah Cohen,
  Associate Dean
  for Development &
  Alumni Relations
Iben Falconer,
  Director of Strategic
  Initiatives
Jillian Kincaid,
  Director of Major Gifts
Alexander C. Muetzel,
  Manager of
  Alumni Relations
  and Annual Giving
Esther Turay,
  Development Office
  Manager

The GSAPP Office of Development and Alumni Relations, established in 2005, is dedicated to building a strong framework for alumni communication, collaboration and networking, and to establishing a strong base of support for the school, its students and its programs.

ARCHITECTURE + URBAN DESIGN

Francesca Fanelli,
Coordinator

Career Services for Architecture & Urban Design programs connects GSAPP students to the professional beyond Avery Hall through engaging panel discussions, workshops, alumni networking events and architecture office tours. Additionally, Career Services offers students an array of tools to help them transition into the workforce after graduation, such as career fairs, peer-to-peer portfolio review, cover letter and resume feedback, a credit-based internship course and alumni mentorship program.

—

HISTORIC PRESERVATION

Melissa Parsowith,
Coordinator

The Historic Preservation (HP) program implemented new initiatives during the 2016-17 academic year to expand Career Services and open professional doors. Program Manager, Melissa Parsowith, supported the HP community year-round in forming and maintaining valuable career connections. With the development of contact databases, the program has effectively streamlined communication and strengthened relations among students, alumni and employers. The HP office now publishes a newsletter, distributed weekly, which offers a central location for internship and job postings as well as opportunities for networking, both local and abroad. HP students are encouraged to take advantage of an open-door policy, and are met with individually to discuss their interests, goals and career trajectory. Each semester, services available include one on one advisement sessions, alumni and mentorship pairings, resume workshops, and annual networking events. The program continues to offer an HP Internship course, valued at 1.5 credits, which allows several students to gain practical field experi-

ence while completing their degree. Exit surveys are administered to graduating students to collect student feedback and track career outcomes for future use.

—

URBAN PLANNING

Margaret Wiryaman,
Coordinator

The Urban Planning Program offers career development resources to help students take advantage of our location in New York City and discover unmatched opportunities for jobs and internships. Our career services include alumni panels, job search workshops, resume and portfolio feedback, visits to select public planning agencies and private consulting firms, and meeting with employers one-on-one at the Career Fair. Each spring, the program connects students to alumni through the annual speed-networking event. The American Planning Association's New York Metro Chapter offers additional networking opportunities through talks, mixers, and local conferences. The program supports travel to the APA national conference each year. We maintain a job board to advertise open full-time, part-time, internship, and fellowship positions—many of which are sent exclusively to students in the UP program. In addition, we distribute a bi-weekly newsletter that advertises upcoming networking opportunities and conferences.

—

REAL ESTATE DEVELOPMENT

Rebecca Andersen
Polimeda, Coordinator

MSRED Career Services reinforces the necessary skills needed for students to succeed in the workforce; communication, critical thinking, collaboration that is built on a foundation of integrity and professionalism. We enable and encourage students to make informed career decisions through diverse and comprehensive services, which can lead to successful internships and employment. We meet with students on an individual basis, providing advice, guidance and strategies for each student's career trajectory in the real estate industry. We work with students on how to articulate their passion and desires for real estate and how to portray themselves when networking and on paper. We specifically teach students how to present their 'package' to be as representative of their skills and capabilities as much as possible. This helps us portray them in an accurate manner to employers

and their specific needs, skill sets and cultural fits within firms and organizations. Services available to students include cover letter and resume critiques; career counseling sessions; a spring career fair and on campus-recruitment; seminars; mentorship program; and a spring internship program. Seminar topics offered throughout the school year included: professional etiquette; effective job searching in real estate; how to leverage linkedin; how to build effective industry relationships; cultural fits in the real estate industry; salary negotiation; informational interviewing; proper presentation and interview skills; the real estate industry hiring process for all real estate asset classes; and real estate industry panels with alumni.

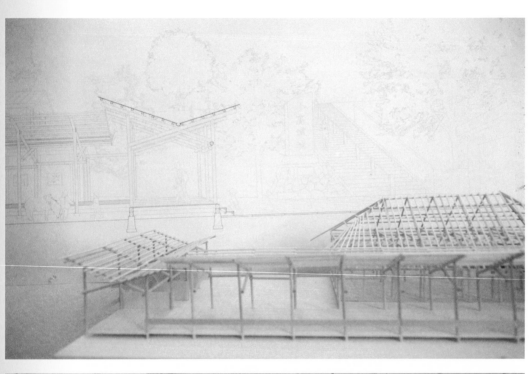

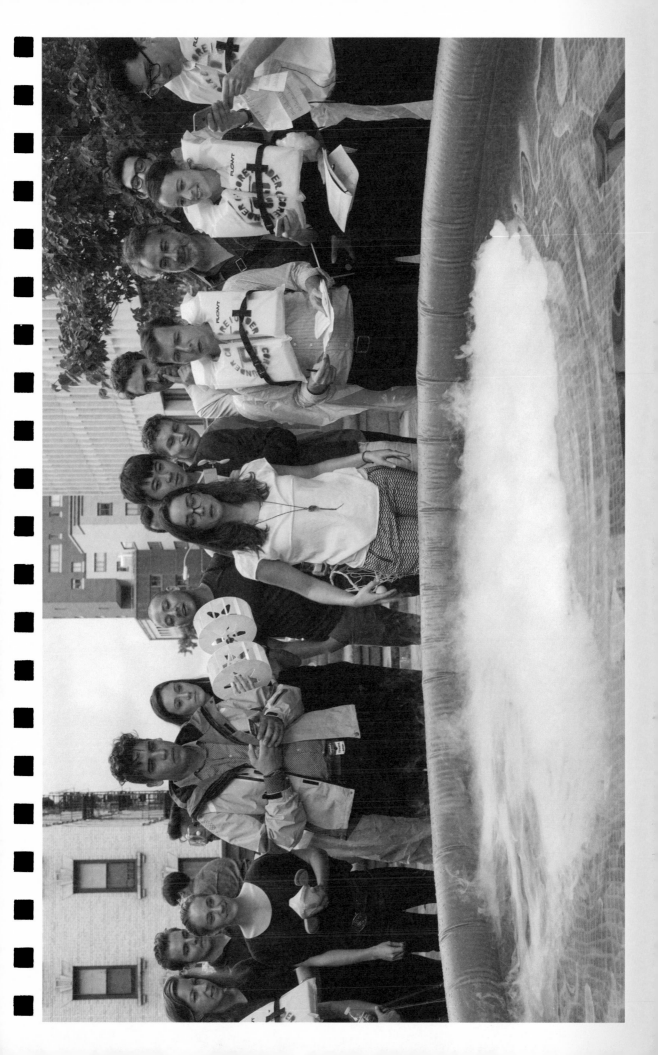

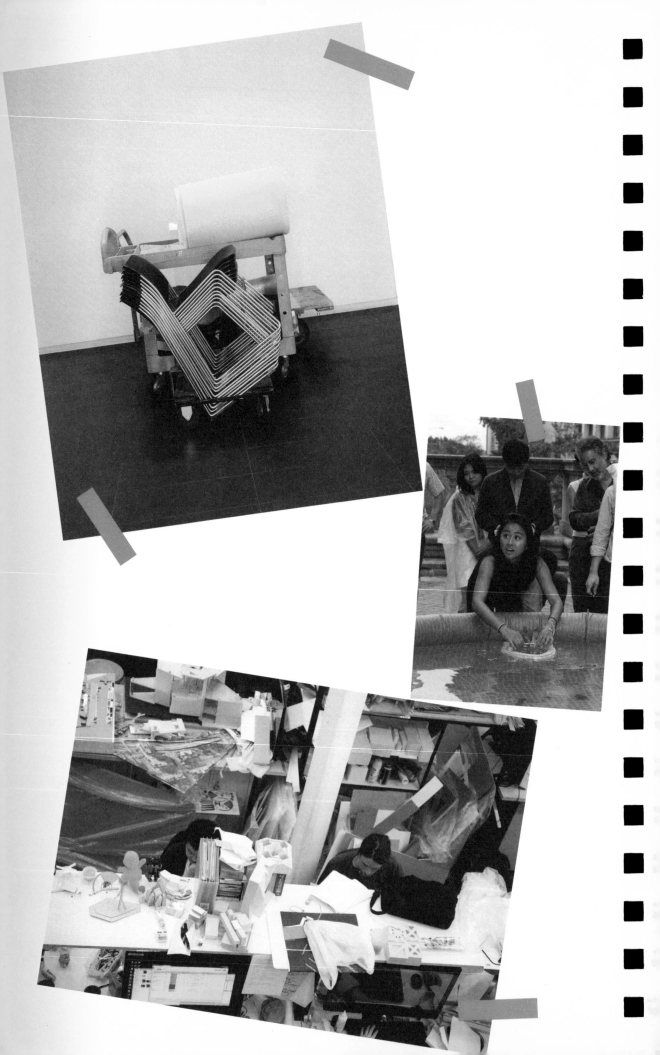